For Brotherhood and Duty

D1522017

AMERICAN WARRIORS

Throughout the nation's history, numerous men and women of all ranks and branches of the U.S. military have served their country with honor and distinction. During times of war and peace, there are individuals whose exemplary achievements embody the highest standards of the U.S. armed forces. The aim of the American Warriors series is to examine the unique historical contributions of these individuals, whose legacies serve as enduring examples for soldiers and citizens alike. The series will promote a deeper and more comprehensive understanding of the U.S. armed forces.

SERIES EDITOR: Roger Cirillo

An AUSA Book

FOR BROTHERHOOD & DUTY

The Civil War History
of the
West Point Class of 1862

Brian R. McEnany

UNIVERSITY PRESS OF KENTUCKY

Published by The University Press of Kentucky

Scholarly publisher for the Commonwealth,
serving Bellarmine University, Berea College, Centre College of
Kentucky, Eastern Kentucky University, The Filson Historical Society,
Georgetown College, Kentucky Historical Society, Kentucky State
University, Morehead State University, Murray State University,
Northern Kentucky University, Transylvania University, University of
Kentucky, University of Louisville, and Western Kentucky University.
All rights reserved.

Editorial and Sales Offices: The University Press of Kentucky
663 South Limestone Street, Lexington, Kentucky 40508-4008
www.kentuckypress.com

Library of Congress Cataloging-in-Publication Data

McEnany, Brian R.
  For brotherhood and duty : the Civil War history of the West Point
Class of 1862 / Brian R. McEnany.
     pages cm. — (American warriors)
  Includes bibliographical references and index.
   ISBN 978-0-8131-6062-7 (hardcover : alk. paper) —
ISBN 978-0-8131-6063-4 (pdf) — ISBN 978-0-8131-6064-1 (epub)
1. United States—History—Civil War, 1861-1865—Biography.
2. United States—History—Civil War, 1861-1865—Campaigns.
3. United States Military Academy. Class of 1862. I. Title. II. Title:
Civil War history of the West Point Class of 1862.
  E467.M16 2015
  973.7'3—dc23   2015006266

ISBN 978-0-8131-7401-3 (pbk. : alk. paper)

This book is printed on acid-free paper meeting
the requirements of the American National Standard
for Permanence in Paper for Printed Library Materials.

Manufactured in the United States of America.

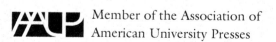 Member of the Association of
American University Presses

For Tully McCrea and the Class of 1862:

Draw the benches under the elms and gather together once more in final reunion.

And for Lillian and Mary Betty

Contents

Preface

There have been many histories written about West Point. Most describe the exploits of some of its famous graduates, but only a few discuss an entire class. *For Brotherhood and Duty* is a collective biography about the experiences of the twenty-eight graduates of the West Point Class of 1862 during the Civil War.

Why this particular class? When I was a cadet, my "adopted" aunt, the late historian Mary Elizabeth Sergent, guided me around the West Point cemetery, regaling me with many tales of the Civil War graduates buried there. I did not become interested in this particular class until much later. While searching for information about the class that graduated one hundred years before my own for a reunion project, I found a group of extraordinary young men that finally sparked my interest.

Digging into the musty cadet records in the West Point Library led me to become immersed in the political unrest that swept this country over one hundred and fifty years ago. The strident voices of Southern cadets were heard everywhere. They argued over states' rights, John Brown's Raid, slavery, popular sovereignty, abolitionist movements, and their oaths of allegiance. Between Lincoln's election in November 1860 and the end of the summer of 1861, the Class of 1862 saw their superintendent and commandant change three times, many of their instructors resigned or returned to their regiments, eleven states seceded from the Union, and half their classmates resigned.

The remaining twenty-eight's shared experiences during the catastrophic events that threatened to split the Union in two created strong beliefs in duty to country. Their class motto embodied those beliefs, *In Causam Communem Conjuncti*—translated as "Joined in a Common Cause." From these beginnings, a brotherhood emerged that would soon be tested in combat.

One former classmate fired the first round at Fort Sumter, and one classmate accepted the surrender of the last Confederate unit in the mountains of North Carolina. One commanded a Union cavalry division within two years of graduation, and three others commanded Union regiments before the end of the war. Most were brevetted for gallantry, some multiple times, and one would receive the Medal of Honor.

This class left West Point realizing there would not be an early end to the conflict, and they joined an army desperately in need of their technical skills. They found themselves assigned as second and third officers to units or staffs led by members of the two classes that graduated ahead of them (May 1861 and June 1861). Their stories are the perspective of junior officers and small units during a war that almost split this country in half.

For Brotherhood and Duty is all about memories. In October 1864, Tully McCrea, a member of this class, returned to West Point to teach mathematics while recovering from a serious wound. He vividly recalled his time as a cadet in a letter to his cousin in Ohio. He was a prodigious letter writer—more than 250 of his letters are held by the Special Collections and Archives Division at the West Point Library. In that October letter, he noted that memories assaulted him every time he passed his old room in the cadet barracks. I have expanded his memories about West Point and the war to compose the short narratives that appear in italics at the head of each chapter. These introductory passages are written in the style of historical fiction but provide important context for the events described in the chapters.

Source material for this book came from letters, articles, official records, regimental histories, historical cadet records, articles, books about cadet life during the Civil War, and data held at several national battlefields. I walked those same battlefields and found where most members of the class stood and fought.

In part 1 the lives of Tully McCrea and his classmates as cadets are described. They were present at the outset of the Civil War at West Point. Each of them was called upon to make the ultimate choice—to either serve the country he swore an oath to uphold or return home to protect his family and state. More than half this class resigned. Before the remaining members of the class graduated, three of their former classmates participated in the bombardment of Fort Sumter.

Part 2 describes the actions and exploits of twelve Union and four Confederate classmates during various campaigns. Two key protagonists are portrayed multiple times. Ranald S. Mackenzie began his career as a second lieutenant of engineers and ended the war as a brevet major general of cavalry. James Dearing resigned in April 1861 and began his career in the Confederate army as an artilleryman, ending it as a brigadier general of cavalry. Both frequently interacted with others in the class.

The other fourteen protagonists served gallantly as well. George Gillespie was awarded the Medal of Honor for actions at Bethesda Church near Cold Harbor many years after the war ended. James Sanderson anchored the gun line at Fairview during the Chancellorsville campaign, and John Calef's battery supported Brig. Gen. John Buford's troopers on McPherson's Ridge on the first day at Gettysburg. Ranald Mackenzie found a regiment for Brig. Gen. Gouverneur Warren to hold Little Round Top on the second day. Former classmates James Dearing and Joseph Blount pummeled Tully McCrea and John Egan with their guns during the bombardment of Cemetery Ridge on the third day. Later, John Egan was captured at Ream's Station when his battery was overrun during Brig. Gen. James H. Wilson's raid to destroy the Staunton River Bridge. Two months later, Albert Murray was captured during the Battle of Atlanta and sent off to a prisoner-of-war camp. Former classmates Oliver Semmes and John West fired on James Sanderson during the Battle of Pleasant Hill in western Louisiana where he was killed. At Appomattox, Ranald Mackenzie's cavalry division helped halt General Lee's army, occupied Lynchburg, and then found James Dearing in a Lynchburg hospital.

The remainder of the class played supporting roles in both the eastern and western theaters during the war. Information about them and most of their former classmates is included in the epilogue along with brief biographical sketches of each member of the Class of 1862.

Morris Schaff, a member of this class, wrote many years ago that he wished his class would meet again at West Point someday. No class in that period of time ever had a reunion. In fact, the hymn sung on the last Sunday before graduation was "When Shall We Meet Again?" and its refrain was "Never—No Never!" After hearing that hymn, Tully McCrea wrote about the improbability of the class ever meeting again. I hope the stories and events within these pages provide the reader with that missing gathering.

PART 1

The West Point Years

1

Aspirations

West Point, December 1865. The cold winter winds swept down the
Hudson River Valley and crept through the cracks and crevices into
Quarters 3 next to the cadet barracks. 1st Lt. Tully McCrea propped his
game leg up on a nearby stool and reflected on events since his graduation three and a half years before.[1]

It was hard to concentrate on studying mathematics when memories
kept flooding back. He could still smell the gun smoke and hear the shells
bursting around him at Gettysburg. When the firing stopped, he could
hear the high-pitched screams of wounded horses and see bodies littering
the ground. "Here come the Johnnies!" came the shout from the stone
wall. Once more he saw the long lines of gray emerge from the tree line
on Seminary Ridge. He and his gunners breathlessly awaited that fatal
charge.

He survived five major campaigns, was brevetted for gallantry three
times, and saw many men fall at Antietam, Fredericksburg, Chancellorsville, and Gettysburg. Wounds in both legs at the Battle of Olustee,
in Florida, left him in constant pain. After a lengthy hospitalization, he
was assigned to West Point to teach mathematics.

He picked up the heavy, leather-bound class album and turned its
pages. There was George Gillespie, his roommate and the only Southerner
to graduate with his class; his close friends Frank Hamilton and Morris
Schaff; and Ranald Mackenzie, who rose to the rank of major general
during the war. Stories about their exploits came to mind as he idly
turned the pages. Those who graduated were all there, but the Southerners had resigned before the class pictures were taken.

Tully vividly recalled his time as a cadet. Memories assaulted him
every time he passed his old room in the second division of the cadet barracks. The barracks were calm now, but West Point had not been exempt

Fig. 1.1. Cadet Tully McCrea. *1862 CA, SCAD*

from the nation's turmoil during the summer of 1860. He recalled the tumultuous months after Lincoln was elected; eleven states seceded, officers left or resigned. One of his ex-classmates even fired the first shot at Fort Sumter, and half his class chose to resign!

It was almost midnight when he began to write his cousin Belle in Ohio. Soon he filled a number of pages about remembrances of his early days and his arrival at West Point in 1858.[2]

Early Days

The city of Natchez stands on the bluffs above the Mississippi River some seventy-five miles south of Vicksburg. By the time Tully McCrea was born, it was the capital of the South's cotton kingdom. Cotton brought wealth to the area, and most of its six thousand white inhabitants lived in large homes with white columns and wide porches. The hot summers were made more bearable by shade from the moss-laden trees that lined the river banks and roads to nearby plantations. Schools were filled with the best books, and the plantation owners often sent their children to the finest schools in the East or Europe.

Tully's father, John McCrea, met and married Mary Jane Galbraith in Natchez, and over the next few years the McCreas had four children. Tully, the oldest, was born on July 23, 1839. His sister Alice arrived in 1842, his brother Percy in 1847, and Walter in 1849. Unfortunately, his mother died shortly after the birth of Walter.[3] Despite his family's situation, John McCrea sensed opportunity in California and with his brother-in-law, James Galbraith, joined the thousands seeking riches during the Gold Rush there. Their grand adventure turned deadly before the end of 1853. James contracted malaria on his return trip to Natchez and arrived in New Orleans delirious with malaria and soon died. John remained in the goldfields, contracted quinsy (an abscess of the tonsils that closes the breathing passages), and died there, leaving his four children orphaned with little means of support. Faced with decisions about the children, the Galbraith and McCrea families exchanged letters between Mississippi and Ohio, and fourteen-year-old Tully and his six-year-old brother Percy were sent north to live with their relatives in Ohio, while Alice and Walter remained in Natchez with Margaret Galbraith Wood, their mother's twin sister.[4]

Addison, Ohio

After a daunting trip north in June 1853, Tully arrived at his uncle William McCrea's home in Addison (also called Christianburg), while Percy went to live with his uncle Wallace McCrea's family a few miles farther west. William McCrea was an established merchant and farmer in Champaign County and had expanded his business to Urbana, the county seat.

Alone and forced to live with relatives he had never met, Tully spent a lot of time behind the washhouse crying. His uncle and aunt, their seven children, and particularly the youngest daughter, Belle, treated him kindly. The little nine-year-old cousin with the dark hair and brown eyes helped him overcome his loneliness. Tully never forgot her kindness.

Before long, the loss of his father and mother and the loneliness of being taken away from Natchez eased, and Tully began enjoying his new life. As he grew older, he worked in his uncle's dry goods store and soon found that he was far ahead of the other students in the local school. His uncle arranged for him to attend the Urbana Academy about sixteen miles away.[5]

Urbana, Ohio

By the time he was seventeen, Tully lived in Urbana to attend school and only came home for vacations. Most days after school, he worked at his uncle's store (Weaver and McCrea Leather Goods) and learned the mercantile business. He opened and closed the store, maintained the books, cleaned up each evening, and soon became well acquainted with local commercial affairs. Soon his uncle William moved his family to Dayton to spend the winter, and at times Tully felt cut off from the only real family he knew. To help pass the time, he began writing letters to his cousin Belle, his sister Alice, and some of his former schoolmates in Natchez.[6]

Tully's business sense proved useful in early 1858. He noticed a local merchant trying to get around paying taxes and mentioned it to his uncle's friend Samson P. Talbot, who passed the information along to the local treasurer. An astute observer of character, Talbot saw something in young Tully that intrigued him. He became convinced that Tully's ambition would serve him well in any career and decided to guide him toward the military, in particular, the United States Military Academy at West Point.[7]

Getting Appointed

Many families sought congressional appointments for their sons. West Point was held in high regard by the citizens of the country after the Mexican War. It provided a free education at the best engineering school in the country, and its diploma offered future financial rewards.

The first step taken by many families seeking a congressional appointment was to establish contact with the local member of Congress. In Tully's case, Sam Talbot, Henry Weaver (his uncle's partner and president of the Champaign County Bank), and his uncle William convinced John Russell, the clerk of the court from Urbana, to contact Benjamin Stanton, the local US congressman, to request an appointment for Tully.[8]

Stanton thought the support of these influential persons was clearly to his advantage and wrote to John B. Floyd, the secretary of war, that "he had the honor of nominating Tully McCrea from Urbana, Champaign County, as a proper person to receive the appointment of cadet at the Military Academy from the 8th Congressional District of Ohio."[9]

Campbell County, Virginia

Meanwhile, other young men contemplated a career in the military as well. James Griffin Dearing lived with his mother and her brother, Charles H. Lynch, after his father passed away. He grew up on an estate near Altavista south of Lynchburg. The Lynch family was well known in the area. Dearing's great-grandfather, Charles Lynch of

Revolutionary War fame, founded the town of Lynchburg. Dearing was well educated and attended Hanover Academy near Richmond in his early teens. The prominence of the Lynch family likely had much to do with him gaining an appointment from Thomas S. Bocock, representing the 5th District of Virginia that year.[10]

Morristown, New Jersey

At roughly the same time, Ranald Slidell Mackenzie decided to follow his late father, Commodore Alexander S. Mackenzie, into the military. While Tully and others began the appointment process through their congressional representatives, the frequent moves and inability of military families to settle in any one area for substantial periods of time limited their efforts to gain favorable congressional nominations. Recognizing this inequity, ten at-large appointments were made available to sons of military officers of the various services. Military officers or members of their families wrote letters to the president, accompanied by letters of recommendation from senior officers or officials, requesting such appointments for their sons.[11]

Mackenzie's mother was not certain that he was taking the right career path. At the urging of her relatives, she had sent him to Williams College in Massachusetts to prepare him for a career in law. But she dutifully wrote a letter to the secretary of war, requesting an appointment for her son. Influence helped once again. One of Mackenzie's uncles was Sen. John Slidell from Louisiana, who also wrote a letter to the secretary requesting the appointment. President James Buchanan agreed, and the appropriate paperwork soon made its way to the War Department.[12]

Washington, DC

All letters requesting nominations to West Point made their way to the US Army's office of the Corps of Engineers. The Military Academy was governed from afar by the head of the engineer corps.[13] The focal point for all West Point correspondence at the War Department was Capt. Horatio G. Wright. He processed all letters received concerning the academy, answered questions from congressmen and families, and placed candidates' names in various entering-year groups for consideration. Candidates could be appointed from thirty-two states, the District of Columbia, and six territories. In 1858 a maximum of 280 cadets were authorized to be present at West Point.[14]

Appointments were made throughout the year, but in March the process came to an end when the selection of the ten at-large presidential candidates was made.[15] Each candidate received a letter signed by the secretary of war, notifying him that he was conditionally appointed as a cadet in the service of the United States. Included with the letter was a copy of regulations pertaining to admission to the Military Academy and a circular that outlined the basic academic and medical requirements, appropriate clothing to be brought, and the required amount of money to be deposited upon arrival. Finally, he added a printed endorsement to be signed and returned to his office if the candidate accepted the appointment. Wright carefully recorded 103 conditional appointments that year, and 94 were returned, including the 10 at-large appointments made by the president.[16]

Addison, Ohio

Tully received a large, official envelope stamped "Adjutants General Office—Official Business" in late March and opened it. The enclosed letter read in part: "You have received a conditional cadet appointment to attend West Point this year. You are required to accept or reject the appointment and if you accept it, you must arrive at West Point between the 1st and 20th of June, 1858."

The enclosed circular noted that each candidate had to pass an entrance examination at West Point that substantiated that he could "read well and spell correctly, to write a fair and legible hand, and perform with facility and accuracy the various operations of the four ground rules of arithmetic, of reduction of simple and compound proportions, and of vulgar and decimal fractions." All applicants were to be tutored prior to an examination at the end of June.

Each candidate was required to bring at least sixty-one dollars for necessary expenses until he was admitted. Finally, the circular noted that if the candidate believed he was deficient in any areas outlined in the circular, he should not consider accepting the appointment. It noted most emphatically that more than a third of those who received appointments failed to complete the course of instruction.[17]

The entrance requirements for West Point in 1858 specified that the applicant must demonstrate a basic level of education. Congress consistently held the Academic Board to the Act of April 29, 1812, that stated, "Each candidate should be well-versed in reading, writing, and arithmetic." The Academic Board at West Point had argued with Congress several times that the entry requirements were too limited, but Congress adamantly opposed changing them. It maintained that the entrance requirements should be "eminently popular, republican, equal conditions of admission." Far more likely was the view that by keeping the entrance requirements to a minimum, fewer candidates would fail to be admitted and disappoint their sponsors in Washington.[18]

Tully signed the required endorsement in John Russell's office on April 5, 1858. During the frequent absences of Tully's uncle William from Urbana, Sam Talbot was now his guardian. Russell added a note stating that he "forwarded the acceptance of Tully McCrea and the consent of his guardian who was regularly appointed as such" to the secretary of war.[19]

The single requirement in the circular that likely bothered Tully the most was the academic examination, a fear undoubtedly held by many others that year. Education beyond that needed for basic literacy was not prevalent across the country, particularly in the South and West in 1858. Most local schools provided only limited grammar and simple arithmetic. Fear of the entrance exam may not have troubled James Dearing, who believed he was so far ahead of other candidates that he could skip the first year at West Point entirely. He was in for a rude awakening. Ranald Mackenzie was equally well educated. He had attended Williams for two years before accepting his appointment to West Point.[20]

Traveling to West Point

The United States Military Academy lies fifty-three miles above New York City on the west bank of the Hudson River. It is the oldest, continuously occupied military post in the country. Since 1778 the sounds of drums and military activities have resounded throughout the Hudson Highlands. It was there that a giant chain was stretched across the narrow elbow in the Hudson River to halt the passage of British ships. On March 16, 1802, President Thomas Jefferson signed the Peace Establishment Act, which created a military academy at West Point.[21]

In 1858 many citizens were anxious for land and riches. The small regular army of 17,469 officers and enlisted personnel was scattered about the country at arsenals and frontier posts and served to protect and defend those striving to reach those goals.[22] Most of the graduates of West Point soon joined those far-flung detachments.

The distances and modes of transportation in the 1850s often required lengthy travel times to reach the Military Academy. There was no transcontinental railroad. Clipper ships from the West Coast or wagon trains across the Great Plains took too long. Recognizing these limitations, candidates were allowed to arrive during the three-week period prior to June 20.

Rail service did not extend directly to West Point from the West. It halted at Suffern, New York, where candidates then climbed aboard a stage coach to travel through Buttermilk Falls (now Highland Falls) to West Point, or it stopped at Newburgh, north of West Point, and the candidates rode through Canterbury (now Cornwall) to reach the academy. Others halted at Albany, allowing some candidates to travel down the Hudson River to West Point by steamer. Those who took trains from the East eventually arrived at Garrison's Landing, a train station on the eastern bank of the Hudson across from West Point. There the daily newspapers, mail, visitors, and candidates were ferried across the river to the south dock of the Military Academy.

Tully packed his trunk, collected the money he needed to pay the treasurer, and visited his relatives before boarding the train to begin his travels to West Point in the first part of June. He took eighty dollars with him, more than enough to satisfy the required deposit and have some extra money left over for travel and food.

More often than not, the new candidates arrived in New York City and booked passage on one of the many steamboats that regularly steamed north to Albany. Perhaps it was the *Henrick Hudson* or the *Isaac Newton* that left at 7 A.M. for the three-hour trip north to West Point. Once the steamboat left New York harbor, it entered the wide Tappan Zee then passed Tarrytown where Washington Irving made his home. It passed through the rugged cliffs that formed the southern gateway to the Hudson Highlands, and in the distance the craggy outline of Anthony's Nose on the east and Bear Mountain on the west formed a narrow channel through which the Hudson River flowed. Soon the town of Buttermilk Falls appeared on the western bluffs where nestled in a wooded ravine south of the village near the river was a small inn run by Benny Havens that was much frequented by cadets and officers alike, although not at the same time. Near Garrison's Landing the captain sounded the whistle, and gradually slowed to approach the south dock.[23]

When the ship halted, lines were quickly thrown ashore and a gangway clattered down. On the shore a lone sentinel stood guard at the end of the dock. The excited candidates who would form the Class of 1862 carried their bags ashore, ready to begin their careers.

2

The Beginnings of Strife

West Point, December 1865. Tully McCrea climbed stiffly out of bed to the sound of fifes and drums the next morning. Looking in the mirror, he saw a swarthy face with brown hair, chestnut eyes, and a mouth framed by a bushy, brown moustache. His 160 pounds were well distributed over a ramrod straight frame.

He pulled on blue, red-striped trousers, donned a white shirt and black bow tie, hitched a pair of suspenders over his shoulders, put on a dark blue vest, and got into a dark blue frock coat with a single row of gold buttons. Gold-trimmed first lieutenant's bars were hooked to the shoulders of the frock coat, and black boots completed the uniform of an artillery officer.

Settling a leather forage cap on his head, he pulled on his heavy wool overcoat and picked up his ever-present cane. Closing the door behind him, he carefully made his way down the hall to the icy steps of the two-story, brick building located between the cadet barracks and the superintendent's house.[1]

The flag atop the clock tower snapped in the winter wind as he headed toward the mess hall. He shivered and wished he had some of Professor Kendrick's brandy-flavored peach slices to fend off the cold. He slowly climbed the stairs to the officers' mess in the south wing of the mess hall; the smell of coffee and biscuits engulfed him as he opened the door. He sat at a table near the window where an Irish steward poured him a steaming cup of coffee and brought him some hot biscuits and honey.

The sounds of cadets leaving their section of the mess hall meant Tully had about half an hour before his mathematics section convened next door in the academic building, also known as the Academy. John Egan sat down next to him. "Dad" Egan was the oldest in his class, and the two of them had been fast friends since they were cadets. Assigned to

Fig. 2.1. Academic Building, Cadet Barracks, and Officers' Quarters. *1878 CA, SCAD*

the same battery during the war, they had spent many nights smoking their pipes, discussing the war and their prospects for promotion.

When the last of the morning's coffee was drained from his cup, Tully made his way next door. As he passed under the bare branches and limbs of the tall chestnut trees standing next to the academic building, he remembered drilling under their welcome shade many times during his first summer at West Point.

West Point—June 1858

It was mid-morning on June 10, 1858, when the steamer from New York City arrived at the south dock. Tully and the other candidates picked up their bags and walked down the gangplank. The sentry halted them at the end of the dock and carefully recorded their names

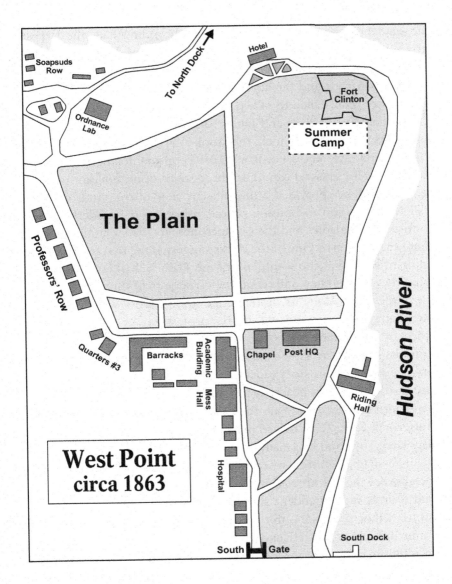

Soapsuds Row

To North Dock →

Hotel

Ordnance Lab

Fort Clinton

Summer Camp

The Plain

Professors' Row

Hudson River

Quarters #3

Barracks

Academic Building

Chapel

Post HQ

Mess Hall

Riding Hall

West Point circa 1863

Hospital

South Dock

South Gate

on his slate—*Tully McCrea, Clifton Comly, Joseph Alexander, Richard Kinney, John West, Henry Wharton*—as he did for each arrival. They put their bags on a horse-drawn cart and followed it up the steep road cut into the granite cliffs. Three-quarters of the way up the incline, the road branched to the right around the riding hall, the largest stone structure of its kind at the time. They followed the cart until it stopped in front of a three-towered Gothic building that housed the post headquarters and the library. They gazed across the open grassy area before them called the Plain.[2]

When Morris Schaff and James Ritchey from Ohio arrived a few days earlier at the north dock, they took a cart up the hill to the West Point Hotel (also known as Roe's Hotel) on the northern edge of a forty-two-acre grassy Plain. The three-story stone building and its spacious porches provided a magnificent view of the Hudson River Valley. In addition to housing official visitors to the academy, many tourists, young ladies and their chaperones, and cadet families stayed there each summer. One of the clerks suggested the two report to the adjutant's office at the south end of the Plain. Schaff later described what they saw as they walked on the carriage road through the middle of the Plain. Along its western edge stood the houses of the superintendent, the commandant, and the professors. An artillery battery stood by the eastern side of the road. Ahead of them at the southern boundary stood the three-story academic building and next to it the massive granite, four-story cadet barracks. On the opposite side of the street stood the post headquarters and the chapel. The road continued south past the mess hall, the hospital, and out the south gate to Buttermilk Falls. They arrived in front of post headquarters where six days later Tully and his small group now stood.[3]

The man in charge when Tully arrived was Bvt. Col. Richard Delafield of the US Army Corps of Engineers. He was serving his second tour as superintendent and supervised the Corps of Cadets, the twelve senior professors, thirty to thirty-four officer instructors, the commandant and his staff, and a post staff of three officers and doctors. In addition, there were several army units: the artillery battery, an engineer company, the West Point band, and the complement of enlisted personnel that made up the military garrison. The academy was home to around 450 soldiers, cadets, and officers, plus their families.

The second-ranking military officer at West Point was Bvt. Lt. Col. William J. Hardee, the commandant of cadets. He was responsible for the military training of the Corps of Cadets and was assisted by four tactical officers who commanded the cadet companies in the Corps of Cadets.

The Corps was organized as an infantry battalion with four lettered companies arranged by height. The cadets were also organized into five academic-year groups or classes as West Point, since 1854, was a five-year institution. The Class of 1859 (the new "first class") would be the first five-year class to graduate. The upper-class cadets eagerly awaited the arrival of young and dusty candidates who now stood in front of post headquarters.[4]

Becoming New Cadets

Tully and the other candidates pulled open the heavy doors to post headquarters and entered. The lower floor housed the offices of the superintendent, the treasurer, the quartermaster, the adjutant, and the academy's library. The second floor contained a lecture hall and Prof. William H. C. Bartlett's Department of Natural and Experimental Philosophy. The prominent central turret on the roof held one of the few observation telescopes in the country and provided cadets with the opportunity to study astronomy.[5]

1st Lt. James B. Fry, the post adjutant, checked each candidate off his list of nominees as they signed a ledger on his desk. He informed them that they could not receive any money from friends or family and asked them to turn in any cash they carried with them, receiving a small account book in return. The money in that account would initially be used to pay for books, clothes, and room rent during their first month. Later it would be augmented by their cadet pay of $30 per month and used to buy uniforms, books, and other materiel.[6]

After they completed their processing, a soldier led them along the carriage road toward the cadet barracks. The granite, four-story, L-shaped building was divided into ten divisions with cadets living in four rooms on each floor. Rooms in the seventh and eighth divisions were sometimes occupied by bachelor officers, and tactical officers maintained offices in the same divisions as their companies.[7]

Fig. 2.2. Post Headquarters and Library. *1868 CA, SCAD*

Tully and the other candidates followed the soldier through a central sally port (or tunnel) into the cadet area and walked up the cast-iron steps into the eighth division where the soldier left them in charge of a cadet officer.[8] Cadet lance corporals descended upon the small band of new candidates when they entered the eighth division and began yelling, "Stand Attention, Sir, Where do you think you are! Take off your cap! Put your heels together on the same line! Little finger along the seam of your pantaloons! Button your coat! Draw in your chin! Throw out your chest! Keep your eyes 15 paces to the front and on that nail over there! Don't let me see you wearing a standing collar again—and stand steady, Sir!"[9]

Tully and his companions were reprimanded incessantly for departing from those instructions. After answering what seemed to be a thousand questions, they were led to their rooms. Many years later, Tully wrote about his first day to his cousin Belle: "How well I remember the first day that I entered the right hand room on the 1st

Fig. 2.3. New Cadet Training. *CULDC, courtesy of Cornell University Library, Making of America Digital Collection*

floor of the seventh division, where Comly[,] Alexander and I were put together as plebes. After camp, I was next on the fourth floor of the second division with Custer."[10]

Their room contained only iron bedsteads, mattresses, a table, a rifle rack, and a locker for clothes. The lance corporal told them they would receive additional furniture, books, articles, and other equipment over the next few days and handed Tully a piece of paper specifying exactly how the room was to be arranged at all times. He then emphasized in no uncertain terms that when the drums began to beat, they must form up in the cadet area. Tully and his new roommates were not alone in the seventh division. Morris Schaff, James Ritchey, and George Gillespie occupied a room on the top floor. Kenelm Robbins and Reuben Higgason were just across the hall.[11]

The drums began rumbling in the sally port just before 1 P.M. Tully and his roommates ran across the cadet area to line up in front of the guardroom. Morris Schaff described his first dinner formation in books and letters written long after he was a cadet:

> We were a column of gawky boys, of all sizes, from five to six feet tall, clad in all sorts of parti-colored raiment; our

eyes fixed, yes, glued to the coat collar of the boy in front
of us; a grim dismalness hanging in every face; all of us trying mechanically to point our toes and to comply with the
fierce orders from sergeants and lance corporals who trod on
the earth proudly on each flank, filling the air with "hep . . .
hep!" Every little while, one of us lost the step or, treading
on the heels of the man in front, threw the whole line into
such a hobbling mass as to cause the sergeant, in a high state
of dudgeon, to plant his heels and roar out "Halt!" The outraged officer then stalked up to the side of the awkward boy
whose eyes were still glued on the coat collar ahead of him,
with a hopelessness more abject than ever in his face, and in
savage tones, threaten the most dire punishment if it should
happen again. After the mighty wrath of the sergeant had
exhausted itself, he would throw a withering glance up and
down the line; then putting himself into an attitude, with
great emphasis he would order the march resumed. Where-
upon the sergeants and lance corporals resumed their yelps
louder and fiercer than ever; and so it went on until we poor
devils reached the mess hall.[12]

After dinner, Tully and his roommates were marched to the commissary storehouse where they were issued bedding, a water bucket,
soap, a coconut dipper, a tin candle box, candles, a candlestick holder,
a washbowl, a broom, a bucket, and a small looking glass to share.
The supply clerk then bundled a slate and two slate pencils, ink,
twelve sheets of paper, and an arithmetic text all together to carry
back to the barracks with the other items. An additional trip provided
them with an iron table that held their wash bucket, bowl, and looking glass. After cleaning his shoes and preparing his clothes for the
next day, Tully finally crawled into bed immediately after a bugler
played "extinguish lights" at 10 P.M.[13]

The next morning, the reveille cannon boomed at 5 A.M., followed by the shrill sound of fifes and the rattle of drums reverberating
off the walls of the sally port. Before the first drum roll ended, Tully

and his roommates were lined up in front of the guardroom again. When the second drumroll began, the other upper-class cadets in the Corps formed in companies near the barracks.[14]

One of the first items of business during their second day was a haircut. The barber listened patiently as each candidate stated how he wanted his hair done, then said, "Aye, aye, sir," and proceeded to shear off his long-cherished curls, unhampered by the candidate's exhortations in the chair to the contrary. Later that morning, the closely shorn Tully and his classmates began receiving tutoring in basic arithmetic and English grammar in preparation for the entrance examination. Next they were issued muskets and divided up into groups of three to six individuals to learn the rudiments of simple formations and the manual of arms. Morris Schaff readily admitted that he was hopelessly awkward and was drilled separately for several days under the horse chestnut trees next to the academic building.[15]

Sometime during their first week, Tully and the others underwent a medical examination. They were weighed, their height measured, and bones checked. An eye test required each cadet to determine if a coin mounted on the wall fourteen feet away was either heads or tails. Based on the examinations, the medical board recommended the dismissal of several candidates and placed some of them on medical probation for varying periods of time. Tully was placed on medical probation for ninety days because of an ingrown toenail.[16]

The Entrance Exam

The cadet adjutant announced at evening parade that the Academic Board would convene on June 22 to examine the new candidates. After breakfast that morning, they were marched to the library in groups of twenty or thirty and told by their tutors to answer questions posed by the superintendent, the commandant, and the senior professors. Morris Schaff vividly described his appearance before the Academic Board:

> That morning, for the first time, I saw the Academic Board. It is made up of the superintendent, commandant, and the

professors, and is a formidable reality to youthful eyes. They were sitting at small desks, arranged in a crescent; the heavy-ballooned epaulettes of the military staff, and the flat, brass buttons on the deep blue, scholastic dress-coasts of the professors, proclaimed the dignity of the solemn array. In the middle of the Board sat Major Richard Delafield—a pudgy man with heavy, sandy eyebrows, abundant grayish sandy hair, and a pronounced eagle nose. He wore glasses and had the air of an officer and a man of cultivation, invested, furthermore, with the honor of a wide and well-earned distinction. Colonel William J. Hardee, the commandant, sat on his left. A tall man with large solid gray eyes, a low forehead, heavy grizzled moustache and imperial, and soldiery bearing. . . . Church, Mahan, Bartlett, French, Kendrick, Agnel, and Weir, the professors, were all beyond middle life; benignant, white locks softened the faces of most of them.[17]

An earlier graduate, Edward Hartz ('55) described his appearance before the board:

About three o'clock the 1st Section of new cadets . . . was marched to the Library building. When there, we were obliged to confront the most rigid, cold and merciless looking set of men I have ever before beheld. They seemed so oppressed by the weight of dignity that rests upon them, that a kind look was as much a stranger to their faces as good living has been to me since I have landed here. There were about twenty of us marched in at once. The mathematical equations consisted of question in vulgar and decimal fractions. . . . We were then called upon to read an extract from Blair which was satisfactorily done. I was then called upon to write [a sentence]. This I done and was sent to my seat. This closed the examination.[18]

Tully answered the questions correctly, and he heaved a huge sigh of relief. Morris Schaff was more to the point. He stated that the examination was so simple that any boy with a common school education should be able to pass it. Not all worried about passing the exam. Several of the candidates had spent one or more years in college before coming to the academy and easily breezed through the questions. In addition to Ranald S. Mackenzie, Charles Suter was educated in preparatory schools in Europe. George Burroughs spent time at Harvard, Frank Hamilton studied at Western Reserve College, and Richard Kinney attended the Virginia Military Institute before he was appointed to West Point.[19]

Fifteen of the eighty-four candidates did not pass the exam. Three more failed the medical examination, leaving sixty-six new cadets admitted as the new Fifth Class on July 1. Capt. Horatio Wright at the War Department soon notified the affected members of Congress. A few days later, twenty people in Athens, Ohio, signed a petition recommending that Rep. Valentine Horton of Ohio's 11th District appoint James Sanderson to fill one of the vacancies. Horton agreed and notified Captain Wright. An appointment letter was soon sent off, directing Sanderson to arrive at West Point between August 20 and 30.[20]

Candidates No More

It was traditional for the Corps to spend each summer living in tents on the northeastern corner of the Plain near old Fort Clinton. The encampment prepared cadets for the camp life of a soldier, a tradition that lasted until 1947. Each year, the camp was named for a well-known person, and in 1858 it was called Camp Jefferson Davis.[21]

The entire Corps was not present during the summer, as the third class left on ten weeks' furlough soon after graduation in June. A month earlier, temporary cadet officer appointments in the new first and second classes were announced, and sixteen members of the fourth class were appointed as lance corporals for the summer to help train Tully and his classmates. Additional cadets were selected to become tutors. Those cadets living in the seventh to the tenth divisions moved out of their rooms around June 1 and doubled up

Fig. 2.4. Cadet Summer Camp. *1857 CA, SCAD*

with the other companies to provide rooms for the candidates until summer camp began.[22]

In preparation for the move to summer camp, the cadets stored their boxes and trunks in empty recitation rooms in the academic building. By noon on the day the camp was to be occupied, the barracks was emptied of everything except their uniforms and gear for the evening parade. At 4 P.M. the band and the color guard led the cadet battalion across the Plain to the summer campsite near the West Point Hotel. Tully and the other new cadets struggled along behind under control of several lance corporals.[23]

Under direction of the upper-class cadets, the new cadets erected eight rows of tents, two rows for each company. Each tent was roughly seven feet square and erected on a raised wooden platform in precise alignment with the others along each company street. The first class officers' tents were slightly larger. Each tactical officer had two large tents that stood facing the rows of his company. Near the entrance to the camp, the cadet quartermaster and the guard tents were erected. The commandant's tent was more richly furnished and larger than any other in the encampment. It was placed centrally along a broad avenue that ran through the center of the camp.[24]

When the last tent peg was driven into the ground, Tully and Robert Noonan were given a portion of a long, wooden chest or locker to store their clothing, cadet gear, and personal items. A water pail and a tin candle box were located in one corner of the tent, and a gun rack stood in another. A shaving glass and their uniforms hung from the rear tent pole. All blankets were carefully folded and piled in a corner each morning.[25]

Life in Summer Camp

From the time a new cadet stirred out of his blankets each morning, the frequent drills, meals, and the evening parade left little free time. Tully spent much of his time cleaning his rifle and preparing for the next inspection. One cadet even asked his family to send him some sandpaper, as he believed all parts of his rifle were required to be taken apart and the steel parts polished until the inspecting officer could see his face in them.[26]

As many cadets had done before him, Tully described life in summer camp in his first letter, which was to his cousin Belle:

In the morning at five o'clock the drums beat about ten minutes, which in military terms is called "Reveille," and before the drums quit beating we have to be up, dressed, and on the parade ground, ready to fall in at a moment's warning. Ten minutes, as you may know, is a very short space of time for a person to get up and dress, but as for washing and hair combing, that has to be put off until some other time. You ought to see the plebes, falling into ranks half asleep and their eyes sometimes half open, and it goes very hard with a great many of them who have been in the habit at home of sleeping until seven or eight o'clock. After Reveille roll call the police drums beat and we have to turn out and police the camp, that is, we have to sweep and clean the camp of every stick and piece of paper as large as a walnut. So you may suppose that the camp is kept in mighty nice order and very clean. After policing, at 5 1/2 o'clock, we have to turn out for an hour's drill, and every mistake that we make we are scolded for it by our drill masters and sometimes put in the guard tent for the most trivial offenses.

After morning drill we have half an hour to prepare for breakfast and at 6 1/2 o'clock we fall in and march a half mile to breakfast. After breakfast we have nothing to do until 11 o'clock when we turn out for another hour's drill. . . . After we are marched in from this drill and dismissed, we have an hour to prepare for dinner and at one o'clock we again march half a mile to dinner. This meal is a little better than breakfast. After dinner we again have nothing to do until four o'clock when we have to police again half an hour and at half past five we again turn out for an hour's drill. After dress parade our delinquencies or demerits are read off. Some get three, four, and even five or six every evening, but I have not had any for four or five days.

At 7 ½ o'clock we go to supper, which consists of bread and butter and coffee and, as I do not drink coffee, my evening meal is bread and water, like some prisoner confined in a dungeon for some capital crime. . . . What we do have is good and well cooked. The bread is the same every day and is very good and the butter is also good; we have nothing but what is good for us to eat, but it does not go very well with me to come from the Hamilton House in Urbana and go to eating this fare here. . . .

After supper we have an hour and a half to go to the river and bathe. At 9 ½ o'clock the drums beat tattoo when we have to fall in to roll call and then we have ten minutes to fix down our blanket, undress, and be in bed. Our bed consists of a pair of blankets laid on the floor of our tents, a pillow, and a coverlid. It is a hard bed but we get used to it and sleep like logs, when the old cadets will let us.[27]

Fifes and drums led the cadet battalion out of the camp to the mess hall three times each day. Inside the cadets sat at twelve long tables with a cadet officer at the head of each. Later Tully described his first few meals:

At 6 ½ o'clock we fall in and march a half mile to breakfast, and after arriving at the mess hall, we find the same regular and never to be forgotten hash . . . as it is called here, but it is Irish potatoes mostly with a very little meat in it, but after we eat it awhile with keen appetites, we find it quite palatable, besides we have bread and coffee and that forms the regular everyday meal . . . dinner, this meal is a little better than breakfast. Today we had soup, boiled beef, boiled potatoes, boiled greens, and for desserts we have bread and molasses and a kind of a pudding made of scraps of bread that is left at the other meals, sweetened I believe with molasses and a good deal of spice.[28]

In the evenings, only the upper-class cadets were allowed to visit the hotel or leave the camp. Dances, or "hops" as the cadets called them, were held three times each week in the fencing hall of the academic building and at least once per week at the hotel during the summer. All were off limits to new cadets. In anticipation of such future thrills, dance classes were offered in polkas, quadrilles, and waltzes at the cost of $2 per month deducted from their pay. Tully was very much attuned to how much money was being taken from his account and did not take the classes.

For the most part, letter writing was the sole form of entertainment for new cadets. There were strict rules about what could be received from home, and all packages were inspected by the cadet quartermaster or the commandant. Even the exact language of addressing their letters had to be followed by friends and family or the cadet would never receive his letters or packages.[29]

At 10 P.M. all cadets were required to be in their tents, and the officer of the day (OD) went through the camp calling, "Get those lights out!" Moving about after dark without approval was prohibited, but some upper-class cadets sneaked back to the hotel to meet young ladies. Others floated boats downriver to Benny Havens's inn for a mug of rum or across the river to Cold Springs. A couple of Tully's classmates, Morris Schaff and Jim Riddle, crept down to one of the coves near the old wharf below the hotel. Schaff later related that they traded their old civilian clothing for a "bottle of mighty poor whiskey and some kind of berry pie, my share being a piece of the pie."[30]

Discipline and Punishment

Constant adherence to orders was a fact of life in the Corps. Infractions were punished in the form of demerits and/or confinement. During the first two weeks of summer camp, demerits for new cadets did not count. After July 15, all demerits were counted against a maximum limit of one hundred each semester. The Academic Board had some leeway in adjusting the total number of demerits, but if a cadet exceeded the hundred-demerit limit, he was usually recommended for dismissal.[31]

On the first day that demerits were counted, the cadet adjutant announced at evening parade that Tully received two demerits for "not going through manual properly at parade" and the next day two more for "not saluting Officer in Charge properly." Upper-class cadets were most attentive to supposed infractions by new cadets, and the most frequent shout heard in the camp was an older cadet yelling, "Turn out the Patrol and take this man to the guard tent!" It was frequently full of new cadets. Tully described his experience in confinement there:

> I was in the guard tent one hour today and I have been in the guard tent three times. Every new cadet has been in the guard tent a great many times and some of them are there nearly all of the time. They are not allowed to leave the tent only when absolutely necessary to go after water, go to meals, go after a book or something of the kind, and when they do

leave the guard tent they are marched with a patrol, that is, they are marched between two armed men. My offense today was for moving my position in ranks to pull on my glove, as any person would naturally do, but if my hat, or even my head, was falling off I would have no right to raise my hand to save it. My hat often falls off in ranks when it is picked up and put on my head by my drill-master, but I now have a military cap which sticks to my head better than my old hat.[32]

Guard Details and Deviling Plebes

The encampment was protected by eight guard posts, manned twenty-four hours a day, rain or shine. After Tully received his uniforms in mid-July, he and his classmates were trained to walk guard. The guard detail was composed of three reliefs of eight men each. Each guard walked his post for two hours and then was off for four hours. They slept on the ground in front of the guard tent, wrapped in their blankets, wearing their uniforms, belts, and cartridge boxes. Each relief was shaken out of their blankets by the corporal of the guard crying out in a loud voice, "Second Relief! Turn Out!" Sometimes the sleepy cadets were subjected to the flat of a cold sword blade across their feet to wake them up. When the guard detail ended, they were marched to Fort Clinton to fire their rifles.[33]

The older cadets played silly pranks when the new cadets began to march guard for the first time. It generally ended up with the new cadet receiving demerits and being sent to the guard tent. In other years, new cadets wrote about being taken away from their guard posts in a wheelbarrow. Some had their rifles taken away, and one was tied to a tree. When a cadet officer approached Morris Schaff during his first guard detail, he was asked to halt and give the countersign. The cadet officer mumbled a response, which Schaff could not understand, but he let the officer pass anyway.[34]

The pranks continued at night as well. Older cadets often reached beneath the tent flaps and grabbed the new cadets by the feet and yanked them out on the ground. Others simply collapsed the tent so it had to be raised in the darkness. By any other name, the pranks were hazing, but at the academy in 1858 it was called "deviling" the plebes.[35]

Military Training

The company tactical officers were responsible for teaching Tully and his classmates the rudiments of infantry and light artillery drills during their first summer. New cadets learned the intricacies of the "cannoneer's hop"—the rotation of crew members to perform the various tasks in the service of an artillery piece. Continued practice in the manual of arms occupied the rest of each day along with marksmanship lessons for two weeks and then bayonet training.[36]

The hot summer sun made the bayonet drills and other formations on the Plain intolerable. The new cadets roasted in their civilian clothes when they first arrived, and it was not much better after they donned their cadet uniforms. Tully described how the heat affected some of his classmates: "We have to stand in a military position for about a half hour and the new cadets, not being used to it, it goes very hard with some of them. Some get very sick and some two or three fainted away. Mr. Chaffee of Massachusetts, a young delicate fellow, fainted away a few evenings ago, and did not come to himself for several moments, but it is not thought of here, as it is a very common occurrence."[37] The continual press of activities, drills, inspections, and parades caused time to pass quickly, and before they knew it summer camp was almost over.

The New Fifth Class

The Academic Board recommended the addition of nine more new cadets to the new fifth class before the end of summer camp. These "seps" (cadet slang reflecting their admittance on September 1) were William Barnard, William Blakistone, George Lovejoy, Samuel McIntire, Arthur Reed, James Sanderson, John Shrewsbury, and James E. Wilson and one "turn-back" (Joseph K. Dixon) from a previous class. They were drilled by selected members of the third class for several weeks during the academic year until they became proficient in marching and the manual of arms.[38]

With the addition of the nine seps, seventy-five new cadets formed the new fifth class on September 1, 1858. In addition to Ranald Mackenzie, only four at-large appointments in the class were awarded to sons of military officers that year: George McKee, the son of the late Col. W. R. McKee ('29); Charles Suter, whose father was an army surgeon; William C. Bartlett, whose dad was one of the professors at West Point; and Samuel Mansfield, the son of Col. J. K. F. Mansfield ('22). The other five at-large appointments were given to E. Kirby Russell, William Beebe, James E. Wilson, Singleton Van Buren, and John R. Blocker.

The members of the class were fairly representative of the country as a whole. Twenty-five entered from the South; forty-eight came from Northern, border, or midwestern states; one from the West; and one from the Nebraska Territory. Some came from well-connected families like Virginian James Dearing. Oliver Semmes from Mobile, Alabama, was the son of navy captain Raphael Semmes (who later commanded the CSS *Alabama*). Singleton Van Buren was the grandson of the former president. Isaac Arnold's uncle was a congressman from Connecticut, and Ranald Mackenzie's uncle was Sen. John Slidell of Louisiana.[39]

Life as a Cadet

The day before summer camp ended, the third class returned from furlough. After visiting the barber shop, they donned their uniforms and reported to the commandant. Soon thereafter, the cadet adjutant sized the cadet battalion. The long line shuffled back and forth until company assignments could be made. The taller cadets were assigned to A and D Companies while the shorter ones landed in B and C Companies. Tully and eighteen others in his class were assigned to A Company.[40]

The next morning room assignments were posted, and the cadets

Fig. 2.5. Cadet Barracks. *1868 CA, SCAD*

moved their equipment into the barracks. That afternoon summer camp ended ceremoniously. One cadet stood by each tent. At the first drumroll, all but one tent rope were loosened. At the second drumroll, all the tents collapsed as one and were folded and stacked. Then with flags flying and the band playing, the Corps marched back to the barracks.[41]

Cadet Barracks

When Tully returned to the barracks, he was assigned a room on the fourth floor of the second division in A Company facing the cadet area. After the sparse accommodations in camp, the spaciousness of the room was overwhelming at first. It had two alcoves, each containing a bed. Overcoats and uniform jackets hung from hooks on the alcove wall between the beds. A rack on one wall held his musket, while a second was used to hang his white cross belts and cartridge box. A wooden wall locker held his clothes, all neatly arranged and straightened. Along with the blankets and comforter issued earlier in June, the room contained a mattress, a bed, a chair, and a foot-locker for his belongings. An iron table and a shaving mirror were shared with his roommate. Everything in the room was required to be arranged at all times.[42]

Suddenly the door slammed open, causing Tully to leap to attention as his new roommate, a blond upperclassman one year ahead of him—a "yearling"—entered the room. His laughing smile told Tully he did not have much to fear from George Armstrong Custer (June '61), who arranged his gear. A carefree youth from Ohio who would soon achieve greatness during the Civil War, Custer claimed the better of the beds and chairs and settled in for the academic year.[43]

Meanwhile, Morris Schaff and John Calef roomed on the fourth floor of the fourth division, one of the two divisions assigned to B Company. Across the hall Jasper Myers and Armond Selby settled in. When Myers arrived in early June wearing a prominent beard, Custer halted him in the cadet area and told him there was obviously a mistake; he was not the one who should be at West Point. He should return home and send his son.[44]

Based on their heights and appointment from Southern states, Joseph Alexander and Joseph G. Blount likely lived in C Company in the fifth and sixth divisions. Six-foot-tall James Dearing, James Barrow, recently arrived James Sanderson, and John West organized their rooms in D Company in the ninth and tenth divisions.[45]

While the entire Corps was easily housed in the ten divisions, the barracks had a number of deficiencies. There was no running water. Each morning the plebes filled water pails at a pump in the middle of the cadet area and carried them back to the upper-class rooms, then returned to fill them once more for their own use. Bathing was limited to swimming in the river during warm weather and required once each week by regulation. During the winter, bathing rooms were located in the basements of the barracks, and a low building located near the tenth division served as a latrine.[46]

The heat was turned on in mid-September and off again in May.

Officers had fireplaces in their rooms, but cadets' rooms were heated by coal-fired furnaces in the basement that distributed heat through flues in the walls. The lack of sufficient heat reaching the upper floors prompted more than a few cadets to write home about studying with blankets or overcoats wrapped around their shoulders. Some even complained about having to thaw out the ink in their writing kits before using it.[47] Tully described how cold his room was during his first winter: "On the north side of the barracks, the cold air generally manages to get in through crevices about the door and window as fast or faster than it does through the flue, so that on a cold day, our room is continually cold."[48]

Academics

Tully's daily activities were completely controlled by drums and bugle calls. A typical daily schedule, constructed from various sources, is shown at table 2.1. Cadets sometimes described the effect the drums that controlled all their activities had on them. Once they began to beat, they rumbled, throbbed, and reverberated in the sally port and cadet area as they pounded out the various rhythms to assemble for meals, classes, parades, or chapel. They were the heartbeat of West Point.[49]

On the first day of academics, Tully rushed down the stairs when Sgt. Louis Bentz's bugle sounded formation for class at 8 A.M. Each section had a specific position in the cadet area, and new cadets searched wildly to find where their section formed up. The first class formed up closest to the academic building and the fifth class farthest away. After the cadet OD received reports from the academically ranking cadet in each section, he commanded them to "March off your sections."[50]

Several of the cadet's instructors, such as 1st Lt. Gouverneur Warren and 1st Lt. Oliver Howard later commanded many of the cadets during the Civil War. Meanwhile, Lieutenant Howard was best known for his Bible classes conducted in the basement of the barracks three times each week. Other instructors, present during

Table 2.1. Daily Schedule	
Monday through Friday	
0500–0510	Reveille
0510–0530	Police call
0530–0700	Study
0700–0730	Breakfast
0730–0800	Washup and class formation
0800–1300	Class
1300–1400	Lunch
1400–1600	Class
1600–Sunset	Drills and evening parade
Sunset	Dinner (30 minutes)
After dinner until 1900	Recreation, study, and free time
1900–2130	Call to quarters
2130–2200	Free time
2200	Taps
Saturday	
0500–0510	Reveille
0510–0530	Police call
0530–0700	Study
0700–0730	Breakfast
0730–0800	Washup and class formation
0800–1300	Class
1300–2200	Free time
2200	Taps
Sunday	
0700–0730	Breakfast
0730–0930	Chapel
0930–1700	Free time
1700–Sunset	Roll call and evening parade
Sunset	Dinner (30 minutes)
After dinner to 1900	Recreation, study, and free time
1900–2130	Call to quarters
2130–2200	Free time
2200	Taps

Fig. 2.6. Academic Building. *1870 CA, SCAD*

these years, would also become well known. English instructor 1st Lt. Adam Slemmer became an instant hero when he refused to surrender Fort Pickens after Florida seceded from the Union. 2nd Lt. Alexander Webb commanded a brigade at the Angle on Cemetery Ridge at Gettysburg. 2nd Lt. Edward P. Alexander taught engineering and later became Confederate general James Longstreet's chief of artillery. 1st Lt. Fitzhugh Lee was the A Company tactical officer before he resigned to become a Confederate cavalry commander.[51]

The new cadets studied mathematics for three hours each day and part of Saturday in Prof. Albert E. Church's Department of Mathematics. The professor wrote a series of math textbooks that were widely used in other institutions. Hardly anyone with a mediocre understanding of mathematics made it through his two-year course, and most academic failures were attributed to his department.[52]

Sections were small, roughly twelve to fifteen cadets assigned by order of merit in a particular subject. Ranking cadets by order of merit and teaching them in small sections began when Col. Sylvanus Thayer, "the father of the Military Academy," served as superintendent from 1817 to 1833. Tully's class was initially assigned to sections alphabetically and then resectioned later in the year according to academic merit.

Each room was arranged with the instructor's desk on a platform facing the door. Blackboards lined three of the walls. The section leader reported the status of the section to the instructor and then all took seats. After any initial questions were answered, the instructor sent each cadet to the blackboards to solve homework problems. At some point, one cadet was asked to "demonstrate" the problem assigned. The cadet picked up a pointer, faced the section, and proceeded to recite what he was required to prove, the assumptions, the facts, and then the solution to his problem. The process was repeated until all cadets had recited. Some sat down after telling the instructor they did not understand the problem or its solution and received a failing grade (a "cold fess" in cadet slang) for the day. Many cadets prayed for the sound of Bentz's bugle to end the session before they were required to recite, but all were graded daily on their work.[53]

After Bentz's bugle announced the end of math class at 11 A.M., Tully raced to find his English section in Prof. John W. French's Department of Ethics and English Studies, where he studied grammar, composition, geography, and rhetoric. On alternate days in the afternoon, Anton Lorenz, the sword master, taught half-hour fencing classes on the first floor of the academic building. The cadets attended classes five and a half days each week.[54]

Every Monday grades for the previous week were posted in the corridor outside the adjutant's office at post headquarters. Those who received proficient grades (2.0 and above on a 3.0 scale) breathed a sigh of relief. Those who failed frequently (overall aggregate grades between 0 and 1.9) were soon assigned to the last section and became the "immortals," those who continually wavered on the brink of dismissal.[55]

Partway through Tully's first month of academics, Secretary of War John B. Floyd announced that the five-year program at West Point was to be discontinued in October. He directed the Academic Board to return to a four-year curriculum. There was much rejoic-

ing among the cadets after the decision, especially those in the second class (Class of 1860), who now would be graduated in June as
well.[56]

Drills, Guard, and Demerits

Practical military instruction was not emphasized as much during the
academic year, while formations and parades remained almost daily
occurrences. When the bugle sounded at 4:30 each afternoon, the
cadet battalion formed up and marched to the Plain where Colonel
Hardee and the tactical officers drilled them for an hour. Hardee had
written a tactics manual for light infantry (*Rifle and Light Infantry
Tactics*) that was adopted by the army in 1855, and he used the Corps
of Cadets to test many of the new drills.[57] Third classman Henry
Dupont (May '61) mentioned how these drills were conducted in
one of his letters home: "He divides up each company in two to form
a battalion of eight companies. We execute all sorts of maneuvers—
form a line facing this way and that, wheeling off to the right or left,
breaking into platoons or fifty things more. The band plays for five to
ten minutes during rest periods. He reviews us when the whole battalion, headed by the band, marches round two or three times before
him. It is guard mount (a formal ceremony held to inspect the new
guard detail) on a large scale. It is, however, the prettiest thing in the
world for the on-lookers."[58]

The only time cadets were excused from military duties was on
Saturday afternoon and after chapel on Sundays. Tully took advantage of those opportunities as many times as he could. One weekend
he and several classmates climbed to Fort Putnam, the crumbling
old Revolutionary War fort that overlooked West Point, and saw the
dungeon where Maj. John André was held prisoner until his trial. At
other times, he liked to roam the woods and pick up chestnuts.[59]

Guard posts were manned in the barracks on Sundays and during study hours during the year. It took every bit as much time to
prepare for guard mount as it did during the summer. After firing his
rifle on Friday evenings, Tully complained that he had to spend all

his evening hours cleaning it in preparation for inspection instead of studying.[60]

Demerits were a fact of life, and Tully and his classmates received many for violations of room regulations. He avoided one set when one of his classmates warned the upper floors that an inspecting officer had arrived:

> You would have laughed if you could have been here just now. While I was writing this letter, I received a "telegraph dispatch" from downstairs stating that an officer was inspecting. . . . My curtains were down and my room was in a confused state generally. I folded my bedding and fixed up the room in a little, the quickest time you ever saw, and had the room ready for inspection by the time that "Old George" got up. . . . You may think that is a little strange about receiving a telegraph dispatch. It was not a telegraph really, but it answers the same purpose and this is what we call it. When on officer begins to inspect on the first floor, the cadets in the lower rooms take a slate pencil or knife and tap on the gas pipe and one can hear it in all the rooms from the first to the fourth floor.[61]

Chapel

Sunday mornings, the Corps marched to church. Attendance was mandatory, as it was at nearly every other college in the country at that time. The cadets squeezed together on the hard benches in the two center rows; the professors, officers, and their families sat in the pews by the walls. Some of the cadets slept bolt upright while others listened to Professor French's two-hour sermons. The cadet choir sometimes showered the cadets below with wads of paper from the loft if the sermon was particularly boring.

The chapel walls were adorned with flags and paintings. Prof. Robert W. Weir, the head of the Department of Drawing and a noted artist in his own right, had painted a mural titled *War and Peace*

Fig. 2.7. Mess Hall. *1867 CA, SCAD*

behind the altar. Flags from the Mexican War hung on one wall, and flags taken from the British at Yorktown hung from the other. Below the flags, black marble shields bore the names of each Revolutionary War general, except for one conspicuously left blank belonging to Benedict Arnold.[62]

Meals

The Corps marched to the mess hall three times each day, rain or shine. William B. Cozzens, the manager of the mess, provided meals from a fairly stylized menu that was often better when the Board of Visitors or congressional delegations came to visit. For breakfast, cadets were treated to the remains of last night's dinner with potatoes and gravy, bread, butter, and coffee. For lunch, the meal most likely included roast beef, veal, fish, or mutton. Most meat or fish was boiled and served with boiled potatoes and bread. Very few vegetables were included, although gardens were set aside at West Point for that purpose. The evening meal consisted of bread, butter, tea or coffee, and perhaps some corn bread with molasses.[63]

Not all of the Corps ate in the mess hall. There were twelve first-class cadets who ate at the home of Mrs. Alexander Thompson and her two sisters in the old military storekeeper's quarters behind the line of brick professors' quarters on the western side of the Plain. Meals were provided there until the last sister died in 1878.[64]

Holidays

Officially the holiday season only included Christmas and New Year's Day, days when cadets were exempted from all duties and the Corps marched to the chapel for services. The officers, soldiers, and their wives tastefully decorated the chapel. Professor French's sermon was lengthy, and the choir was much improved by the addition of female voices.

After chapel on the holidays, the mess hall tables were filled with extra condiments, cakes, and pies. The additional foods were funded by charging each cadet a small fee. One cadet remarked that it was almost impossible to get a passing grade the next day, as study time in the barracks was spent eating all the good food. The respite from military duties did not include the guard detail, and Tully had the misfortune to walk guard on Christmas Eve.

The tactical officers generally overlooked the receipt of boxes of presents during the holidays. Holiday packages often contained sweets, spices, or delicacies, such as peaches, brown biscuits, ginger cakes, cooked sausages, and mutton suet. Tully looked forward to receiving packages from his relatives, but the best gift he received as a cadet was a new pair of warm, white gloves given to him by one of his classmates. Gifts of money were prohibited, but cadets found ways to avoid confiscation. Tully received very little, and whatever he received came from Sam Talbot. James Dearing's uncle made arrangements for money to be sent him from a firm in New York

City. By the end of each year, many cadets were still in debt to the quartermaster.[65]

On New Year's Day, Tully was introduced to the army custom of making calls on his commanding officer. He and his roommates donned their full dress uniforms and visited the homes of the superintendent, the commandant, and some of the officers and professors. The visits sometimes included food and drink even for those on pledge. Morris Schaff remembered enjoying a dinner of fine Virginia ham at Professor French's home. Prof. Henry L. Kendrick was particularly known for his spiced peaches laced with brandy that he readily made available to visiting cadets.[66]

While brandy-laced peaches satisfied some, getting caught drinking while a cadet was a dismissal offense. The only way to avoid dismissal was for all of his classmates to take an oath or "pledge" not to drink until they graduated. Tully's class avoided having to sign such a pledge until their first-class year. It was unlikely they abstained from drinking—just no one was caught until then.[67]

Winter Blues

When winter weather arrived, reveille was adjusted to 6 A.M., and afternoon recreation time increased to an hour and a half. Still, the monotony of the daily schedule, the limited opportunities for outside recreation, and the continual pressure of studying created a depressing atmosphere at the academy. It weighed heavily on the cadets and was rightfully called "gloom period" by generations of cadets. Evening concerts in the library each week offered additional respite from the dreary atmosphere. The Dialectic Society sometimes offered skits and readings in the large, high-ceilinged room over the central sally port.[68]

Outside recreational activities sometimes enlivened the bleak environment. Superintendent Delafield surprised them in late January by arranging sleigh rides. In most years, the depressions on the Plain, one or more ponds, and the reservoir offered places to skate. When the river froze over in early January that year, it immediately became a large skating rink in the afternoons.[69] Tully told Belle:

This is the best place to skate that I ever saw. The Hudson River is frozen over and we can skate for miles up and down the river . . . and it is quite a lively sight, and sometimes very funny to see those that are from the southern states and never saw skating on a pair of skates, trying to break the ice with their heads. . . . We have to get permits to skate. . . . A few weeks ago, three soldier's wives attempted to cross on the ice, before it was frozen very solid and the ice broke in with them, and one of them was drowned.[70]

Examinations and Warrants

Right after New Year's Day, orders were published announcing that exams would commence on January 4, and the Academic Board began with the plebe class. Many cadets stumbled bleary-eyed into formation at reveille after studying late into the early morning hours. Their careworn appearances were often noted by the professors as examinations grew closer.[71]

On the first day of examinations, the OD walked through the barracks and called out, "Second Section, Mathematics, 5th Class, turn out!" That section marched to the academic building where they responded to questions by the Academic Board about the subject at hand. The oral recitations measured each individual's demonstrated command of a particular subject, and satisfactory responses to questioning meant passage to the next semester or year.[72] For some, there was the immediate gratification of doing well. For others, their ashen faces after the exam said it all; they were at the mercy of the Academic Board.

The Academic Board released its results around the middle of January when all examinations were completed. For the first time, the fifth class received both a class standing in each subject and an overall class ranking, a combination of their academic standing and conduct. Some of Tully's classmates—William Bartlett, James Hamilton, Cliff Comly, and William Blakistone—came perilously close to the hundred-demerit limit. Twelve members of Tully's class failed one or more subjects and were recommended for dismissal. Five more were "turned back" to join the next entering class.[73]

Successful passage of the January exams also ended the probationary period for each new cadet. A formal ceremony was held in the chapel for them to receive their cadet warrant, a commission that ranked them somewhere between a warrant officer and a second lieutenant in the US Army. Signing the warrant meant agreeing to serve five years at West Point and three more years in the army. On the day his warrant was issued, Tully also took an oath of allegiance. When his name was called, he stepped forward, raised his right hand, swore the oath, signed the warrant, paid the Orange County clerk twenty-five cents, and returned to his seat.[74] The wording of the cadet warrant shown below became more critical two years later:

> I, Tully McCrea, of the State of Ohio, aged 18 years and eleven months, having been selected for an appointment as Cadet in the Military Academy of the United States, do hereby engage, with the consent of my Guardian, in the event of my receiving such appointment, that I will serve in the Army of the United States for eight years, unless sooner discharged by competent authority.
>
> And I, Tully McCrea, do hereby swear that I will bear true faith and allegiance to the United States of America and that I will serve them Honestly and Faithfully against all their enemies or opposers whatsoever, and that I will observe and obey the orders of the President of the United States, and the orders of the officers appointed over me, according to the rules and articles of war.[75]

Spring Semester and Return to Drills

The second semester brought the fifth class more math classes, continued English studies, and fencing classes in the afternoon on alternate days. The two upper classes eagerly awaited graduation in June, but hopes were dashed on April 4, 1859, when the secretary of war abruptly reversed his decision to return to a four-year program. Stating that the five-year program had not been subjected to a complete trial, the Academic Board was directed to continue the five-year course of instruction.[76]

Recreation and free time evaporated soon after the winter snows left the Plain, as military drills began again. The upper classes often trained with a "flying battery." When a bugle call rang out, the artillery battery crashed to a halt near one corner of the Plain. Within minutes, the cannons were loaded and at a signal, fired in unison. Just as suddenly, they limbered up and whirled away to another section of the Plain to repeat the process once again.[77] When horses, guns, and cadets operated together, it was a mixture of high adventure and danger. Tully related a close call he had in April:

> Everyone had to be wide awake and attend to his duties at the same time keep out of the way of the horses. In one drill, there were 63 horses, 25 soldiers as drivers of the caissons, and 62 cadets to work the battery. One officer drilled the battery. In the midst of conducting the drill, I stepped back to avoid the horses belonging to one section coming very near me and stepped into the wheels of my own piece. The wheel struck me in the back and knocked me down. Fortunately, I received no more than a bruised knee. If the horses had been traveling at a faster pace, the outcome might have been different.[78]

A Plebe No More

June brought examinations once again, and studying took precedence over most other events. Orders announcing the exams were published, and the Academic Board began with the first class.[79] Tully prepared as well as he could. Charles Warner wrote to his family about how hard it was to study for examinations: "You must not expect me to write much or take pains because it is so near the examinations that

I have to study hard and time is precious. I must improve the short time that remains to me and then oh! What a nice rest I will have."[80]

The first year took a heavy toll on Tully's class, and only fifty-six classmates remained at the beginning of the summer of 1859. The cadets ranked at the top of the class were George Burroughs, Henry Wetmore, William Marye, Jasper Myers, and Ranald S. Mackenzie. Discipline problems continued to plague several. Cliff Comly, William Bartlett, James Hamilton, and William Blakistone each received more than 150 demerits for the year. William Bartlett led the class with 194, just short of the maximum limit allowed. His father, Professor Bartlett, was very uncertain about how long his son might remain a cadet if the trend continued. Three more classmates were found "not proficient" by the Academic Board and "turned back" to join the next class.[81]

Summer Camp

Graduation parade in June 1859 ended their tenure as plebes, and the members of the Class of 1862 became yearlings. Within a few days, orders announcing cadet appointments for the new cadet detail and summer camp were published: "Special Orders 89: Kress, Burroughs, Murray, Farley, Gillespie, McCrea, Marye, Bolles, Hamilton, Moreno, Dearing, West, Chaffee, Blount, Barrow, and Wetmore to be lance corporals." A week later, John Kress, Albert Murray, Henry Farley, and George Gillespie were also appointed to the color guard. Tully would wear his corporal stripes only until September because corporals were only appointed from the third class during the academic year.[82]

In 1859 the summer encampment was named Camp Robert E. Lee in honor of a previous superintendent. After the Corps occupied the camp, Tully directed his squad of new cadets in the art of erecting tents in precise, straight rows, filling water buckets, and arranging the contents of their tents in A Company.

The daily camp schedule was similar to last year's—nothing changed very much at West Point. Most of Tully's days were filled with training his squad, and he was assigned as corporal of the guard once every four to five days. The one good thing about guard duty this year was that he could read, write, or talk while occupying the guard tent, but he was repeatedly called upon by his classmates to dole out punishment to new cadets who were inadvertently tricked into violating guard instructions. As much as he thought the pranks were funny, he risked losing his corporal stripes if he participated in any of those activities.[83]

For the first time, Tully's class took advantage of the summer social season. Tully repeatedly told Belle that he did not dance and spent most evenings in his tent writing to her. Dances were not the only social entertainment during the summer. Young ladies might be asked if they were available to walk about the grounds with a chaperone discreetly following behind. Cadets sometimes had to abruptly leave their young charges and return to the camp at a dead run to avoid being late for formations.[84]

Near the end of August as Tully remembered it, the third class returned from furlough while the rest of the Corps was at chapel on a Sunday morning. After chapel there was a lot of hand shaking and talking about friends at home. Some returning cadets admitted that the most unpleasant time they spent was coming back to the academy after ten weeks of leave. Within a few hours, they were all in their gray uniforms, grudgingly resigned to continuing their lives as cadets.[85]

After the battalion sizing formation and new room assignments, the cadets carried their belongings to the barracks and returned to the camp. Southerners in the class continued congregating in D Company where Frank Maney, Joseph Blount, James Dearing, James Sanderson, and James Barrow settled down. Not all the Southerners were in D Company. George Gillespie now roomed with Tully in A Company.

There were too few rooms allotted to each company that fall, and Morris Schaff from B Company found himself rooming with John West from D Company in the eighth division. Two turn-backs from Custer's class, James Lord and James Rollins, joined Tully's class on September 1, bringing the class strength temporarily to fifty-eight.[86]

Life as a Yearling

Coincident with return to the barracks, cadet appointments for the academic year were announced. Four cadet captains were selected from the first class, and the first name on the list became the first captain. The first ranking lieutenant in the first class became the adjutant, and the next senior lieutenant was the quartermaster. The senior ranking sergeant in the second class was appointed the sergeant major, and the second ranking sergeant became the quartermaster sergeant. Each cadet company had three lieutenants promoted from the first class, four sergeants from the second class, and four corporals from the third class. All other cadets, regardless of class, were privates.[87]

Tully and George Gillespie moved into a room on the fourth floor of the second division in A Company. Gillespie had attended Western Military Institute before entering the academy and finished near the top of Tully's class during his first year.[88] Just a few days into the academic year, Tully and Gillespie were excitedly counting the months, weeks, and days until furlough the next summer: "We are the furlough class of 1860. Speed the time and hurry the happy day that shall release us from this prison and return us to the loved ones at home from whom we have been so long separated. We count the time by days until we will be relieved. My roommate and I have a furlough calendar written on a post in our room with pencil with the number of days calculated until next June. By referring to it, I see that it is 274 days until furlough."[89]

The academic year soon became an unending cycle of studying, meals, classes, studying, drills, and more studying. Tully continued taking math and English and learned the art of fencing and use of the small sword and saber. Many key engineering and scientific papers, tactical studies, and weapon manuals were written in French, and Tully's class was required to study French in Prof. Hyacinth R. Agnel's department.[90]

Cadets formed opinions of their professors readily. Tully offered a number of observations about all his instructors and officers too. He was particularly convinced that Professor French was not an effective instructor. Morris Schaff soon declared that Professor Church was "an old mathematical cinder, bereft of all natural feelings."[91]

By this time, most cadets in Tully's class knew everyone in the Corps fairly well. Such close relationships often resulted in nicknames that had to be endured. Tully's nickname was "Widow," and the story behind it unfolded in a later letter to Belle. When an upperclassman asked him during his plebe year if he was any relation to the "Widow McCrea" (a character in a popular song of the day), Tully's classmates picked it up and the nickname stuck.[92]

Others picked up nicknames based on age. The oldest cadet in the class was generally accorded the name "Dad," and John Egan of New York carried that nickname for the rest of his career. Henry Wharton, the youngest cadet, was likely called "Little Dad." There were several "Micks" and "Macs" in the class, and George Gillespie picked up the name "the General" from his habit of reading many military histories. With three years difference in ages between Frank Hamilton from Ohio and James Hamilton from South Carolina, James immediately became "Little Jim." Morris Schaff picked up the name "Ole Shoaf" when his tactical officer incorrectly linked him with the prominent Shoaf family of Virginia.[93]

John Brown's Raid Impacts West Point

That fall the Corps was not immune to the passions that swept the rest of the country. Polarization between Northern and Southern cadets did not take place all at once—it just grew more slowly at West Point than in the rest of the country. Ten or fifteen years earlier, cadets seldom argued over sectional issues. Most respected political conservatism, polite manners, and an ordered social structure. Over the years, the professors and instructors removed offending text from books used by the cadets and refused to allow any such discussion in the classroom. Colonel Delafield even put the Presbyterian Church in Buttermilk Falls off limits because the minister preached abolitionism. But John Brown's Raid at Harpers Ferry in the autumn of 1859 became an event that polarized the cadets.[94]

In October, John Brown and a band of twenty-one conspirators launched a raid against the federal arsenal at Harpers Ferry in western Virginia. Several hostages were taken, and a few citizens were killed in the attacks. Governor Henry A. Wise of Virginia called out the militia and wired Washington for federal assistance. Rumors spread fast that there was an insurrection among the slaves in Virginia, sparking terror among its inhabitants.

The secretary of war placed Col. Robert E. Lee ('29), a former superintendent who was home on leave from his command in Texas, in charge of a federal relief force—a Marine company. He was joined by 2nd Lt. J. E. B. Stuart ('54) and both boarded a late night train to Sandy Hook across the Potomac River from Harpers Ferry. At first light on October 18, Stuart went to the fire-engine house where Brown and his party were holed up, under a flag of truce to negotiate the release of the hostages. He was rebuffed at the door, and Lee immediately launched an attack with the Marines. Brown was captured, several conspirators and two slaves belonging to the hostages were killed. The hostages were released with the loss of one Marine killed. A hunt for other members of Brown's band began immediately. Brown was soon brought up on charges in a Virginia court, found guilty, and sentenced to hang.[95]

Brown's raid had considerable impact at the academy. Not only had two graduates been prominently involved, but one of the hostages taken by Brown was the father of fifth classman James Washington. Washington's room in D Company soon became the focal point for information. Tom Rowland, one of Washington's classmates, wrote home about the event: "There has been quite an excitement here for the last few days occasioned by the startling and almost incredible news of the insurrection at Harper's Ferry. Washington was particularly interested in the state of affairs as his home is only four miles from Harper's Ferry, and his father is a prominent slaveholder of that region. Very fortunately his sister had left home for Baltimore the day before the insurrection occurred, but his father was the first person taken by these desperate men. They came to his house during the night and woke him up, telling him that he was their prisoner."[96]

Church bells in the North pealed, and cannons were fired when Brown was executed. Most Southerners were appalled by the North's behavior. Meanwhile, letters filled with indignation about the incident flew back and forth between cadets and their families. Second classman Henry du Pont (May '61) wrote: "There has been a great deal of talk here about John Brown. A great many seem to think the Union is going to be dissolved. What an outrageous affair at Harpers Ferry. The most disgusting part of the business though, I think, are the meetings of the republicans in Chicago and various towns in Massachusetts to express their sympathy for Brown and regret at the failure of his plans—a great deal of political capital will be made of this affair."[97]

The voices and views of Southern cadets became more strident after Brown's raid. Morris Schaff later wrote that during Brown's trial and just after guard mount one morning, second classman and Southerner Pierce M. B. Young swung his sword around him in an arc and loudly proclaimed, "By God, I wish I had a sword as long as from here to Newburgh, and the Yankees were all in a row. I'd like to cut off the head of every damned one of them."[98] Schaff later attempted to relate how many Yankee heads were required to reach Newburgh: "Newburgh, faintly visible up the river, lies about eleven miles from West Point or something over fifty-eight thousand feet. If we allow two heads per foot, Pierce would have beheaded over a hundred thousand Yankees at a slash, which might have made a material difference in New England's ability to fill her quota two years later."[99]

Tully finally broke his silence about the event when he wrote how Young was responsible for hanging John Brown's effigy from a tree. Schaff recalled that "many of the Southern cadets broke out into natural and violent passion, denouncing in unmeasured terms all abolitionists and everyone in the North who shared their antipathy to slavery." Southern emotions spilled over the day after Brown's execution in early December.[100]

During the evening meal, a confrontation occurred between second classman Emory Upton (May '61), an outspoken abolitionist, and first classman and Southerner Wade Hampton Gibbes ('60).

Gibbes made some comments about Upton's association with female African Americans at Oberlin College, a school he attended before the academy. Upton demanded an apology. Gibbes refused, and the two agreed to settle their differences that evening.[101]

After returning to the barracks, the two antagonists crowded into one of the second-floor rooms in the first division with their principals and seconds. The sentinel on duty called out loudly for the corporal of the guard, but no one took him seriously. Thuds and crashes were heard from inside the room and at the end, Upton came out of the room with blood streaming down his face and went upstairs while Gibbes was seen with a blackened eye. Ned Willis ('60) of Georgia and Felix Robertson (ex-June '61) of Texas led the clamor of Southern cadets calling for Gibbes to finish the fight with bayonets. John Isaac Rogers (May '61), Upton's second and his roommate, came to the top of the stairs and cried out, "If there are any more of you down there who want anything, come right up!"[102]

Tempers cooled until the Dialectic Society met in December. Animated swordplay between Judson Kilpatrick (May '61) and John "Jack" Garnett (ex-June '61) received considerable encouragement from the audience. The Southern cadets yelled "Kill him, Jack" and the Northerners, "Go it, Kil." Although the academy was not a hot-bed of sectionalism or abolitionism, the intensity of views professed by cadets increased as the year progressed.[103]

Politics and Dissension

The underlying tensions brought about by John Brown's Raid and the Upton–Gibbes fight tapered off after exams in January when politics became the hot topic among cadets. They avidly read the New York newspapers and took a lively interest in ongoing congressional debates. The widespread and angry comments in the press often prompted heated arguments between Northern and Southern cadets. Cries of disunion were heard for the first time in the barracks.[104]

In the spring of 1860, the national political parties went about the task of selecting their candidates for president. The Republicans met in Chicago and nominated Abraham Lincoln, a moderate on slavery. John Bell was nominated by the National Constitutional Union party as an independent candidate. The Democratic Party split in two over the extension of popular sovereignty into the territories. The Northern Democrats nominated Stephen Douglas as their candidate. The Deep South Democrats eventually nominated John C. Breckinridge as their choice. His vice-presidential running mate was Sen. Joseph Lane from Oregon, the father of third classman John Lane (ex-June '61) in D Company.[105] His classmate, third classman William Harris (June '61), summarized some of the views held by cadets in the spring of 1860:

> Slavery may be a curse, but I cannot help thinking that Anti-Slavery is a greater one. Perhaps not in theory, but it certainly seems so in practice. The resistance to the execution of the Fugitive Slave Law, the measures which are being taken in some parts of the country to allow negroes to vote, and others of a similar nature, spring from heads to whom I should not like to be subjected. . . . I know that I have as much sectional pride and love of my state as any other man, but I cannot help feeling that the United States has a prior claim on me, especially since the solemn oath I took three years ago. The everyday, reckless talk about Disunion is particularly disgusting to me.[106]

Punishment Woes

Tully began his second semester engaged in a full-fledged personality conflict with his French instructor. 1st Lt. Beekman Du Barry reported him for seemingly inconsequential infractions as the months went by, and Tully took to staring at him in class.[107] Fortunately, his disrespectful actions did not warrant a court-martial, but some of his classmates were not so lucky.[108] In March 1860, Henry Wetmore was court-martialed for being out of his room during study period and missing three assigned guard tours. His punishment was to be served in a "light prison"—a room in the guardhouse where the curtains were opened and bedding was placed near the front of the room. He remained confined to his room at all other times, performed guard tours on Saturdays, and was confined to the limits of the Plain until June 1. Asa Bolles, Cliff Comly, James Drake, John West, and James Sanderson received slightly different punishments at the same time. They were to be confined halfway through their allotted furlough until July 15.[109]

End of the Second Year

Politics took a back seat to studying for exams when June arrived. The "immortals" of the French class—Cliff Comly, James Drake, Joseph Blount, and John West—needed help to make it through the exams, and Morris Schaff described how he helped prepare them: "Preparation for recitation consisted in gathering in our room about five minutes before the bugle blew, and having me translate the reading lesson. If I read over the 'Benefactor Recompenses' to that crowd once, I read it a dozen times. If any one were to stop me with an inquiry, 'How's that, Morris?' or, 'What's that, Morris?' he would be squelched immediately by all the others exclaiming indignantly, 'Oh, for God's sake! What's the use of stopping him for that? Go on, Morris, *go on*! The bugle will blow in a minute.'"[110]

At the end of his second year, Tully finished seventeenth in the class, with a total of ninety-one demerits that year—most of them caused by his personality conflict with Lieutenant Du Barry in French class. His roommate George Gillespie, Ranald Mackenzie, William Marye, the confined Henry Wetmore, and Charles Suter were ranked as the top five distinguished cadets.

The Academic Board dealt harshly with John Blocker, Joseph K. Dixon, Henry Farley, Henry Dodge, Richard Kinney, Albert Murray, E. Kirby Russell, and J. Eveleth Wilson. They were found deficient in one or more academic subjects and recommended for dismissal. Eight more were close to the annual demerit limit. William Blakistone, James Hamilton, and Frank Maney actually exceeded it, and the Academic Board ordered them to be dismissed.

Secretary Floyd did not always accept the recommendations of the Academic Board and made a regular practice of commuting cadet dismissals. When the final results were adjudicated later that summer, no cadets were dismissed in Tully's class. Two were "turned back," and the class strength was reduced to fifty-four members. The final decisions came too late for Frank Maney, who left the country in late June to join Giuseppe Garibaldi's army in Italy.[111]

Furlough Delayed

Meanwhile, the Class of 1860 received their diplomas and departed, but Tully's class still remained at West Point. Their bags were packed and their furlough uniforms hung ready, but the superintendent delayed releasing them. Angry and disappointed, Tully wrote: "No doubt you expected me home. I expected to be with you before this time, but 'old Dell' seems determined to keep us back here as long as possible. The 1st class was relieved last Saturday, and there is no reason under the sun why we should not be. In all probability I will not be home before sometime next week. Do not expect me until you see me."[112]

Before their release came, Tully's rebellious attitude exceeded his good sense. He and several of his classmates were reported for throwing a potato at a new cadet. In addition to the five demerits he received for unmilitary conduct at dinner, he was ordered into confinement, and his long-awaited summer leave was suddenly in jeopardy.[113]

3

Crises of Conscience

West Point, December 1865. Tully's classroom was on the second floor of the academic building. After hanging up his overcoat, he limped to his desk and awaited the arrival of the first group of cadets. He was an acting assistant professor in Professor Church's Department of Mathematics teaching algebra, geometry, and trigonometry to first-year cadets. He shared his duties with two other officers. The plebes studied algebra for one and a half hours each day along with a similar amount of time spent studying English. During the second term, two hours of French were added to the schedule on alternate days.

The cadets entered and stood at attention while the section leader reported, "Sir, Second Section, all present." "Thank you, Mister Harris. Take seats!" Tully quickly turned to the day's lesson. After several general questions, he announced that a review of the semester's work would begin next week in preparation for the semiannual examinations in January.

He then sent each cadet to the slate blackboards to solve problems from the previous night's homework. Soon only the scratching of chalk could be heard. A half-hour later, Tully ordered all work to halt. This was the hardest time for the cadets. They wiped sweaty hands on their trousers, and their stomachs churned uneasily as they awaited the dreaded call to demonstrate their solutions.

"Mister Harris, please explain the first problem." Cadet Harris stood at attention and began by saying, "Sir, I am required to solve the following problem," and then using the pointer, discussed his solution point by point. Tully asked several questions to ensure that various teaching points were covered. Harris received full credit for his work that day.

Each of the other cadets discussed their solutions. Tully ended one presentation when it became obvious that the cadet did not understand

Fig. 3.1. Post Headquarters and Chapel. *1867 CA, SCAD*

the basic concept. He received a failing grade for that day. When the crisp, clear notes of Bentz's bugle announced the end of the period, he said, "Class is dismissed. Good day, gentlemen!"

Tully limped over to the open window and closed it. He remembered how long he had stared out those same windows after his classmates left on furlough while he was confined and in danger of losing part of his summer furlough.

Furlough—June 1860

Furlough, that elusive event that each member of Tully's class planned so carefully, finally arrived on June 19. They donned their furlough uniforms, slung their bags over their shoulders, and walked down the hill to the south dock. Tully looked through his window and tried to keep up appearances as he watched them leave.

Fig. 3.2. Cadet Furlough Uniform. *1863 CA, SCAD*

The furlough uniform worn by his classmates consisted of an army blue uniform coat with a single row of brass buttons, a standing collar, and blue trousers. A white shirt and dark tie were worn under the coat. A black hat with a brass plate and "U.S.C.C." (United States Corps of Cadets) emblazoned on it completed the uniform. Stuffed in their bags was a supply of cadet buttons that could be strung together to form bracelets that were much favored by young ladies.[1]

Cliff Comly and Morris Schaff likely traveled together to Dayton and Kirkersville, Ohio, respectively. Bill Marye came from California and more than likely did not go home because of the distance, but he had relatives in Baltimore. Ebenezer "Rube" Ross and George Gillespie traveled to Tennessee. Sadly, the delay in releasing the class caused Gillespie to arrive in Chattanooga the day after his father's funeral. James Dearing traveled south to his uncle's home near Alta Vista, Virginia, south of Lynchburg. Fellow Virginian Richard Kinney returned to Staunton and probably met some of his old classmates from the Virginia Military Institute. Henry Farley headed farther south to Laurinsville, James Hamilton to Charleston, and John Blocker to Edgefield, all in South Carolina. It is possible that Joseph Blount traveled partway with them on his way to Talbolton, Georgia. William Bartlett walked across the Plain to his father's quarters on Professors' Row, dropped his bags, and most likely contemplated visiting Ranald Mackenzie in New Jersey or George Burroughs in Boston to simply get away from West Point.[2]

Mackenzie's mother lived in Morristown, New Jersey, and she was very accommodating to his classmates. Many stayed at her farm when they were allowed to leave the Military Academy. When she found out that Tully was an orphan, she immediately "adopted" him as a member of her family.

Much of the time spent on furlough that year was not immediately recorded at the time, but several common events were described in letters written later. Some cadets wrote about giving riding lessons; others wrote of eating meals in homes full of company. Endless discussions ensued about how difficult it was at West Point and stories about some of their pranks and close escapes from the tactical officers. Some even wrote about meeting Mexican War or Indian War veterans, which usually ended in displays of the manual of arms and how it had changed over the years.[3]

Five days after his classmates left, Tully and several others were finally released by the commandant, except for John West whose confinement extended throughout the summer. Tully returned to Ohio for the first time in twenty-four months, free from discipline and orders until August 28.[4]

As planned, he visited Sam Talbot and his family in Urbana and his brother Percy near Addison. His small bag of brass buttons probably found their way to Belle's wrist. He and Belle spent July 4 with some of his cousins watching the fireworks light the sky over Dayton. The days flew by, and before long it was mid-August and time for Tully to return to the academy. Now completely infatuated with his sixteen-year-old cousin, his emotions spilled over on the train when thoughts of being away from her for three more years brought him to tears.

His return trip took him first to Urbana to have dinner with Sam Talbot and his family. Talbot was the father Tully never really knew, even giving Tully extra spending money to help make his trip east easier. After leaving Addison, Tully spent the next evening with Morris Schaff and his family in Kirkersville. The next morning they attended a Republican mass meeting, which must have been quite an experience for Schaff, an avowed Democrat. At the meeting Tully met Benjamin Stanton, the congressman who appointed him, and he asked about the possibility of a change to a four-year curriculum. Stanton replied that Sen. Jefferson Davis's commission was meeting at West Point and would likely support a continuation of the five-year program.

Having delayed as long as they could, the two classmates boarded the Baltimore train and headed east. When it stopped at Harpers Ferry, they wandered about the town, saw the bullet holes in the walls of the fire-engine house, and were amazed that John Brown and his companions held out for such a long time. A piercing whistle brought them running back to the train to continue their trip east. Arriving in New York City, they spent two days visiting museums, art galleries, and Central Park and even crossed the river to get a better view of the city. They boarded the steamer *Alida* early on August 28 and landed at the south dock about 11 A.M.[5]

Return to West Point

Tully and his unhappy classmates returned to the academy all morning long. John West was so happy to see them that he wept like a child. In short order, they found their trunks, donned their uniforms, and joined the long line at the barber shop to shear away their mustaches, side-whiskers, and long hair. At 2 P.M. they marched to the encampment and reported to the commandant. Two classmates did not answer when the roll was called. The location of Frank Maney remained unknown, although some thought he had left the country, and James Drake was reported sick at home in Indiana.

Later after the initial round of tall stories about leave ended, the prospect of spending three more years at the academy finally caught up with Tully. With memories of leaving Belle still vivid, he suffered an "awful attack of the blues." He was in good company, because his roommate, George Gillespie, was still grieving the loss of his father that summer. Although Tully believed he could shrug off the sadness soon, he wasn't sure that some of his classmates could do so. Cliff Comly had begged his father to let him resign while he was home on leave but was wisely told to stick it out.[6]

Before summer camp ended, new appointments in the Corps for the academic year were posted outside the adjutant's office. The list included Kress, Gillespie, Mansfield, F. Hamilton, Clayton, Lovejoy, Semmes, Rollins, Barrow, J. Smith, Moreno, Suter, James, McCrea, and Alexander, who were to be promoted to lance corporal. Tully was surprised. He thought his punishment in June had destroyed any chance for an appointment that year.[7]

Morris Schaff and John West wanted to room together, but Schaff had to get into D Company first. Putting pads of newspaper in his shoes before the sizing formation gave him just enough added height to make the cut. Tully and George Gillespie were assigned a room on the fourth floor of the second division in A Company. That evening, a mellow voice and the strumming of a banjo in camp was traced to James Dearing. He sang a catchy new song learned over the summer—one from minstrel shows then touring the country called "Dixie's Land."[8]

The status of James Lord was finally decided late in the summer. Already turned back once to join Tully's class, he was found deficient in French in June and ordered to be dismissed. The letter-writing efforts of a general officer, a congressional representative, and his father proved successful, however, and Secretary Floyd decided not to dismiss him. He rejoined the class on September 1.[9]

While Tully and his classmates were on furlough, Sen. Jefferson Davis's commission convened at the academy to examine the efficacy of the five-year program. The superintendent, the commandant, the academy staff, all the professors, and selected cadets were interviewed. The committee produced a comprehensive review of cadet academics and made recommendations for changes to the curriculum by September. As expected, the committee recommended continuation of the five-year program.[10]

Several personnel changes took place that summer as well. New instructors joined the academic staff, and most cadet companies had new tactical officers. Bvt. Lt. Col. John. F. Reynolds ('41) became the new commandant. Colonel Hardee would soon resign his commission to become a general officer in the Confederate army.[11]

Academics Begin—September 1860

When Tully and his classmates came back, they were steeped in politics and reinvigorated regional prejudices. The strident Southern voices in the Corps became louder. Henry Farley, a redheaded firebrand in Tully's class from South Carolina, frequently and loudly argued against the possibility of a Lincoln victory. Morris Schaff's views, colored by living with Georgian John West at the academy, offered a Southern view of states' rights during his furlough one evening and received a violent rebuke from his uncle: "Morris, I tell you slavery has no rights either before God or man, it is a curse and a disgrace to this land, and the South shall not bully us under the threat of disunion into its defense any longer!"[12]

With these unprecedented events beginning to unfold around them, fifty-four members of the Class of 1862 began their third-class year. Glad to be rid of math and English, Tully and his classmates studied philosophy (physics) in Prof. William H. C. Bartlett's Department of Natural and Experimental Philosophy. Professor Bartlett ('26) authored a series of popular college textbooks, pioneered the use of photography in astronomy, and was one of the foremost astronomers in the country. He was a brilliant theoretician but possessed a nervous temperament that made the cadets believe he was not a good teacher.[13] Tully offered his own description of the professor:

> "Old Bart" is an odd looking little man. He has a little sharp pointed face, and little eyes that are always dancing around and watching everything that is going on. His hair sticks out straight all over his head, and he is so nervous that he cannot keep to himself still for a minute. He has a habit of twitching his chin and mouth that looks very comical until we get used to it. The cadets say he is trying to see if he can catch the end of his ear. He has been trying it for a great many years but has not yet succeeded and the ear does not seem to mind it but has got used to it and takes it very patiently.[14]

His next class was civil engineering in Prof. Dennis H. Mahan's ('24) department. Next to mathematics, it was the second most important course taken by cadets. Professor Mahan was the senior professor, and it was his decisions and arguments that often swayed the Academic Board. He testified for the academy before congressional committees and the secretary of war. Well respected in academic circles, he authored many scientific works on engineering, and his book on civil engineering was accepted as the best text on the subject in the country. But most cadets felt the professor was intolerant of those who could not keep up with his thinking.[15]

Much to his disgust, Tully found himself studying French in Lieutenant Du Barry's section once more. Personality clashes between them were evident from the first day, and it worsened as the year progressed. Tully also studied topology and mapmaking in Prof. Robert W. Weir's Department of Drawing. Professor Weir, a nongraduate, was noted for his portraits, landscapes, architectural drawings, and etchings. In addition to the mural in the chapel, his *The Embarkation of the Pilgrims* adorned the rotunda of the US Capitol.[16]

For the first time, Tully went down the hill to take riding classes. Tully's experiences were no different from countless other cadets:

> I have been to riding drill four times, and strange and as wonderful as it may seem, I am still alive, and my neck is not yet broken. I have not been throwed [*sic*] yet, although I came very near it last Friday, when my instructor gave my horse a cut with his whip, he jumped sideways very suddenly, and like to have spilled me off. One of the squad named Smith was throwed five times the same evening, and another one was throwed once. It is mighty good fun to go to riding when I can get a good horse that does not trot too hard and watch some for the other cadets that cannot ride very well. . . . There is not much danger of getting hurt when we are thrown because we ride in the riding hall which is a large building with a floor covered in tan bark which makes a very soft place to be thrown. We always get the worst horses; the best ones are used by the First and Second classes.[17]

Many cadets complained of injuries sustained while riding or the viciousness of their mounts. Their relationship with the horses was definitely antagonistic. Rumors persist that after being reported by his instructor for cruel and inhumane treatment after he kicked his horse, one cadet unsuccessfully appealed his punishment in a letter to the commandant by stating that the horse kicked him first.[18]

The Monotony Continues

Tully's life remained a continuous and monotonous routine of academics and drills with little free time. He often complained there was little respite from preparing for inspections, even on Sundays:

> Sunday is not to us a day of rest, for I have been preparing for inspection ever since I got up at reveille this morning. Immediately after breakfast we are marched onto the parade ground where our muskets and accoutrements are inspected and woe to the cadet that has a gun that is not bright and clean. Lt. Griffin, the present commanding officer of my company is much more particular and rigid in his inspections than Lt. Saxton, our old officer. After this inspection is over we have to prepare for inspection of quarters at which our rooms have to be in "apple pie order." The floor cleanly swept, every article of furniture in its place and cleanly dusted, and our shoes neatly blacked. The place for our shoes is at the foot of the beds, ranged in a row. I forgot to put them in your picture but you can take a pencil and put some in yourself. There are three pair at the foot of my bed and two pair at the foot of Gillespie's.[19]

Isolated events enlivened their lives and the visit of the Prince of Wales in October held their attention for a week or so. A huge crowd gathered to see the royal visitor. The West Point band played several martial tunes, and the Corps paraded for the prince and his entourage. Next morning when Tully demonstrated a particular principle at the blackboard and responded to questions from one of the royal visitors, the prince and several British officers were surprised at the amount of detail and performance required of each cadet.[20]

James Drake returned pale and thin just before the end of October. The post surgeon declared that if he stayed through the winter, his illness might cause his death, so the secretary of war sent him back home to Indiana on a six-month leave. Word was received from Frank Maney, the other missing member of the class, that finally confirmed that he was a captain in Garibaldi's army in Italy.[21]

With a little free time one evening, Tully gave some thought to his career as an officer:

> When I graduate, I will be 24 years old. I will have a short furlough then of a few months, after which I may be allowed to remain at some eastern post for a few months longer. Then I will be ordered out to some fort in the heart of a wild territory in the midst of Indians and there to remain for four to eight years, deprived of home, friends, society, and everything else but a hard, laborious and monotonous life. This is a great sacrifice, but it is required of us by the government to recompense them for the expense that they been at in giving us an education. I never should be willing to take one away from a home where she had been surrounded by society and refinement all her life, and ask her to share all these deprivations with me. A fort in the midst of the wilderness surrounded by crafty and savage Indians is not the place for a lady.[22]

Straw Votes

The upcoming national elections caused the Southern cadets to place a ballot box in the cadet area, and all were urged to vote for their choice for president. With Joseph Lane's father running for vice president with Breckinridge, he was anticipated to win. Morris Schaff later wrote that as a result, "some evil spirit stole his way into West Point. . . . A better scheme than a straw ballot to embroil the Corps and to precipitate hostilities between individuals which soon involved the States, could not have been devised."[23]

When the votes were counted, ninety-nine had been cast for

Breckinridge and Lane, forty-four for Bell, forty-seven for Douglas, and twenty-four for Lincoln. When the Breckinridge ticket won the straw poll, it led to a "disunion" meeting where many Southern cadets made threatening statements about Lincoln and the real election. Henry Farley emphatically stated that he would resign if Lincoln was elected.

The Southern cadets were particularly upset at the number of votes Lincoln received, prompting them to send tallymen into the divisions to find out who voted for him. When one made a disparaging remark in Tully's room after Tully informed him that he voted for Lincoln, the tallyman was ordered to leave. A few days later, a large Kentuckian picked a fight with Tully, leaving several scars on his face in the process. Tully's outspoken views did not set well with his Southern orderly sergeant (first sergeant) either, who reported him for numerous trivial offenses. Tully successfully appealed the offenses to his tactical officer, and the commandant canceled the reports.[24]

The Presidential Election and the Aftermath

After the election of Abraham Lincoln, turmoil at West Point increased during the next eight months. Within a few weeks, cadets were forced to make difficult choices between allegiance to home, families, and state or to the Union. Prior to the election, the cadets from South Carolina received instructions to come home if Lincoln was elected. Already outspoken in their criticism of Lincoln, some sent a letter to the *Columbia Guardian* swearing to stand by their state if it seceded. Others swore to resign and never serve under Lincoln as their commander in chief. Acts of support for secession soon began to appear. Some Southern cadets began wearing a blue ribbon tied to a button on their caps that Tully called "the South Carolina cockade."[25]

Amid rejoicing by Northern cadets at Lincoln's election, the newspapers carried word that South Carolina had convened a secession convention. Letters soon arrived from Mississippi. Alice wanted to know how Tully voted, and he described his response in a letter to Belle: "I told her my choice was Ole Abe. This I suppose will shock my southern cousins and they will think that I am a hopeless Abolitionist. William Wood, the editor of the Free Trader has sent me his paper for nearly four years. I am afraid that when he hears I am a "black Republican" he will send it to me no longer. He is a great disunionist and thinks the north has grievously wronged the south in electing Lincoln and thinks it is best to form a southern republic."[26]

Capt. Edward C. Boynton's history of West Point recorded there were 278 cadets in the Corps in November 1860. Included in that number were eighty-six Southerners. The Southern contingent was not a majority of the Corps. There were eighteen Southerners remaining in Tully's class (to be consistent with other accounts, the term "Southerner" only refers to those who came from one of the seceded states). After the election, earlier threats to resign soon became reality. Henry Farley became the first member of the Corps to submit his resignation after he received his parent's or guardian's permission. On November 19, he was released and headed home. Four days later, two more South Carolinians, James "Little Jim" Hamilton and John R. Blocker, submitted their resignations.[27]

The earlier cadet letters to the *Columbia Guardian* caused a stir, but the small number of resignations in December failed to upset Washington. In fact, journalists looked for other reasons for the defections. One Philadelphia reporter concluded that low class standings rather than lack of patriotism was the real reason for the departures. John Blocker took personal affront at that speculation and requested that his resignation be canceled until after exams in January. By late December, however, he resubmitted his resignation.[28]

Meanwhile, Secretary John B. Floyd and the chief of engineers, Brig. Gen. Joseph G. Totten, debated over who should replace Colonel Delafield as superintendent. Congress seemed bent on changing the current policy of only appointing engineer officers to that post. To preempt that change, General Totten nominated a prominent Southern graduate and engineer, Maj. Pierre Gustave Toutant Beauregard ('38) of Louisiana to relieve Colonel Delafield in January 1861.[29]

While Southern emotions were escalating, Tully's hot temper landed him in serious trouble with Lieutenant Du Barry. Three weeks after Tully began staring at him in class, leading to reports of insubordination, he was in arrest and confined to quarters with the loss of all privileges. Once again he appealed his punishment to his tactical officer, and surprisingly the commandant restored him to duty without even a reprimand.[30]

Secession Begins

On December 20, the South Carolina secession convention proclaimed South Carolina to be an independent commonwealth. When the ordinance of secession was signed, Charleston erupted with boisterous, cheering crowds. Headlines screamed "The Union Is Dissolved!" Bonfires lit up the sky, church bells tolled, and the long-awaited break from the Union had finally taken place.[31]

Now other Southern cadets began to worry what actions they should take if their own states followed South Carolina's example. Initially there was a strong belief in many parts of the land that there would be no disunion. Cadets sought advice from family, friends, and politicians. Many were told to stay the course and graduate. For the first time, there were conflicting views on whether a cadet not of legal age was legally bound by the oath he had signed as part of his cadet warrant.

The Southerners in the first class were particularly conflicted. They had struggled for five long years to gain a highly valued diploma from West Point. Each knew that after they left the service three to four years hence, their education at West Point could lead to lucrative professional jobs. Letters to politicians flew home or to Washington. First classman Tom Rosser (ex-May '61) wrote to Sam Houston, the governor of Texas. He may not have liked the answer he received in return:

> Much as excitement has wrought the public mind, I cannot for a moment entertain the belief that any cause for disunion exists, or that the masses of the people would be ready or willing to precipitate the country into the horrors of civil war. Such a picture should not be contemplated, but we should

look to the union as the main pillar in the temple of our independence. Under her wise protection, we hold our dearest rights and enjoy our greatest blessings. My advice is that you give your whole time and attention to your studies in order that you may be prepared to assume that position to which your graduation would entitle you.[32]

Another first classman, John Pelham (ex-May '61) of Alabama, wrote several letters to his father and to Judge A. J. Walker, who advised him to resign immediately if Alabama seceded. His father delayed responding until events had already spiraled out of control. Fourth classman Tom Rowland (ex-May '61) of Virginia wrote that Virginia's governor, John Letcher, had "advised all cadets from Virginia to remain here and do their duty until their native State shall absolutely require their services."[33]

Of primary concern to the cadets was to whom did they owe allegiance—to the state they were appointed from or to the Union, which they had sworn to uphold? Fifth classman Edward W. Anderson (ex-'64) from Virginia asked his parents about the oath he took when accepting his appointment. His mother responded: "You are not exactly a commissioned officer yet. You are under a sort of bond to serve the United States eight years and you are under this bond as a minor. Now I think you are bound by that contract, but of course, no country ever contemplated that a man should fight his own countrymen. I think you should remain where you are until called upon to kill your own brethren, then sheath your sword and tell all men, law or no law, you will draw it for your country's enemies."[34]

The federal government, of course, believed the oath taken to support the Union was paramount. Conflicting instructions and advice coupled with pressures from home and other cadets simply confused the issue. Within Tully's class, letters from friends and family prompted many discussions over what actions they should take. George Gillespie's family was part of a small Union minority in East Tennessee. Before his father passed away, Gillespie promised him that if Tennessee seceded, he would remain with the Union.[35]

Muted Holidays

The heated rhetoric lowered somewhat during the holidays. The extra money paid by the cadets resulted in extra spices, meats, and desserts, but "Old Bratt," the mess hall manager, withheld the mince pies until the day after Christmas. Tully described his Christmas dinner in "this delightful institution of science and learning":

> At my table we had a glorious old patriarch of a turkey. He must have died of old age, as he was awful tough and lean, but the toughness did not save him, for he was soon parceled out to ten unmerciful cadets who went to work with knives and forks with a desperate and resolute look. In the course of half an hour, the unshrinking cadets had succeeded and nothing was left, but a mass of aged looking bones. . . . Christmas pies for dinner were given to us on the Saturday or Sunday after Christmas. I suppose the reason we do not get them at Christmas is that "old Bratt" is afraid we would kill ourselves with so many good things at the same time.[36]

Just before Christmas Eve, Joseph K. Dixon of Mississippi returned to his room in D Company to tell Morris Schaff and John West that he had submitted his resignation. He sent a telegram to the governor of Mississippi stating, "The war is begun, I leave tomorrow."[37]

With the loss of Farley, Blocker, Hamilton, and Dixon, only fifty classmates faced examinations in January 1861. Tully predicted that many more would follow when their states seceded:

> Southern cadets are beginning to leave very fast. Two of the best in the second class started this afternoon. They were accompanied to the dock by a large crowd of their friends and carried part way on the shoulders of the crowd of secessionists who cheered them as they left. One of them was my orderly sergeant with whom you will remember I had trouble last fall. . . . Both were from Alabama. . . . They think 50–60 will go home next month. The Academic Board will pro-

nounce about 20 wanting in their different branches of studies. Besides, almost every cadet from the extreme southern
states had their resignations ready to hand in to the Supt. as
soon as they hear that their states have seceded. In all probability, six states will secede.[38]

Charleston Harbor

Maj. Robert Anderson ('25) reached the conclusion that his tiny garrison at Fort Moultrie near Charleston would never be able to resist
an assault by the South Carolina militia. Rereading the exchange of
letters with Washington and the verbal instructions he received from
Secretary Floyd's office, he concluded he had some discretion in
deciding how best to defend his position.[39]

After dark on December 26, Anderson shifted his small garrison
to Fort Sumter in the center of Charleston harbor. At first light, a
greatly excited Gov. Francis Pickens immediately demanded its evacu-
ation. Major Anderson refused, stating that he had not reinforced
Fort Sumter, merely shifted his garrison from one fort to another.[40]

Washington erupted with the news, and Northerners quickly elevated Major Anderson and his little band to hero status. After lengthy
and contentious arguments within his cabinet, President Buchanan
reluctantly decided to send provisions to the fort. Secretary Floyd
from Virginia violently disagreed and was ultimately forced to resign.[41]

When the news about Sumter arrived at the academy, Southern
cadets loudly proclaimed that Anderson's actions were yet another
affront to Southern sovereignty. Amid the swirl of these events, Tully
happily realized that for the first time in three years he was not part of
the guard detail during the holidays.

The Parting of Ways

The daily newspapers arrived just after the first classes ended on January 9. Emblazoned across the top of the *New York Times* was a banner
headline announcing that Mississippi had seceded. Two days later,

Florida and Alabama followed suit. On the 19th, Georgia seceded, and within another week so did Louisiana. Texas waited until February 1. The cotton states' militias quickly occupied post offices, federal installations, and arsenals within their boundaries.[42]

With the cadets pressured by family, friends, politicians, and other cadets to return home, resignations became more frequent. The superintendent forwarded each letter of resignation, the required parent's permission, the cadet's academic and conduct standing in his class, and the superintendent's recommendation to General Totten in Washington. All resignations were required to be approved by the secretary of war before they were allowed to leave the academy.[43]

Meanwhile, two Northerners, Henry Dodge of New York and William Barnard of New Jersey, failed their January exams and were recommended for dismissal. Dodge was turned back one year and later graduated with the Class of 1863, while Barnard is believed to have joined a New Jersey infantry regiment. Unrelated to the current series of events, John Kress, an excellent student who stood high in the class, submitted his resignation because of a drastic change in his family's circumstances in New York.[44]

Leadership Changes

Major Beauregard, who once looked like the ideal candidate to replace Colonel Delafield, now became cause for alarm. In early January, Beauregard stopped in Washington on his way north and mentioned that he would probably resign if Louisiana seceded. General Totten and newly appointed secretary of war John Holt did not want the superintendent of the United States Military Academy to resign. Prompted by Louisiana's pending secession, Holt directed Colonel Delafield to resume his duties as superintendent until a new officer could be appointed. Major Beauregard served exactly five days as superintendent and later resigned his commission on February 20. He was soon appointed a brigadier general in the Confederate army.[45]

The Regulars Depart

In Washington, Lt. Gen. Winfield Scott believed there was a strong possibility of civil unrest when the electoral votes were counted in January or during the inauguration of President Lincoln in March. In preparation for these eventualities, he ordered a small number of regular units to come to Washington. 1st Lt. Charles Griffin, Tully's tactical officer, was ordered to prepare the West Point artillery battery to depart, and in mid-January the engineer company also left for Washington.[46]

When the two units left, they took all the horses with them, leaving none for riding instruction for several months. The small group of enlisted men left behind was consolidated into a single unit, and Sgt. Thomas McEnaney appointed its first sergeant. Eventually enough horses, guns, and enlisted personnel were located among paroled troopers and soldiers to restart cadet instruction.[47]

Conflicting Allegiances

The creation of the Confederacy in the middle of February likely prompted more resignations, but the necessary permissions from parents or guardians took time to arrive. Resignation did not come easily for any cadet, save those from South Carolina. The few remaining cotton states Southerners in the first class believed their five-year goal to gain a diploma was almost within their grasp. John Pelham from Alabama refused to accept any appointment in the Confederacy while he was under obligation to the United States. He wrote to the new president of the Confederacy for advice: "Being still a member of the Military Academy, I don't think it would be exactly proper for me to offer my services to the new government, but I am anxious to serve it to the best of my ability. If you think it would be better for me to resign now, than to wait and graduate, a single word from you will cause me to resign. As soon as my resignation is accepted, I will consider myself under your orders and repair to Montgomery without delay."[48]

Pelham later noted that several members of the first class received letters from Davis advising them to wait and graduate. His father hoped for a peaceful settlement and reconciliation between the states but finally gave his permission to resign. When some Northern states began offering commissions to cadets and officers as their state militias were increased, General Scott directed that all officers or cadets must resign their existing commissions in the regular army before accepting a volunteer commission.[49]

A Patriotic Holiday Creates a Pause

Washington's Birthday proved exciting that year. All academic duties were suspended at 11 A.M., and the commandant led the Corps into the chapel. 1st Lt. Fitzhugh Lee followed at the head of A Company, then 1st Lt. Alexander McCook with B Company, 1st Lt. Robert Williams with C Company, and finally 1st Lt. William B. Hazen with D Company. As George Washington's Farewell Address was read, Morris Schaff wondered how his words about the importance of maintaining unity of government were received by the remaining Southern cadets.[50]

The crash of drums and bugles at tattoo caused Tully and George Gillespie to rush to the windows fronting the Plain. Schaff was on the third floor of the eighth division with Custer and others. Below them were Rosser and other Southerners on the second floor. Schaff related that he never heard such a burst of music when the West Point band emerged from the sally port into the cadet area playing the "Star Spangled Banner." A thunderous cheer begun by Custer broke out. The Southerners in D company began calling for "Dixie," and they were answered by ringing cheers from A and B companies beyond the sally port. Cheer after cheer began with Rosser's group at one window and Custer's at another. It was a grand night.[51]

More Resignations

The cadets honored the arrival of Bvt. Col. Alexander H. Bowman ('25) as the new superintendent on March 1. Not all mourned the departure of Colonel Delafield that day. When one of the officers commented that the colonel had left, an old Irish worker reportedly said, "Deed [*sic*] Captain an' he has, . . . and its [*sic*] many the dry eye followed him!"[52]

Among the first issues facing the new superintendent were the resignations of all the Georgia cadets. John West returned from a disunion meeting in early March to tell Morris Schaff that he, Joseph Blount, Joseph Alexander, and the remaining Georgia cadets had decided to resign. Alexander initially did not want to resign, but his father pleaded with him to return home to avoid confiscation of all their property.[53]

Unexpectedly the governor of Georgia complicated their release. He commissioned them as second lieutenants in the military forces of Georgia, and the list was published in the *New York Herald*. Colonel Bowman required Blount and West to write an additional letter emphatically stating they had not accepted any commission in the Georgia force before submitting their resignations.[54]

After their release, Schaff sorrowfully waved to West as he walked down to the south dock with the other Georgia cadets. Blount would serve in a Virginia artillery battery. Alexander returned to Georgia but refused to join the Confederate army until drafted. A few days later, Stephen Moreno followed the Georgia cadets down the hill after he resigned to return to Florida. Oliver Semmes's father, a recently resigned US Navy officer, was in New York obtaining machinery and munitions for the Confederate navy. He paid his son a visit, wrote out his permission, and Oliver resigned on March 18 and traveled south to Mobile. West soon joined him in the First Regular Confederate Artillery Battery in Alabama.[55]

A few Northerners left that month too. Benjamin King of the District of Columbia and William Spurgin of Indiana resigned and later joined the Union army. John Kress notified the superintendent that he wanted his earlier resignation canceled. A benefactor had provided funds to care for his family until he graduated, so he asked to be reinstated. After the Ides of March, none of the other cotton states seceded, and the number of resignations slowed. With few notable exceptions (Pelham and Rosser), all the cadets from the cotton states were gone.

In Washington during Abraham Lincoln's inauguration, the engineers and sappers from West Point formed part of his escort, and Lieutenant Griffin's battery unlimbered near Capitol Hill. Near the end of his address, Lincoln warned the citizens of the seceded states: "In your hands, my dissatisfied fellow countrymen, and not in mine, is the momentous issue of civil war. The government will not assail you. You can have no conflict without being yourselves the aggressors. You have no oath registered in heaven to destroy the government, while I shall have the most solemn one to "preserve, protect, and defend it."[56]

The Onset of War

April began calmly. Virginia, still uncertain of her path, was watched carefully by the rest of the country. Governor Letcher informed the Virginia cadets to remain and graduate. The apparently calm atmosphere led fifth classman Edward Anderson (ex-'64) to discuss hotel reservations at West Point for his family that summer.[57]

In the background, friends and relatives continued to write and ask what their cadets were going to do. Southern governors continued to commission cadets in their state forces. First classman Henry A. du Pont (May '61) explained how his classmate John Pelham reacted when their appointments were received: "Take Pelham for instance, and a man of nicer and more honorable feelings never lived. . . . But like many others, they have appointed him a first lieutenant, that is, have published it in the newspapers his appointment; there having been no application made for the place. He does not intend to serve in the army but will resign as soon as he graduates, which is quite right under the circumstances, as he cannot be expected to fight against his home and friends."[58]

In early April the superintendent was made aware that the fifth class did not receive their cadet warrants in January. In the confusion of the initial secessions, the press of examinations, and the changes in superintendents, the warrants were never received from Washington, and the plebes never took their prescribed oath of allegiance. Colonel Bowman requested that Washington send their warrants to the academy and planned a formal ceremony in the chapel for April 18.[59]

The First Shot Is Fired

Since mid-March, Lincoln and his new cabinet had intensely tried to solve the ongoing situation in Charleston Harbor. The South received mixed signals from members of the cabinet about what the new administration was going to do. Lincoln finally decided to send a federal relief expedition to peacefully resupply the garrison at Fort Sumter and sent a message to advise Governor Pickens of the attempt to provision the fort.

The city of Charleston was gripped by a war fever as its citizens anxiously awaited the arrival of the federal relief fleet. Volunteer regiments manned the fortifications around the harbor. Confederate president Davis ordered P. G. T. Beauregard, now a brigadier general and in command of all Confederate forces around the harbor, to reduce Fort Sumter if the garrison did not surrender before the fleet arrived.

The best of plans often do not survive the first shot and it soon became apparent that this was the case at Charleston. A series of messages between Major Anderson and General Beauregard failed to cause Anderson's small band to leave the fort. The imminent arrival of the relief fleet prompted one last early-morning message on April 12, saying that unless the fort were surrendered, a bombardment would begin within the hour. Anderson again refused. Left with no choice, Beauregard ordered the bombardment to begin.[60]

His order went to Fort Johnson on James Island, the site of two batteries of the First South Carolina Artillery. 1st Lt. Wade Hampton Gibbes ('60) went up the hill to prepare his mortars. At the beach battery, 2nd Lt. Henry S. Farley (ex-'62) awaited the order to fire. Capt. George S. James, the battery commander, later joined Farley at the beach battery as the time grew near. At precisely 4:30 A.M.,

James's hand dropped, and Farley yanked the lanyard, sending a signal shell arcing high into the air. Some years later, Farley noted: "The circumstances attending the firing of the first gun at Sumter are quite fresh in my memory. Captain James stood on my right, with watch in hand, and at the designated moment gave me the order to fire. I pulled the lanyard, having already carefully inserted a friction tube, and discharged a thirteen-inch mortar shell, which was the right of the battery. In one of the issues of a Charleston evening paper which appeared shortly after the reduction of Fort Sumter, you will find it stated that Lieutenant Farley fired the first gun, and Lieutenant Gibbes the second."[61]

Henry Farley was not the only former member of the class to participate in the bombardment. 2nd Lt. James Hamilton (ex-'62) was home sick in bed when the bombardment began. Determined not to miss such an important event, he rose from his bed and took up his duties until the fort surrendered. 2nd Lt. John Blocker (ex-'62) was assigned to Mortar Battery No. 2, east of Fort Moultrie. Thirty-four hours later, the interior of Fort Sumter was in flames, and its walls were breached in some sections. Major Anderson and his weary band were out of supplies and finally forced to surrender.[62]

Major Anderson received permission to salute the US flag before the garrison left, and his cannons thundered out a national salute. Sparks from ongoing fires flew about and likely caused the powder in one cannon to explode prematurely, wounding several crew members and killing one. Anderson carefully tucked the tattered Union flag under his arm and followed his soldiers and their wounded comrades out the gate. Behind them, the South Carolinians joyously raised the Palmetto Flag over the fort.[63]

The News Reaches West Point

The news of the attack on Fort Sumter arrived the next day just as the cadets changed morning classes. The *New York Times* had arrived containing the first dispatches from Charleston, including the string of messages between General Beauregard and Major Anderson. Textbooks and lessons were set aside, and the cadets talked of nothing else except the initiation of hostilities. Southern cadets loudly proclaimed that the North had violated Southern rights but were soon cowed by the outpouring of patriotic spirit from the Northern cadets. Tully expressed the feelings of many when he wrote that his "thoughts are with Major Anderson and his little band fighting so bravely against such fearful odds at Ft. Sumpter [*sic*]." The same feeling spread rapidly across the country, uniting the Northern states and their people in a common cause to halt further dissolution of the Union.[64]

Lincoln and Washington React

In the days after Fort Sumter surrendered, President Lincoln issued a proclamation stating that the seceded states were in rebellion against the laws of the United States. He called for seventy-five thousand three-month volunteers to restore the Union and ordered a blockade of the Southern coast. Within a month, he increased the strength of the regular army and the navy, added forty regiments of US volunteers, and called for Congress to convene in early July. Northern governors enthusiastically began raising volunteer regiments to defend the Union. The border states' governors vehemently refused to raise a hand against their sister states.[65]

The Turmoil Continues

Cadets from the border states and Virginia now saw their future challenged. Fourth classman Tom Rowland (ex-'63) of Virginia wrote to his aunt shortly after the news about Fort Sumter reached the academy. He eloquently described the choices each cadet confronted on April 16, the day before Virginia made its decision: "All Virginians and all cadets from Border States, for they are almost the only southerners left here now, anticipate the immediate secession of Virginia and the other Border States. What else can they do? . . . We cannot hesitate, we must either make up our minds to fight under the "Stars and Stripes," wherever our services may be called for, or we must resign at once and free ourselves from that solemn oath to serve the United States "honestly and faithfully, against all their enemies or opposers whatsoever."[66]

Meanwhile, the continuing resignations of officers and cadets were creating such a national outrage that West Point came under verbal attack from citizens and Congress alike. One day after the firing on Fort Sumter, Simon Cameron, the new secretary of war, ordered all cadets and officers at the academy to take an oath of allegiance to the United States, and Colonel Bowman set the ceremony for May 13.[67]

Crisis of Conscience

On April 17, Virginia's legislature voted to secede. Arkansas, Tennessee, and North Carolina followed suit one month later, adding three more states to the Confederacy. The day after Virginia's decision, it was time for each member of the fifth class to pledge to support the Union, knowing full well that it might place them in a difficult position of raising their sword against relatives, family, or even their own classmates. Classes were canceled, and the Corps marched to the chapel to observe the ceremony. Absolute silence descended upon the gathering. No one knew what would happen if someone failed to take the oath. None had ever done so before. The plebes were called up to the altar five at a time. Each cadet put his left hand on the Bible, raised his right hand, took the oath, and sealed it with a kiss on the Bible. Tully later described what happened:

> An exciting scene was witnessed in the chapel on Thurs. afternoon. The fifth class was assembled to take the oath of allegiance to the United States, as we have all willingly done heretofore. Everything is done on such occasions to make it as solemn and impressive as possible. As it was supposed that some from the Slave states would refuse to take the oath, a great many cadets of the other classes had assembled to witness the ceremony. The oath is administered in the chapel in

the presence of the military and academic staff in full uniform. Ten of the class refused to take the oath, and of course will be dismissed. When the first one refused a few southern cadets tried to applaud him by stamping on the floor, but he was immediately greeted with such a unanimous hiss that he could clearly see the sentiments of the great majority present. This shows what a change has come over the country, for never before did a cadet refuse the oath of allegiance, but on the contrary was proud of the opportunity, and hailed with delight the day when he was a plebe no longer.[68]

Later fifth classman Edward Anderson (ex-'64) wrote to his mother describing the anguish he suffered when he failed to raise his hand that day:

It was a solemn occasion for me. All my class was in the Chapel. Many of the other classes were there to see the ceremony. The officers of the army were there in their dress coats and epaulets and we wore our side arms. We went up five at a time to take the oath. Before it was taken, it was explained that "Cadets constituted part of the land forces of the United States," and as near as I gather "took this oath in the same spirit that officers and soldiers take it." Well Mama, I didn't take the oath, and they may pack me off in short order, or dismiss me. . . . Nine other cadets of my class refused to sign with me. I don't believe a true Southerner signed it. He couldn't.[69]

After the ceremony, Colonel Bowman telegraphed Washington that ten cadets in the fifth class had failed to take the oath. He expected many others to join them and requested instructions. In short order, the secretary of war authorized him to process the resignations of any cadet who failed to take the oath or to send away any cadet he felt was causing disorder. The lengthy process of securing approval from Washington was ended.[70]

"A Stampede of Cadets"

The authority to process resignations came none too soon. Colonel Bowman's office was soon inundated with resignations after Virginia seceded. With the oath of allegiance pending for all other officers and cadets, many remaining Southerners attached permission letters already in their possession and turned in their resignations. Over the next few days, the telegraph wires were jammed with messages from parents approving their cadet's decision to resign. First classmen John Pelham and Tom Rosser saw their long-sought goal of graduating slip away. They submitted their resignations and packed their bags.

A week after the surrender of Fort Sumter, more than thirty cadets from all classes had submitted their resignations. Eight Southerners from the Class of 1862 now awaited Colonel Bowman's ruling. Ebenezer Ross (Tennessee), Horace Twyman (Virginia), and George Lovejoy (North Carolina) submitted their resignations right away. James Dearing (Virginia) turned in his paperwork as soon as he received his uncle's permission. Richard Kinney (Virginia), George Marchbanks (Tennessee), William Blakistone (Maryland), and Robert Noonan (Maryland) each handed in the required paperwork to Bowman's office. Concerned that the Southern cadets might be mobbed in New York on their way home, the superintendent advised them to leave through Albany instead and withheld any announcement of their resignations until after they departed.[71] Tully wrote that he never saw such an alarmed crowd as those who left here at the beginning of the week:

> This has been an eventful week in the history of West Point. There has been such a stampede of cadets as was never known before. 32 resigned and were relieved from duty on Monday and since then enough to increase the number to more than 40. There is not very few cadets from any southern state here. My roommate, a good Union man from Tennessee, is still here and intends to remain as long as he can possible do

so with honor. He has no sympathy with the southern rebels, and thinks that the Union feeling is overwhelmed in his state for the present, but will prove true and loyal in the end.[72]

When the last of the resignations was approved, a total of eighteen Southerners in Tully's class had left the service of the nation since the election of Lincoln. With the addition of three others who joined Northern units, his class was now reduced to thirty-two members. Only one Southerner, George Gillespie, remained.[73]

The raising of volunteer regiments in various Northern states frequently brought offers of early promotions and commands to the officers as well. 1st Lt. Alexander McCook, the B Company tactical officer, accepted the colonelcy of an Ohio regiment and returned to recruit and raise volunteers. Several other officers either tendered their resignations or requested permission to return to their regiments soon after Virginia seceded. The commandant, Colonel Reynolds, left for his Union regiment and was replaced by Capt. Christopher Augur ('43) in August. Professors' families were also caught up in the turmoil as the sons of Professors Weir, Church, Bartlett, and French volunteered to fight for the Union.[74]

Patriotic Resurgence

The attack on Fort Sumter stirred a rise in patriotism in various cities across the land. Tully described some of the events that month:

> Several cadets of the First Class were at New York City yesterday and they give a wonderful account of the stirring scenes going on there. A large mass meeting met in the park to endorse the course of the administration and welcome Major Anderson. It is said to be the largest and most enthusiastic meeting ever seen in New York. . . . The buildings were literally covered with the stars and stripes and every man, woman and child had either a flag or rosette attached to their clothing. The ladies are commencing to wear red, white and blue

dresses and trim their bonnets with the same glorious combination. Hurrah for the stars and stripes "Long may it wave,
over the land of the free and the home of the brave." . . . The
cadets brought some paper flags back from New York and we
have put up some paper flags in our rooms. Lt. Lee, my tactical officer and a secessionist, made me take mine down as all
ornaments are forbidden by regulation. Lt. McCook found
flags in all the rooms in B Company, but did not make the
cadets take them down.[75]

Morris Schaff later recorded that Tully took down his flags then defiantly painted his water bucket in bands of red, white, and blue for
which there was no academy prohibition.[76]

Tully's tactical officer, 1st Lt. Fitzhugh Lee ('56), a nephew of
Col. Robert E. Lee ('29), submitted his resignation the day after
Virginia seceded. With Tully's stationery now emblazoned with the
words "THE UNION IS FOREVER" at the top and a US flag prominently displayed on the envelope, he described Lieutenant Lee's
farewell:

On Friday night, the officers serenaded Lt. Lee, who is a Virginian, and has resigned because his state has seceded. He
was the most popular officer that I have ever seen at West
Point. He was liked by the officers, cadets, ladies, and in fact
by every one that knew him. It was a bitter day for him when
he left, for he did not want to go, and said he hated to desert
his old flag. But he thought it was his duty to do as Virginia
did. He was the Commandant of my company, and on Friday
evening he came to bid us goodbye. He went to every room
and shook hands with every one of us, with tears in his eyes,
and hopes he said that our recollections of him would be as
happy as those that he had of us. On Saturday morning after
breakfast the cadets gathered in front of barracks to see him
off. As he passed in the omnibus we took off our hats and
waved them as he passed.[77]

Early Graduation of the First Class

The first class learned that their colleagues at the Naval Academy had received permission to graduate early soon after Fort Sumter surrendered. A class committee quickly drafted a letter for all to sign requesting permission to graduate early. Although General Totten initially disapproved the requests, the secretary of war thought it was a wonderful idea. On April 29 Totten sent instructions to "take steps to have the First Class graduated as soon as practical, and take immediate action for the completion of studies of the Second Class with view to graduating that class also." Additionally, he approved the recommendation that the graduating class be required to take an oath of allegiance.[78]

The cadets in the first class had already purchased their uniforms, rings, and class albums in preparation for graduation in June, but the Academic Board was not about to graduate them without examination. The other cadets were examined later in June.

On May 6, two days after they completed their examinations, forty-five members of the first class, which included Edmund Kirby, Henry du Pont, Judson Kilpatrick, Adelbert Ames, Emory Upton, and Samuel Benjamin, received their coveted diplomas and became the West Point Class of May 1861. All raised their hands and took their oaths as officers. Tully described the scene when the first class entered the mess hall:

> They afterwards entered the mess hall and were received by the other classes with such rounds of applause as was never heard before. The oldest waiters and employees about the mess hall, who are used to seeing such demonstrations on the departure of graduating classes, were perfectly astonished. In the exuberance of my joy, I knocked a mess hall stool all to pieces, which will cost me a few dollars. But the applause and excitement reached its height when Henry Kingsbury, the adjutant entered. He is one of the best and smartest men of the class and by far the best soldier. He was deeply affected by

the compliment which the other cadets gave him, and made a
speech in behalf of himself and his class, which brought tears
to many eyes."[79]

The newly commissioned officers were ordered to report to
Washington as soon as possible. Disappointed that they would have
no leave, they traveled to New York City where they purchased pis-
tols, swords, and additional uniforms before taking a late train to
Washington. Upon their arrival in Philadelphia, they were arrested by
armed police and asked to surrender their swords and revolvers. After
being shown a copy of their orders from the War Department, the
mayor immediately apologized. He had received a telegram from the
well-meaning mayor of Jersey City that a band of armed Southerners was on the train heading south. Within two months, however, six
Southerners in that class resigned their commissions and joined the
Confederate army.[80]

Just after the May class left, the Academic Board prepared a compressed course of instruction in first-class subjects for the new first
class. The board was under considerable pressure. They had to prepare the new first class to graduate early and begin creating a four-
year course of instruction to replace the five-year program finally laid
to rest by the secretary of war. Subsequent messages from Washington indicated the possibility that a third class (Tully's class) might be
required to graduate later in the year.[81]

Tully's class was now the new second class, and cadet officer
appointments for the summer were posted on the wall outside the
adjutant's office. Kress was to be sergeant major; Wetmore was to be
quartermaster sergeant; Gillespie, Hamilton, Rollins, and Smith were
to be first sergeants; and Mansfield, Suter, James, McCrea, Lancaster,
Arnold, Marye, Egan, Burroughs, and Calef were to be sergeants.[82]

Graduation of the first class and departure of the furlough class
left many empty rooms in the barracks, and the remaining cadets
were consolidated into the first four divisions in the cadet barracks.
Tully and George Gillespie moved to the second floor of the first
division.[83]

Continuing Pressure to Resign

At first Tully heard little from his Southern relatives in Natchez until Alice asked when he was going to resign and return to Mississippi. He wrote to Belle after he responded to Alice:

> She wanted to know when I was going to resign and come home like other southern cadets. I told her that as I had received my appointment from Ohio, I was a Buckeye and not a southern cadet, and in all probability, it would be some time yet before I resigned. I told her all about the uprisings in the north and how they regarded the actions of the southern people. I would like to see some of my secessionist cousins read the letter for I know they will think that I have degenerated into a terrible abolitionist and everything else that is bad. Alice also said that Bob and Mark Wood had joined the Miss. Volunteers and were on their way to Washington.[84]

Alice's letter was followed a short time later by a similar letter from his cousin Maggie Wood. Tully was prevented from responding when President Lincoln ordered all mail to the seceded states stopped. Tully didn't think he would hear from his Southern relatives again for some time and was surprised to find one last letter from Alice on his desk one afternoon. Again she implored him to return to the South, and her words pained him greatly. He poured out his bruised feelings in a lengthy letter to Belle:

> I received a letter from Alice on Monday that caused me a great deal of pain. Tears seldom come to my eyes, but they were filled while reading her letter. She implores me by everything that is sacred and dear to resign my position here and return to the south. . . . She writes my letter created great astonishment and regret in my uncle's family, who seem to think I have become demoralized into an abolitionist, and

everything else regarded as horrid by the southern people. . . .
Aunt Margaret says she would rather see me dead and in my
grave than advocating such principles. Alice says Aunt Margaret took it very hard when she heard what conclusion I had
come to and was taken sick on account of it. Alice beseeches
me by the memory of our mother to reconsider the cause of
the present difficulties, for I would be sure to see the south
was not to blame and would resign and return to the land
of my birth. This argument did not have much weight, for I
know my mother would not have counseled me to dishonor
and disgrace by proving false to mother, my Country, my
oath, and my duty, in its hour of danger.[85]

The Class Struggles to Complete the Year

New first classman Francis Parker (June '61) wrote that his class only
took the most important and practical parts of their first-class courses.
Two weeks later, he complained, "This method of cramming a year's
course into two months' time is rather hard on us. I never studied so
hard and did so poorly as I am doing now."[86] Additionally, he and his
classmates ordered their officer uniforms, equipment, class rings, and
photo albums. For the most part, they studied in the barracks while
Tully's class took charge of the Corps.

Meanwhile, West Point was under attack by Congress, the president, and the secretary of war over those who were educated by
the nation and then left it in its time of need. In the face of certain
civil war, eleven states had seceded from the Union, the superintendent and the commandant changed three times, and many of Tully's
instructors resigned or returned to their regiments. If civil war did
occur, the scene was set for classmates to meet on various battlefields,
something that Tully predicted earlier:

The future in the present unhappy state of our country is
wrapped up in more than usual uncertainty, and there is no
means of foreseeing what will be the state of this country

one year from now. I hope the people of the south will have
returned to their reason and allegiance to the government
before that time. But I fear that this is a frail hope, and
that we are destined to have a long and bloody civil war, in
which brother will be fighting against brother and untold
suffering and misery will be experienced on both sides. God
grant that the new Congress that meets next month, may
present a better set of men than the last, and that some of
them may devise means for bringing this fratricidal conflict
to a speedy end.[87]

Amid the ongoing turmoil, Tully found trying to study for his
exams most difficult. Hoping to bring back his concentration, he
pulled out pen and paper and wrote:

I have been vainly endeavoring to study and feel discontented
and provoked with myself because I cannot bring my mind
to my lessons. I have been sitting with my book in hand but
my thoughts were far away, and I have at last come to the
conclusion that it does about as much good to study Sanscrit
or Hebrew as try to learn Philosophy when not taking an
interest in it. It is the same with my classmates and cadets of
the other classes. It is impossible to form an interest in the
abstract principles of science when there are such great events
occurring around us every day of such practical importance
to us all. The professors are in despair and have tried every
means to prevail upon cadets to study more. But their appeals
have been in vain, and we are all as poorly prepared for the
examination that commences next week as we could conve-
niently be.[88]

He threw himself into his studies but was woefully unprepared
for the exams. When the results were posted a week later, he was
greatly surprised to find that he had finished fifteenth in his class.
George McKee and William Beebe failed their examinations and were

turned back to the next class. With their loss and the Southerners who resigned, the class strength was down to thirty.[89]

Tully had a little time to reflect on the chaotic events that had taken place over the past eight months. Another class was about to graduate, and his class would take over the Corps. He had seen half his class willingly take more than one oath to protect and support the Union. By this time, half his class had not! He was convinced that a shooting war would soon erupt, and he and his classmates were uncertain whether they would graduate early enough to join the rapidly forming army around Washington.

4

"When Shall We Meet Again?"

West Point, December 1865. Tully finished grading the boards just as Bentz's bugle sounded again. Daily grading was one of the bedrock principles established by Col. Sylvanus Thayer many years before. Each cadet was measured daily on a 3.0 scale; less than 2.0 was considered a failure. He sent the grades to the post adjutant weekly and soon the hallway was filled with cadets marking down their grades. Groans or cheers could be heard as they read off their standings.

There was time before lunch to find problems for the January examination that Professor Church had requested each instructor prepare. Tully worked until he heard the sound of drums and the shouted commands of cadet officers as the Corps marched to the mess hall. He carefully locked the test problems in his desk and walked to the mess hall where he found three classmates, John Egan, Frank Hamilton, and Jim Lancaster, engrossed in a discussion of artillery support at Gettysburg. They had arranged silver pitchers and salt and pepper shakers around the table to represent the various artillery positions on Cemetery Ridge.

Grabbing a cup of coffee from one of the stewards, Tully joined in the lively discussion. He and Egan had suffered greatly on the third day at the hands of General Lee's artillerymen, including two of his former classmates, James Dearing and Joseph Blount, during Maj. Gen. George Pickett and Brig. Gen. J. Johnston Pettigrew's charge. Watching his classmates interact, Tully remembered the long discussions held in his tent during the cadet summer encampments after the attack on Fort Sumter. All of them had high hopes that the Union would prevail in any conflict with the South. Those hopes were dashed when the Union army was defeated at the First Battle of Bull Run. Now that his class led the Corps after early graduation of the two upper classes, conversations also addressed the possibility of their early graduation as well. Tully hoped to

Fig. 4.1. Cadet Class Formation. *1869 CA, SCAD*

be assigned to the artillery, but all was contingent upon the availability of positions for junior officers in the various regiments.

Summer Camp 1861

The heroic actions at Fort Sumter led to the encampment being named Camp Robert Anderson that summer. Just before camp began, Henry Wetmore applied for a leave of absence, but when his initial request was denied, he compounded the problem by getting caught absent without leave, thereby losing his appointment as quartermaster sergeant for the summer. Tully was appointed to replace him.[1]

Tully's new appointment had one major advantage. He shared one of the larger tents with the quartermaster, a first classman who was heavily engaged in studying in the barracks and seldom present. The spacious tent soon became a gathering place for Tully's classmates, as it offered one of the few tables in the camp where they could write letters.

Forty-five days after the May class graduated, the thirty-five members of the Class of June 1861, including Patrick O'Rorke, George Woodruff, Alonzo Cushing, Justin Dimick, and George Armstrong Custer, were examined and then graduated on June 24. They too were ordered to Washington without leave—all except Custer who was in arrest until July 17. A few were immediately promoted to first lieutenant as their regiments were expanded in the rapidly building army around Washington.[2]

Now with the graduation of the new first class, only seventy cadets remained to train the new cadets that summer, not counting a few Southerners still awaiting their official release. Robert Noonan (Maryland) finally received permission to return home to Frederick where he joined a Confederate unit despite his parents' Union sympathies. E. Kirby Russell (New York) received his mother's permission, and Colonel Bowman approved his resignation although fearful that a flood of resignations to join Union regiments would begin.[3]

Tully's class advanced from third class to first class in the space of forty-five days, and now orders announcing new appointments in his class for the summer encampment were published. The list showed Marye, Kress, Gillespie, Egan to be captains, Hamilton, Smith, McCrea, Mansfield, Burroughs, Murray, Arnold to be lieutenants, and Lancaster to be lieutenant and adjutant.[3]

Bill Marye was the first on the list and became the first captain. He, John Kress, George Gillespie, and John Egan commanded the four cadet companies during the encampment. James Lancaster took up his duties as the adjutant, while the lieutenants became platoon leaders. Tully successfully argued with his tactical officer to retain the quartermaster's tent, sewed on his lieutenant's stripes, and enjoyed the privileges of being a first classman. Most important, passes to leave the encampment became more frequent.

Holidays and Discipline Woes

Several classmates continued their battles with the academic and tactical departments during the summer. Henry Wharton stood high in the class but collected more demerits than allowed. Consequently the Academic Board recommended he be turned back one year. His status was not resolved until late in August when the Secretary of War reversed the board's decision and allowed Wharton to continue with Tully's class.[5]

Frederick James began experiencing severe chest pains whenever he ran up and down the stairs in the barracks. The doctor recommended that he apply for a leave of absence to recover, and he was placed on leave until September 1. His father, a well-to-do banker from New York City, and his family lived across the river on a two-hundred-acre estate overlooking Cold Springs during the summer.[6]

On the Fourth of July, the cadets paraded on the Plain, and the cadet battery fired a national salute of thirty-four rounds despite the fact that eleven states had seceded. After the parade, the Corps marched to the chapel to hear George Burroughs read the Declaration of Independence and Morris Schaff give the oration. Schaff later admitted that when he looked over the large crowd, he was too scared to begin his speech. Then someone inadvertently stepped on the tail of a small dog that had crept into the chapel. The sharp yelps provoked laughter and eased the tension in the room. Schaff suddenly remembered his speech and delivered it without any further ado.[7]

Life as a First Classman

The daily routine of summer camp left little for the new first class to do except run the guard detail and attend increased drills and exercises. Tully was assigned as officer of the guard once every six days and often complained about the lack of sleep. He was also annoyed by the incessant requests and utterances by the new plebes in the guard tent.[8]

At times guard duty was fun. One evening Tully saw several of his classmates leaving camp to meet some ladies. Not finding their names on the list of those authorized to leave, he mischievously ordered out the guard detail and marched it up to the carriages where his classmates stood. Calling out in a sharp, cross voice, he ordered them all to report to the guard tent. The ladies were terribly frightened, but his classmates knew Tully was only kidding. One of them told him later that one lady gave his hand such a squeeze in her fright that it would have been worth a week's confinement in the guard tent.[9]

The new tactical officers that summer were universally disliked. Tully characterized his tactical officer as "too mean to live and hated by everyone with an intensity that is surprising considering the short time he has been here." In less than five days, Tully received as many demerits as he had in the previous six months.[10]

The new officers passed out severe punishments for seemingly small errors during guard detail. Attempting to avoid the same fate, Tully tried to make his inspections more detailed and precise, but his good intentions were for naught. He received three demerits for his tent walls not being lowered, four demerits for allowing citizens to loiter in the vicinity of the guard tent, and four demerits for allowing cadets to loiter around the guard tent at parade. Incensed, he wrote a caustic appeal to the commandant that several classmates pleaded with him not to send. He ignored their advice and delivered it anyway. It was declared disrespectful, and Tully received five more demerits. A few days later, his appointment to cadet lieutenant was revoked. He was placed in arrest, confined to his tent, and Ranald Mackenzie was appointed to replace him.[11]

Tully complained bitterly to Belle about his punishment:

My unfortunate disposition, or temper if you please, has again placed me in conflict with the authorities. I am in arrest again, and have lost my office in the battalion of cadets. My offense, "submitting a disrespectful excuse to the Commandant." On last Friday I was officer of the guard. I tried to attend to my duties and did attend them properly, and the next morning after I marched off guard, I was congratulating myself how fortunate I was that I had succeeding [*sic*] in pleasing the officer in charge and had not received a single report. But to my great astonishment in the succeeding afternoon, when the delinquencies were published, I found I had been reported for three different offenses in either of which there was not a particle of justice. You may imagine how I felt, after trying my best to do my duty, and not getting any demerits, to be thus reported by the wholesale, giving me nearly as much demerit in one day as I had for the whole of the last six months.[12]

As Tully sat in his tent one afternoon, John Russell, one of the men who helped him get his appointment to the Military Academy, arrived to visit him. Mortified to have Mr. Russell find him in disgrace and confined like a common criminal, Tully apologized profusely. He hoped that his change in status would not be communicated back to Ohio, and Mr. Russell assured him that it would not.[13]

Tully's hot temper had too often placed him in situations where he got in trouble. Russell's visit certainly caused him to reflect on keeping it in check in the future. As the days passed, his confinement was not all that dreary or isolated. Classmates came by every day to write letters on the table in his tent or to have long discussions about their future in the army. Within a week, Tully was released from arrest and his punishments rescinded, but he was not reappointed to his prior cadet rank.

Tully's temper almost got him in trouble again. When his request to visit the West Point Hotel was not approved, his discussion with the commandant became heated. He explained that Tully "had better keep cool and not get excited." Tully later saw it as a lesson in dealing with subordinates that would stay with him during his career as an officer.[14] He kept his temper in check, and there were no further outbursts before graduation.

For the rest of the summer, Tully was a "high private" with few responsibilities. He regularly attended hops and often went "walking" with lady friends to Fort Putnam, all the while wondering why he had not done so earlier. One young lady patriotically offered to raise a company to fight in the war. Tully was to be the captain and she a first lieutenant. She and Tully entered into a conspiracy: she gave him a small ring to send her when he decided to take command of the company, because she knew her father would never understand. Laughingly, Tully wrote to Belle that now was the time for her to enlist.[15]

The First Battle of Bull Run

The Union army's defeat at Bull Run on July 21 dampened the atmosphere at West Point. The news arrived just as Morris Schaff was passing a group of excited officers standing around Professor Church near the barracks. The professor stopped him and said, "Mr. Schaff, it has just been received that our army has met with defeat and is fleeing to Washington in utter rout." Schaff later noted that some of his classmates gathered in the company streets that evening and sang patriotic songs to raise their spirits.[16] Tully also described what happened when the news arrived: "An excitement here last Monday when we heard of the defeat of Gen. McDowell's army was very intense. There were scarcely any, either cadets, officers, or soldiers but had some friend or relation in the routed army. But the distress was the greatest among several ladies whose husbands had been ordered off a few days before to take part in the battle. There were a great many poor women too that had husband, brothers, and some dear friends in Griffin's West Point battery which was reported cut to pieces and then captured, and Capt. Griffin killed."[17]

Initial reports from any battlefield are invariably incorrect. The battle to end the war took place thirty miles west of Washington. Brig. Gen. Irvin McDowell attempted to halt the Confederate advance in the afternoon by advancing two regular batteries, Capt. Charles Griffin's "West Point Battery" (Battery D, Fifth US Artillery) and Capt. James Rickett's Battery I, First US Artillery. Both batteries were overrun as federal forces were forced to withdraw. By late afternoon, he ordered the federal forces to retreat toward Washington. What began as an orderly retreat quickly turned into a rout as scared civilians watching the battle became entwined with frightened men fleeing the battlefield. A few Confederate artillery rounds on a

crowded bridge started a panic that did not halt until the much fragmented force was back in Washington.[18]

1st Lt. John Pelham (ex-May '61) of Stuart's horse artillery probably recognized the captured Union cannons on Henry House Hill
as those he had trained with at West Point. A little farther south near
Blackburn's Ford, 2nd Lt. James Dearing (ex-'62) survived his first
brush with combat just five days after his assignment to the Washington Artillery.[19]

Three days after the battle, President Lincoln appointed Maj.
Gen. George McClellan ('46) to head all the federal forces. By mid-
August, General McClellan organized most of the units around Wash-
ington and the Shenandoah Valley into a new organization called the
Army of the Potomac. He quickly brought order and discipline to his
new command as equipment and horses poured into Washington.[20]

Later battlefield reports show that Captain Griffin was not killed,
but his guns and a number of his men were lost. West Point drowned
in sorrow for the losses sustained. As a result of the defeat, the secretary of war ordered Colonel Bowman to prepare Tully's class for
early graduation. On July 27 his class returned to the barracks to
begin a highly compressed program of studies. Lights burned late as
they tried to cram two years of knowledge into a few weeks. Rumors
spread that they would graduate in September.[21]

Less than a week later, Tully and his classmates were shocked
when Secretary Cameron reversed his decision. Tully recounted what
happened later:

> I was in the section room yesterday afternoon, reciting in
> artillery tactics, when the adjutant entered and told the
> instructor to dismiss the section as there would be no further
> recitations. You should have seen the blank astonishment and
> despair that come over the faces of the cadets. As soon as they
> were out of the hearing of the officers, their suppressed anger
> was relieved in such a round of swearing as you never, and
> I hope may never, hear. Cadets are noted for their profanity,
> but I think the most profane would have been shocked if he

could have heard the swearing when we got to barracks and told the rest of the class the news. One of them speaks three languages, and it would have been amusing had it not been so wicked to hear him swearing in all the different languages. Comly was so mad, he turned perfectly pale.[22]

Beginning Their Final Year

Tully shrugged off the angry and resentful arguments of his class-mates, lamenting their retention at West Point for another year. He believed that staying one more year would make him a better officer. Meanwhile, it was his good fortune and that of ten of his classmates to be selected to eat meals at the Thompson's residence for the rest of the summer. He no longer had to march to meals and thoroughly enjoyed the good food and conversation.[23]

After his classmates resumed their duties in summer camp, they received an invitation from Fred James to have dinner with him and his family in Cold Springs. Secretly Tully and fifteen classmates crossed the river in an overloaded small boat to join them for dinner. After two hours of pleasant conversation and a sumptuous seven-course meal, the cadets successfully returned to the academy without being caught. It would be the last time anyone left West Point for a while. Smallpox was discovered in Buttermilk Falls, and the superintendent immedi-ately quarantined the post in early August. No one could enter or leave, effectively cutting off any nightly forays to Benny Havens's inn.[24]

Taking chances with regulations and being a cadet officer proved unlucky for Ranald Mackenzie. Always close to the borderline in demerits, he was reported for being off limits near the end of July and demoted only a month after taking up his duties as a lieutenant. Morris Schaff was appointed in his place.[25]

A More Specific Oath

Verbal attacks on West Point increased after the loss at Bull Run. Even Secretary of War Cameron attacked the Military Academy in his annual statement. In his message to Congress when it convened, Lincoln chastised those who had left the army in its hour of need. Radical Republicans such as Benjamin Wade and Zachariah Chandler mirrored the outrage in the country. They found enough votes in Congress to halt any increase in the number of cadets when West Point's annual budget was submitted. West Point was clearly under siege and had lost the respect of the country.[26]

Congress was angry that such a large number of officers and cadets had resigned. In retaliation, it passed new legislation that made clear the supremacy of the Union over the states. In the middle of August, all officers and cadets were required to take a new oath of allegiance. Each of the cadets in Tully's class raised his hand and swore the following: "I, (_____), do solemnly swear that I will support the Constitution of the United States, and bear true allegiance to the National Government; that I will maintain and defend the sovereignty of the United States, paramount to any and all allegiance, sovereignty, or fealty I may owe to any State, county, or country, whatsoever; and that at all times obey the legal orders of my superior officers, and the rules and articles governing the armies of the United States." [27]

The wording of the oath taken by all officers and cadets was changed again the following year when Congress legislated the "iron clad oath." In addition to the words of the earlier oath, the following, more restrictive wording was added:

I (_____) do solemnly swear that I have never voluntarily borne arms against the United States since I have been a citizen thereof; that I have voluntarily given no aid, countenance, counsel, or encouragement to persons engaged in armed hostility thereto; that I have neither sought nor accepted nor attempted to exercise the functions of any office whatever under any authority or pretended authority in hostility to the United States; that I have not yielded a voluntary support to any pretended government, authority, power, or constitution within the United States, hostile or inimical thereto. And I do further swear or affirm that to the best of my knowledge and ability, that I will support and defend the Constitution of the United States against all enemies, foreign and domestic, that I will bear true faith and allegiance to the same, that I take this obligation freely, without any mental reservation or purpose of evasion, and that I will well and faithfully discharge the duties of the office on which I am about to enter, so help me God.[28]

West Point—Fall 1861

The new third class returned from furlough on the last day of August. The sizing formation took place, and Tully and George Gillespie were assigned to a room in the second division. The grand illumination held on the last night of camp was much enjoyed by a large number of spectators as Tully described later:

We had fun last night and afforded amusement to a large crowd of visitors. Camp always closes up by a stag dance during the last week. . . . The parade ground is illuminated by candles which are placed on the ground. We had about 400 last night. Candles are placed on the four sides of a large parallelogram, inside of which the dance takes place. Outside the outer row of candles are the spectators. The cadets are dressed in all kinds of ridiculous ways and the different caricatures afforded great amusement to the crowds. One was fixed up to represent a cow, another, a pelican, several were dressed as women, your humble servant was an Indian, but the majority were dressed in some ridiculous military costume. Six cadets played fiddles, banjos, etc. They led the procession, and followed by the rest of us, passed twice around so the visitors could have a good look at all. The dance with all its variations took about an hour and wound up with three rousing cheers. Everything went off splendidly and everyone seemed to be pleased.[29]

The festivities clearly missed the additions of Southerners James Dearing's banjo and Stephen Moreno's guitar. As soon as they were over, the cadets changed into their dress uniforms and attended their last hop at the West Point Hotel.[30]

Orders announcing the appointment of first-class officers for the academic year were published: The published list showed that Kress, Gillespie, Marye, and Mansfield were to be captains, Lancaster to be adjutant, Egan to be quartermaster, and Rollins, Burroughs, Smith, Murray, Arnold, Sanderson, and Schaff to be lieutenants. George Gillespie kept his captain's stripes and took charge of A Company, but not all the lieutenants were appointed yet. One week later, the new commandant, Bvt. Lt. Col. Christopher Augur ('43), released the last appointments: "To be Lieutenants: Myers, Calef, McCrea, and Wharton." Tully sewed lieutenant stripes back onto his uniform and took charge of one of the platoons in A Company.[31]

First-class privileges extended to the class during the encampment were continued when they returned to the barracks. Their rooms were no longer inspected at night, and lights could be left on until 11 P.M. or later without fear of punishment. If they received fewer than thirty demerits in a three-month period and were not in debt to the quartermaster, passes and permits to leave the academy were frequently allowed.[32]

Final Struggles with Academics and Discipline

When the academic year began, Charles Warner, a turn-back from Custer's class, joined them. The biggest change facing Tully's class was the new four-year academic program. It looked a lot like the pre-1858 version, but their first-class courses were different. The Academic Board merged two years into one, and classes soon proved to be hectic. On September 1, Tully's class began studying engineering, chemistry, law, artillery, infantry and cavalry tactics, ordnance, and gunnery. Chemistry and drawing from the second class were added to the existing first-year courses already heavily oriented on engineering.[33]

The heaviest emphasis came from Prof. Dennis H. Mahan's Department of Civil Engineering. Tully and his classmates studied the construction of fortifications, use of barrier material, design of entrenchments and the protection of camps and battle areas, all of which later proved beneficial. The intensive study requirements and opinions about Professor Mahan soon flew back to Ohio:

> I am extremely disgusted tonight with Engineering, Professor Mahan and everything connected with the Engineering Department. Last night I had 2 bridges to draw for this mornings [*sic*] lesson. I sat up until after 12, took a great deal of pain in my drawing and was confident they were right. But to my chagrin, Professor Mahan informed me, and eleven others that our drawing did not suit him and they would have to be drawn over again and brought to the section room on Monday. Perhaps I did not cuss some, and perhaps I did. . . . Professor Mahan is the most particular, crabbed, exacting man I ever saw. His is a little slim skeleton of a man and is always nervous and cross. If a cadet dropped a ruler or point or makes a little noise, he is sure to hear "Gentlemen, please make a little less noise"—"Keep your eyes open and see what you are doing"—" You can't go through this world asleep"—or some other expression of the kind.[34]

The various academic departments were still short of instructors at the beginning of the academic year as well. To satisfy the shortfalls, the superintendent authorized the appointment of top-ranking first- and second-class cadets to fill some of the absent positions. Ranald Mackenzie, Jasper Myers, and George Burroughs were appointed as acting assistant professors of mathematics. Charles Suter and George Gillespie taught French. Clemens Chaffee, Bill Marye, and Frank Hamilton taught English along with Morris Schaff, John Egan, and Henry Wharton later in the year. In recognition of their new status as instructors, some earned an additional ten dollars per month and were allowed to walk to all meals and classes. A few, like Mackenzie, had the numbers of rows of brass buttons on their uniform jackets doubled to show their appointments as instructors.[35]

An hour every other day was spent studying chemistry in Professor Kendrick's Department of Chemistry, Mineralogy and Geology. Professor Kendrick was the only head of a department who had actually served in a regular regiment. He was not as well known or academically acclaimed as some of his fellow professors but was better liked by the cadets who lovingly called him "Old Hanks." Tully enjoyed listening to his stories about the Mexican War and the Indian campaigns.[36]

Rounding out his class schedule, Tully studied law in Professor French's Department of Geography, History, and Ethics. Colonel Augur and the Tactical Department increased the study of cavalry and artillery tactics with emphasis on drills and practical military engineering.

Class instruction in artillery and riding was limited after the artillery battery and engineer company departed with most of the horses. The superintendent requested their replacement several times and even located paroled soldiers and units at Seneca, New York, to fill the absent positions. Finally, seventy-six new horses and a contingent of soldiers arrived. The first class drew lots to pick their own horses and name them. Tully named his horse "Nina" in honor of an accomplished horsewoman whom he knew. Others quickly picked up names such as McClellan, Hardee, Daisy, and Victoria.[37]

The increased academics made finding time to study much more difficult. Engineering alone occupied Tully's entire study period from 7:30 P.M. to midnight each evening. After reveille, he often sneaked in more sleep until breakfast, then went back to the books until just before class. He rode from 11 A.M. to noon and then studied law for an hour. Classes ended at 4 P.M. and then, in Tully's words, "we have the extreme pleasure of a drill" before supper, leaving only half an hour free before call to quarters started. One Saturday morning, Tully and the rest of his classmates were even locked into a section room and a sentinel posted at the door until they completed their exercises in "stone cutting" to Professor Mahan's satisfaction. It was, in Tully's words, "the darkest and gloomiest month he ever spent as a cadet."[38]

The pressure of academics did not dissuade Tully from attending the weekly hops, although he complained about the strict Victorian etiquette imposed on ladies and gentlemen at such functions. On several weekends, when all his grades were above 2.0 and he wasn't in debt to the quartermaster, he left the academy and traveled to New York City to visit some young ladies he met that summer.[39]

The newly appointed first captain, John Kress, ran into serious trouble at the beginning of the academic year. During the first week of September, he donned civilian clothes and went to Roe's Hotel in Buttermilk Falls where he was reported by an officer for being off limits. Colonel Bowman ordered him into arrest and convened a court-martial that found him guilty of "conduct to the prejudice of good order and discipline." He was ordered into confinement, lost his appointment as a cadet officer, and was sent to the "light prison" for one month. His several requests to resign were all denied. Subsequently a series of letters between Washington and Colonel Bowman led to the secretary of war ordering him to be released. He was allowed to resign, subsequently joined the staff of the adjutant general in Washington, and was later appointed a major in the Ninety-fourth New York Infantry Regiment, US Volunteers.[40]

The appointment of a new first captain for the Class of 1862 was never officially recognized. Subsequent lists of the first captains at the Military Academy skip over the Class of 1862. Tradition would have the next cadet listed in the appointment order take up those duties, but the next-ranking cadet on the published list, George Gillespie, was not given that opportunity. Perhaps the fact that he was from Tennessee may have given the commandant reason to skip over his name. For whatever reason, it is believed that the appointment went to Bill Marye, the third cadet on the order, who had performed those duties earlier during the summer encampment. When John Kress's resignation was announced in October, Jim Rollins became a captain, and Bill Bartlett was made a cadet lieutenant to replace Rollins. A month later, Jasper Myers turned down his appointment as a lieutenant and was replaced by Asa Bolles.[41]

Riding Classes, Punishments, and Holidays

All cadets have favorite classes, and Tully loved riding. Each afternoon, he donned his riding jacket, pulled on heavy leather gauntlets, strapped on a heavy cavalry saber, and walked down the hill to the riding hall.[42] The rapid advancement of Tully's class limited the number of hours normally devoted to riding instruction. To offset this deficiency, he and his classmates were allowed to ride twice a day, once during their own class and then again with the second class. Long rides south of the academy often took them through Buttermilk Falls where Thomas McEnaney's children probably waved to the cadets as the riders passed through the village. Sergeant McEnaney and his family moved to "Soapsuds Row," the enlisted quarters below the level of the Plain, a few years later.[43]

Riding injuries were not uncommon. Tully's horse reared up and fell over backward when it approached a hurdle one day, dumping him ingloriously on the tanbark floor of the riding hall. Unhurt, he dusted himself off and waved to several young ladies in the gallery with whom he was acquainted.[44]

As the year progressed, Tully and Henry Wharton often rode with the second class on long trail rides. Whenever possible, the two rode near the end of the column and collected any lost equipment. One afternoon, several young ladies from Buttermilk Falls handed a lost blanket to them. As they rode to catch up with the column, Wharton's hat fell off. Tully galloped back and found the same lovely lass holding it for him.[45]

Guard duty came more often than ever before, and Tully often complained how cold and dreary it was in the guard house. There were few amenities for the detail or those serving confinement. Tully often wrote letters "with a shocking bad pen and by the brilliant light of a couple of oil lamps . . . [in] the only building in which there is no gas." His frequent tours included monitoring the punishment of one of his classmates, James Lord. Court-martialed for rendering a disrespectful excuse to the commandant, he was required to attend all classes and drills, walk sentinel every Saturday from 2 P.M. until retreat, and spend the rest of the day and all day Sunday until tattoo in the guardhouse for one month. At all other times, he was confined to his room in the barracks. It was not the first time he was confined; he frequently ran afoul of cadet regulations. The previous year on a bet, he tried to grow a moustache, a flagrant violation of cadet regulations. The B Company tactical officer didn't think much of his attempt. Much to the amusement of his classmates, Lord was simply reported for "trying to have hair on upper lip." In later years, cadets would try the patience of their tactical officers with an intentional play on words. One typical example was to try and be reported for "housewife on bed"—a "housewife" being the sewing kit issued to each cadet.[46]

Such a Delightful Institution of Science and Learning

The compressed first-class curriculum forced Tully's letters to become shorter and shorter as the year progressed. Sam Talbot, John Russell, and Belle repeatedly chastised him for their brevity. He missed being able to send letters to his relatives in Natchez even though the last letter from Alice was not the friendliest.[47]

George Gillespie's spirits rose when a colonel commanding one of the Tennessee volunteer regiments offered to pass messages to his family. This had to be done carefully, as any mail sent directly to any Unionist family in Tennessee was intercepted and opened by the Confederates. He immediately sent him a long letter to pass along.[48]

Ranald Mackenzie opened the morning newspaper on November 17 to learn that his uncle, ex-senator John Slidell of Louisiana and the designated Confederate commissioner to France, had been captured at sea. The boarding of the British ship *Trent* by the US Navy in international waters created a serious diplomatic issue for President Lincoln. Citing a major violation of international law and diplomatic rules of etiquette, the British government angrily demanded that Slidell and another commissioner be released. By mid-January, Lincoln finally submitted to the unrelenting international pressure and sent the Confederate representatives on their way to Europe.[49]

The expanding Union army needed officers, and more often than not this created frequent vacancies in the Tactical and Academic Departments. Colonel Augur was appointed a brigadier general of volunteers near the end of November and left the academy. The superintendent appointed Capt. Kenner Garrard, the riding instructor, as his replacement.[50]

On New Year's Eve, Tully spent the evening writing to Belle and his family. He bid them all a merry Christmas and a happy New Year and described his last holiday at West Point: "On Christmas morning I went to church, the only time but one I have voluntarily done so since I have been here. The church was so cold the religious ardor was froze out of me before the service was over. . . . Same Christmas dinner we have had for four years back, seems even Christmas dinners must conform to the monotony that hangs over everything connected with this delightful institution of science and learning."[51]

Last Semester as a Cadet

On New Year's Day, Tully and George Gillespie made their official calls, including a stop at Professor Kendrick's quarters for some waffles and laced peaches. Later Tully went skating on the frozen river, only to suffer several cuts and bruises:

> I am exceedingly awkward as you know at all times, but when I get on the ice, my awkwardness approaches perfection. One of my classmates was making fun of me, skating and in trying to catch me, tripped me up and away I went. Of course, I struck head first as is the case with all unfortunate skaters. I did not know I was hurt until the blood came streaming down my face from a wound above the eye. It turns out to be only a flesh wound and is now nearly healed up, but has left

a very black eye and a scar that is the exact counterpart of the one above my other eye. I have a fair prospect of becoming a "scar worn soldier" even before I graduate.[52]

The first-class rooms were much quieter in the evenings. Everyone studied hard, as no one wanted to be "turned back." As was customary in January, the plebes were examined first. The senior members of the Academic Board devoted themselves to examining the first class while the other instructors examined the other classes. While the professors were grading and discussing their findings, the Tactics Department weighed in with their own recommendations.

Punishments were doled out more liberally during the fall semester. Fred James and Charles Warner came close to dismissal with ninety-nine demerits. Even Bill Marye, the first captain, had over seventy demerits next to his name, while Tully had forty-eight.[53] Morris Schaff lost his lieutenant's stripes just after the beginning of the New Year. He and another classmate helped two young ladies recross the frozen Hudson River to Cold Springs and returned just as church formation was in progress. Since Schaff was an acting professor, he did not have to march and decided to sleep in. Unfortunately, his absence was noticed, and he was placed under arrest that evening. He was relieved from his duties as an acting professor and demoted to a high private. Ironically, the other classmate who crossed the river with him, Cliff Comly, was now appointed a lieutenant to replace him.[54]

At the end, Tully successfully passed his exams along with most of his classmates. There were four more losses. James Drake was dropped from the rolls as a result of his continuing illness. William Beebe and George McKee were turned back to the next class. With John Kress's resignation in October and Charles Warner joining them in September, the Class of 1862 now numbered twenty-eight, half the size of a year ago and two-thirds less than when they first arrived in 1858.

The spring term began with heavy doses of military engineering, cavalry, infantry and artillery tactics, riding, ordnance, gunnery, mineralogy, and geology. Again, the class drew lots for horses, and Tully was assigned the troublesome Don Quixote. More than once, his letters called attention to problems with that horse:

> Don Quixote concluded he would not jump and it took all I could do with whip and spur to make him jump. I succeeded at last much to the amusement of my classmates and several ladies in the gallery. When he at last concluded he had to go, the horse raised himself on his hind feet and gave such a spring that it came very, near throwing me out of the saddle and my cap went off one side, my saber on the other, and I went cavaulting [*sic*] up into the air as I never did before. I was fortunate in lighting again in my saddle right side up with care. But the Rubicon was passed, for after the first jump the others were not such terrible affairs. Although my new horse is as big a fool as his illustrious namesake Don Quixote, I am beginning to like him in spite of his meanness.[55]

Branches, Uniforms, and Rings

As graduation came closer, Tully's class arranged to purchase uniforms, rings, and class albums. The albums were a relatively new tradition in the Corps. Since 1857 each cadet in the graduating class purchased albums filled with photos of their classmates, instructors, and other interested officers. Each was unique and represented the desires of the cadet to whom it belonged. Tully described what he wanted in his album:

> When I graduate or as soon as I am able, I want to get a photographic album and collect the photographs of as many of my friends as possible. When I graduate I will get one of all my classmates, the Professors, the Supt. and the Commandant. This has been the custom of graduating classes for several years, and my class intends to follow it still. Several that I have seen of the last few classes were magnificent books

Table 4.1. Uniform List	
Ring	$25.00
Class Album	$46.00
Flannels	$17.50
Uniform Coat	$43.00
Uniform Trousers	$10.00
Sword	$15.00
Pistol	$24.00
Baggage	$7.50
Underwear	$23.37
Boots and Spurs	$9.00
Total	$220.37

and cost from $25 to $30 a piece. They are well worth it and in fact such a book would be perfectly invaluable to me, for when we part here on graduation day we don't know but it will be the last time, for never have a class all met again after graduating and leaving WP.[56]

Tully and his classmates often gathered in the evenings to discuss their future assignments. Because class rank at graduation drove assignments to the various branches, those who stood at the top of the class entered the Corps of Engineers as engineers or topographic engineers. Those in the middle were qualified to enter ordnance, the artillery, or the infantry, while those near the bottom generally ended up in the cavalry.

A tailor from Philadelphia arrived at the end of February to measure Tully and his classmates for their blue officer uniforms. The cost of outfitting themselves staggered the cadets. Morris Schaff estimated the total cost of graduating to be between $200 and $250, as shown in table 4.1. Tully's recurring indebtedness with the quartermaster left him with little money for any major purchases. He was already writing to Belle on long, coarse sheets of paper because he did not have enough money to buy proper notepaper. He discovered that a second lieutenant's pay in his chosen branch, the artillery, was $105.50 per month, composed of $45 as actual pay with an additional $36 per month for subsistence and rations. The remainder of his pay supported a servant and forage for a horse. When he included the cost of his class ring and class album to his uniform list, he knew he would have to borrow money, but from whom?[57]

Since 1835 each graduating class developed mottos, designed a class crest, and purchased rings. A class committee was formed, and their first product was the class motto, *In Causam Communem Conjuncti*—roughly translated as "Joined in a Common Cause," an apropos phrase considering the events that shook the Union to its very roots that year. Those events had driven each member of the class to embrace duty to serve his country. The class committee next designed a class crest that incorporated a sword crossed with an axe embedded in a bundle of rods, or fasces. The sword, ax, and rods were the tools of lictors, the men who bound the hands of criminals and took them before the Roman magistrates for judgment. Again, it seemed apropos for those who sought to bring the Confederacy to judgment. Once the design was approved by the class, the firm of Ball & Black set to work to make their rings.[58]

More Cadet Life

As the year progressed, Tully and his classmates often gathered nightly after tattoo. Their lengthy discussions often prohibited any further studying, so all were equally ill prepared for the next day's lessons. Frank Hamilton, serving confinement for an earlier offense, took a chance one evening and joined Tully and others in their evening discussions but was found absent from his room. As a result, he too lost his lieutenant's stripes and received six Saturday guard tours and a number of demerits. As a cadet officer for the past two years, he had never walked guard tours, and the thought of it chilled his mind. He now sat at Tully's table in the mess hall and marched in the ranks as a high private. Tully wrote Belle that he would try to keep Hamilton out of mischief during his last few months at the academy.[59]

Over in B Company, John Egan and Henry Wharton often smoked their pipes with a small group of classmates after tattoo. One classmate had an annoying habit of borrowing tobacco from them almost every night. Deciding to teach him a lesson, Egan and Wharton stirred colored wood shavings into the tobacco tin before the evening session began. When the individual asked for a "pipe full," Egan passed him the special blend and returned to the ongoing discussions. After watching the huffing and puffing for several minutes, Egan asked the individual how he enjoyed the new blend. His response was, "not too much; it was too woody," brought peals of laughter from the group.[60]

One of Belle's letters asked if Tully planned to come home after he graduated. But Tully had given up all hope of going home. He had a premonition about a "long and bloody war, in which brother will be fighting against brother and untold suffering and misery will be experienced on both sides." He explained:

> You say I must not think of [me] coming home to stay less than two or three months. In the first place I am not so sure I will have an opportunity of coming home at all, and in the next place it will not be at my option how long I stay. A soldier is not his own master, but has to give a blind obedience to the orders of his superior officers, no matter how unpleasant and distasteful they may be to him. If you think of it properly you yourself would not want me to stay at home so long a time next summer. The war will be waging dreadfully in all parts of the country, and every soldier and officer will be needed at his post. If I should be so fortunate as to have a couple of days I will be satisfied.[61]

Before the end of February, Tully was caught sleeping in bed during the day and ordered into confinement. This gave him plenty of time to study and stare out the window. One evening he wrote to Belle about "stretching an elephant":

I spent the first of the evening stretching an elephant. You
need not be surprised at the magnitude of the undertaking,
for it was only a paper elephant. It is the name given to
the heavy drawing paper that we use to draw our problems
in engineering. The paper has first to be wet and soaked.
Then it is laid on the drawing board, and the edges pasted
to the board. If it is properly stretched the paper will be as
tight as a drumhead when it dries, which makes it much
more convenient than if the paper were laid on the board
loose. But as the paper is as large as a common sized table,
it is very difficult to get it properly fastened to the board.
I succeeded admirably with mine last night, and am sure
no one in the class has an elephant stretched better than
mine.[62]

Although he received numerous letters from Ohio, he missed
hearing from his family in Natchez. His spirits brightened when a
friend at Fort Monroe offered to forward his letters under a flag of
truce to Norfolk, a practice that had grown up since the prohibition
on mail began at the beginning of the war. At the end of February,
he was excited when a short letter from Alice arrived. She wrote that
the family was well but that his uncle, William Woods, had passed
away. She did not mention much about the war except that she was
engaged to a Mr. Parker who had gone off to Tennessee. Tully's
response never made it to Natchez, as the secretary of war halted the
practice of forwarding mail that month.[63]

The War Sputters On

The calm atmosphere at West Point was in stark contrast to that of
Washington in early 1862. Congress and the president grew increasingly agitated at the lack of action by McClellan's army, and a frus-
trated Lincoln finally issued a general war order requiring the Army
of the Potomac to move west to occupy Centreville before the end
of February. The methodical General McClellan eventually reached

Centreville only to find that the fortifications were empty when the
first Union soldiers arrived.[64]

Meanwhile along North Carolina's Outer Banks, Brig. Gen.
Ambrose Burnside's expedition secured Roanoke Island and Pamlico
Sound, resulting in the capture of twenty-five hundred prisoners. The
lists of prisoners published in the newspapers a few days later included
one of Tully's former classmates. 1st Lt. John R. Blocker of South
Carolina was captured when his unit, Fifty-ninth Virginia Infantry
Regiment, was overrun during the attack. He was paroled at Elizabeth City, North Carolina, near the end of February and exchanged
later that year.[65]

Farther west, Maj. Gen. Ulysses S. Grant's forces captured
Fort Donelson on the Cumberland River in Tennessee. Tully
searched the prisoner and casualty lists for signs of Alice's fiancé,
Mr. Parker, or his cousin, Mark Wood. Instead he found another
former classmate, Capt. Frank Maney of Tennessee. Maney had
returned from Italy to raise an artillery battery, which was heavily
damaged during the attack at Fort Donelson. He was wounded
and his second officer killed. All those captured were sent north to
prisons in Ohio.[66]

The fall of Fort Donelson was quickly followed by the state
of Tennessee falling under Union control. President Lincoln soon
appointed Sen. Andrew Johnson as its military governor. George Gillespie was now able to contact his family in Kingston. Tully wrote:
"My roommate is jubilant over the news from Tennessee, as it is driving the rebels from the state and restoring the federal authority. He is
writing home tonight, the first time in seven months. He is going to
send the letter to the clerk of the House of Representatives who goes
to Nashville with Governor Johnson."[67]

Within a short time, Gillespie received a letter from his family.
Everyone was well, but they were closely watched by secessionists.
Even though the state was under Union control, it was not yet safe
enough to carry on a regular correspondence. In short order, Tennessee offered him a lieutenant colonelcy in a federal volunteer regiment. Earlier he was offered a colonelcy in a Confederate regiment,

but he chose not to be placed in a position of fighting against friends or relatives and turned all offers down.[68]

By now casualty lists were becoming daily reading. One morning, the name of Robert Noonan was listed as killed in action at Kernstown near Winchester, Virginia. After he resigned, Noonan had volunteered with Company C, Twenty-first Virginia Infantry Regiment, while awaiting an artillery appointment in the Confederate army. He was the first of the Southerners who left the class to die in battle.[69]

Getting Ready to Graduate

The Tactical Department increased the number of first-class drills after the snow and ice left the Plain. In May, Charles Warner described one of his gunnery classes:

> We had artillery drills and fired a dozen rounds from two Parrott guns, one hundred and thirty-pounders. I had to go for the ammunition and I carried all the hundred-pound balls some distance and lifted them into the bore of the piece. They were greased to diminish the friction and I got quite a lot of the grease and soot all over myself, but I had on old clothes so that it did not make any difference. They are wonderful things to shoot. The distance was nearly a mile and they went into almost exactly the same spot every time. Some of the shells burst and spread all over the water. It was not intended but there was something the matter with the fuses.[70]

With six more weeks left until graduation, Tully and his classmates were uncertain if they would receive any leave. The last two classes were immediately sent to Washington and within days involved in the battle at Bull Run. The Army of the Potomac had now shifted its operations to the Virginia Peninsula, and the cadets avidly read accounts of General McClellan's army fighting near Williamsburg.

With the possibility of joining the army quickly after graduation quite high, the cost of purchasing all his officer uniforms and gear still remained a problem for Tully. When Sam Talbot asked to come to graduation, the question of the cost of Tully's uniforms and equipment arose. Talbot offered to lend Tully $300 to cover their purchase, and Tully swore to repay the loan as soon as he could after graduation.[71]

The Engineering Department's reputation as having one of the hardest courses at West Point was well earned. After working on a single problem for three weeks, Tully still couldn't find the error that would correct it, and the instructor was less than willing to assist. Once again, the hot-tempered Tully was in "an irrepressible conflict" with an instructor. This time, thankfully, it did not result in any punishment.[72]

Tully related that George Gillespie had received a letter from one of his cousins, a prisoner of war, in Tennessee. He stated that his cousin reported that Frank Maney had escaped from prison and was back in Dixie once again. Most prisoners captured at Fort Donelson were first sent to Camp Chase near Columbus, Ohio. A few months later, the officers were transferred to Johnson Island near Sandusky, and Maney escaped during the transfer. He now commanded the Twenty-fourth Tennessee Sharpshooter Battalion in Cheatham's Division, Buckner's Corps, Army of Tennessee.[73]

The Excitement Grows

In May a Mr. Frederick arrived from New York to take pictures of the cadets for their class albums. A few days later, Morris Schaff visited the West Point Hotel to ask the recently retired Lt. Gen. Winfield Scott if he would give him a picture for his class album. Most albums only contained photos of the surviving members of the group that had trudged up the hill in June 1858, some of their professors, and General Scott. No one thought to add pictures of their departed Southern classmates, but a few pictures of those who were turned back to the next class in January were included.[74]

Sam Talbot planned to arrive on Wednesday and stay until Saturday of graduation week. As Tully could only take a limited number of uniforms and gear with him when he left the academy, Talbot agreed to take most of his other clothes, books, and the class album back to his family in Dayton.[75] Tully's brand-new blue uniform hung in his room awaiting his last day as a cadet.

First-class exams began on June 3 and lasted four days. Tully ended his career as a cadet exactly in the middle of the class at number fourteen. Luckily, none of his classmates was found deficient or turned back. Ranald Mackenzie, George Gillespie, George Burroughs, Charles Suter, and Jared Smith were academically ranked as the top five, and their names were published in the *Army Register*.[76]

After the exams ended, Tully and his classmates found a much more relaxed atmosphere for a change. The second class gave them a hop on Saturday evening, and another hop was held at the West Point Hotel the following night. Classmates such as Fred James who lived nearby were given short leaves between required formations. Tully accepted an invitation to spend a few days at Ranald Mackenzie's home in New Jersey as the prospect of remaining in the virtually deserted barracks was quite unpleasant.[77]

Graduation

The Class of 1862 attended chapel for the last time on Sunday, June 8. The cadets listened as Asa Bolles's tenor voice led the choir. Tully later wrote that Professor French's sermon was "eloquent and affecting, and a great many realized the truths it contained." As was the custom, one hymn, only heard during graduation week, was sung by the choir. It commenced with the words "When shall we meet again" and the concluding words were "never, no never." In all probability, Tully and his classmates would never meet again as a class.[78]

The Final Parade

Graduation parade was held on June 10. Spectators ringed the Plain, and a large group of cadet families gathered in front of the superin-

Fig. 4.2. Formation for Parade. *1863 CA, SCAD*

tendent's house. The West Point band marched to the edge of the Plain. James Lancaster, the cadet adjutant, took up his position by the band. At precisely 4:50 P.M., the drummers beat First Call in the cadet area for the parade.[79]

After winding his red sash around his waist and adjusting his belts and saber for almost the last time, Tully McCrea joined his platoon forming on the carriage road in front of the cadet barracks. Frank Hamilton was already in the rear rank with the rest of the high privates in A Company. In C Company, Charles Warner adjusted his belts and cartridge box. He looked fondly at his old musket and left it in the rack by the wall. On this day, all the high privates marched without arms. He walked down the steps to the carriage road and joined the rear rank of his company with Morris Schaff and Ranald Mackenzie.[80]

At 5 P.M., when the band stepped off, playing "The Dashing White Sergeant," George Gillespie led A Company onto the Plain. The rest of the Corps of Cadets followed, with the color guard carrying the national colors marching between B and C Companies. After Retreat and the lowering of the flag, the Corps came to parade rest while the band played two traditional graduation airs, "Home Sweet Home" and then "Auld Lang Syne." Tully realized this was the last time he would ever hear the West Point band or march in a parade as a cadet. Tears clouded his eyes, yet he could not raise his hand to wipe them away.

Each company snapped to attention at the command "Pass in review." The companies marched smartly around the Plain, and the officers' sabers snapped up and down in salute; each cadet turned his head and eyes to the right as his platoon passed the commandant. The companies then resumed their original positions on the Plain. There was one more important ceremony to conduct.

Bill Marye called out, "Graduating class, front and center!" The first-class privates joined the officers in front of their companies. Marye and his staff then marched forward to join the two gray lines forming before them. As the band played a stirring march, the two lines of cadets marched forward. When the class reached the commandant, it halted, and in unison the cadets lifted their hats off in a salute. The commandant swept his dress hat off in return and announced, "Gentlemen, I congratulate you." Behind them, the second-class sergeants took command of the cadet companies and marched them off the field.[81]

The commandant then dismissed the first class, and a great cheer arose. The cadets threw their hats into the air and broke ranks to join their families. Several cadets took pleasure in kicking their heavy dress hats along the grass ahead of them as they would never wear them again. Smiles abounded on every face as classmates clapped one another on the shoulder and fathers rushed up to congratulate their sons. Sam Talbot was there to wish Tully good luck.

The superintendent and the professors made their way among the families congratulating each of the graduates. Later the cadets walked back to the barracks, jauntily swinging their cartridge boxes by the white belts, vowing never to clean their breastplates ever again. They quickly donned clean uniforms and prepared for the evening's festivities. With a few minutes left before the hop, Tully wrote his final letter from West Point to Belle:

This has been an eventful week for me. I have graduated and am now awaiting orders from Washington. I do not know exactly how long we will have to remain here, or where we are to be ordered to. My class, since we finished our examinations on Thursday, have had nothing to do except a few military duties. The balance of the time we have been allowed every possible privilege and have had a pleasant time. On Friday night, the Second Class gave us a hop. Last night, we had a hop at Cozzen's Hotel and danced until Sunday morning.[82]

The Graduation Ceremony

The next day, the Class of 1862 received their diplomas, "one at a time, and without ceremony," according to Morris Schaff. It was likely a ceremony similar to that conducted the previous year for the June class at the cadet chapel.[83]

The band led the graduating class up to the chapel followed by the rest of the Corps. Tully and his classmates stood in line in order of merit order awaiting the final act. Professor French delivered a short sermon and blessed the class. Then the event they had longed for so long, the event denied their Southern classmates, began.

Colonel Bowman walked to a table where an open drumhead contained the diplomas and read off the name of the first cadet in the class. Ranald Mackenzie walked forward to the table where Colonel Bowman announced, "Cadet Ranald Mackenzie, you are commissioned a second lieutenant in the Corps of Engineers." Mackenzie accepted his diploma with a slight bow, then turned and walked back to his seat. The rest of the class followed suit and marched up one at a time to receive their diplomas when their name was called. When Tully's turn arrived, Colonel Bowman announced, "Cadet Tully McCrea, you are commissioned a second lieutenant in Battery M of the 1st Regiment of Artillery." After accepting his diploma with a slight bow, Tully turned and returned to his seat, holding the long-sought diploma high over his head. Minutes later, excitement grew as Charles Warner, the last man in the class, received his diploma.[84]

At the end, seven engineers, four ordnance officers, fifteen artil-lerymen, and two cavalrymen were graduated that day. Two were pro-moted as brevet second lieutenants until a vacancy in their assigned regiments appeared. The entire list of members of the Class of 1862 in commissioning order and their initial assignments are shown in the epilogue.

Final Days

The new graduates reported to the hospital for a medical examina-tion on June 12. At some point that week, they put on their new blue uniforms and took their oath of allegiance as officers. Although the official date of graduation was established as June 17, the class was released from the academy on June 14 and ordered to report to the adjutant general in Washington on July 15 to receive their final assignments.[85]

Tully completed packing his bags and prepared to leave the acad-emy. He thought about the long journey that began four years ago when he climbed the hill from the south dock. He was pleased that he graduated high enough to get commissioned in his favorite corps, the artillery. He had a month's leave but would go to Washington to try to get his orders early. He donned his new blue uniform, picked up his bag, closed the door to his room for the last time, and headed down the hill to the south dock, impatient to begin his career.

PART 2

The Civil War Years

5

McCrea Joins the Army
of the Potomac

West Point, December 1865. The next morning, the blaring sounds of bugles and drums at reveille resounded off the walls in Tully's quarters. Fortunately, he did not have to get out of his warm bed yet. Today he was scheduled to begin reviewing the semester's lessons in preparation for the January examinations. Finally, he threw off the brown comforter and readied himself for class.

Thirty minutes later, he left for the mess hall. His limp was not as pronounced now as he navigated the carriage road with a cane. He pulled his overcoat tighter as the biting, cold wind cut right through him after he turned the corner by the academic building. The cadet companies were just entering the mess hall, and the morning meal was about to begin.

Over breakfast, Tully, Frank Hamilton, and John Egan commiserated about the slowness of promotions now that the war had ended. Each of them had received several brevet promotions during the war but still remained first lieutenants in the regular army. Less than six months before the army was close to one million men. Now it was reduced to one hundred and eighty thousand and scheduled to get much smaller.

The changes in the army were more evident when the Class of 1865 graduated just after the war ended in June. The graduates assigned to the infantry were immediately promoted to first lieutenants because the number of infantry regiments had increased. Those assigned to the engineers and ordnance were also promoted to first lieutenants. The new graduates in the artillery and cavalry branches were unhappily promoted to second lieutenants because the number of their regiments remained constant. Tully could only see much slower promotions in the future.

Just then, Bentz's bugle announced first call for class. Bugles had

Fig. 5.1. Old Harrison Mansion at Harrison's Landing (Arthur Lumley). *LOC*

regulated his life for so many years—it was hard not to react to them. Tully remembered the stirring bugle calls in the early morning hours in the camps near Harrison's Landing when he first joined the Army of the Potomac.

Transition—June 1862

After graduation, Tully traveled to Morristown, New Jersey, to spend a few days with Ranald Mackenzie's family, then on to Brooklyn to participate in a wedding. His dancing created great havoc with his wildly swinging saber striking left and right. Perhaps he should have taken those dance lessons after all. The next day he was off to Washington to try to get his orders early.

Upon arrival he found lodging in the same boardinghouse that Maj. Gen. Winfield Scott, the general in chief of the army, had occupied when he was in the city. The next morning, he walked to the War Department where the clerks in the Adjutant General's Office advised him that all cadet nominations had to await confirmation by Congress and there was no telling when that would take place.[1]

He tried several more times to get his orders that week but quickly ran out of money and faced the prospect of not being able to pay his hotel bill. Unexpectedly, Ranald Mackenzie and his mother found him at the hotel. After hearing his tale, Mrs. Mackenzie paid his hotel bill and rail fare to Morristown. Tully returned there with them, extremely grateful for the assistance, but was now deeper in debt. He tried to explain in a letter to Belle why he chose to go to Washington instead of returning to Ohio:

> I feel I ought to be thankful for having so many kind friends. The only drawback to my pleasure here is that I would like to be with you and feel that you will all think strange of my spending my furlough away from home. But you must not blame me for I should have gone home if I had not been so greatly in debt. And I thought that by going to Washington I could get immediate orders, go in the army, and be earning money to pay my debts. But the very thing I tried to avoid, I fell into for I have been unable to obtain my orders and my traveling around has cost me more than if I had gone home. I am now completely out of money and I was indebted to Mrs. Mackenzie for paying my board bill in Washington and my railroad fare here.[2]

The vibrant family life at the Mackenzies' kept Tully busy. He was never at a loss for things to do and read the *New York Times* daily. On July 7 he found the following notice tucked away on an inside page:

Artillery Officers at West Point

The artillery officers of the graduating class from West Point, excepting those retained for the summer duty at the Military Academy will repair, without delay, to the headquarters of the Army of the Potomac, and report to Major General McClellan.[3]

It is likely that he was disappointed. He had looked forward to joining his permanent or assigned battery in Beaufort, South Carolina, but Maj. Gen. George B. McClellan's directive overrode his initial orders, and he would now join the Army of the Potomac in Virginia. Tully left Morristown on July 11 and traveled back to West Point to visit George Gillespie where he, Henry Wharton, Jim Rollins, and Jared Smith were retained for the summer, and Gillespie was not too happy about it. Tully spent the weekend commiserating with his classmates before traveling to Washington on July 15 to pick up his new orders.[4]

When he arrived in Washington this time, Tully learned he was now assigned to Battery I, First US Artillery, Second Army Corps, with the Army of the Potomac. After receiving instructions about how to reach his new assignment, he loaded his trunk and bags on a wagon and headed for Alexandria to find a steamer headed south. At the quartermaster's wharf at the foot of Montgomery Street, he found Ranald Mackenzie awaiting transportation there as well. The two classmates shared expectations of what lay ahead as the steamer slowly made its way down the Potomac.[5]

The ship was one of several that regularly plied the waters between Alexandria and Harrison's Landing, the headquarters of the Army of the Potomac. It left Alexandria in the evening and arrived off Old Port Comfort and Fort Monroe around 7 A.M., the next morning. When the ship reached Fort Monroe, Mackenzie left to join the regular engineer battalion while Tully stowed his extra baggage in a nearby warehouse before climbing back aboard the steamer for the final leg of his trip.[6]

The steamer headed west through Hampton Roads and entered the mile-wide mouth of the James River. The captain kept to the center of the river to avoid rebel sharpshooters. Tully observed great expanses of cultivated land and large plantations on both banks, many of which stood empty since the arrival of Federal troops. Near the end of his trip, the steamer passed the Westover plantation with its docks and nearby fields filled with supplies for the Army of the Potomac. Ahead he saw the masts of numerous ships in the river marking the location of Harrison's Landing and the end of his voyage. Tully's arrival on July 17 coincided with a heavy rainstorm, and he elected to stay on board until morning.[7]

Joining the Army of the Potomac

The next morning a small boat took Tully to the dock, and he carried his bags up a dirt road toward the Berkeley mansion. Once the home of the former President William Henry Harrison, it now served as a hospital with a signal station perched precariously on its roof. In a grove of trees near the plantation house, Tully found the adjutant's tent and signed in.[8]

Gen. Robert E. Lee, the recently appointed commander of the Army of Northern Virginia, had halted McClellan's advance toward Richmond. Beginning on June 26, his army had forced McClellan's larger force to withdraw from Mechanicsville to Malvern Hill where, on July 1, McClellan's artillery contributed greatly to halting Lee's offense. Still, McClellan chose not to take advantage of that engagement and pulled his army back to Harrison's Landing on July 2.

The army was in a good defensive position. Its encampment stretched for miles along a great arc centered on the Berkeley plantation with both flanks anchored on the river. The Third, Fourth, and Sixth Corps defended along the arc. The Second Corps and Fifth Corps were in reserve and located around the Berkeley and Westover mansions, respectively.[9]

The Second Corps was commanded by sixty-seven-year-old Maj. Gen. Edwin V. "Bull" Sumner. It was located on both sides of the River Road, which split the vast camp in half. Tully probably walked along its regimental streets until he found Battery I in a grove of trees. (Artillery units were also called "companies" during the Civil War.) He dropped his bags near one of the larger tents, pulled aside the flap, and ducked inside. The battery commander, 1st Lt. Edmund

"Ned" Kirby likely looked up when Tully entered and called out, "Halloo, McCrea. Welcome to Company I. John Egan is already here. I am assigning you to command the first section. John has the third, and Frank French will handle the center. Find your tent, and we'll see you at supper."

John "Dad" Egan met him as he walked toward the three Sibley tents that housed the battery officers. Egan had a droll sense of humor, a slight build, blue eyes, and brown hair. A pipe always seemed to hang out of his mouth, something that surely must have tried the patience of safety-conscious gunners around the ammunition chests. Tully's tent mates were 1st Lt. Frank S. French and the surgeon, Dr. J. H. Baxter. Egan helped Tully build a bed from a few hardtack boxes nailed together and added some saplings under his blankets for comfort.[10]

Food in the camps was plentiful as ships frequently brought fresh meat and vegetables up the James River from Fort Monroe. The soldiers' meals were quite basic: a portion of cooked pork, some bread, and coffee. Officers' meals were different. Charles Warner, assigned to 1st Lt. Edward B. Williston's Battery D, Second US Artillery, Sixth Corps, kept a meticulous account of his expenditures during the war and described his officers' mess and meals in a letter to his sister: "For supper tonight, we had chicken, fresh pork, macaroni, warm bread, good fresh butter and crackers and coffee. We have a good cook and waiter. My mess bill is from 25 to 30 dollars per month. We have an occasional Sherry wine and claret and things of that kind, which I care little about, but am willing to pay my share for."[11]

Each officer paid into a mess fund to supplement the normal menu. But, as Tully explained later, their rations and gear were loaded onto one of the battery wagons that often went astray, leaving them hungry and without their baggage for periods of time.

At 9 P.M., the buglers sounded "Tattoo," and the officers and soldiers soon slipped off to their tents—all except Tully, who had difficulty going to sleep the first night. He found his writing materials and wrote his first letter from the field:

We are very pleasantly encamped in the pinewoods about one-half mile from the river. We have three tents for the six officers and another for a mess tent where we take our meals, write, smoke and play cards. All around us is scattered the army camped in little huts. I have not yet been around the army much but expect to do so in a few days when my horse gets better. I have seen a great many of the graduates of the academy with whom I am acquainted and there are a great many more here that I have not seen. There is fifteen of my class here and one of them is with the same battery. The others are miles away with other divisions of the army. I expect to remain here several weeks, as it is thought that General McClellan will not do anything until he gets reinforcements.[12]

Tully was excited about his assignment. He was pleased to be assigned to one of the best units in the Army of the Potomac. Battery I was always in the thick of battle, and opportunities to bring honor to the name of McCrea would soon appear:

I knew Kirby at West Point. He has distinguished himself very greatly since he graduated. He has been in seven pitched battles since Bull Run and now has the reputation of having the best battery in the Service. Besides him, there is Lt. Woodruff of the class before mine. Egan one of my own classmates, Lt French, who is not a graduate, and Doctor Baxter, a young doctor from Cincinnati, making six officers in all. We have 140 men and 130 horses, all bays except four. Our battery is composed of six bronze 12-pounder Napoleon guns and has the reputation of being the best in the army. I think myself extremely fortunate in getting my present position for it is a battery that is in every fight and sees more active service than any other in the army.[13]

"Ned" Kirby, a West Pointer from the May Class of 1861, was born in New York, the son of an army general. He joined Battery I right after graduation, suffered through the disaster at the First Battle of Bull Run, and brought what was left of Battery I back to Alexandria where he twice reorganized it.[14]

His second officer was another West Pointer, 1st Lt. George "Little Dad" Woodruff (June '61) from Michigan, who was currently sick in the hospital at Fort Monroe. Woodruff had joined Company I right after the First Battle of Bull Run. The two West Pointers both suffered recurrent bouts of typhoid fever and since the fall of 1861 were "taking turns" as battery commander as Kirby styled it. The third officer, 1st Lt. Frank S. French, was not an academy graduate and was the son of Maj. Gen. William H. French, who commanded General Sumner's Third Division. He was wounded at Ball's Bluff, and his father kept trying to get him assigned to a less demanding position. Doctor Baxter was from Cincinnati and on most days could be found at the brigade medical tent.[15]

Still not ready to go to sleep, Tully put his ink and paper away, lifted the flap of his tent, and walked outside. Around him thousands of campfires gleamed in the darkness, and he likely saw what an army chaplain later described in a letter: "Thousands of white tents among the beautiful green trees, with fires gleaming here and there for miles over an extended plain, providing light and comfort to over a hundred thousand armed men, while darkness gently spreads its mantle over all."[16]

Camp Life with the Army of the Potomac

A gunboat on the river fired the morning gun at 5 A.M. prompting buglers to quickly sound "Reveille" throughout the camps. The bugle call evoked Tully's memories of cadet life and rushing down the stairs into formation. It was somewhat easier now as an officer. He donned his uniform for the day. He wore a dark-blue, thigh-length uniform coat with a single row of brass buttons down its center. Two gilt-edged red tabs—a second lieutenant's insignia—were pinned on its shoulders. A red stripe on the legs of his blue trousers denoted his artillery assignment. He pulled on heavy boots, placed a forage cap on his head, strapped on his sword, and headed out to the morning formation.

The men of Battery I lined up in the road in front of their tents as the section sergeants called the roll. The battery's officer of the day took the report, and the first sergeant dismissed the formation. The bugler soon sounded "stable call," and the morning chores began while the cook boiled water for coffee. The smell of coffee brewing soon drew Tully to the officers' mess tent. The soldiers had coffee, a piece of bread, and perhaps a piece of boiled pork for breakfast. Sometimes there might be corn bread if the cook knew how to make it.[17]

After breakfast, Kirby gave Tully and the other officers their duties for the day. Tully made his way to his gun section to examine the two twelve-pounder Napoleons assigned to him and found them clean and in good shape. Each gun had a limber with an ammunition chest. Each gun also had a caisson with two ammunition chests, and its limber carried another. Each chest contained 32 rounds for a total of 128 rounds for each gun. Tully found all the section tools clean and lashed down. Bags of grain for the horses were tied down on all the caissons.[18]

Tully walked down the picket line and looked at the horses. Some were limping, others showed battle scars, but most seemed to be recovering with rest, and there was plenty of forage available at the camp. He saw the horse assigned to him was recovering from a few battle wounds. He ran his hands down its legs and knew it was fit to ride but needed a few more days of rest to heal properly.[19]

Horses were a very important part of an artillery battery. A team of six drew each cannon and its limber. Another team of six drew the caisson and its limber with the ammunition. The drivers rode on the left horses while the rest of the crew rode on the caisson, spare horses, or marched alongside. The senior sergeants, officers, bugler, and the guidon bearer all rode on horseback. Three other teams of six pulled the three battery wagons that carried the cook's equipment, rations, officer gear and their rations, the battery forge, and the tents used in camp.

Battery I was designated as light artillery. "Light" may have been a misnomer, as the gun, limber, and ammunition weighed almost 3,900 pounds. Currently, there were some 140 men, 6 officers, and about 130 horses present; a few more men and fewer horses than authorized, but that was expected with the casualties it had suffered. Battery and section drills were frequently conducted, and Tully soon became quite familiar with the crews that manned his guns.[20]

By mid-July, the combined personnel losses due to sickness and wounds caused General McClellan to send officers back to their hometowns to recruit replacements. Tully's classmate Cliff Comly went home to Dayton to buy horses and recruit cavalry personnel to replace losses suffered during the Seven Days Battles. Tully heard all about the trip when Cliff returned and berated himself for making that futile trip to Washington instead of going home after graduation. Compounding his disappointment over not going home was the lack of mail arriving for him.[21]

Illness Strikes

With temperatures sometimes over a hundred degrees, heat-related casualties among the soldiers were common. Unsanitary conditions were also quickly generated when large numbers of soldiers camped in a relatively small area. Seeking to avoid the "swamp miasma" or "marsh fever," Kirby's battery drew its water from the same source as General Sumner's headquarters. But the illnesses struck randomly, and large numbers of soldiers were sent off to hospitals. By the middle of July, the losses were so great that only the most critically sick were allowed to leave camp. It did not take long before Tully joined the long lines in front of the doctor's tent.[22]

Ill or not, Tully was expected to perform his duties. With little or no rebel activity to stir his army, General McClellan insisted on inspections, drills, and parades to maintain a high state of discipline. Grand reviews were held near the Weston plantation near the end of July, and Tully later recounted what happened to him:

Since I wrote you last, I have been sick with the fever, but am now getting better. A week ago, Sumner's Corps to which my battery belongs, was reviewed by General McClellan. I was kept in the saddle in the hot sun from 8 until 12. I think that perhaps this was the cause together with the miserable water that I had to drink. I stood it well for a while but after I had been in the hot sun for half an hour, I began to feel weak and came near fainting while on my horse. I obtained permission to leave the battery and returned to camp. I intend to return to duty this evening, although I feel barely able to do so. It makes the duties so much more for the other officers when I am sick that I feel ashamed of myself.[23]

He knew the men saw his repeated illnesses as a sign of weakness and wondered what would happen if his condition became worse. When Brig. Gen. John Sedgwick's Second Division and Kirby's battery were sent to Malvern Hill in early August, Tully became so sick he could not ride his horse and ended up riding in the ambulance. This was not West Point where fainting at parade brought demerits and guard tours. Here his absence limited the battery's capability to respond to enemy attack.

Sick or not, junior officers were often assigned additional tasks outside their units. Still recovering, Tully was ordered to muster out all the volunteer units that had reached the end of their enlistments in General Sedgwick's division. He had to reconstruct entire personnel rolls from scratch several times as there were few unit records available. Three days later, he was rewarded for his efforts by being assigned as a judge advocate for thirteen prisoners awaiting trial by court-martial.[24]

Leaving Harrison's Landing

Under direct orders from Washington in early August, General McClellan's army began to slowly leave Harrison's Landing and the Peninsula. Several classmates were transferred with their units while the movement north was under way. Five batteries were transferred to join Maj. Gen. Ambrose Burnside's newly formed Ninth Corps at Fredericksburg. With them went James Lord, Albert Murray, and William Bartlett. Bartlett's transfer was delayed as he fell sick and entered the hospital at Fort Monroe for a period of time. He would not rejoin his battery until much later. Ranald Mackenzie found himself assigned to Burnside's engineer staff.[25]

Tully knew there were sixteen classmates currently assigned to the Army of the Potomac. In addition to himself, John Egan, and the Ninth Corps contingent at Fredericksburg, J. Eveleth Wilson and Isaac Arnold were with the Third Corps, Sam McIntire and John Calef were with the Fifth Corps, and Charles Warner was in the Sixth Corps. Frank Hamilton and James Lancaster rode with the horse artillery brigade and James Sanderson with the Artillery Reserve. George Gillespie was now assigned to the US Engineer Battalion in the engineer brigade. Cliff Comly and Fred James rode with the two cavalry regiments.

The other twelve members of the class were scattered around Virginia, at West Point, in one of the western departments, or with Maj. Gen. John Pope's Army of Virginia. Jared Smith, one of the engineers in Pope's army, was wounded at Cedar Mountain and lay in a hospital in New York City, the first in the class to be wounded.

On August 15, the Second Corps left Harrison's Landing. During his second road march, Tully again became too sick to ride and was forced to endure an unpleasant trip in the back of an ambulance for several days. While Battery I and the Second Corps boarded steamers and headed north, the doctor sent Tully to the hospital at Fort Monroe:

> I left Harrison's landing with the army a week ago, so sick that I could not stand up, and was consequently obliged to ride in an ambulance. We were six days marching through and arrived here Thursday Night [August 21]. I was taken with the fever again three days before I left Harrison's Landing and as everything that could be shipped in transports had

been sent off, I had to go without medicine, and I had none until the day when I got here. I am not confined to bed and feel very well except the portion of the day when the fever is upon me. I am very weak and greatly reduced. On the march we officers had nothing to eat except what we could beg and borrow from the other officers. By some mistake the wagon that contained our mess chest and eatables was sent on with the wagons of the train of another division, and we did not see it from the time we started until we stopped at the end of the march. It should have been with us every night. I went the first day 26 hours and the second 18 without anything to eat, and then when I did get it, it was not fit for a sick man.[26]

Tully's ward in the hospital was filled with patients recuperating from various wounds and illnesses. He soon wrote to Belle about the treatment he received:

I may be here three weeks, and you surely can write me a letter so that I will get it here. I have received no letters from you for two months. Direct to Old Point Comfort, Va., in care of the Post Adjutant. . . . Have taken a great many large doses of medicine, principally quinine. I have had no fever for several days, but am very weak. The least exercise fatigues me very much. I have been in the hospital since last Monday and find it much more pleasant than I anticipated. Everything is kept very clean. I have a very obliging and attentive attendant, and we have good food and a good variety. The doctors have been changed three times since I have been here. They were all good, but I think the present one is the best. He is a young surgeon of the regular army and very attentive. In the same ward as me is one of my classmates, Wm. Bartlett, son of Prof Bartlett. When I came Monday there were six beside myself, but now there are only Bartlett and myself. . . . There are about 12,000 sick soldiers in the hospitals near here mostly belonging to the army of the Potomac. . . . The

1st Lt and second in command [Woodruff] is here also sick and there are only three officers with the co. I do not know where my battery is exactly, but if I can find out and the doctor will let me go I will leave here tomorrow or the next day.[27]

The quinine he was given made him feel much better, and he enjoyed a regular menu for a change. On the last day of the month, news came that General Pope's army was defeated at Second Bull Run, and Ranald Mackenzie's name was listed as killed in action. Saddened by the news, Tully became more determined to rejoin Battery I and renewed his efforts to leave the hospital.

6

McCrea, Egan, and the Maryland Campaign

West Point, December 1865. John Egan mentioned in passing that the order convening the various academic committees to examine the cadets was just posted. As usual in January, the full Academic Board examined the fifth class first. As soon as that class was finished, the board began examining the first class while the other instructors tested the other three classes.

Tully was afraid that one of his sections was slipping behind as the dreaded semiannual examinations rapidly approached. Professor Church's Mathematics Department claimed almost fifty percent of all deficiencies during the first two years. Tully could tell by looking at the sleepy-eyed cadets that the lights were already burning late in the barracks. His favorite technique with a sleeping cadet was to come around behind him, lean down next to his ear, and in a low voice say, "Mr. W., please explain why X is greater than Y," much to the amusement of the other cadets.

All the academic departments were still short of instructors, but it was getting better now that the war was over. The superintendent appointed several members of his class to teach the plebes during their first-class year in an effort to offset some of those shortages. Washington's answer was to assign to the academy a few paroled Union officers who were unable to return to active service until exchanged as well as some disabled graduates. Having spent two months or more confined to his bed last year, Tully was all too aware that disabled officers spent much of their time recovering from wounds or on extended leaves of absence. Their continued absences left the remaining staff with heavier burdens, as he was finding out. At the same time, arguments by some representatives and senators that West Point should be abolished because it failed to train its graduates properly had tapered off.[1]

Fig. 6.1. Lee Crossing the Potomac (Alfred Waud). *LOC*

Tully was amazed that Congress was so appreciative of the military and West Point after the war. His training in the "cannoneers' hop" with the artillery battery on the Plain had helped him train his gunners into formidable soldiers. He wished those outspoken members of Congress had seen his well-trained crews work their guns in front of the East Woods during the Battle of Antietam.

The Maryland Campaign—September 1862

General Lee's Army of Northern Virginia had given Maj. Gen. John Pope's Army of Virginia a serious drubbing during the Second Battle of Bull Run in August. As Pope's defeated troops slowly moved toward the safety of the Washington defenses after the battle, Maj. Gen. Thomas "Stonewall" Jackson attempted to cut off Pope's withdrawal at Ox Hill (Chantilly) on September 1. The engagement brought part of the Union Third Corps and the Ninth Corps into contact with Jackson's command, resulting in the loss of Union generals Philip Kearny and Isaac Stevens. James Lord with 1st Lt. Samuel N. Benjamin's (May '61) battery supported the action at Ox Hill and then withdrew.

General Lee now saw an opportunity to keep Richmond safe by shifting the fight to the north where he could resupply his tattered army from the untouched northern farmlands. He sent Longstreet's and Jackson's commands across the Potomac River into Maryland at White's Ford on September 4. Riders soon galloped across the Chain Bridge and the Long Bridge into Washington bringing news that an invasion of the North was under way.[2]

Congress, the cabinet, and the president had seen their hopes for a speedy end to the war dashed again after the Battle of Second Bull Run. Once more, one of their armies was in disarray. All about the city, stragglers from Pope's army lay in the streets, officers and soldiers looked for their units, and passing wagon trains created massive traffic jams. Although his cabinet strongly opposed him, President Lincoln knew there was only one person who could bring organization out of the chaos swirling around them. On September 2, he and Maj. Gen. Henry Halleck asked General McClellan to help defend Washington and reorganize the Army of the Potomac for future operations.[3]

McClellan soon directed Pope's Army of Virginia and the Army of the Potomac to occupy defensive positions around the city. At the same time, a visible change took place in the city. Order was restored, the streets were cleared of stragglers, and missing soldiers were reequipped and reunited with their units. Newly arrived volunteer regiments were assigned to divisions or the defenses around Washington. The Army of the Potomac began to hold its head up again.

The movement of Lee's army into Maryland caused McClellan to quickly order the Army of the Potomac to consolidate around Rockville, north of Washington. At the same time, Pope's three corps were integrated into the Army of the Potomac as the First, Eleventh, and Twelfth Corps. McClellan left the Third, Fifth, and Eleventh Corps

Table 6.1. Class Organization in September 1862

Army of the Potomac		Other Commands
US Engineer Bn.:	**Gillespie**	Army of the Cumberland: Engineer Dept.: **Burroughs, Wharton**
Quartermaster's Guard	1st US Cav.: Reno (**Comly, James**)	
1st Corps	Engineer Staff: **Suter**	
2nd Corps	I/1 US Arty.: Kirby (**McCrea, Egan**)	Arsenals:
3rd Corps	H/1 US Arty.: Dimick (**Sanderson**)	St. Louis: **Marye** Allegheny: **Myers**
	K/4 US Arty.: Seeley (***Arnold***)	Watervliet: **Chaffee**
5th Corps	K/5 US Arty.: Van Reed (**Calef**)	Ft. Monroe: **Schaff**
	I/5 US Arty.: Weed (**McIntire**)	
6th Corps	D/2 US Arty.: Williston (**Warner**)	West Point: **Rollins, Smith** Sick/Wounded: ***Arnold,***
from 4th Corps	G/2 US Arty.: Butler (**Wilson**)	**Mackenzie**
9th Corps	E/2 US Arty.: Benjamin (**Lord**)	Recruiting Service: **Bolles**
	A/5 US Arty.: Muhlenberg (**Murray**)	Suffolk, VA—7th Corps Staff: **Mansfield**
	L&M/3 US Arty.: Edwards (**Bartlett**)	
Cavalry Div.	M/2 US Arty.: Haines (**Hamilton**)	
	C&G/3 US Arty.: Gibson (**Lancaster**)	

Notes: Members of the Class of 1862 (shown in bold type) remained with these units throughout the war unless otherwise stated in the text. Other names are commanders of their units at this point in time. Italicized names signify transfers between units.

behind to protect Washington, and the Fourth Corps stayed at Fort Monroe.[4]

The Maryland campaign brought seventeen members of the Class of 1862 into the Army of the Potomac. They remained assigned to the units identified in table 6.1 throughout the war unless otherwise stated in the text. Others in the class were initially located at various arsenals, at West Point, or assigned to units or staffs in the western theater of war.[5]

McClellan's order for the Army of the Potomac to consolidate at Rockville caused thousands of seasoned veterans in dust-covered uniforms to begin passing through Washington. One column headed north through Georgetown, another up 7th Street, and a third marched up 17th Street into Maryland. Confederate spies frantically signaled Lee that the federal army was on the move.[6] Charles Warner later wrote about his experience marching up the 17th Street corridor on September 7:

> Last night we got orders to be in readiness to move. At 6 o'clock, we started out and passed over the Long Bridge, through Washington and Georgetown, and on to where we are now, about eight miles from Washington. We marched in all about fourteen miles and until about one thirty in the afternoon. I was not very well when we started and was never so tired in my life. At the end of the march we just spread out blankets and I never enjoyed sleep better in my life than I did until seven this morning. . . . As we passed McClellan's HQ, he was vociferously cheered on his balcony on 17th Street across from the War Department. . . . The streets were thronged with people, ladies as well as others who were out to see us. We passed through 3 or 4 miles with houses so thick on both sides of the road. I had no idea Washington was so large but I did not think that Georgetown was a continuation of the city.[7]

Tully was finally released from the hospital at Fort Monroe on September 3. He found space aboard a steamer headed for Baltimore, then climbed aboard a train for Washington. Much to his relief, the newspapers now listed Ranald Mackenzie as wounded, not killed. Upon arrival in Washington, he headed to the army's camps near Alexandria to get paid (he had not been paid for two months) and then went to look for Mackenzie.[8]

He stumbled into George Gillespie while wandering around the camp. Gillespie had just arrived from West Point and was assigned to C Company in the US Engineer Battalion. He told Tully that Mrs. Mackenzie had taken her son back home to Morristown to recover.[9]

Over dinner that evening with George Gillespie, Charles Suter, and George Custer (June '61 and now a captain in the Cavalry Division), Tully listened as Gillespie explained that Mackenzie was assigned to the 9th Corps delivering messages when he was struck down by a musket ball that plowed across his back. Knocked off his horse, he lay on the ground nearly immobilized by his wounds. Two rebels took his pistol, watch, and papers. He was not found until the next day and then sent to a hospital in Washington. His brother, Sandy, searched through many hospitals and churches until he found him. Being wounded in the back was considered a sign of cowardice, and Mackenzie adamantly told his mother when she arrived at the hospital, "I am wounded in the back, but I was not running away!"[10]

The next morning, Tully received word that the Second Corps was located near Tennallytown (now the Washington neighborhood Tenleytown). He crossed the Potomac River and traveled north by wagon until he found Kirby's battery camped near Fort Pennsylvania (now Fort Reno) outside of the village. John Egan was glad to see him and explained they had moved across the river from Fort Marcy and Fort Ethan Allen on September 3. Woodruff was now in charge after Kirby fell victim to typhoid fever and was again hospitalized.[11]

Tully was glad to be back. He put his bag in the battery wagon and hoped to stay at the fort for several days, but late that afternoon, marching orders were received. The Second Corps was ordered north to Rockville. A few days later, Tully found time to write a few lines to Belle: "I rejoined my company the next day at Tenallytown where we had a pleasant camp. The men and horses were completely worn out with long marches and as we had a pleasant place to camp I was hoping we would stay there long enough to have the company rested. But a few hours later we were ordered to prepare to move."[12]

Marching North into Maryland

Early in the morning of September 9, the drummers beat out the long roll and the Army of the Potomac began marching toward Frederick, Maryland, on three converging routes. McClellan's objectives were to protect Washington and to find and defeat Lee's army. A few days later, Maj. Gen. Fitz John Porter's Fifth Corps was released from Washington, adding a seventh corps to McClellan's growing army.[13]

Tully and Battery I followed John Sedgwick's Second Division up the Rockville Pike to a position just east of Rockville where they camped for two days. Meanwhile James Lord and Lieutenant Benjamin's battery in Burnside's Ninth Corps marched northwest toward Frederick with the First Corps. Charles Warner and Williston's Battery with Maj. Gen. William B. Franklin's Sixth Corps moved along a road parallel to the Potomac with the Twelfth Corps. Warner later described his experiences to his sister: "We had first rate living lately. Ripe apples and peaches in abundance. Splendid mutton, chickens, duck, milk, buttermilk, honey, jelly, etc., and I have had such an appetite as to enjoy them to the fullest extent. . . . I hope we bag the secesh army and not allow a single one to return to the sacred soil of Virginia. When we have affected it then I shall be able to enjoy other things."[14]

Each evening, the guns in Battery I were unlimbered and readied for action in case of an attack. Once the cannons were separated from their limbers, the gunners began their evening chores. Bags of grain were unlashed from the ammunition caissons and the drivers fed and watered the horses before tying them to a picket line that was stretched from flank to flank of the battery. The Army of the Potomac consumed vast amounts of supplies each day. Critical among those supplies moved daily was forage. For example, each horse consumed about fourteen pounds of hay and twelve pounds of grain each day, so hundreds of tons of forage were required to be carried for the tens of thousands of horses and mules that moved the wagons and other conveyances of the army.[15]

Later Tully leaned up against a tree and recounted the events of the past few days in a letter to Belle written on his knee. The weather turned cold that evening, and the battery wagons went astray, leaving him and the other officers without their gear or rations:

> The first day we were here the wagons were all sent several miles to the rear with all our baggage. We had to drive that afternoon on bread and cheese, and sleep on the ground without tents or bedding. I had nothing but my cloak, and like to have frozen. I got up in the night and went to the picket line to see if there might not be some hay the horses had not eaten, but they had been so long without feed they had eaten every straw. I then looked around for a horse blanket, but the men had taken them all to make themselves comfortable. So I had to pass the time as particularly as possible until day. I have been very much afraid since I returned that I would take the fever again. The days are very warm and the nights very cold, with very heavy dews. I get up in the morning and find my top blankets as wet as if they had been rained upon. . . . I feel much better now. I still take a little medicine every day to prevent the return of the fever. And I have also taken to drinking whiskey, which no doubt you will be shocked to hear as I have always been such a teetotaler. Everyone, the Dr. included, recommends it as a guard against the continual change of the water.[16]

The clear, crisp notes of "Reveille" announced the beginning of each new day. Blankets were tossed aside and soldiers staggered into the morning formation. Breakfast was nearly always the same: hard-tack crackers and salt pork, washed down with coffee. As soon as "Boots and Saddles" sounded, commands were yelled to harness the horses, the cannons were limbered, and everyone took his place in preparation for another day on the march.

The long blue columns started moving north and halted each hour to rest. Within minutes, fires sprang up and water was boiled for coffee. When the bugles sounded "Assembly," a few minutes later, the infantry kicked out the fires, struggled back into their packs, grabbed their muskets, and lurched into formation, ready to start plodding forward once more. By noon the steady rhythm of the march by thousands of feet left everyone coated with a thin coat of white dust.[17]

Near Hyattstown, Woodruff's battery passed through well-tended fields of beans and corn and intermittent forests along the Rockville Pike. The corn stood seven to eight feet tall, and its golden tassels waved in the slight breeze. Friendly faces greeted Tully and John Egan as they passed through each village. Children and women stood by the roads with pails of water to cool the throats of the thirsty soldiers. At the Monocacy River, the horse teams struggled to pull the cannons across a mud ford and up a nearby hill. At the crest of the hill, the church spires of Frederick were visible in the distance and, just beyond, the purple-tinted slopes of Catoctin Mountain.[18]

When its leading elements marched into Frederick on September 12, McClellan's army was treated as liberators and with cheers from its citizens. But soon its narrow streets became a huge bottleneck, and McClellan finally ordered his corps to bypass the town. Setting up camp the next evening, two sergeants found a copy of Lee's Special Order 191, which sent Jackson's Corps to attack Harpers Ferry and Longstreet's corps north toward Hagerstown. As soon as the order reached McClellan, he excitedly began planning to attack before Lee could reunite his scattered army.[19]

Two days later on the morning of September 15, Sumner's Second Corps broke camp near Frederick. Tully, John Egan, and Battery I crossed Catoctin Mountain on the Shooktown Road. It narrowed rapidly as it rose from the valley floor, and it was filled with numerous steep grades and tight curves. The shouts of officers and cursing gunners yelling at the straining horses did little to move the guns faster up and over the mountain. Tully described the move later: "We marched that day from Frederick city over the mountains on one of the worst roads for artillery that I have ever seen. We arrived at the summit about 12 o'clock and we could see and hear the battle on another range of hills about six miles distant. We were all anxiety to catch up and take part in it, but before we arrived there, the enemy had been whipped and retreated."[20]

Late that afternoon, they crossed South Mountain at Turner's Gap. A series of engagements had already taken place as evidenced by the large numbers of dead and wounded lying alongside the road and in nearby field hospitals. The men halted along the way to cheer McClellan and his staff as they passed through unit after unit on their way toward Boonsboro.[21]

The Second Corps bivouacked near Keedysville where Woodruff placed the battery in a field. Tully later climbed a nearby hill and described a brief brush with death:

> We marched that night beyond the village of Keedysville and camped just behind the brow of a hill on which the artillery that was to open the battle was posted. In the morning, our artillery opened upon the enemy, which was soon returned by them. The shells began to come over the hill and fall amongst the troops, but fortunately no one was injured in my company. Just in front of me a cannonball went through a man cutting him to pieces. Another man had his foot cut off. Before the rebels opened their batteries I was up on the brow of the hill trying to discover their position with a field glass. As I was watching, they fired four batteries simultaneously and the way that the shells did fly around was new to me. One struck in front of me about ten feet, bounded over my head and struck in the midst of some infantry.[22]

Sometime during the day, Maj. Fred Clarke, the Second Corps chief of artillery, ordered Woodruff's and another battery to cross Antietam Creek at the Upper Bridge that night and be ready to support the next morning's attack. The three Second Corps divisions remained east of Antietam Creek along the Boonsboro Road. After crossing the Antietam, Woodruff located his battery near the Hoffman farm at the northern end of the battle area that evening.[23]

The Battle of Antietam

General McClellan watched the battle unfold from his headquarters at the Pry House on the heights above Antietam Creek on the morning of September 17. Beginning at dawn, Maj. Gen. Joseph Hooker's First Corps pushed Lee's soldiers back along the Hagerstown Pike and through Miller's cornfield, but his advance was halted by a savage counterattack. Maj. Gen. Joseph K. F. Mansfield, the newly assigned commander of the Twelfth Corps, was ordered into the attack around 7:30 A.M. A few minutes later, Sam Mansfield's father was killed upon entering the battlefield. The divisions of the Twelfth Corps pressed the rebel soldiers back through Miller's cornfield and reached the area around the Dunker Church where they too were halted. Part of the First Corps occupied positions near the Dunker Church and the West Woods.[24]

When the Twelfth Corps began its attack, McClellan ordered Sumner to move the Second Corps across Antietam Creek in support. Within minutes, a few shouted commands along the Boonsboro Road brought Sedgwick's and French's divisions to their feet. Maj. Gen. Israel B. Richardson's division remained east of the Antietam for another hour until it was released from its reserve mission.[25]

Sumner led Sedgwick's division down the slope from the Boonsboro Road in a column of three brigades to ford the Antietam at Pry's Ford, a half-mile south of the Upper Bridge. With water still sloshing out of their boots, the soldiers climbed the opposite bank and marched up a slight slope and then across farmlands until they arrived near the East Woods around 9:00 A.M. There Sumner ordered Sedgwick to change front into line of battle and cross the open cornfield into a gap he believed existed between the First Corps in the North Woods and the Twelfth Corps around the Dunker Church. Sedgwick's brigades moved across the field in three lines as if on parade, climbed the fences along the Hagerstown Road, and entered the West Woods.

Sumner assumed that French's division was right behind him. In

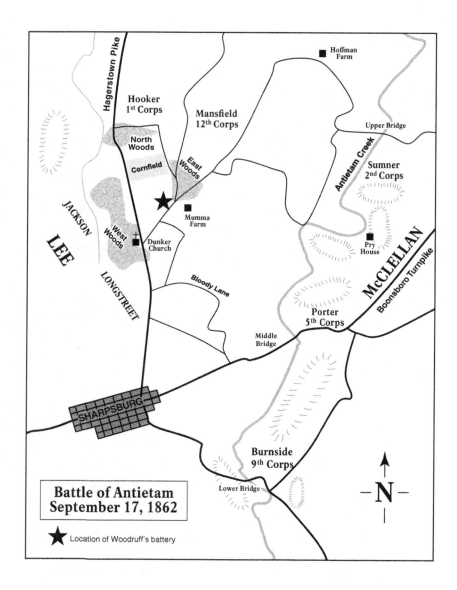

**Battle of Antietam
September 17, 1862**

★ Location of Woodruff's battery

reality, French crossed the Antietam, marched forward about a mile, then turned south to bring his division up on Sedgwick's left flank. But rebel artillery slammed into his first line, diverting him farther to the south without French seeing any Second Corps units. Meanwhile, Richardson's division, finally released from its reserve mission, crossed the Antietam to support French's division. As a consequence, Sedgwick's division marched into the West Woods without any support on his flanks or in the rear.[26]

Tully and John Egan surely heard the sounds of battle taking place from their location near the Hoffman Farm as the First and Twelfth Corps attacked southward that morning. Woodruff and the other Second Corps batteries moved down a country lane to the Smoketown Road and halted behind a wooded area around 8:30 A.M. Major Clarke found them more than a mile north of the East Woods between 9 and 10 A.M. He ordered Battery I to move into the open field in front of the East Woods as quickly as possible to support Sedgwick's attack.[27]

Woodruff and the guidon bearer rode ahead while everyone else scrambled to take their places. Tully likely pumped his arm up and down and yelled, "Trot, ho!" as Battery I moved down the road, desperately trying to keep Woodruff in sight. A mile or so later, he spotted Woodruff turn off the Smoketown Road into an open field in front of the East Woods. The need for artillery support came quick enough. Just after Sedgwick's brigades entered the West Woods, Maj. Gen. Thomas "Stonewall" Jackson's graybacks launched a surprise attack. Casualties were heavy, and Sedgwick's soldiers struggled out of the woods and fled up the Hagerstown Pike or across the fields toward the East Woods.[28]

Sometime between 9:30 and 10:00 A.M., Battery I careened into the field, limbers bouncing up and down, gunners and drivers holding on for dear life. Woodruff was in the middle of the field pointing the direction of fire with his saber and yelling, "Action front!" With wounded and dead soldiers strewn about, the drivers changed direction sharply to avoid running over them. Smoke from the nearby burning Mumma farm initially obscured the battery from the rebel infantry near the Dunker Church as the six guns unlimbered and readied to fire. For the first time, Tully and John Egan heard the eerie buzzing sound of musket balls speeding past as the battle erupted around them. Now they concentrated on the fleeing soldiers from Sedgwick's division streaming into the field in front of their guns.[29]

At the end of the Smoketown Road and closer to the Dunker Church was Captain J. Albert Monroe's Battery D, First Rhode Island Artillery, from the First Corps. When Sedgwick's division was surprised in the West Woods, Monroe's infantry support pulled back as rebel infantry closed on his position as well. Monroe yelled "Limber to the rear!" and four of his sections successfully pulled back in front of the East Woods, just to the left of Woodruff's guns. While his men were trying to limber his fifth gun, rebel musket fire killed two of the horses; the others went wild with the smell of blood, broke their harnesses, and fled. Monroe yelled for nearby soldiers to help drag the gun back by hand. His sixth gun was destroyed by artillery fire before it could be moved.[30]

Within the hour, eleven cannons stood on a line in front of the East Woods loaded with canister. Monroe and Woodruff rode out in front of the gun line and waved their swords and arms to alert the fleeing Federal soldiers to get out of the way. Tully could see gray uniforms running close behind. He likely tried to control his impatient men calling out, "Hold, hold, wait for the signal to fire!" Finally Monroe and Woodruff abruptly turned their horses, rode back through the line of cannons, and gave the order to fire. The guns erupted, and hundreds of small pellets slammed into the oncoming gray lines.[31]

Tully's and John Egan's gunners serviced their guns like clockwork. Their continual training paid off, each gun easily fired two rounds each minute. When rebel infantrymen were two hundred yards away, Woodruff ordered double canister, and the gunners rammed home two canister shells and fired. Ammunition handlers ran back and forth to the caissons as the gun crews shot up what was left in their limber's ammunition chest. Behind the gun line, General Sedgwick tried to rally what was left of his division, but he was struck down by musket fire and his horse killed. Within minutes, Monroe's battery ran out of ammunition and withdrew, leaving Woodruff's guns alone on the field.[32]

Woodruff's battery was not immune from the gunfire either.

John Egan's and Frank French's horses were struck, and several gunners were shot down. When a rebel detachment approached from his left, Woodruff ordered his guns pulled back closer to the East Woods. Quickly limbering their guns, Tully's crews pulled them back just in front of the wood line, dropped trails, and readied their guns for action. Woodruff's sword came down again, and the guns roared, forcing the gray lines back beyond the Dunker Church. Minutes later when the smoke dissipated in front of his guns, Tully saw piles of dead strewn about in the field in front of the East Woods.[33]

A few days later, he described in a letter what happened:

The firing commenced the next morning about dawn and continued all day. At first it was only an occasional shot from our skirmishers, but it soon increased until the roar of artillery and musketry was continual. We were kept in the rear until 11 o'clock when we were ordered to the front, took up a position in the rear of a brigade of infantry that were flying like sheep. The rebels were pursuing them, but our men persisted in running before the guns, in spite of all endeavors to get them from before the battery, so we could fire at the rebels. At last our cannoneers became so impatient to fire, that it was impossible to restrain them any longer, and the battery opened.[34]

He elaborated much later when the history of the First Regiment of Artillery was prepared:

We opened upon the rebels with canister at short range, the volunteer battery on our right doing the same. It soon became too hot for them and they began to fall back, and soon regained their position on the other side of the Sharpsburg road. We had no inf. in support except some stragglers as Sedgwick and some other officers could rally on our flanks. Both Egan and French's horses were shot. Luckily we only lost six men and 4 horses. General Sedgwick was standing in the rear of the battery and was wounded twice and his horse killed. His brother was also mortally wounded. After the battle, we counted over 200 dead rebels in the field, most of them killed with canister shot.[35]

John Egan also contributed his observations in the history of the First Artillery Regiment:

Around 10 o'clock Major Fred Clark ordered us into position. Woodruff started at a trot and under cover of fragments of the division succeeded in getting us into a field unseen by the rebels, about 150 yards in front of and a little to the right of the Dunkard [sic] Church. Waving out of his front Sedgwick's retreating men, Woodruff opened fire with canister which the enemy got as nicely as could be wished. About 30 rounds were fired before the rebels were checked. . . . The battery remained until firing began across its front. We retired about 75 yards and again opened and continued to fire until a line—part of the 2d Corps—marched across the field of fire.[36]

Between 11:00 and 12:00, Woodruff's battery stood alone in front of the East Woods, the barrels of his Napoleons too hot to lay a hand upon. His guns were the last remaining Union force in the center of the battlefield. Just when it looked as if the battery would be forced to withdraw in the face of renewed rebel advances, the flags of the Sixth Corps appeared behind them, and new artillery batteries pulled up on either side. Later, after withdrawing to refill their ammunition chests, Tully and Egan considered themselves lucky. They had "seen the elephant" (survived combat for the first time, in the phrase of the time) and were pleased with the actions of their men. Both were later brevetted to captain for gallantry at Antietam. Although McClellan's campaign to rid the North of Confederate invaders proved successful, both knew that it would be a long war.

7

Egan at Fredericksburg

West Point, December 1865. The early morning snow had now turned to rain. After breakfast, Tully braved the wet weather to reach the academic building. Even with the festivities and decorations during the Christmas holidays, West Point was not like being at home. He missed his aunt's tables laden with food and the camaraderie of his cousins. Three years of war had taken that away from him. He was not sure when he would be able to return home and fully expected to be assigned to some far off frontier post as soon as his medical condition resolved itself.

Belle's letters arrived somewhat regularly, although they did not contain the same carefree discussions she and he engaged in before he was wounded. His failed attempt to bring their relationship to a different level while he was recovering in Ohio caused her to build a wall between them that only time would bring down. Tully always looked forward to receiving her letters.

He heard the cadets in the hallway outside his classroom and involuntarily shivered when the door opened and a blast of cold air blew in. It brought back memories of the bitter cold at Fredericksburg where he tried to stay warm by stamping his feet and leaning up against his horse on Stafford Heights—he just wanted someplace safe and warm. It prompted him to remember that he did not have the same harrowing battle experience as John Egan who had transferred to a new battery after the battle of Antietam. It crossed the upper bridges into the town during the battle and held in position along the river until his division was ordered forward. His harrowing experience supporting the assault against Marye's Heights amazed everyone who heard the story.

Fig. 7.1. Crossing the Rappahannock (Alfred Waud). *LOC*

The Army Moves South—November 1862

More than a month after the Battle of Antietam, the drummers sounded the long roll, and McClellan's army began leaving Maryland over bridges constructed across the Potomac River by George Gillespie, Charles Suter, and the engineer brigade at Berlin (now Brunswick). John Egan was transferred to 1st Lt. George Dickenson's (June '61) Battery E, Fourth US Artillery, and left Pleasant Valley to cross at Berlin on October 26. They and the rest of the Ninth Corps followed Brig. Gen. Alfred Pleasonton's cavalry southwards along the eastern slopes of the Blue Ridge.[1]

Twenty-three-year-old John "Dad" Egan was now a veteran. His new assignment with the Ninth Corps brought him in contact with a battery shattered by the loss of its officers at Antietam and a new gun to learn. Battery E was equipped with four 10-pounder Parrott rifles and organized as a horse artillery battery. It supported Brig. Gen. Samuel D. Sturgis's Second Division.

Two of his classmates were also assigned to the Ninth Corps. William Bartlett was in Capt. John Edwards's Battery L&M, Third US Artillery, a part of the Ninth Corps artillery reserve, and James Lord was with 1st Lt. Samuel Benjamin's Battery E, Second US Artillery, in support of the First Division. With the exception of himself, the rest of his class in the Army of the Potomac remained with the same units and corps they fought with at Antietam (see table 6.1 for assignments), though some artillery batteries had new commanders.[2]

The weather turned cold as Egan rode south. By the time he reached Waterloo on the Rappahannock River southwest of Warrenton on November 6, an early heavy snowfall had changed to rain and made the bivouac very uncomfortable. His men hunkered down under blankets and oilcloths trying to escape the effects of the freezing wet weather.[3]

Meanwhile, President Lincoln fretted over the leisurely pace of McClellan's army as it moved south. He reasoned that if McClellan allowed the rebels to get between his army and Richmond, he would remove him from command. Within days, Longstreet's First Corps arrival in Culpeper made it clear that McClellan had failed the test. On November 7, 1862, Lincoln signed the orders relieving McClellan and appointing Maj. Gen. Ambrose Burnside as the new commander of the Army of the Potomac.[4]

The Fredericksburg Campaign

Soon after taking command, General Burnside planned to take his army rapidly east to Fredericksburg and then along the rail line toward Richmond, a different approach from what Lincoln and McClellan had discussed earlier. While Burnside awaited approval of his plan, he created three large troop organizations called "grand divisions" of two corps each under Generals Sumner, Hooker, and Franklin, and a reserve of two corps under Maj. Gen. Franz Sigel. On November

8, Brig. Gen. Orlando B. Willcox was now in command of the Ninth Corps as it and Maj. Gen. Darius N. Couch's Second Corps were now a part of the Right Grand Division under General Sumner.[5]

Burnside reacted quickly after receiving approval of his plan. Lee's army awakened on November 15 to a fierce artillery bombardment followed by part of the Ninth Corps and cavalry crossing the Rappahannock River. Alarmed, Lee ordered the withdrawal of Longstreet's First Corps to Culpeper and more defensible terrain. While this diversion was under way, Sumner led the Right Grand Division east toward Fredericksburg followed by the rest of the Army of the Potomac.[6]

General Pleasonton's cavalry division acted as the rear guard when the Ninth Corps withdrew from Sulphur Springs (also known as White Sulphur Springs or Warrenton Springs) and Rappahannock Station. Sturgis's division was taken under fire, and a number of his wagons were struck by rebel artillery when it began leaving. Egan's battery fired frequently as the units withdrew and took the road toward Falmouth. Two days later, Sumner's Right Grand Division arrived near Falmouth on November 17.[7]

Couch's Second Corps camped on the north side of the town just off the Telegraph Road. Willcox's Ninth Corps passed through the town and occupied the railroad depot and the area east of Falmouth. Both corps remained far enough away from the river to avoid direct observation by the Confederates. Dickenson's battery and Sturgis's Second Division were located along the road to Belle Plains where they occupied the old Ninth Corps camp sites used the year before.[8]

Burnside's army was forced to remain idle for the better part of a month. His plan called for pontoons to arrive at Falmouth when the rest of the army did, but they were weeks late. Lee's entire army soon occupied the heights behind the town, the five-mile range of hills that stretched south and west toward the river, and along the river to Port Royal. Meanwhile, Burnside's engineers searched the riverbanks above and below the town, trying to find adequate crossing sites. As time passed, Burnside became convinced that only a rapid crossing near the town would allow his army to successfully defeat Lee's widespread forces before they could consolidate against him.[9]

The Crossings

After sufficient pontoons finally arrived, the attack of Fredericksburg required the volunteer engineer battalions to build upper and middle bridges near the town. About two miles south of town, the US Army engineer battalion and part of a volunteer engineer battalion would build the lower bridges for the First and Sixth Corps to access the lower plain. At the same time, Brig. Gen. Henry Hunt, the chief of artillery, would position four large artillery groupings on the high ground above the river to support the crossings.[10]

After dark on December 10, several of Egan's classmates moved forward to Stafford Heights. Their gunners wrapped cloths around the trace chains to deaden any sounds during movement. Finally the officers quietly passed the word. The horses snorted great clouds of steam into the night air as they pulled the heavy cannons down the icy roads through two inches of fresh snow. The four artillery group commanders led their batteries into positions along the heights above the river. By 11 P.M. four miles of Stafford Heights were lined with 147 cannons.[11]

Sometime after midnight, the heavy pontoon bridge trains moved forward toward their designated crossing points. Working as quietly as possible in a heavy fog, the crews began construction. The artillery crews above them likely stamped their feet and pulled their overcoats and blankets tighter to keep warm as the temperature dropped to nearly twenty degrees. Their officers continually cautioned them to be quiet. When one pontoon slipped into the ice-covered river at the upper bridge site with a resounding crack, all work stopped to see if the rebel pickets, four hundred feet away on the far shore, heard the noise. Not hearing anything, the engineers quietly completed the first section and began work on the next. By 5 A.M., the upper and middle bridges were more than halfway across when two signal rounds were fired on the opposite shore alerting Confederate forces that a crossing

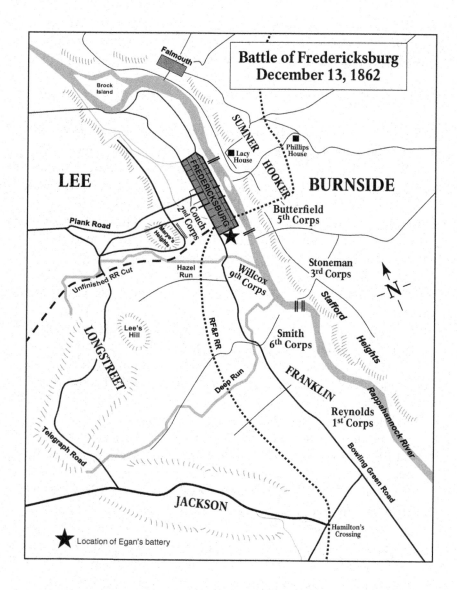

was in progress. Rebel riflemen rose up along the riverbank and fired blindly into the fog. Startled cries and splashes meant some of their rounds hit the engineer crews.[12]

Construction came to a complete halt by mid-morning. Every

time the engineers tried to extend the bridges, rebel sharpshooters picked them off. Even with artillery continually bombarding the opposite shore, it was difficult to continue work in the face of almost instant death. With progress stalled, Hunt called more artillery batteries forward to the riverbanks. His orders quickly brought Tully McCrea in Kirby's battery, Albert Murray in 2nd Lt. James Gilliss's Battery A, Fifth US Artillery, Isaac Arnold with 1st Lt. Francis W. Seeley's Battery K, Fourth US Artillery, and three other batteries to the Lacey House. Kirby's and Murray's batteries and two others went into position above the upper bridge site while Seeley's battery and one other were sent to the riverbank near the middle bridge site. The combined fires of their 12-pounders did little to reduce the continuing fire from rebel sharpshooters across the river.[13]

Near 2 P.M., Hunt suggested to General Burnside that infantry be sent over the river under the cover of artillery fire, clear out the first street, and let the engineers finish the bridges. Burnside reluctantly agreed if the assault was made by volunteers. Two regiments from the Second Corps crept down to the riverbank near the upper bridge, while a regiment from the Ninth Corps moved closer to the middle bridge. The infantry waited until the batteries on the heights finished a thirty-minute bombardment. They loaded into the ungainly pontoons and rowed furiously to the opposite shore, the first amphibious assault ever conducted by the US Army. They stormed ashore and entered the closest buildings, mills, and houses, finally evicting the persistent rebel riflemen. With each bridgehead now secured, the upper and middle bridges were quickly finished, and Union troops began moving into the lower town.[14]

The next morning (December 12), Egan and Battery E moved forward with Sturgis's division to the plateau behind the Lacey House and awaited orders to cross into the town. The other two Ninth Corps divisions moved behind the middle bridge. Around 11 A.M., Sturgis's soldiers began moving down the ravine in front of the Lacy House to cross the upper bridge behind the Second Corps. With little vegetation along the riverbanks, any movement toward the bridges was dangerous. After leading his battery down the river road to reach the

Fig. 7.2. View of Upper Crossing Site (Brady Collection). *LOC*

bridge site, Dickenson likely waved his hand above his head and cried out, "At a gallop, ho!" The gun sections raced across the open plain. When they reached the bridge, both officers cautioned the drivers to carefully lead each gun section over the swaying span so as not to unbalance the pontoons. Intermittent rebel artillery rounds from Marye's Heights splashed water and shell fragments over their heads frequently, adding to the excitement of the crossing.[15]

John's crossing likely paralleled what Tully McCrea described in a later letter: "We had to cross the open plain in full sight of the rebels. When we crossed, they began to shell us, and the shells burst around us quite merrily. We went across with the horses at a gallop and succeeded in reaching the river without having anyone hurt. The battery in front of ours had three men wounded by a bursting shell. We crossed the river and staid [*sic*] in Fredericksburg all day without any battle."[16]

Once on the opposite shore, Sturgis's division turned south and marched parallel to the river. Dickenson's battery moved with the infantry along Caroline Street into the southern part of the town. Egan likely saw columns of black smoke funneling into the sky from burning or collapsed buildings from the earlier shelling all around him. A few civilians gradually emerged from the ruins and darted across the streets where wounded and dead soldiers from both sides lay. Yellow flags hung from the rooftops of unoccupied houses or stores, announcing the locations of regimental hospitals.[17]

There was little sleep in the lower town that night. Anticipating the inevitable order to assault Marye's Heights the next morning, many soldiers believed the town was a prize of war and began entering empty houses and stores in search of tobacco, a valuable commodity. What began as a few isolated incidents soon turned into a rampage. Before long, soldiers stole whatever struck their fancy, and within a few hours Fredericksburg became the first American city to be sacked since the War of 1812.[18]

The Battle of Fredericksburg

The next day, on December 13, two violent and bloody attacks took place more than four miles apart. The first attack was made early in the morning on the lower plain where the First and Sixth Corps assaulted "Stonewall" Jackson's Second Corps defending the heights near Hamilton's Crossing. The second attack began closer to noon in Fredericksburg when the Second and Ninth Corps moved toward Marye's Heights and Longstreet's waiting rebel soldiers.

Prior to the attacks, a thick early morning fog from the river crept over the town and lower plain. The men of Couch's Second Corps stood in tightly packed formations in the lower town, readying themselves for the order to advance. Hoping to cause panic and casualties, rebel artillery atop Marye's Heights fired blindly into the fog, sending shells bursting over the streets.[19]

Meanwhile, Willcox's Ninth Corps was ordered to connect with General Franklin's Left Grand Division near Deep Run in the lower plain. Sturgis's division shifted near the train depot, forming the right flank of the Ninth Corps and linked up with the Second Corps in the lower town. The other two Ninth Corps divisions pushed south to link up with the Sixth Corps at Deep Run. John Egan and Battery E occupied positions near the river with the other Ninth Corps batteries.[20]

An hour before noon, Sumner ordered Couch's Second Corps forward and Willcox's Ninth Corps to support the attack. Sturgis's division moved across the railroad tracks into the lower town and brought his brigades on line behind Brig. Gen. Winfield S. Hancock's division from the Second Corps. Ahead of them lay a field broken up by some houses and a few substantial fences or walls from behind which rebel sharpshooters fired repeatedly. When Sturgis moved his brigades into the town, he ordered Dickenson's battery forward to the rising ground on the left of the railroad tracks to provide cover for his advance.[21]

At the bivouac area along the river, a bugle probably sounded "Boots and Saddles," and the gunners leapt into their saddles. With the caissons left behind, Egan and Battery E likely followed Dickenson up graveled city streets to reach the brickyard. Close to 12:30 P.M., Battery E unlimbered on an elevated rise in front of the brick kilns immediately south of the railroad and about twelve hundred yards from the nearest rebel positions. Closer to town and just behind them, the Fifty-first New York Infantry provided protection.

Meanwhile, Sturgis's division was already under fire from sharpshooters behind a stone wall to their front, and rebel artillery on Marye's Heights raked the field before them as the blue columns advanced. Dickenson's exposed position on the rise quickly attracted the attention of rebel artillery, which wounded several of his men. Unfazed by the initial shelling, Dickenson directed his fire on the enemy guns and earthworks in front of Sturgis's advance. Within minutes, a fierce bombardment of Battery E's position began.[22]

Barely fifteen minutes after his guns began firing, twelve cannoneers were dead or wounded, and Dickenson was struck down, mortally wounded. First Sergeant Moran, now acting as second in command, remained at his post even after being severely wounded

in the cheek. The intense shelling caused the gun crews to be driven from their pieces twice, but all returned without being ordered.

Egan immediately took command of the devastated unit and later described in his report what happened:

Before the first piece was in position, the enemy opened from his earthworks, and sharpshooters from concealed places singled out men of the battery. For the first ten minutes, seeing no infantry, we replied to their fire from the earthworks, but to no effect. After seeing a few skirmishers, we directed our fire upon them while the battery was in position. In the meantime, the enemy changed his projectiles from solid to shell and case shot, which burst just at the point to make it most destructive, and continually their fragments and bullets hailed upon the battery. In less than twenty minutes, the commanding officer and 12 of the cannoneers were killed or wounded. Twice all the cannoneers were driven from the pieces.[23]

Egan, likely remembering his earlier experiences at Antietam, determined that it was disastrous for the battery to remain where it was. Less than thirty minutes after the battery arrived, he called out "Limber to the rear!" With shells continuing to explode around them, the surviving gunners hastily limbered their guns, picked up their dead and wounded, and followed Egan back to the river and safety.[24]

His battery remained near the river for two days. His crews tried to keep warm as the temperature dropped precipitously. No fires were allowed as the slightest glimmer of light brought shells raining down from Marye's Heights. Everyone was hungry as their rations were long gone.

Their stay in Fredericksburg ended after Burnside met with his senior commanders on December 15 to order a general withdrawal. The infantry tied down their loose gear, and the engineers spread hay and dirt over the pontoon bridges to deaden the sounds of wagons and men crossing. Darkness hid the Union exodus from the city and the lower plain. Not a word was spoken as the long lines of soldiers, wagons, and ambulances moved toward the bridges. Between 7 P.M. and midnight, Egan's gunners loaded baggage on the limbers and caissons, wrapped the trace chains, and quietly recrossed the river. By dawn the entire army was across, and the bridges were cut loose and swung against the shore in friendly hands.[25]

Egan led the battery back to its old camps along the road to Belle Plains, having become the first in his class to take command of a unit under harrowing combat conditions. His decision to withdraw the battery undoubtedly saved it from destruction. Although he was cited in several official reports for his gallantry, he was not brevetted for his actions that day.

8

Sanderson, Arnold, McIntire, and Warner at Chancellorsville

West Point, December 1865. Meanwhile, the cadets had entered Tully's classroom and stood behind their chairs, waiting for the section leader to deliver his report. They were uncomfortable when Tully stared at them before class, as instructors often issued demerits for uniform infractions. Fortunately, the cadets were now wearing uniforms that were not torn or full of holes. The war had driven the cost of repairs and cleaning far above their cadet pay. This was especially hurtful in an organization that prided itself on clean, fresh uniforms each day. Recognizing that need, the superintendent changed the regulations to allow cadets to receive money from home for the first time.[1]

It was only a short time until Christmas Day, and the cadets hoped the tactical officers might look the other way when they received boxes of food and presents from home. When Tully thought of the holidays, he remembered how much he enjoyed receiving those boxes and letters when he was a cadet. Writing letters evoked memories of having to unfreeze the ink before he could write letters in the field. There were times when he lacked enough paper and wrote on scraps, turning the pages sideways to write across lines already written.

After General Hooker took command of the Army of the Potomac, changes in organization improved the life of the soldiers. New recruits and supplies improved the atmosphere in the camps near Falmouth. Tully recalled the high hopes he and his classmates had that General Lee would finally be defeated the next time the armies clashed. Those hopes were dashed during the Chancellorsville campaign. While his battery did not play a major role, four of his classmates—Sam McIntire, James "Sep" Sanderson, Isaac Arnold, and Charles Warner—were heavily engaged during that battle.

Fig. 8.1. Hooker's Headquarters at Chancellorsville (Edwin Forbes). *LOC*

The Chancellorsville Campaign—April 1863

Late in the evening of April 30, a tired and dusty James Sanderson was located near Hartwood Church after a rapid sixteen-mile march from the lower bridge crossings south of Fredericksburg. Maj. Gen. Daniel Sickles and the Third Corps were ordered to join the rest of the army at Chancellorsville no later than daybreak on May 1.[2]

The preceding days had been filled with much anticipation and preparation. Maj. Gen. Joseph Hooker had replaced Ambrose Burnside as the commander of the Army of the Potomac three months before. His plan to attack General Lee and the Army of Northern Virginia required fast-moving columns, and each infantry corps was directed to reduce the number of wagons to a bare minimum. All extra ammunition was carried on mules, and only one artillery battery marched with each division. The remaining wagons, ammunition, and guns marched with the army trains. The day before they left, the soldiers were issued eight days' rations and sixty rounds of ammunition. The veterans packed their haversacks and knapsacks and, sensing heavy action ahead, found space to carry twenty more rounds.[3]

Classmates Reassigned

James Sanderson knew that less than half his class remained with the Army of the Potomac by this time. A number of transfers took place after the Battle of Fredericksburg. More took place when General Hooker took command of the Army of the Potomac. He quickly dismantled the grand divisions and sent Burnside's Ninth Corps with three divisions off to Fort Monroe. Over General Hunt's objections, Hooker dismantled much of the Artillery Reserve and its batteries were returned to division control, substantially changing the artillery command structure that had worked well at Antietam and Fredericksburg.

James's remaining classmates were still assigned to the same units they fought with at Antietam and Fredericksburg (see table 6.1), again with a few new battery commanders. Several batteries were shifted between corps, the Artillery Reserve, and the horse artillery brigade. John Egan and Battery E, now under command of 1st Lt. Samuel S. Elder, were reassigned to the horse artillery brigade in support of Brig. Gen. George Stoneman's Cavalry Corps. When the Ninth Corps was sent off to Fort Monroe and the Department of Virginia, William Bartlett in Hayden's battery, James Lord in Benjamin's battery, and Albert Murray in Gilliss's battery headed south with the three infantry divisions.[4]

New orders from Washington transferred Charles Suter to the Department of the South at Hilton Head Island. Ranald Mackenzie was now acting as an aide to Brig. Gen. Gouverneur Warren, the chief engineer on Hooker's staff. The Ordnance Department shifted Morris Schaff from Fort Monroe to the ordnance depot at Aquia Landing, making him a member of Hooker's ordnance staff. Frank James left the First US Cavalry, where he had been assigned on "detached service" since graduation, to join his permanent unit in the Third US

Cavalry in Kentucky and Tennessee. Asa Bolles's death in California saddened the class in April. Tully McCrea was heard to say, "He is the first; who will be next?" After all the transfers and reassignments ended, just thirteen members of the class remained with the Army of the Potomac.[5]

Not all thirteen were present during the Battle of Chancellorsville. Stoneman's cavalry with close to nine thousand troopers and four batteries of horse artillery had already departed on a lengthy raid to destroy the railroads supplying General Lee. Cliff Comly rode with the First US Cavalry. Frank Hamilton, with 1st Lt. Robert Clarke's Battery M, Second US Artillery, and John Egan with Elder's battery rode with the long lines of blue troopers. Soon after the army consolidated at Chancellorsville, John Calef's and James Lancaster's batteries from the Artillery Reserve were sent to protect the fords along the Rappahannock.

The Army Gathers at Chancellorsville

Hooker's right wing (Fifth, Eleventh, and Twelfth Corps) left Falmouth on April 27 and began a wide turning movement to cross the Rappahannock and Rapidan Rivers far in the rear of Lee's lines. Maj. Gen. John Sedgwick's two corps demonstrated along the Rappahannock River south of town while Stoneman's cavalry tried to cut Lee's supply lines. The right wing reached Chancellorsville on April 30, and by nightfall the Second Corps joined them.[6] Tully McCrea and Battery I unlimbered in the rear of the Chancellor House with Edmund Kirby now back in command of the battery. Sam McIntire and 1st Lt. Malbone F. Watson's (May '61) Battery I, Fifth US Artillery, were located just east of the Chancellor House where Maj. Gen. George Sykes's division in the Fifth Corps was entrenched.

Hooker's plan also called for the First and Sixth Corps to cross onto the lower plain on April 28 in an attempt to confuse Lee as to the main attack. To support these crossings, George Gillespie and the Engineer Battalion moved its heavy pontoon trains to Franklin's

Fig. 8.2. Franklin's Crossing, Lower Bridge Site (Alexander Gardner). *LOC*

Crossing, and the volunteer engineer battalions went to Pollock's Mill. Just after midnight, Gillespie's men moved the pontoons down to the river's edge with the assistance of some infantry. By this time, they were experts in laying bridges at this particular place. Behind them James Sanderson's and Isaac Arnold's batteries came forward to provide security for the crossings.

Between 4 A.M. and 5:00 A.M. on April 28, an infantry regiment from Brig. Gen. William T. H. Brooks's division in the Sixth Corps climbed into the ungainly wooden pontoons and quietly rowed across the Rappahannock River through an early morning mist without an artillery bombardment. Rushing up the riverbanks after landing, the infantry quickly neutralized the rebel pickets but not before they signaled that a crossing was in progress. Gillespie's engineers then went to work. Within the hour, a single span was completed, and Brooks's division crossed over. Charles Warner and Williston's battery soon followed and initially occupied a position near a line of rifle pits along the banks of the river.[7] In a letter to his sister Emma, Warner later described the crossing:

The night was cloudy and very favorable for our movements. We could see very well for short distances, but the rebels could not see us. The boats were launched very quietly, and two or three hundred men got into them and rowed across just before daylight. When they were about in the middle of the stream the rebs gave them a crashing volley, but it did not stop our men, who landed, charged the rebel rifle pits and took quite a number of prisoners. . . . A division was thrown over to hold the ground until the bridges were built. It was our division. We considered it quite an honor that our battery should be chosen to defend the crossing, as it was a very responsible and dangerous duty. . . . We are about one hundred yards from the south bank of the Rappahannock, and the battery is in position behind a rifle pit that the enemy built to resist the crossing. The bridges are just in front of us.[8]

Early on May 1, Maj. Gen. Daniel E. Sickles's Third Corps crossed the Rappahannock at US Ford. One brigade along with Isaac Arnold and 1st Lt. Francis Seeley's Battery K, Fourth US Artillery, were left behind to protect the crossing site. When the Third Corps arrived at Chancellorsville later that morning, five corps and eleven divisions with seventy thousand soldiers were present in the area.[9]

James Sanderson's battery bivouacked near the Bullock House (also known as the White House) with Maj. Gen. Hiram G. Berry's division. With the Third Corps in reserve, 1st Lt. Justin Dimick (June '61) put Battery H, First US Artillery, "in park," and the horse teams were unharnessed. The drivers watered the horses at a nearby stream, and the gunners spread out their wet tarpaulins, blankets, and overcoats to dry. Most of the men started cooking their evening meal and relaxed after the forced march from the lower plain.

Sam McIntire Fights on the Road to Fredericksburg

Before the last of the Third Corps arrived, Maj. Gen. George Meade received orders to begin moving two Fifth Corps divisions along the

Fig. 8.3. Watson's Battery on Orange Turnpike (Alfred Waud). *LOC*

River Road and General Sykes's division down the Orange Turnpike toward Fredericksburg. Sam McIntire with Watson's battery trotted behind Sykes's lead brigade. Rebel artillery firing from the crest of the shallow valley beyond Mott's Run prompted a call for McIntire's battery to come forward when Sykes's infantry was initially halted. Around 11:30 A.M., the battle for Chancellorsville began.

Watson initially put two guns in position astride the road and sent McIntire into the nearby tree line with the other four guns, which responded to the rebel battery on the far crest for close to an hour. Meanwhile, Sykes's infantry regrouped and pressed the rebel skirmishers and infantry back up the eastern slope of the valley. McIntire's battery leapfrogged its way up the slope, occupying farmyards along the way. When it reached the crest, it engaged a rebel battery in the rear of a farmhouse at roughly five hundred yards. In the exchange, McIntire's battery lost two men wounded and five horses killed or disabled, and one limber was blown up, but the rebel battery was forced to withdraw. Sykes's infantry now held the crest, but for how long? Beyond was the open terrain where the Union infantry sought to maneuver, unrestricted by the confines of the area known as the Wilderness.[10]

Confederate reinforcements soon began arriving on the flanks of Sykes's division, threatening his hold on the ridge line, and he called for assistance. In response, Hooker sent Hancock's division from the Second Corps along with orders for Sykes to withdraw. McIntire's battery along with two batteries from the Second Corps withdrew by bounds, providing covering fire for the infantry to withdraw from the crest before they were overwhelmed.

Generals Couch, Hancock, Sykes, and Meade were convinced that it was unwise to give up access to the open terrain beyond the ridge and wanted to press forward, but Hooker began issuing a series of confusing orders and counterorders. Couriers raced back and forth, and an angry and disappointed Couch found Hooker on the front porch of the Chancellor House. Hooker told him not to worry—Lee must now fight him on his own ground. The net effect was to adopt a defensive posture. By nightfall the advanced elements were withdrawn to the vicinity of the Chancellor House. Later that evening in a grove of trees east of Chancellorsville, General Lee and General Jackson conducted a key meeting that would greatly disrupt Hooker's vision of how the battle would be fought over the next two days.[11]

"Sep" Sanderson Anchors the Gun Line at Fairview

As a result of the late night meeting, Lee's artillery on the eastern side of Chancellorsville opened up between 6 A.M. and 7 A.M. on May 2, scattering wagons and everything loose around the Chancellor House.[12] At the same time, Jackson's divisions followed a local guide down the Catherine Furnace Road. His ten-mile-long column was seen by a sharp-eyed picket near Hazel Grove, but the Union generals believed the report was visible evidence that Hooker's plan was succeeding—Lee's army was retreating.

Sometime between 3 P.M. and 4 P.M., Jackson's tired divisions emerged from the forest where the Brock Road intersects the Orange Turnpike well west of Chancellorsville. They crossed the road and formed a line of battle almost a mile wide perpendicular to the turn-

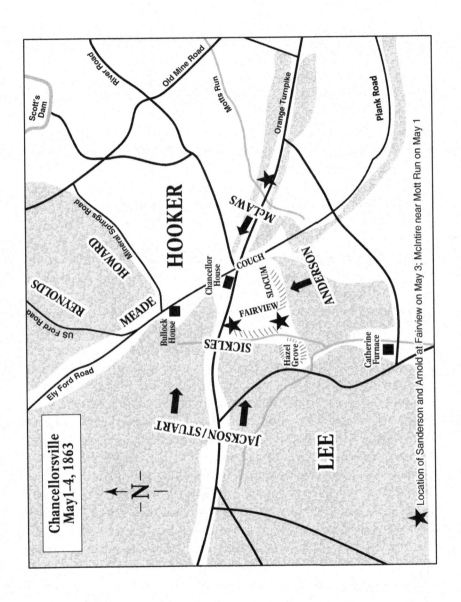

Chancellorsville
May 1–4, 1863

Location of Sanderson and Arnold at Fairview on May 3; McIntire near Mott Run on May 1

pike. The Wilderness's brambles and thickets caught at the men's clothing, low-hanging branches scratched their faces, and it was almost impossible to see more than twenty or thirty feet in any direction. Finally, they kneeled down and waited for the order to attack. Sometime between 5:00 and 5:30 P.M., Jackson nodded to Brig. Gen. Robert E. Rodes to go forward. Bugles sounded, and the long line moved forward into the unsuspecting right flank of Maj. Gen. Oliver Howard's Eleventh Corps.[13]

Due to unusual weather and terrain conditions that afternoon, the initial sound of firing in the west was not heard at the Chancellor House. Hooker, sitting on the front porch, was suddenly confronted with a disorganized mob of men, wagons, and horses coming toward him on the Plank Road. He mounted his horse, yelled orders to his staff to send whatever units were available westward and any artillery units to Fairview, then galloped toward the Bullock House. Behind him, Kirby's battery quickly shifted across the road to help stem the tide of the fleeing Eleventh Corps soldiers. Tully McCrea later wrote that his battery was located in a low, swampy area and along with army engineers helped block the road. In one account, the stampede of Eleventh Corps soldiers was only slowed by the swords of the officers and the sponge staffs of Kirby's battery drawn up across the road. Tully and Battery I were soon withdrawn to US Ford and then sent back to where the First and Fifth Corps were building breastworks at the intersection of US Ford and Ely Ford roads during the ensuing battle around the Chancellor House on May 3. Meanwhile, Kirby was ordered by General Couch to take charge of Capt. George Leppien's Fifth Maine Light Artillery battery near the Chancellor House after all its officers were wounded or killed. Subjected to heavy shelling after he arrived, he was seriously wounded and evacuated from the field.[14] George Woodruff, Kirby's second in command, now took command of Battery I.

When Hooker reached Berry's division near the Bullock House, he reined up and exhorted the men to stem the tide of the fleeing Eleventh Corps and halt the rebel attack. Berry's regiments grabbed their muskets and moved quickly toward the sound of the guns.[15]

Across the road, James Sanderson's head likely snapped up when Dimick's bugler suddenly sounded "Assembly," and he yelled for his horse teams. Dimick and the guidon bearer mounted their horses and rode off toward the Plank Road. Quickly limbering the guns, Sanderson and Battery H followed Capt. Thomas W. Osborne, the Third Corps chief of artillery, out to the road, leaving the battery caissons to follow later.[16]

As soon as Sanderson and Battery H reached the road, they ran into hordes of fleeing Eleventh Corps soldiers, wagons, horses, and mules that clogged the way ahead. Osborne later reported: "As we passed General Hooker's headquarters, a scene burst upon us which, God grant, may never again be seen in the Federal Army of the United States. The Eleventh Corps had been routed and were fleeing to the river like sheep. The men and artillery filled the roads, its sides, and the skirts of the field, and it appeared that no two of one company could be found together. Aghast and terror-stricken, heads bare and panting for breath, they pleaded like infants at their mother's breast that we would let them pass to the rear unhindered."[17]

Undeterred, Sanderson forced his way through the mob, desperately trying to keep Dimick in view. About four hundred yards ahead of him, he saw the red battery guidon move off the Plank Road into the Fairview clearing. Pushing aside the masses on the road before him, Sanderson swung his four guns into the clearing just off the Plank Road. With Sanderson's guns acting as the anchor, Osborne then directed the following Third Corps batteries to form a gun line immediately to the left of Battery H along the crest of the hill in the Fairview clearing.[18]

In the interim, Dimick took the other two guns another four hundred yards down the road and unlimbered in the middle of the Plank Road behind Berry's infantry, who were hard at work building breastworks and barricades. Soon, Maj. Gen. William French's division from the Second Corps arrived on Berry's right, and Brig. Gen. Alpheus Williams's division from the Twelfth Corps linked up in the forest on the left. A stiffened Union defense was being created on the fly to stem the tide of graybacks flowing toward it.[19]

At the opposite end of the Fairview clearing, Capt. Clermont L. Best, the Twelfth Corps chief of artillery, quickly reoriented his fourteen guns to join the rapidly forming gun line. Within the hour, thirty-eight cannons from eight different batteries were in position firing against Jackson's attackers. By one account, they fired over one hundred rounds per minute against the advancing rebel infantry.[20]

By 7 P.M., an invigorated Union defense had slowed Jackson's attack. Dimick's two guns on the road, the gun line at Fairview, and more Union artillery at Hazel Grove belched canister and shot at such a furious rate that they cleared the Plank Road of advancing rebel troops more than once. When time permitted, Sanderson's gunners frantically dug low lunettes around each of their gun positions for protection.[21]

The evening hours robbed Lee of Jackson's services forever. Riding beyond his lines in the darkness near the Plank Road, Jackson was seriously wounded by friendly fire. He and his staff were further subjected to shelling from Dimick's guns before he was evacuated and taken to a field hospital. Maj. Gen. J. E. B. Stuart was placed in command of Jackson's Second Corps in the interim.[22]

Sanderson and Arnold Are the Last to Leave Fairview

After arriving from US Ford before dawn on May 3, Isaac Arnold and Battery K were given little rest before Seeley was directed to join the gun line at Fairview. The battery was sent six hundred yards beyond the far left of the gun line to help cover the Third Corps divisions that Hooker ordered withdrawn from the now tenuous Union positions at Hazel Grove. Seeley later described his position near the Twelfth Corps as "on rising ground in the angle made by the formation of our infantry."[23]

Before the sun rose, two Third Corps divisions slipped through the narrow corridor between Hazel Grove and Fairview under enemy fire. The two divisions then took up a second line of defenses behind the Twelfth Corps divisions around Fairview and Berry's division across the Plank Road.[24]

Around the same time, Stuart's gray lines rose up from where they halted the night before and headed east. Rebel yells resounded across the fields as they approached the stiffened Union defenses. Dimick's two guns and Berry's infantry came under heavy fire almost immediately. Gray columns twice tried to force their way past them only to be repulsed. For over an hour, the furious attacks continued as rebel infantry crept closer and closer, killing Berry in one exchange. Stuart's regiments finally forced in the flank of one of Berry's brigades on the northern side of the road, and at the same time a Twelfth Corps regiment unexpectedly withdrew uncovering Dimick's guns on the southern side. Osborne quickly ordered him to withdraw.[25]

His horse teams came forward, and one gun was successfully dragged away, but concentrated rebel musket fire killed several horses in the second team, leaving the others frantically thrashing about trying to escape. Several gunners were killed or wounded in the continuing fusillade. Minutes later, Dimick's horse was killed. He attempted to gather harnesses from the dead horses and was struck in the foot by a musket ball. Then a second round struck his spine and he toppled to the ground.

When the news reached Fairview, James Sanderson saw the lone gun standing in the middle of the road. He yelled for a limber and a team and galloped down the Plank Road through smoke, musket fire, and exploding rounds to recover the gun and his fallen commander. With musket balls whizzing past, he helped limber the gun, loaded Dimick and the other wounded onto its limber, and ordered the crew to pull away just before the gray lines overran the position. When he returned to Fairview, Sanderson immediately took command of the battery, shifting gunners between pieces to man all six guns once again. Dimick was evacuated to a field hospital but died two days later.[26]

Action now shifted to the opposite end of the Fairview gun line. Confederate units occupied Hazel Grove soon after Sickles removed his two divisions that morning. Stuart ordered it filled with artillery. Soon upwards of forty rebel cannons were massed there, and the Union infantry and cannons at Fairview came under heavy attack from two directions.[27]

Isaac Arnold's battery was now the most visible part of the gun line at Fairview. In the early morning haze, a rebel battery ducked behind one of the small knolls that broke up the open ground between Fairview and Hazel Grove and began firing. Arnold's half of Seeley's battery immediately returned fire, but most of its rounds passed over the crest of the knoll without doing much damage. When a rebel brigade crept closer, Arnold shifted his fires to the left to confront it while Seeley's half of the battery shifted trails to the right to blast canister into the tree lines to hold back another rebel unit. At the same time, the continuing fires from the rebel battery killed or wounded several men and horses in the battery.[28]

Elsewhere along the Fairview gun line, the rate of fire slackened noticeably between 8 A.M. and 9 A.M. as the guns began to run out of long-range ammunition. Complicating the lack of ammunition was the absence of the guiding hand of General Hunt. No batteries were designated to replace them nor any ammunition resupply provided. Hunt was ordered to Banks's Ford by Hooker earlier and was not present at Chancellorsville until near the end.[29]

Stuart's gunners soon noticed the slower rate of fire from the Union guns and increased their own, causing a terrible crossfire to fall heavily on Fairview from guns at Hazel Grove and along the Plank Road. Capt. Charles Morse, a member of one of the Twelfth Corps regiments at Fairview, later wrote home about the terrible shelling that morning: "The air was full of missiles, solid shot, shells and musket balls—I saw one shot kill three horses and a man, another took the leg of one captain of the batteries—more than half the horses were killed or wounded; one caisson blown up; another knocked to pieces, in ten minutes more, the guns would have been isolated."[30]

By this time, Arnold's battery could barely hold its position on the far left of the line. For over two hours, artillery fires savaged the battery. With his ammunition chests almost empty and the infantry pulling back on both sides, Seeley finally yelled, "Limber to the rear!" as the rebel infantry started up the slope, some 250 yards away. Horse teams galloped up from a grove of trees in the rear. The guns were hastily limbered, and the battery pulled back near the Chancellor

House to refill its ammunition chests. It was forced to leave Fairview in such haste that a number of wounded and dead were left behind.[31]

At the opposite end of the gun line, Sanderson's guns were subjected to the same heavy fires and he was also forced to withdraw, but his battery was sent to US Ford. That evening he reviewed what occurred that day: Dimick and two men were killed, eighteen were wounded, a number of horses were killed or disabled, and one caisson was lost.

Upon withdrawal from Fairview, Arnold was not out of danger yet. Seeley's battery was sent to the Chancellor House and then ordered into a field on the opposite side of the Plank Road. The heavy rebel cross fire continued, and each of his gun sections now had two or three wounded, including Arnold who suffered a non-life-threatening wound.

During a lull in the action, Seely's gunners repaired the spokes of several wheels so the guns could be extracted. As the infantry fell back around him, he gathered as many harnesses from dead horses as he could but had to leave a caisson behind when given permission to withdraw. By this time, he had only two or three horses to draw each gun away. Late that night near US Ford, he reported that his battery had lost seven killed, one officer (Arnold) and thirty-eight men wounded, and fifty-nine horses killed or disabled. More casualties were suffered in his battery that day than any other artillery unit during the entire war.[32]

Hooker's army withdrew from around the Chancellor House to strong defensive positions at the intersection of the Mineral Springs and US Ford roads a mile away. In the meantime, riotous celebrations began at the Chancellor House. As Lee rode through his cheering soldiers, a messenger appeared with news that the Federal Sixth Corps was approaching from the east.

Warner and the Battle at Salem Church

Late on May 2, Hooker ordered Maj. Gen. John Sedgwick's Sixth Corps to fight its way toward his position from Fredericksburg as quickly as possible. Before dawn broke, two Sixth Corps divisions left the lower plain and, after several concerted efforts, finally breached the Confederate defenses on Marye's Heights. They continued west along the Orange Turnpike for about a mile and then halted, exhausted. Meanwhile, Sedgwick directed Brooks's division to come forward from the lower plain and take the lead west that afternoon.

Brooks's infantry, along with Charles Warner and Williston's battery, left the lower plain, climbed Marye's Heights, and pushed west along the Orange Turnpike until they passed the other two divisions. Small Confederate detachments skillfully delayed Brooks's advance. Just after his division passed the toll house, his two brigades became engaged in heavy fighting along the wooded ridgeline upon which the Salem Church stood. The arrival of rebel reinforcements from Chancellorsville and stiffened rebel defenses along the ridge forced his brigades to fall back before the other two Sixth Corps divisions came up. The wooded terrain limited the use of his artillery up to this point, but now the batteries rushed forward into the open fields below the ridge.[33]

Warner described his part in the battle a few days later:

We marched over the heights on the Chancellorsville Road about two miles. Our 6th Corps was detached, you know, from the rest of the army which was with Hooker. Well, when about two miles from Fredericksburg, we came across the enemy, strongly posted in a dense piece of woods. Our men had to go a long distance on a level plain, exposed to a heavy fire before reaching the woods, but they advanced in splendid style and then the slaughter commenced. . . . I saw our men go into the woods, line after line, with banners streaming, and then heard a perfect roar of musketry for perhaps fifteen minutes. Then our men began to fall back. They fought well, but the rebels were too strong. Some fell back slowly and in good order, disputing the ground inch by inch, while others fled ingloriously, perfectly terror stricken. The rebs followed them a short distance out of the woods, and perhaps the

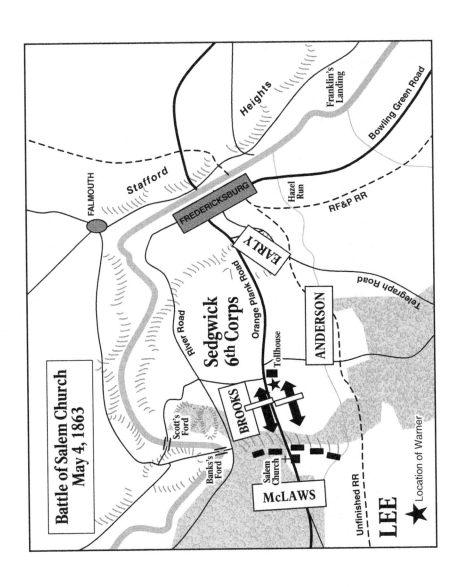

Battle of Salem Church
May 4, 1863

FALMOUTH

Stafford

Heights

Franklin's Landing

Bowling Green Road

FREDERICKSBURG

Hazel Run

RF&P RR

EARLY

River Road

Orange Plank Road

Sedgwick 6th Corps

Telegraph Road

ANDERSON

Tollhouse

Scott's Ford

BROOKS

Banks's Ford

Salem Church

McLAWS

Unfinished RR

LEE

★ Location of Warner

repulse might have become general rout, if the rebs were not
driven back.[34]

Williston's guns careened through the retreating blue uniforms
at a gallop. He sent Warner with four guns to the left of the road near
the tollhouse and took two other guns to the right. The drivers swung
the guns around and dropped trails. For the moment, Warner's guns
were hidden behind a dip in the ground, and his gun crews quickly
readied their pieces without the threat of musket fire. The road and
field before him was a different story. Confused Union soldiers filled
the field, closely followed by rebel infantry, which offered an opportunity to fire into the flanks of the enemy. His gunners waited impatiently until Williston gave the order to fire.

When his sword came down, the first volley ricocheted off the
hard-surfaced turnpike. Orders to switch to shell caused subsequent
rounds to burst over the heads of the rebel infantry, forcing them
back into the tree line. Williston then yelled, "Fire at will!" When a
second group of graybacks headed directly for Warner's guns, he fired
canister with great effect at three hundred yards. The concentrated
fires of Williston's battery forced the enemy to withdraw into the
woods.[35]

Warner later continued his description of the battle:

> The air was full of bullets which went whistling by and it
> was almost impossible to stop the stragglers. Our battery was
> already in position nearby. It was ordered up to the front at
> a gallop, to cover the retreat of our men and drive the rebels
> back into their holes. We were in action perhaps half an hour
> and it is said did very good service. I believe we did. Some
> say we would have been driven into the river if it had not
> been for our battery. I think we killed a few and scared a great
> many more. We were under a pretty warm fire. Our horses
> were just in the rear of us hitched to the limber chests, which
> carry the ammunition. I was so busy with my firing that I did
> not notice much that was going on, but happened to turn

around once, I saw two of my horses on their backs kicking their last. That was our only loss. They fired no artillery at us here. We had several horses wounded and several men grazed. General Sedgwick was right there, and seemed much pleased with our practice.[36]

By 6 P.M., the Sixth Corps was bloodied by a force one-third its size. Sedgwick began to withdraw his divisions into a strong defensive position. Unable to force his way past Salem Church to join Hooker's forces at Chancellorsville, Sedgwick organized his three divisions into a horseshoe-shaped defense around Banks's Ford and Scott's Ford, with his flanks securely anchored on the Rappahannock River. The engineers were quick to throw two bridges across the river to provide a means of escape should he need it.[37]

Warner's words will likely resonate with many soldiers who have gazed upon battlefields after the guns ceased firing:

That night, I must say, I was horrified. In that repulse we lost a great many men, quite a number that I knew very well. Between us and the woods, about eight hundred yards, I could see black spots all over the ground. They were dead bodies. A great many of our dead and wounded fell in the edge of the woods. The woods were afterward set on fire by the rebs, and a great many must have been burned. We were near a house, where some dead and wounded were brought. They were all alone and uncared for, and one who was gasping very nearly his last, rolled his eyes around at me. I do not forget how he looked. I suppose I am not very much of a soldier or I would not mind such things, but I never was so much impressed with the horror of war as I was that night.[38]

After dark, Warner's battery withdrew to the rear, refilled its ammunition chests and replaced some of its lost horses. It then relocated to a commanding position in the center of the area near Banks's Ford. His letter described how tired he was that evening:

That night we moved back about a mile, unharnessed the horses and made preparations for passing the night. I never was so tired in my life. As soon as I could get my blankets out of the wagon I dropped down on them and was asleep in no time without intending it. After a while I was (with difficulty I am told) aroused to take a cup of coffee. I stayed awake scarcely long enough to do it and the next morning, did not remember anything about it. We had slept only about an hour the night before and had been on the battlefield since daylight. It was the longest day I ever knew. I never slept so soundly in my life, and the next morning was as good as new.[39]

Camp near Falmouth

On May 6, Hooker's army withdrew from the Chancellorsville area, recrossed the Rappahannock, and marched back to Falmouth in the pouring rain. This time there was no music to welcome them when they arrived at their old camps. Tully McCrea later wrote that Battery I "started around dark and marched all night through the murderous rain, reaching our old camp around 9 A.M. the next day, completely worn out."[40]

James Sanderson led his battery back to their old camps near the Bellaire mansion and set about rebuilding the unit. At the same time, Williston's battery was ordered north to Richards's Ford to protect against any attacks by rebel cavalry. Tired, wet, and still drowsy from lack of sleep, Charles Warner's gunners harnessed their teams and Battery D trotted north while the rest of the army slowly marched east to Falmouth. They remained at Richards's Ford until May 7 before returning to their old camp near White Oak Church.[41]

Sanderson's actions to recover Dimick and the advanced gun under heavy fire caught the attention of several senior officers, and he was mentioned in three official reports. Sickles's report stated that Sanderson "advanced with a limber through a storm of musketry, disdaining death, and withdrew the last gun of his battery from the grasp of the enemy." With the loss of Dimick, Sanderson became the second member of his class to take command of a regular unit under combat conditions.[42]

The brave actions of these four classmates failed to gain them brevet promotions after the battle. A review of personnel records shows that only one member of the class, Ranald Mackenzie, was brevetted for his actions at Chancellorsville, but it is unclear what those actions were. Shortly after the army returned to Falmouth, Isaac Arnold transferred to the Ordnance Department along with James Rollins from West Point. It is likely that an offer of early promotion enticed them, as both were immediately promoted to first lieutenant after they reached their first new assignments.

James Sanderson, Isaac Arnold, Sam McIntire, and Charles Warner had left Falmouth at the end of April believing they would never return. Instead, they came full circle back to their starting points, their hopes of an early end to the war dashed. Most of the soldiers and officers did not believe they were beaten, but their confidence in Hooker was now seriously eroded.

9

Calef, Mackenzie, McCrea, Egan, Dearing, and Blount at Gettysburg

West Point, December 1865. The morning class focused on key principles covered earlier in the year. Hands shot up and questions were asked. Tully then sent the cadets to the boards to solve homework problems. The room quieted as the cadets developed their answers. The only sound was the noise of chalk scratching on the blackboards.

Halfway through the session, Tully halted the work at the blackboards and, pointing to one cadet, asked him to explain his problem. The cadet stood at attention, picked up one of the long pointers from the chalk tray, and proceeded to identify the facts and method he had used to correctly solve the problem. Tully gave him high marks for his recitation.

By the time the class ended, Tully knew most of the cadets understood enough to get through the exams. However, one cadet asked no questions, and Tully was convinced that he would not make it through the exam. He had been "skinned" by his tactical officer for studying after lights-out at least once this month and yawned in class many times. Perhaps Tully could get some of the demerits removed—the cadet needed all the help he could get to remain at West Point.

After class, Tully heard the jangle of trace chains and went to the window just in time to see the artillery battery clatter up the carriage road. It stirred memories of riding alongside his guns—the thrill of seeing the drivers swing the guns into line, the swirl of activity as the gunners readied their pieces, and the smell and taste of gun smoke were still with him.

Gettysburg was different. He now knew that John Calef had been heavily engaged on McPherson's Ridge on the first day and that Ranald

Fig. 9.1. Artillery Advancing over Difficult Terrain (Edwin Forbes). *SP*

Mackenzie had greatly assisted General Warren at Little Round Top on the second day. The third day was etched forever in his mind. Tully could still feel the impact of the incoming rounds during the heavy bombardment that John Egan later declared was the greatest in any war. Nothing took away the sounds of crashing tree limbs around him and horses screaming in pain during General Lee's assault of the Union center. The memories all flooded back in an instant!

The Battle of Gettysburg—July 1863

2nd Lt. John Calef and his battery rode into Gettysburg with Brig. Gen. John Buford's First Cavalry Division. The troopers were ordered to "proceed to Gettysburg no later than the night of June 30." Buford's division was part of Maj. Gen. George Meade's vast army that stretched along the Maryland-Pennsylvania border, awaiting word of the location of Lee's army. Meade, the newly appointed commander of the Army of the Potomac, had just replaced Hooker on June 28. Around the same time, John Calef became the first in his class to take command of a regular unit, Battery A, Second US Artillery (also known as Tidball's battery).[1]

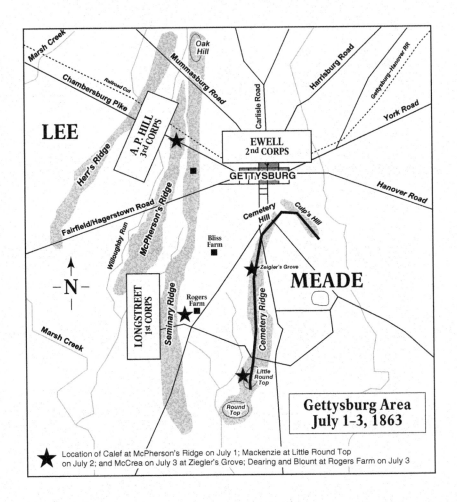

Map caption: Location of Calef at McPherson's Ridge on July 1; Mackenzie at Little Round Top on July 2; and McCrea on July 3 at Ziegler's Grove; Dearing and Blount at Rogers Farm on July 3

Gettysburg Area July 1–3, 1863

Calef was the only member of his class to reach Gettysburg that day. Waiting on the Pennsylvania-Maryland border were nine other classmates who would also participate in the Gettysburg campaign. Frank Hamilton in 1st Lt. Alexander C. M. Pennington's ('60) Battery M, Second US Artillery, supported Brig. Gen. Judson Kilpatrick's (May '61) Third Cavalry Division, while Jim Lancaster in 1st Lt. William D. Fuller's (June '61) Battery C, Third US Artillery, rode with Brig. Gen. David M. Gregg's Second Cavalry Division. Sam

McIntire in 1st Lt. Edward Heaton's Battery B&L, Third US Artillery, was in reserve with the First Horse Artillery Brigade.[2]

Tully McCrea and John Egan in George Woodruff's battery were bivouacked near Uniontown with the Second Corps Artillery Brigade. Egan had transferred back to Battery I after Chancellorsville. Charles Warner and Williston's battery were at Manchester with Sedgwick's Sixth Corps. Jim Sanderson had turned Battery H over to more senior 1st Lt. Chandler P. Eakin as part of the Artillery Reserve. Ranald Mackenzie and Morris Schaff were both located at Meade's headquarters at Taneytown. George Gillespie, after collecting the bridges across the Potomac at Edwards Ferry, would remain in the army's rear with the regular engineers.

Isaac Arnold and James Rollins were now assigned at the arsenals in Washington and Watervliet, New York, respectively. Charles Suter was part of the engineer staff of the Department of the South, and Jasper Myers was appointed chief of ordnance for the Department of Virginia. In the West, William Marye was on temporary orders from the St. Louis arsenal to assist Maj. Gen. Ulysses S. Grant's Army of the Tennessee, while Clemens Chaffee was transferred from Watervliet to the ordnance staff of the Department of Tennessee near Vicksburg.[3]

For the first time, several former classmates opposed them on the field of battle. Capt. James Dearing's artillery battalion and 1st Lt. Joseph Blount's Lynchburg battery were part of Maj. Gen. George Pickett's division in Longstreet's First Corps. Richard Kinney marched in Maj. Gen. Jubal Early's division with the Fifty-second Virginia Infantry in Lt. Gen. Richard S. Ewell's Second Corps. 2nd Lt. Henry Farley, the first to fire at Fort Sumter, had given up his artillery commission and was now riding with Stuart's cavalry somewhere in Pennsylvania.

Calef on McPherson's Ridge

Gettysburg's citizens were more than happy to see Buford's troopers arrive, because a Confederate regiment had recently passed through searching for supplies. Schoolchildren dressed in white stood on the street corners singing patriotic songs and handing out cold water,

Fig. 9.2. Union Artillery on McPherson's Ridge (W. Taber). *BLCW, vol. 3*

bread, and butter as Calef's gunners passed by. A young miss handed him a large bouquet of flowers as he rode through town. He thanked her and hurried to catch up with Col. William Gamble's Second Cavalry Brigade while trying to keep his horse from eating the flowers.[4]

Calef unlimbered his guns about a mile west from the town square near Gamble's camp on the left or southern side of the Chambersburg Pike. Gamble's brigade occupied the ridgeline south of the Chambersburg Pike to the Fairfield road, while Col. Thomas Devin's brigade was responsible for the area north along the ridge to the Mummasburg Road. An unfinished railroad cut, one hundred yards north of the pike, ran across both McPherson Ridge and Herr's Ridge, the next ridgeline.[5]

By 10:30 P.M., a thin line of cavalry vedettes (four-to-five-man cavalry pickets) were spread over a wide arc to the west covering the Fairfield Road and the Chambersburg Pike and as far north as Rock Creek. One of the vedettes made contact with one of A. P. Hill's pickets that evening. Messengers soon galloped away from Buford's headquarters to inform Maj. Gen. John Reynolds and Maj. Gen. Alfred Pleasonton that a major element of Lee's army was close to Gettysburg.[6]

At 5 o'clock in the morning on July 1, Maj. Gen. Henry Heth's soldiers from A. P. Hill's Third Corps began marching east along the hard-packed Chambersburg Pike toward Gettysburg. With an artillery battery and an infantry brigade in the lead, Heth's men had five miles to march. An hour later, Buford's vedette near the Marsh Creek Bridge, three miles west of the town on the Chambersburg Pike, saw dust spiraling up into the warm and cloudy sky. Dust clouds meant infantry marching, and messengers galloped away to warn Buford at his command post at the Blue Eagle Hotel, just west of the Gettysburg town square. At roughly the same time, a signal corps lieutenant atop the tower of the Lutheran Seminary spied the flags of Heth's division through his telescope and alerted Buford's command post. Lee's army was on the march toward Gettysburg, and the only Union forces to stop him were Buford's two cavalry brigades and Calef's battery.[7]

In Gamble's camp, buglers sounded "Boots and Saddles," and his troopers scrambled forward to defensive positions on McPherson's Ridge. His advance guard rode across Willoughby Run and quickly formed a thick, dismounted skirmish line on Herr's Ridge about five hundred yards west of McPherson's Ridge. Every fourth trooper held the reins of the horses behind the crest and awaited the order to withdraw.[8]

The bugle call caught Calef saddling his horse to ride into town for supplies. Within minutes, his guns were limbered and on the road toward McPherson's Ridge, with his wagons and caissons left near the seminary for the time being. Near the crest of McPherson's Ridge, he waited to move his guns into position while pioneers tore down some intervening fences. When Buford arrived, he had a different idea. He directed Calef to spread his guns out along the ridgeline to give the impression that more artillery was present.[9]

Reacting quickly, he left 2nd Lt. John Roder's section of 3-inch rifles on the northern side of the Pike and directed 1st Sgt. Joseph Newman's section to move to the southern side between the road and McPherson's barn. He then led Sgt. Charles Pergel's section to the southeastern edge of McPherson's Woods, spreading his guns along the ridgeline for almost six hundred yards.[10]

Meanwhile, a classic meeting engagement was now under way as the lead elements of Heth's column ran into Buford's dismounted skirmishers on Herr's Ridge, forcing Heth to deploy his units into a line of battle almost a mile wide. While Calef was positioning Pergel's two guns near the southeastern side of McPherson's Woods, some of Heth's infantry and several mounted men crossed Herr's Ridge, north of the Chambersburg Pike. Roder yelled, "Number one, fire!" and the chief of his left piece yanked the lanyard of his 3-inch rifle, sending the first Union artillery round in the battle of Gettysburg toward the oncoming rebel column.[11]

Heth reacted slowly, and his artillery fired for the better part of half an hour before his infantry advanced around 9 A.M. Buford's advance guard had done its job well. They delayed the rebel advance long enough for Buford's main line of defense to be established on McPherson's Ridge before withdrawing to join the rest of the division. When Heth's infantry finally advanced beyond Herr's Ridge and across Willoughby Run, Buford's fast-loading carbines and breech loaders made it seem that a large infantry force was present. In fact, A. P. Hill would later report that he fought against cavalry supported by infantry that morning.[12]

Meanwhile, Calef rode back and forth between his three sections to ensure they fired deliberately at Heth's artillery on Herr's Ridge. At one point, Buford reined up beside him saying, "Our men are in a hot pocket, but, my boy, we must hold this position until the infantry comes up; then you withdraw your guns in each section by piece, fill up your limber chests from the caissons and await my orders." The sky suddenly filled with exploding shells and musket balls, and their horses reared up in fright, but they escaped any injury. Calef later wrote that the sounds of "the demonic whir-r-r of the rifled shots, the 'ping' of bursting shells, and the wicked 'zip' of the bullet, as it hurried by, filled the air."[13]

For two long hours, Buford's cavalrymen and Calef's guns fought outnumbered against Heth's rebels. Buford frequently rode back to Seminary Ridge and climbed to the cupola of the Lutheran Seminary to observe the battle unfolding before him. Confederate lines were beginning to overlap the flanks of his brigades, and he was concerned that he could not hold out much longer.[14]

On his last trip up the tower, his signal corps lieutenant pointed out sunlight glinting on bayonets and the flags of the Union First Corps coming up the Emmitsburg Road. According to one account, Reynolds and his staff reined up at the base of the tower, and Reynolds shouted up, "What's the matter, John?" Buford responded by saying, "The devil's to pay!"[15]

Within a short period of time, Reynolds sent one messenger galloping off to Brig. Gen. James S. Wadsworth's First Division, the lead element marching up the Emmitsburg Pike, directing him to come up as quickly as possible. Another aide was told "ride with all speed, to ride his horse to death if he had to," to Taneytown to inform Meade that the First Corps would hold the ground west of Gettysburg as long as possible, fighting in the streets of the town, if needed. A third messenger galloped away to urge Maj. Gen. Oliver Howard to hurry the Eleventh Corps forward as fast as possible.[16]

The First Corps Arrives

Near 10 A.M., the lead regiment of Wadsworth's division started across the fields from the Emmitsburg Pike at the double-quick, loading their guns on the run. Capt. James A. Hall's Second Maine battery bumped across the fields behind them while Hall rode forward. Reynolds directed him to replace Calef's battery on McPherson's Ridge and distract the rebel artillery as much as possible while the infantry deployed.[17]

In the interim, Calef's battery was now under heavy fire from eighteen guns on Herr's Ridge. When directed to withdraw, Calef ordered Newman's section to "limber to the rear" first. Rebel infantry climbing the slope toward the battery saw horse teams arriving and concentrated musket fire on them. One gun was quickly drawn away. Suddenly a shell burst killed four of the six horses in the other team. Calef yelled to Newman to leave the piece, but he stubbornly refused to leave the gun. With a Herculean effort, it was drawn off by its crew and the remaining two horses. By this time, the enemy infantry was so close that Newman had no time to remove the harnesses from the dead horses before he pulled away, something he rectified later in the day.[18]

Once Newman's guns were gone, the advancing rebel soldiers shifted their fire to Roder's section. He moved one gun by hand about seventy-five yards to the rear to cover the movement of the first. Firing canister to keep the rebel infantry at bay, he successfully hitched up both guns and pulled away. Satisfied that two of his sections were out of danger, Calef rode to McPherson's Woods to withdraw Pergel's section before it was overrun.

Before Roder's section was too far away, Buford noticed rebel infantry attempting to pour through the railroad cut. He halted Roder and asked him to stop them. Roder took one of his guns to the lower end of the railroad cut and unlimbered. One of his gunners was shot down as rebel soldiers rushed forward to capture the piece. Another gunner picked up the double charge of canister and ran for the gun. By the time it was rammed home, the rebel infantry was so close that the canister blast literally tore them apart when it was fired. Roder's efforts secured the cut, and he led his gun back to the seminary to join the rest of the battery.[19]

Shortly thereafter, Reynolds sent Wadsworth's lead brigade north of the Chambersburg Pike to replace Devin's cavalry brigade. The column halted as Hall's battery rushed through its ranks to occupy Calef's old position on the ridge. As soon as Hall tried to unlimber the guns, however, the battery came under heavy artillery fire.

South of the Chambersburg Pike, Gamble's troopers were gradually being forced back into McPherson's Woods by Heth's steadily advancing soldiers. In the swale behind the ridge, the next brigade arriving from Wadsworth's division was directed up the slope to their support. The gray lines had already reached the crest when the sound of musket fire swelled, and Heth's soldiers knew they were no longer facing just dismounted cavalry. The flags of the First Corps and the "damned black hats" of the First Division's Iron Brigade, its reputation well earned during the Battle of Second Bull

Run, were now visible to the advancing rebel infantry in McPherson's Woods.[20]

While the infantry battle swirled around them, Calef ordered Pergel's section to "limber to the rear," before it was overrun. By 10:30 A.M., all of his sections were back at the seminary, replenishing their ammunition. Back on the ridge, the Iron Brigade pushed Heth's soldiers out of McPherson's Woods, chased them back across Willoughby Run and up the slopes of Herr's Ridge before halting. It captured over one thousand soldiers and their brigade commander. It was not accomplished without a critical loss. Reynolds was shot and killed as he directed arriving units to their positions.

The initial success on the southern side of the road was not matched on the north. After Wadsworth's lead brigade replaced Devin's troopers, they were forced to pull back to Oak Ridge, the extension of Seminary Ridge north of the pike, leaving Hall's battery unsupported. Within thirty minutes, Hall was forced to withdraw his guns. About this time, Howard and his staff arrived near Cemetery Hill and were advised of Reynolds's death. Howard then took charge of the battle.[21]

Just before noon, more First Corps batteries clattered up to the seminary. Wadsworth tried to order them to the ridge to support his infantry, but Col. Charles S. Wainwright, the First Corps chief of artillery, believed it too hazardous and refused to send them forward. Failing to get any First Corps batteries forward, Wadsworth ordered Calef's battery to return to its old position. Over Buford's strenuous objections and, according to one account, after Wadsworth's threat of court-martial, Calef finally agreed. He led four guns back up McPherson's Ridge, cautioning his drivers to drive carefully to avoid the many dead and wounded lying on its reverse slope.[22]

Puffs of white smoke from rebel batteries on Herr's Ridge and a cross fire from the newly arrived Ewell's Second Corps batteries on Oak Hill to the north signaled that Calef's guns were noticed. He later wrote that the rounds from Oak Hill sent "projectiles skipping in a playful manner between my line of guns and their limbers." At one point, Calef was absolutely amazed how his horse teams were so completely indifferent to the chaos around them. The horses calmly chewed their oats amid the thunderous roar and exploding shells around them and did not even raise their heads when horses in the same team were killed.[23]

By mid-afternoon, Howard's two Eleventh Corps divisions deployed northwest of the town were under heavy attack from Ewell's Second Corps. At the same time, fresh troops from A. P. Hill's Third Corps launched another attack against the First Corps on McPherson's Ridge. Calef's four guns proved to be no match for the combined artillery of both rebel corps. His crews suffered a number of casualties, and his position became untenable. When a First Corps battery was finally sent to replace him, it suffered heavy shelling before it could even unlimber and was forced to withdraw. Seeing graycoats streaming through the railroad cut to his right, Calef limbered his guns and withdrew across the fields behind McPherson's Woods to the Seminary.[24]

Sometime between 3 P.M. and 4 P.M., Howard reluctantly ordered a withdrawal of the two Union Corps to Cemetery Hill. His two divisions were already streaming through Gettysburg. When the First Corps began its withdrawal from Seminary Ridge to Cemetery Hill, a column of Confederate soldiers approached from the south to cut off its retreat. Gamble's weary troopers, covering the left flank of the First Corps near the Fairfield Road, and Calef's battery rushed to a nearby wood line (Shultz's Woods) south of the seminary and dismounted behind a low stone wall along the Fairfield Road. The troopers' rapid fire and Calef's deliberate rounds delayed the advancing rebels long enough to protect the First Corps's orderly withdrawal.[25]

Gamble's brigade and Calef's battery first withdrew to Stevens' Run, south of the town, and later that evening joined the rest of Buford's troopers bivouacked in a peach orchard east of the Emmitsburg Pike about a mile south of Cemetery Hill.[26]

After dark, Calef took stock: twelve men and thirteen horses were killed, wounded, or disabled. Even by shifting men between guns, the battery could only man five guns the next day. Out of the darkness, Buford quietly guided his horse into the middle of his camp and called out to the exhausted gunners, "Men, you have done splendidly. I never saw a battery served so well in my life."[27]

Mackenzie at Little Round Top

The next day, July 2, the battlefield quieted around noon, with only a few desultory exchanges of fire between the pickets on the valley floor. Maj. Gen. Winfield S. Hancock and the Second Corps had arrived and occupied positions in the center of the Union line on Cemetery Ridge. Its soldiers piled stones atop the low wall along the center of the ridge high enough so they could lie down behind it. Shortly after 1 P.M., their attention was drawn to the lower portion of Cemetery Ridge when Maj. Gen. Daniel Sickles's Third Corps suddenly moved forward about a thousand yards to occupy a rise and a peach orchard along the Emmitsburg Road.[28]

The forward movement opened a large gap in the Union lines, fully exposing the left flank of the Second Corps. General Meade rode to meet General Sickles and ordered him to return to his original position. At the same time, Hancock was directed to shift a division farther south. Maj. Gen. George Sykes's Fifth Corps, bivouacked in the fields east of the Taneytown Road, was ordered to fill the rest of the gap.[29]

While Meade was conferring with Sickles in the peach orchard, Warren and his aides rode up to the summit of a wooded hill at the end of Cemetery Ridge, and they found it empty except for a small signal detachment. One aide was immediately dispatched to notify Meade of its importance and request at least a division to defend the area. Warren then looked across the convoluted terrain in the valley below. Believing there might be rebel infantry in the woods beyond, Warren sent one of his aides to a nearby battery with instructions to fire a few rounds into the trees. Bayonets glinted in the sunlight as heads under the foliage turned at the explosions, convincing him that help was needed as soon as possible.[30]

Warren then directed the last of his aides, Ranald Mackenzie, to find a brigade to occupy the wooded hill (Little Round Top) and send it to him as quickly as possible. Mackenzie mounted his horse, passed behind the large rocks and crags along the summit, rode down the narrow pathway to the road, and galloped off to find Sickles in the valley. Maj. Gen. John B. Hood's Texans had begun their attack and were relentlessly pushing the Third Corps back. Upon receiving Warren's request, Sickles, according to Mackenzie, "refused to do so, stating that his whole command was necessary to defend his front or words to that effect."[31]

Realizing that it was imperative to hold Little Round Top, Mackenzie galloped back to the crest of Cemetery Ridge where he met Sykes and the lead elements of the Fifth Corps coming forward. He explained what Warren needed and pleaded for a brigade to occupy Little Round Top. Sykes immediately ordered Brig. Gen. James Barnes's First Division to provide one of his brigades. Along with one of Barnes's aides, Mackenzie rode off to deliver the message.

Stretched along a nearby dirt road was Col. Strong Vincent's brigade of the First Division, Fifth Corps. It is unclear if Mackenzie was present when the final instructions were passed to Vincent, but Vincent enthusiastically accepted the mission. "What are your orders?" he called out and then rode quickly up the narrow trail to the top of Little Round Top. Musket fire and artillery rounds struck the summit when Vincent's flags appeared among the rocks and trees, and he moved his horse and staff behind the crest. Col. Joshua Chamberlain's Twentieth Maine Infantry, the first regiment to arrive at the top, was sent to the far side of the hill with orders to hold that position at all costs.[32]

In the interim, Warren rode down to the road across Cemetery Ridge and diverted one of the Fifth Corps regiments passing by. The stalwart defense of Little Round Top by these few units served to secure the Union left flank against multiple attacks. At some point during the day, Mackenzie was wounded for the second time.

McCrea, Egan, and Dearing during Pickett's Charge

That same morning, Capt. John Hazard, chief of the Second Corps Artillery, directed his five batteries into positions between the divisions and brigades of the Second Corps along Cemetery Ridge. Tully McCrea and John Egan in Woodruff's battery occupied a crescent-shaped grove of trees called Zeigler's Grove on the right flank of the Second Corps. The Second Corps had moved up the Taneytown Road from Uniontown, Maryland, in the afternoon of July 1 and bivouacked near the Round Tops. Just after dawn, the long columns marched toward Gettysburg and halted just east of Cemetery Ridge until ordered to occupy positions in the center of the Union line.[33]

Edmund Kirby had died from his wounds received at Chancellorsville, and Woodruff was officially the battery commander. Tully was in charge of the right section, 1st Sgt. John Shannon controlled the center, and Egan commanded the left. Soon after occupying his position, Woodruff argued with the commander of the 108th New York Infantry over the closeness of the infantry supporting his guns. Incoming artillery rounds soon solved the problem as the infantrymen quickly scrambled away from the guns.[34]

That evening, as Lee's plans for an attack on the Union center with Longstreet's First Corps evolved, he finally agreed to keep Longstreet's two divisions near the Round Tops where they had ended the fighting the day before. In their place, he ordered A. P. Hill to add Brig. Gen. James J. Pettigrew's and Maj. Gen. Isaac R. Trimble's divisions from the Third Corps to Maj. Gen. George Pickett's newly arrived division to conduct the attack. The assault would be made with nine brigades, with two additional brigades available as immediate reinforcements.[35]

The Attack on the Union Center

During the morning hours of July 3, Ewell's Second Corps attempted to secure Culp's Hill on the Union right flank. Repeated rebel attempts to force their way up the steep slopes to assault the Union Twelfth Corps included Richard Kinney and the Fifty-second Virginia Infantry with Brig. Gen. William "Extra Billy" Smith's brigade from Early's division. All attempts were thrown back.

While the attack on Culp's Hill was under way, Maj. James Dearing's batteries arrived with Pickett's division and trotted forward to the first rise short of the Emmitsburg Road near the Rogers farm around 10 A.M. His right flank battery came on line next to Col. Edward P. Alexander's gun line, and Capt. Joseph G. Blount's Lynchburg Artillery occupied the far left flank of Dearing's battalion.[36]

Colonel Alexander, commanding Longstreet's artillery for the attack, gave Dearing specific targets on Cemetery Ridge. In addition, he wanted the battery commanders to be prepared to follow Pickett's infantry after they passed through the gun line. The roughly twelve-hundred-yard range to the oak grove where Tully and John Egan awaited the attack was well within range of Dearing's Napoleons and an easy shot for his rifled guns. Dearing identified three Union batteries to the left of the clump of prominent trees selected by Lee as the center of the attack and three batteries to the right.[37]

Around 11 A.M., General Hunt rode along Cemetery Ridge and saw the long line of rebel batteries on the valley floor going into position. He anticipated a heavy bombardment from those guns and would need every gun in the Artillery Reserve to be ready. Realizing the need to conserve ammunition for the infantry assault that was sure to come, he and his aides notified each battery in position along Cemetery Ridge to withhold their fire for fifteen minutes after the Confederate bombardment began.[38]

A deceptive quiet descended across the battlefield around noon. It was stifling hot, with the temperature already above eighty degrees. Most soldiers relaxed behind the stone wall or under the trees behind the crest, while others rolled up in their blankets and tried to sleep. Brig. Gen. John Gibbon, commanding the Second Division in the center of the Union line, invited Hancock and Meade to join him for lunch. Within the hour, several generals were seated around the cook fire, plates perched on hardtack boxes. Their aides sat on the ground nearby.[39]

At the same time Dearing, trying to gain more information about the targets to his front, rode almost up to the line of skirmishers along the Emmitsburg Pike. Within minutes, a courier from Lee trotted up with a message: "I do not approve of young officers needlessly exposing themselves, their place is with their batteries." Chastised, Dearing turned and rode back behind his gun line.[40]

Just before 1 P.M., two signal shots from the Washington Artillery sounded, and all along the nearly two-mile line of guns, rebel gunners pulled lanyards, beginning a massive bombardment of the Union center. Heads snapped up along the stone wall on Cemetery Ridge. Cries of "Get down, get down!" were heard as the valley floor erupted in smoke and flame. Soldiers tried to become as small a target as possible behind whatever cover they could find. Regimental flags were pulled down to avoid being damaged in the shelling.[41]

The initial rebel volleys passed overhead and landed in the rear among the second and third lines of the divisions, as well as scattering the cooks, orderlies, and ambulance drivers and the generals at lunch. Meade's headquarters was struck repeatedly. Charles Warner's recently arrived battery and the rest of the Sixth Corps artillery moved away from the rain of shells that fell beyond the Taneytown Road. Once the rebel batteries finally got their range, the center of the Union line was deluged by thousands of shell fragments.[42]

Fifteen minutes later, the Union guns responded, and for at least an hour and a half more than two hundred guns roared back and forth. Their thunderous sound was heard as far away as Harrisburg, and the rising gun smoke blocked out the sun. John Egan would later call it "the grandest artillery effort of our or any other war."[43]

1st Lt. Frank A. Haskell, one of General Gibbon's aides, described the scene on Cemetery Ridge in a letter to his brother after the battle: "The thunder and lightning of these two hundred and fifty guns and their shells, whose smoke darkens the sky, are incessant, all pervading, in the air above our heads, on the ground at our feet, remote, near, deafening, ear-piercing, astounding; and these hailstones are massy iron, charged with exploding fire."[44]

On the valley floor, Dearing rode his horse up and down behind his guns, defiantly waving his battalion flag while Union shells crashed all about. More than once, his gunners looked back anxiously. Most thought his antics did nothing except attract more attention from the guns on Cemetery Ridge.[45]

At Zeigler's Grove, casualties from exploding shells, tree limbs, and branches took their toll. Tully and Egan repeatedly removed branches and limbs that landed on their guns. Behind them, limbers exploded; horses lay dead while others fell to the ground kicking and screaming. The commander of the 108th New York Infantry reported that it lost men simply by being too close to Woodruff's battery.[46]

After suffering under the onslaught for about an hour, Hunt came to the conclusion that if the Union guns ceased firing, it might confuse the rebels as well as conserve ammunition for the assault. He and his aides galloped along the ridge to notify the batteries. Meade, an old artilleryman, had already reached the same conclusion and simultaneously sent orders to initiate the cease-fire.[47]

As the firing from the Union batteries diminished, Hancock angrily ordered the Second Corps's batteries to continue to fire. Then, one by one, they grew silent as they ran out of long-range ammunition. The men of the 108th New York helped Tully and Egan push their guns into Zeigler's Grove to protect them as much as possible before the inevitable infantry assault.[48]

The rebel cannonade ceased near 3 P.M., and the battlefield grew silent. Hazard rode along the ridge and took stock of his batteries. The destruction was heavy. Horses lay dead or dying, bodies were flung about, and here and there limbers and caissons were in flames. Woodruff's battery was still able to man six guns, but he had lost a number of horses, limbers, and caissons. Capt. William A. Arnold's A Battery, First Rhode Island Artillery could only man two guns at the wall. Farther south at the corner of the wall where Gibbon's division manned the wall as it jogged south (known as the Angle), 1st Lt. Alonzo H. Cushing's (June '61) A Battery, Fourth US Artillery, only had two guns left. Most of his officers were killed or wounded, and he was in a great deal of pain after being twice wounded. Still farther to the left, Capt. James J. Rorty's B Battery, First New York Light Artillery was heavily damaged, and 1st Lt. Fred Brown's B Battery, First Rhode Island Artillery had lost three of its guns, thirty horses, and suffered many casualties. With the assault yet to come, Hazard

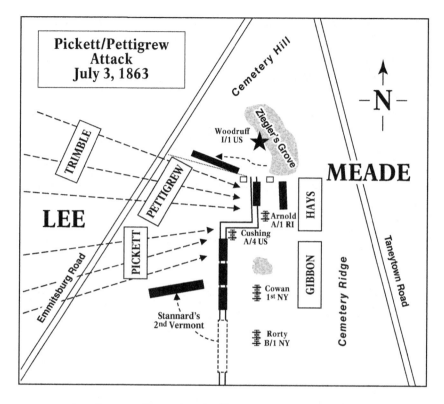

requested assistance from the Artillery Reserve and ordered Rorty's and Brown's batteries to withdraw.[49]

Hunt quickly responded. Five batteries from the Artillery Reserve were ordered forward. Before those batteries arrived, however, cries went up along the stone wall as soldiers excitedly pointed across the valley, "Here they come! Here come the Johnnies!"[50]

The withdrawal of the disabled Union batteries did not escape the notice of Colonel Alexander. He sent a courier galloping to Pickett with the message "For God's sake come quick. The 18 guns are gone!" When Pickett asked permission to advance, Longstreet reluctantly nodded, and Pickett galloped off into history.[51]

Minutes later, drums beat and bands played, and there was movement in the tree line all along Seminary Ridge. Out of the smoke that still blanketed the valley floor strode a line of skirmishers. Behind the first line of infantry, a second line appeared and then a third. When all the brigades were aligned, some thirteen thousand Virginians and North Carolinians stood in an unbroken line that stretched over a mile in length across the valley floor.[52]

The soldiers on Cemetery Ridge knew full well what was coming. Many years later, the sight was still etched in Tully's memory: "I could see this mass of men, in three long lines, approaching our position, and knowing that we had but one thin line of infantry to oppose them, I thought our chances for Kingdom Come or Libby Prison were very good."[53]

Dearing's gunners cheered as Pickett's infantry passed through their gun line, but their ammunition chests were empty and they could not follow. Alexander found eighteen guns with ammunition still remaining and led them forward behind Pickett's gray lines.[54]

The men of the Second Corps watched the gray lines come closer and closer. Woodruff's voice rang out, "By hand, forward," and the gunners ran the six Napoleons out of Zeigler's Grove. The Union guns on both flanks fired mercilessly into Pickett's and Pettigrew's advancing units, but the Second Corps guns stayed silent until the lines of silver came within canister range. Tully recounted that part of the battle some years later:

> As soon as it was seen what was coming, a look of stern determination settled upon every man's face, artillery and infantry alike. This was, it must be remembered, the afternoon of the third day, and every sneak and coward had found safe shelter in the rear long before. There were now there none but men determined to do or die. . . . As soon as the rebel line advanced, all of our artillery, to the right, left, and front of them, that could be brought to bear opened upon them. They soon discovered that we were not badly demoralized. Battery I, having smoothbores, loaded with canister and waited for them to get nearer. When we opened on them one could see great gaps swept down. There were three lines, remember; it was impossible to miss. We had

forty rounds of canister to each gun and they got the most of it.[55]

Along the stone wall north of the Angle soldiers emptied their cartridge boxes on the ground for quicker reloading. Extra rifles captured the day before were loaded and laid on the ground next to them. Their officers cautioned them to keep down and await the call to fire. Just to the left of the Bryan house and barn, Brig. Gen. Alexander Hays brought his First Brigade up behind the wall, creating a line of rifles almost four men deep. Regimental and national colors were unfurled.[56]

On the right, Tully watched the gray regiments climb the slope toward him: "They had to cross an open plain and march twelve hundred yards to gain our position. There was no shelter for them other than a small orchard. A house and barn near the orchard had been burned the day before, and the skirmishers had thrown down the fences. A slight depression or valley was between their position and ours. Could a finer target for artillery practice be imagined? Three lines of infantry, two deep, advancing over such ground in the face of our artillery."[57]

When the rebel regiments reached roughly three hundred to four hundred yards away, Woodruff ordered his guns to commence firing. Round after round of canister fire from the Union artillery along Cemetery Ridge now smashed into Pickett's and Pettigrew's brigades as they approached the Emmitsburg Pike, tearing the lead brigades to shreds.[58]

When Pettigrew's soldiers reached the two stout fences that bordered the Emmitsburg Pike, Woodruff commanded, "Double canister!" and "Fire at will!" Tully's and Egan's gunners bent to their tasks, firing as fast as they could load across the open field as the Confederates attempted to cross the road. At the same time, Hays cried, "Fire!" and his thick line of soldiers stood up behind the stone wall on both sides of the Bryan barn, leveled their rifles, and fired as one.[59]

At two hundred yards, the effect was murderous. It decimated Pettigrew's front ranks and swept the fence clear of those trying to cross behind them. No longer a formation, a mass of gray raised the rebel yell and rushed toward the wall. Simultaneously, three New York regiments and a company of sharpshooters swept forward on the right flank to fire into their flank.[60]

To the left of Hays's lines, a fierce battle was under way at the Angle. Hancock rode to his left and watched as Brig. Gen. George Stannard's Second Vermont brigade from the First Corps crossed the wall and fired into the flank of Pickett's division. With the Vermont regiments on the left and the New Yorkers on the right, Pickett's and Pettigrew's divisions were caught in the middle.[61]

Tully's guns were now unable to fire because friendly troops ran into the field in front of them. His crews stood by their guns, the barrels too hot to lay a hand upon. Then amid the smoke and firing, Hays reined up looking for Woodruff. Arnold's Rhode Island battery was severely damaged and needed assistance. Woodruff immediately ordered Egan to move his two guns toward the Bryan barn to assist. As Woodruff turned to ride back into the trees, he was struck by a musket ball and toppled from his horse. Egan rushed to his side and tried to assist him, but Woodruff refused. Holding his side, Woodruff gasped, "I ordered you to the left, sir. Do your duty and leave me!"[62]

Complying with Woodruff's order, Egan led his guns toward Bryan's barn, but Hays directed him farther along the wall toward the Angle. Much later in life, Egan described the location of where his section went into action as "a little to the right and front of Cushing's battery and 15 to 20 yards in the rear of the stone wall." His guns fired point blank into the mass of rebels crossing the wall, completely destroying what was left of Cushing's guns.[63]

Meade and his son and aide, George Jr., rode up beside Egan just as he fired his last rounds. General Meade cried out, "Egan, have they turned?" and Egan shouted back, "Yes, they have!" A few minutes later, it was all over. Union flags waved back and forth along the ridgeline as the Army of the Potomac reveled in victory. A clearly elated Meade rode up and down the Union line from Cemetery Hill to Little Round Top, accepting the cheers of the soldiers as he passed

Fig. 9.3. Cemetery Ridge after Pickett's Charge (Edwin Forbes). *BLCW, vol. 3*

by. Hays jumped his horse over the wall near Arnold's guns and dragged a rebel flag behind him while his men cheered.[64]

Tully continued his description of Lee's great assault: "They marched bravely up in face of it all and part of them penetrated our line on the left of our position. But their numbers had then been so reduced that they could make no fight and were taken prisoners. Directly in front of where we were, when not fifty yards off, they hesitated and wavered. Then our infantry charged and captured the greater part of what was left."[65]

When the smoke cleared away, Tully finally realized that only four guns remained in Zeigler's Grove. He looked to the left and saw Egan bringing his guns back from the Angle. They quickly looked for Woodruff and found him propped up against an oak tree. Through clenched teeth, Woodruff told Tully that he was now in command of the battery and only then allowed himself to be carried to the aid station. Later that evening, a Dr. Buck, the battery surgeon, informed them that a musket ball had torn up Woodruff's insides, causing him terrible pain. Lying on a stretcher, Woodruff simply asked through gritted teeth, "Have we beaten the enemy?" When Egan replied in the affirmative, "an expression of gladness spread across his face."[66]

Captain Hazard and General Hunt assessed the damage to the Second Corps batteries. Woodruff's battery had lost a number of men, horses, and limbers but could still man six guns. Cushing's battery had ceased to exist. Arnold's, Rorty's, and Brown's batteries were severely damaged and needed much refitting before they were ready to fight again. Tully and Egan were the only Second Corps battery officers who were not killed or wounded. With the possibility of another attack likely, Hunt and Hazard decided to consolidate the two Rhode Island batteries and combine Woodruff's and Cushing's batteries with Tully in command of the regulars.[67]

Later Tully and Egan found Woodruff awake but in pain. Tully dripped water on his clenched lips and clasped his hands, hoping to ease some of the pain. Woodruff knew by this time there was little hope of his recovery and expressed a wish to be buried near the battlefield. After he passed away on the evening of July 4, Tully and Egan tenderly buried him beneath an oak tree near the Granite School House. They carefully marked his grave and sent a letter to Woodruff's father with a detailed description of its location.[68]

The next morning, Tully sat down on his camp stool under one of the oak trees, pulled out his writing kit and wrote a short note to Belle: "I take a hasty chance tonight to let you know that I am safe. We were in a terrible fight on the 2nd and 3rd. Woodruff was killed. All the officers of A Co. of the 4th were killed or wounded. I am in command of that and my own company. Please write to Eliza and Sam Talbot. I have no time, as I march immediately."[69]

Gettysburg was a defining moment for the Union and the Class of 1862. Tully and John Calef were both brevetted for gallantry again. Calef's actions on McPherson's Ridge were noted in official reports by both General Buford and General Hunt. Hunt reported that the firing of Calef's guns enabled Buford's troopers to hold their line against a considerable force for two hours. He was later brevetted for gallantry at Gettysburg and other actions near the end of the war.

Ranald Mackenzie's actions earned him his third brevet promotion for gallantry during the war. In the meantime, Tully readied his now consolidated battery while his ex-classmates, James Dearing, Joseph Blount, and Richard Kinney slipped away from the battlefield after nightfall.

10

Mansfield, Semmes, and West at Port Hudson

West Point, December 1865. After the last cadets left the classroom, Tully continued to identify problems for the final exams. He included a few problems he used in the classroom to give some cadets a few points on the exam if they remembered their homework problems. After finishing the list, he carefully locked them away in his desk. George Armstrong Custer (his former roommate) told him that one time he was almost caught looking at a similar list when he was a cadet after sneaking into the quarters of one of his professors. Tully smiled and placed the key to the desk in his uniform coat pocket.

He pulled on his overcoat and limped down the stairs. At the mess hall, he found John Egan and Frank Hamilton arguing artillery tactics again. Tully laughed at their antics and offered a few ideas of his own about the employment of light artillery. Perhaps someday he would write them down for one of the military journals.

All seemed eager to attend this evening's performance by the Dialectic Society. Last year's performance had drawn people from as far away as New York City, and all the officers and their wives stationed at the Academy attended as well. Tully enjoyed listening to the cadets make fun of the institution and some of those connected with it.

The three of them offered various tales about their classmates as they finished their meal. One story involved Sam Mansfield, the first in the class to take command of a volunteer unit. After his father was killed at Antietam, Mansfield returned to Connecticut and was appointed to command one of its regiments. After a harrowing voyage to New Orleans, he and his regiment fought in the swamps and bayous of Louisiana against two of his former classmates, John West and Oliver Semmes. Later he participated in the siege of Port Hudson

Fig. 10.1. Nineteenth Corps en Route to Bayou Sara (F. S. Schell). *BLCW, vol. 3*

before returning to Connecticut where the regiment was mustered out of federal service.

Department of the Gulf—January 1863

Col. Samuel M. Mansfield, US Volunteers (USV), left his tent on the grounds of the US Arsenal at Baton Rouge, Louisiana, and gazed around at his camp. It was January 1863, and his regiment, a part of the Nineteenth Corps, had recently occupied the city. His days were filled with company and battalion drills to improve the discipline and training of the Twenty-fourth Connecticut Volunteer Infantry.

After graduation from West Point, Mansfield was initially assigned to the staff of his father, Maj. Gen. Joseph K. F. Mansfield, with the Seventh Corps at Suffolk, Virginia. He remained behind when General Mansfield took command of the Union Twelfth Corps, two days before the battle of Antietam. Unfortunately, his father was killed shortly after the Twelfth Corps was committed. After his father's death, Mansfield returned to his childhood home in Middletown, Connecticut, where he was appointed a colonel, USV, and to command the Twenty-fourth Connecticut Volunteer Infantry in October. He and the regiment were mustered into federal service on November 18 and immediately left for Long Island where it became part of Maj. Gen. Nathaniel Banks's reinforcements sent to the Department of the Gulf at New Orleans.[1]

The eleven-day voyage south began on December 2 and was filled with adventure and mishaps. The steamer *New Brunswick,* a small, overloaded, side-wheel riverboat, was wholly unsuited for a winter voyage. It encountered a gale and heavy seas that put the regiment in peril for more than a day. The ship barely limped into the Dry Tortugas, took on coal, and then sailed for Ship Island off the Mississippi coast. Shortly after its arrival in New Orleans, Mansfield and the Twenty-fourth Connecticut became part of the Second Brigade of Brig. Gen. Cuvier C. Grover's Fourth Division, a part of the Nineteenth Corps. Grover's division steamed up the Mississippi River to occupy Baton Rouge on December 17.[2]

At this point in time, there were no other members of his class assigned to General Banks's Department of the Gulf. However, two of Mansfield's former classmates, Maj. Oliver Semmes and 1st Lt. John A. West, were part of Maj. Gen. Richard Taylor's rebel army in western Louisiana. Semmes commanded the First Confederate Regular Light Artillery Battery, and West was one of his section leaders.[3]

Meanwhile, Banks planned to open the Mississippi River in support of General Grant's Vicksburg campaign. He was convinced that he could not accomplish that task until the heavily fortified Port Hudson was captured. Located on steep eastern bluffs above the Mississippi River 150 miles north of New Orleans, the fortification was manned by several thousand men, and its siege guns had resisted every attempt by Union forces to pass up the Mississippi River since the beginning of the war. As long as Port Hudson commanded the river, the Confederate supply lines over the Mississippi River remained safe.[4]

Battle of Port Hudson, 1862
Red River Campaign, 1864

Shreveport

Mansfield

Pleasant Hill

Natchitoches

Alexandria

Simsport

Opelousas

Irish Bend

Franklin

Fort Brisland

Gulf of Mexico

Vicksburg

Red River

Mississippi River

Sabine River

Natchez

Bayou Teche

Bayou Sara
Port Hudson

Baton Rouge

Donaldsonville

Grand Lake

Lake Ponchartrain

Bayou LaFourche

NEW ORLEANS

Ship Island

★ - - ▶ Location of Sanderson 1864
☆ - - ▶ Location of Mansfield and 24th Connecticut 1862

In mid-March, Mansfield's regiment and the Fourth Division were sent to assist Adm. David G. Farragut's gunboats to force passage past Port Hudson. But Farragut started north before the ground support arrived. His ships became highlighted by huge bonfires on the banks, and the heavy siege guns on the high bluffs destroyed several of his vessels. Only a few were able to pass and proceed north toward Vicksburg. Mansfield's regiment spent a few unpleasant nights in a swamp in the rain before returning to Baton Rouge.[5]

He soon learned that Banks planned to send three divisions up the Atchafalaya River, the Red River, and the network of bayous, including Bayou Teche, that connected with the Mississippi River to attack Port Hudson from the north. It was expected that Taylor's rebel army and Semmes's First Confederate Regular Artillery battery would attempt to delay them several times.[6]

Mansfield and the Twenty-fourth Connecticut learned a great deal about amphibious operations during that lengthy march. Leaving Baton Rouge on March 28, Grover's Fourth Division loaded on steamers, sailed south to Donaldsonville, unloaded, marched to the rail station at Terrebonne, and were transported by rail to camp at Bayou Boeuf on April 4. When Banks attempted to engage Taylor's rebel army with two divisions along the Teche, Grover's Fourth Division embarked on transports to sail up the Grand Lake to turn Taylor's position at Fort Bisland. On April 9, Mansfield's regiment marched to Brashear City to load on gunboats. The available transports were so limited that it took almost two days to find additional boats and rafts to fully load Grover's division. Heavy fog further delayed their departure until the morning of April 12.[7]

Meanwhile, Taylor's infantry engaged the two advancing Federal divisions along Bayou Teche. West's 3-inch rifles were placed between the swamp and Bayou Teche on the far right of Taylor's lines. At the same time, Semmes and his gunners manned a captured Union gunboat, the *Diana*, and commenced firing on the advancing divisions. In the hotly contested engagement, the *Diana* was disabled and forced to withdraw for repairs, with two killed and five wounded. That evening Taylor learned that Grover's division was attempting to land in his rear, and he immediately began to withdraw toward Franklin.[8]

In the interim, Grover's movement was plagued by delays. Several landings were attempted, but shallow waters limited his ships from getting any closer to the shore than a hundred yards. Finally, enough rafts were found to allow a landing to commence. One brigade disembarked and started down the road toward Franklin, while the rest of Grover's soldiers disembarked more slowly and prepared to move inland. No wagons or trains were on board. Supplies were limited, and the soldiers were issued as much hard bread and coffee as they could carry.

The next morning, Mansfield and the Twenty-fourth Connecticut were part of the reserve line as Grover's brigades attempted to cut off Taylor's retreat at a place called Irish Bend. Taylor deployed a rear guard to protect his withdrawal. Semmes and a repaired *Diana* fired lobbed shells into Grover's column while West's rifled guns peppered them from the opposite shore. When Taylor's rear guard withdrew in the face of the Union advance, the *Diana* was left unsupported. Semmes and his gunners were forced to burn the gunboat and then tried to escape, but he and his men were captured within hours. Meanwhile, West's guns were more successful in delaying Banks's and Grover's advance. They protected Taylor's withdrawal and covered the burning of a bridge within a couple of miles of Franklin. Taylor's official report spoke highly of the part West played in the engagements that day.[9]

After the engagement, Semmes and his men were taken to New Orleans and then sent north by ship. After picking up more prisoners at Fort Monroe, their ship started up the Chesapeake Bay toward Fort Delaware, but Semmes and twenty-four others overpowered their guards and captured the boat, escaping through the Dismal Swamp to Richmond. He eventually returned to Louisiana where he commanded an artillery battalion in Taylor's command until the end of the war.[10]

After the engagements at Irish Bend and Franklin, Taylor's army was pushed north by Banks's three divisions almost to Alexandria, then Banks's men turned east, crossed the Red River, retraced their steps to Simsport (now called Simmesport) at the mouth of the Atchafalaya River, and boarded steamers to sail down the Mississippi River. After seven weeks and 180 miles, Mansfield and the Twenty-fourth Connecticut disembarked at Bayou Sara on May 21, ten miles north of Port Hudson.[11]

The Attack and Siege of Port Hudson

Over the next two days, Banks's three divisions marched south from Bayou Sara to join the rest of the Nineteenth Corps arriving from

Baton Rouge and New Orleans. Port Hudson's fortifications consisted of a series of linked redoubts, forts, and trenches that took advantage of the numerous swamps, steep ravines, and hilly terrain that surrounded it. Every bit as strong as Vicksburg to its north, the defenses stretched for some four miles in an arc anchored on both ends by steep bluffs overlooking the river. Siege guns covered the water approaches. On May 24 and 25, the Twenty-fourth Connecticut struggled through the virtually impregnable thick forests, tangled underbrush, and steep terrain on the north to push back a line of enemy skirmishers. A sketch artist with *Harper's Weekly* recorded the advance of Grover's division and the Twenty-fourth Connecticut that day.[12]

Three days later, a major attack was made against the fortifications, but the rebel lines withstood all assaults. Over the next three weeks, the regiments dug trenches closer and closer in preparation for a second attack on June 14. That morning, Mansfield's men were each directed to carry two thirty-pound gunny sacks filled with cotton, rush forward, and throw them into a ditch in front of the rebel parapets for the following storming parties to cross during the attack. Heavy fire from the rebel fortifications disrupted the plan. Instead, Mansfield's men rushed forward to the crest of a little hill under heavy fire and piled up their gunny sacks within fifty yards of the enemy's works. It is likely that Mansfield's engineer experience helped that evening. Before dawn, the men turned the line of bags into earthen breastworks. Its sudden appearance the next morning almost caused Union artillery to begin bombarding it before its real defenders were identified.[13]

The Twenty-fourth Connecticut's line now became a valuable strategic point for future operations. A zigzag approach was dug up to the enemy's ditch in front of the fortifications, and in time a forty-two-foot-long tunnel was dug under the enemy's works. The ever-encircling Union trench lines and breastworks eventually cut off all supplies from reaching Port Hudson. Both sides suffered losses from the hard work, oppressive heat, and severe living conditions.[14]

When Banks learned that Taylor's army had reappeared along the

Teche and was slowly approaching Donaldsonville downriver from Port Hudson, he had to act quickly to seize Port Hudson and return to defend his headquarters and base of supply. When word of the surrender of Vicksburg reached him in early July, he immediately sent word through the lines to the garrison commander, but it took until July 8 before he finally became convinced of the truth of the surrender and asked for terms.[15] When President Lincoln was made aware of the surrender, he said in a letter to a friend, "The Father of Waters again goes unvexed to the sea."[16]

The men of the Twenty-fourth Connecticut manned their advanced breastworks for twenty-five days until withdrawing after the surrender of the rebel garrison. A few days later they embarked on steamers for Donaldsonville where Mansfield's regiment and Grover's division engaged in a sharp fight with Taylor's rebel army. Subsequently assigned to the defenses of New Orleans at Ship Island for the next few months, the Twenty-fourth received welcome news on September 9—they were going home.[17]

The steamer *Continental* took nine days to transport them back to New York City where they immediately boarded the steamer *Granite State* for Middletown. Cheering crowds, the ringing of church bells, and the firing of cannons celebrated their arrival. On October 2, 1863, almost a year after they formed the regiment, the men were mustered out of federal service. Of course, not all returned from the Department of the Gulf. Eighteen men and officers were lost to enemy action and fifty-seven others to disease in the swamps and bayous of Louisiana. After the regiment was mustered out, Mansfield was promoted to brevet captain for gallant and meritorious services at Port Hudson. At the same time, he doffed his volunteer rank of colonel, USV, for the silver bars of a first lieutenant in the regular army. He did not attempt to regain an appointment with a volunteer unit and supervised the construction of forts and defenses at various ports and cities in New England until the end of the war.[18]

11

McCrea and the Battle of Olustee

West Point, January 1866. One week later, the dreaded exams were under way. The corporal of the guard made his rounds calling, "Section 1, fourth-class mathematics, turn out!" Anxious cadets nervously shuffled their feet in the corridor outside the exam room, awaiting the inevitable call to enter.

Professor Church, head of the Department of Mathematics, and the other members of the Academic Board sat around a long table inside. Tully and the other instructors sat at smaller desks nearby. When all were ready, Tully, the junior lieutenant, stood up, straightened his uniform coat, and limped to the door to allow the first four cadets to enter the room.

The cadets lined up in front of Professor Church, apprehension vividly displayed on their faces. He gruffly stated, "Each of you will come forward, one at a time, and draw a slip of paper from the table in front of you. On each slip of paper is a problem you are to solve. You will have fifteen minutes to reach a solution, and then be prepared to answer questions from the board."

Tully watched the cadets' faces after they drew the problems. If they knew the answer, their faces lit up and they immediately went to work. If they did not know how to begin, they shuffled their feet, a vision of a "frigid zero" for the session crowding out all other thoughts. Sometimes an idea suddenly struck them, and there was a furious scratching of chalk on the blackboard. After much erasing of boards and clicking of chalk, one cadet had barely sketched out the problem before the time period ended. Finally Professor Church announced, "Cease work!" He pointed at one cadet and directed him to defend his proof. The cadet picked up a long, wooden pointer and stood at attention in front of his board, and the long process of examining each cadet's knowledge began.

Fig. 11.1. Federal Troops at Sanderson. *LOC*

At the end of the session, Professor Church cautioned the cadets not to discuss their problems with anyone until the examination of all the plebes was completed. Then he released them.

The guard was already in the barracks calling out the next section to march to the examination room, and the officers took a short break before the cadets arrived. In the interim, Tully stood idly at the window as the rain beat down on the Plain. The cold weather and rain reminded him of Olustee and General Gillmore's ill-fated expedition to northern Florida where he was wounded.

Department of the South—January 1864

Just after the New Year began, 1st Lt. Tully McCrea was temporarily detailed to Brig. Gen. Truman Seymour's staff at Maj. Gen. Quincy Gillmore's headquarters on Hilton Head Island. He found his new duties a welcome reprieve from the boredom of camp life. His experience with the Army of the Potomac stood him in good stead. Seymour officially commended him for his performance, an act that raised Tully's status among his fellow officers.[1]

It had been four months since he left the Army of the Potomac. The previous August, he requested transfer to his permanent unit in the Department of the South after losing command of Battery I. In typical army fashion, he was first assigned to command one of the horse artillery batteries in the Army of the Potomac by General Hunt, and then orders from Washington arrived sending him to Beaufort, South Carolina, in the Department of the South. After a brief leave at Ranald Mackenzie's home in New Jersey, he traveled by steamer to Beaufort to join Capt. Loomis Langdon's ('54) Battery M, First US Artillery, a part of the Union Tenth Corps.[2]

Life was good in Beaufort, but the calm days and limited activity soon grated on Tully. In November the battery was ordered to Hilton Head Island. He welcomed the change, although the new location was not in any way comparable to Beaufort. The chilling winds, ever-present sand, and continual battles with the commissary and quartermaster for equipment and supplies left him praying for any sort of action. His promotion to first lieutenant at the end of November only heightened his desire to return to the Army of the Potomac. More than ever, he felt he was no longer contributing to the war effort.[3]

The Florida Expedition

By January 1864, General Gillmore was actively planning an expedition to Florida. He sent several messages to Washington outlining his objectives and requesting more troops and equipment. Florida had become the major source of meat and other supplies for Southern forces after the fall of Port Hudson and Vicksburg effectively closed Confederate sources of supply from west of the Mississippi River. Consequently, Gillmore planned to control the railroads and access points in northern Florida to hamper any northward movement of supplies. His plans were soon the object of political intrigue and economic opportunity that began right in Lincoln's cabinet. The treasury secretary, Salmon Chase, sought the nomination for president in the upcoming national election, and he controlled patronage appointments of tax collectors in various states. His Florida tax collectors repeatedly assured him they could provide sufficient Union sympathizers to bring Florida back into the Union and, with it, potential votes at the next convention.[4]

Secretary Edwin Stanton and General Halleck informed Gillmore that he would have to find his own resources for the expedition and that, at all times, he must keep pressure on Charleston. Gillmore took this final message as approval of his plans and created a task force composed of seven thousand men and sixteen guns in four brigades from among the various units in his department. On February 5, he ordered General Seymour, his deputy at Hilton Head Island and Tully's old drawing instructor, to execute the plan. Orders went out to the units in the task force to draw six days' rations and sixty rounds of ammunition and to load the arriving ships in Port Royal Sound.[5]

Tully was the only member of his class to participate in the expedition to Florida. Only one other classmate was assigned to the Department of the South at that time. Charles Suter was the assistant chief engineer, and he had recently returned from participating in the campaign to capture Battery Wagner near Charleston Harbor, for which he received a brevet promotion for gallantry. He was now in charge of engineer operations at Hilton Head Island and Port Royal Island.[6]

Leaving Hilton Head

Tully finished loading Battery M onto the steam ferry *John Adams* and the schooner *F. R. Cogshall* early in the morning on February 6. He had written Belle the night before, explaining that after five months of inactivity he was going into action once more:

"A large expedition is leaving here today. I think the destination is somewhere in Florida, but that remains for us to find out after we arrive there. There are a large number of vessels in the harbor waiting to load troops and I suppose that we will start tomorrow. General Seymour, my favorite general here, is in command and, if we have an opportunity, there will be some hard fighting and someone will be hurt."[7]

Thirty-eight ships, tugs, gunboats, and transports left Port Royal Sound on February 6. Once the steamers were at sea, sealed orders were opened. Tully was correct: they were bound for Florida and

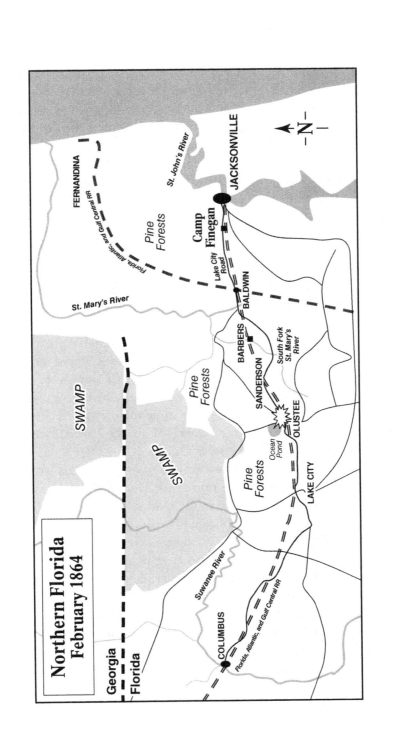

Northern Florida
February 1864

Georgia
Florida

FERNANDINA

St. John's River

JACKSONVILLE

Camp Finegan

Pine Forests

Florida, Atlantic, and Gulf Central RR

St. Mary's River

Lake City Road

BALDWIN

BARBERS

SANDERSON

South Fork St. Mary's River

OLUSTEE

Ocean Pond

Pine Forests

SWAMP

SWAMP

Pine Forests

LAKE CITY

Suwanee River

COLUMBUS

Florida, Atlantic, and Gulf Central RR

–N–

Jacksonville. One day and 160 miles later, the ships stood off the mud bar at the entrance to the St. John's River. When the task force entered the river, Tully's steamer and several others were too heavy to cross the mud bar and remained stuck until the tide lifted them over. They did not arrive at the docks until 4 P.M. the next day.[8]

Meanwhile, the rest of Seymour's task force unloaded at the nearly vacant wharfs when they reached the docks. Jacksonville was mostly a ghost town, and only a few rebel pickets contested their arrival. It had partially burned during the last Union occupation, and most of its population had fled. Soon, Col. Guy V. Henry's (May '61) brigade of cavalry, mounted infantry, and horse artillery moved west along the Lake City road. They were followed more slowly by the infantry brigades and artillery as their ships arrived and unloaded. The appearance of two regiments of "colored" troops (as they were called then) marching through the streets of Jacksonville with Col. James Montgomery's brigade frightened the few remaining inhabitants.[9]

Henry's mounted brigade pushed west to Camp Finegan so quickly that the few Confederate forces in their way were quickly overwhelmed and captured. Tully and Battery M were assigned to Col. William B. Barton's brigade of three infantry regiments. They followed Henry's fast-moving troopers along the Lake City Road to Baldwin where they camped the first night.[10]

The village of Baldwin consisted of a few shanties, a tavern, and a rail depot. It lay at the intersection of the Florida, Atlantic, and Gulf Central Railroad and the Florida Railroad. One rail line ran toward Tallahassee, and the other connected Fernandina on the eastern coast with Cedar Keys on the Gulf of Mexico. There was no direct rail connection to the rest of the South because a gap of over twenty miles existed between Georgia and the Tallahassee rail line. The next day, Tully and Langdon's Battery M advanced as far as the train depot at Sanderson, some forty miles west of Jacksonville, before returning to Barber's Plantation (now called Macclenny) on the southern fork of the St. Mary's River.[11]

Tully's description of these events was fairly close to the official reports:

As soon as we had disembarked, we were started for Camp Finegan, about nine miles from Jacksonville, where the rebels had about six hundred men and where we expected to have a fight. We arrived at Camp Finegan about midnight and found that the Rebels had fled only a few hours before, leaving us in possession of everything. They left so hurriedly that they did not have time to collect all their men and when ours entered their huts and informed them that they were prisoners they were perfectly surprised. A whole family was captured in one of the huts. In this family was an old woman, who was the most perfect Meg Merriles that I ever saw. Her face was full of wrinkles and from sitting around a pine fire, her face was covered with black soot. Altogether she was the most perfect old hag that I ever saw. The soldiers here had left coops filled with chickens and turkeys and our men had a perfect carnival and feasted on poultry. We captured seven cannon and a large quantity of small arms. We pushed ahead every day until we arrived here last night, fifty-two miles from Jacksonville. We have been subsisting almost entirely on the country and find it very slim living. We have named this camp "Camp Misery" because we are halting here in the rain without anything to eat, either for ourselves or our horses. I find the campaigning is not done here as it is in the Army of the Potomac, with system and order.[12]

Brig. Gen. Joseph Finegan, the Confederate commander of the District of East Florida, sent frantic messages to Gen. P. G. T. Beauregard at Charleston requesting reinforcements. In the meantime, he gathered his few scattered and fragmented units at Lake City some fifty miles west of Jacksonville where he built a line of breastworks and awaited the Union attack. It was not long in coming. Henry's brigade engaged a small Confederate cavalry unit just west of Barber's Plantation at the bridge over the southern fork of the St. Mary's River around noon on February 10. After a sharp encounter, his troopers forced the crossing and then rode twenty more miles to Lake City without further resistance. The next morning, his troopers attacked Finegan's breastworks. Two hours later, Henry believed he faced a much stronger force than expected and withdrew his brigade to Sanderson to meet with General Seymour.[13]

Command Disagreements

By February 13, Gillmore was satisfied with the progress of his expedition, and he returned to Hilton Head, leaving Seymour in command of the newly formed District of Florida. However, in an exchange of messages after Gillmore left, Seymour began to disagree with the strategy. He did not see any great numbers of sympathizers rallying to the Union cause as promised and initially recommended returning to Jacksonville and Baldwin. But on February 17, something changed his mind. He notified Gillmore by message that he planned to sever the Confederate supply link to the north over the Suwannee River at Columbus. Upon receipt of the message, Gillmore immediately ordered him to go no farther than the southern fork of the St. Mary's River, but weather delayed his messenger, and by the time he reached Florida it was too late.[14]

In the interim, Finegan sent the rebel reinforcements some thirteen miles east of Lake City to Olustee where a long series of rifle pits and entrenchments were constructed across the rail line between Ocean Pond and a swamp. By February 20, he had fifty-four hundred infantry, cavalry, and twelve guns organized into two brigades under Brig. Gen. Alfred Colquitt and Col. George P. Harrison.[15]

One of Tully's former classmates, Lt. Col. James Barrow, was the second-in-command of the Sixty-fourth Georgia Infantry Regiment, a part of Harrison's brigade. After recovering from wounds suffered during the Peninsula Campaign, Barrow helped train the regiment near Savannah before deploying to Quincy and Tallahassee in November 1862. Barrow's time was spent training his regiment in Quincy, and he looked forward to enjoying a normal life in the future, including the courting of a young widow in the town. They were engaged to marry and planned an early wedding when the Yankee threat was over.[16]

The Battle of Olustee

At dawn on February 20 at Barber's Plantation, Seymour's soldiers rolled their tents, gulped a quick cup of coffee, and shivered in the cold waiting to move. The original task force was now organized into four brigades of fifty-four hundred men and sixteen guns. The rest protected his supply lines and the base at Jacksonville.[17]

Henry's mounted brigade and a battery headed west first, then Col. Joseph Hawley's, Barton's and Col. James Montgomery's brigades left at one-hour intervals. They marched west on the Lake City Road, crossing and recrossing the railroad tracks several times. When Hawley's brigade reached Sanderson, one regiment shifted to the railroad bed and the other two marched through the pine forests along the Lake City Road.[18]

At the same time, Finegan decided to draw Seymour's soldiers into his prepared defenses at Olustee. Before noon, Barrow led the Sixty-fourth Georgia, some cavalry, and part of another infantry regiment two miles east of Olustee Depot along the Lake City road to a point just short of the first rail crossing east of the station. The graycoats hunkered down in the underbrush and waited for the Union soldiers to appear. An hour later, Finegan impatiently ordered Colquitt to start moving part of his brigade and artillery forward to reinforce Barrow.

When Hawley's lead regiment appeared along the railroad track near 2 P.M., Barrow's skirmishers opened fire. But Hawley's heavier firepower from quick-loading Spencer rifles forced Barrow's skirmishers to retreat almost a half mile. Barrow grabbed the regimental flag and tried to rally his men but was killed in one of the initial volleys. Meanwhile, hearing the sound of the guns ahead, Hawley's other two regiments hurried forward along the forest road followed by Barton's brigade. Montgomery's brigade halted at Sanderson less than five miles away.[19]

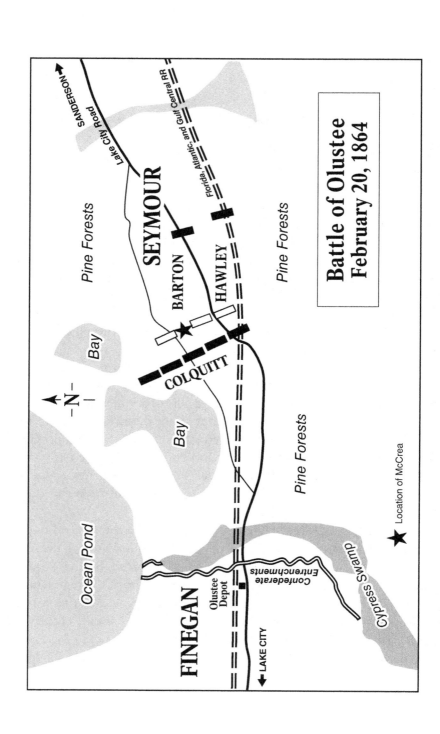

Battle of Olustee
February 20, 1864

The timely arrival of Colquitt's initial reinforcements pushed Hawley's regiments back into the open pine forest north of the railroad crossing. One regiment was routed and scattered, leaving a gap in the Union lines. Barton heard the boom of cannons and musket fire and urged his three regiments forward along the forest road. Around 2:30, an aide from Seymour reined up beside Langdon. His guns were needed forward on the left. Tully and Battery M swung out of the column and trotted forward.[20]

Within minutes, another messenger galloped up urgently seeking Langdon's assistance. Up and down pumped Langdon's arm, and the signal to gallop flew down the line. As the guns approached the smoke and confusion in the pine forest, one of Seymour's aides directed Langdon to deploy one section to the right to help cover a gap in the Union lines. Langdon waved Tully's section in that direction while he led the other guns into position behind the already deployed guns between the forest road and the railroad tracks.[21]

Tully quickly positioned his guns between the widely spaced pine trees, and trails dropped to the ground. The limbers quickly pulled back several yards to the rear. The noise of musket and cannon fire now rose to a steady roar, and it was clear that the Union advance was halted.[22]

Barton's arriving regiments quickly deployed on either side of Tully's guns as the battle raged among the waist-high palmetto plants and tall pine trees for the next hour or so. Both sides advanced and fell back as ammunition ran low. Cartridge cases were quickly emptied. Soldiers grabbed ammunition from the wounded and searched for more among the dead. Reinforcements on both sides were committed piecemeal as soon as they arrived.[23]

As soon as his section chiefs were ready, Tully probably yelled, "Canister, load, fire at will!" Hundreds of pellets sliced through the underbrush, but the only visible targets were puffs of smoke that rose above palmetto plants. Tully was likely worried. His situation here was far worse than he experienced at either Antietam or Gettysburg. Rebel soldiers were too close! Around him, musket fire dropped several of his gunners and horses.[24]

On the opposite side of the clearing, the arrival of additional rebel units sent forward by Finegan allowed Colquitt's rebel line to continue to advance. Langdon, hearing the increase in musket fire north of the road, shifted two guns in that direction and fired across the field at the advancing gray lines. Tully yelled, "Double canister!" and his crews blasted away. When Barton's supporting infantry began to give way in the face of Colquitt's advances, Tully called out, "Limber to the rear!" His teams galloped forward, but musket fire dropped many of the horses. The gunners cut them loose from their traces, and one gun was pulled safely to the rear. Suddenly, a musket ball struck Tully in the legs, and he toppled to the ground in great pain. Two gunners carried him to the rear just before a wave of gray swept over his remaining gun.[25]

When Finegan's last remaining reserves and ammunition reached Colquitt around 5 P.M., it enabled his line to overlap both Union flanks, and he pushed Seymour's soldiers farther into the forest. It was not long before Langdon's battery met the same fate as Tully's. He shifted his four guns to the rear once before rebel musket fire left him with only eight men in his gun crews. As his supporting infantry fell away, Colquitt's gray lines swept forward. With no time left, Langdon was forced to leave his guns or be taken prisoner.[26]

Back at Sanderson, Montgomery heard the sounds of a major engagement in the distance and ordered his two colored regiments (one of which was the famous 54th Massachusetts) to start moving toward Olustee. Both regiments dropped their knapsacks and haversacks along the route and primed their guns on the march. One marched astride the railroad bed; the other quickened its pace along the forest road and double-quicked the last mile into battle.[27]

After four hours of heavy fighting, Seymour now believed he faced a far superior force and ordered a general withdrawal between 6 and 7 P.M. In reality, the numbers on both sides were nearly even, but piecemeal commitment of units as they arrived had given Finegan's force the advantage at the end. Henry's cavalry and the arrival of Montgomery's two colored regiments provided Seymour's rear guard as his foot-weary soldiers trudged seven to eight miles back to Sanderson.[28]

After a short rest at Sanderson, the motley collection of wagons and ambulances began moving again. Only the cries of the wounded broke the silence as the wagons bounced over the rough roads in the dark and cold. Early in the morning of February 21, the column straggled into Baldwin, where more than 250 desperately wounded Union soldiers were quickly loaded onto railcars and sent ahead to Jacksonville.[29]

2nd Lt. Peter Michie ('63) found Tully lying on a cot after his wounds were dressed. Tully asked him to pen a short note to Sam Talbot in Ohio:

> At the request of Tully McCrea, I write to you that you may have no unnecessary uneasiness as to his condition. You will probably see by the papers, that he is wounded and of course, as is natural, in such cases, picture the worst. It is a pleasure to me to assure you that he is quite well and I shall tell you his condition exactly, so that you can feel no alarm whatever. We engaged the enemy at about 2 ½ PM yesterday at Olustee about 30 miles from here and were beaten. I saw McCrea just as he was bringing his section in to action and I could not help feeling glorious myself at the gallant manner in which he did it. Most of his men and horses were killed or wounded before he was carried from the field. He has two wounds, one in each leg. That in the right leg is a flesh wound in the calf, the other, I think, is a little more serious, but not by any measure so as to afflict the use of his leg hereafter. He has behaved most gallantly and has won the envy and admiration of all about him. Gen'l Seymour told me himself yesterday that McCrea was a most gallant and heroic officer and that he had the highest regard for him. I write this in a hurry as I know McCrea is anxious you should not be alarmed by the exaggerated newspaper reports. He would write himself but has just arrived at Baldwin and is now having his wounds dressed by the surgeon. He bears up very bravely and to outward appearances you would not know as he lies in bed

smoking a segar [*sic*] that he was wounded at all. He wished that you tell Belle, and Uncle Wallace too, that they need not worry.[30]

On the road to Baldwin, Tully was again painfully jolted over bumpy dirt roads in an ambulance before arriving in Jacksonville early in the morning of February 22. He and most of the other wounded were soon loaded onto ships and sent north.[31]

When Tully's ship arrived in Beaufort the next day, he was carried to General Hospital Number 7 where his wounds were dressed again. This time his left leg was immobilized in a wooden frame packed with sand bags. It was close to a week before Tully was able to write home:

> I suppose that you have heard ere this that I was wounded in the late battle in Florida. I was shot through both legs— compound fracture of the left and a flesh wound through the fleshy part of the right, both below the knee. Neither wound is dangerous but the one in the left leg has been very painful. I was compelled to ride two nights and one day over the rough road in an ambulance and all the next day was at sea in a steamer bound for this place. The torture was very great and I have never before suffered such physical pain. As soon as I arrived here everything was done that was possible and I have received every attention from kind friends among whom are several ladies. I have everything that I can desire and as I am now getting over the prostration caused by the bad journey. I am feeling quite comfortable and getting along famously. I will probably be amongst you Buckeyes about the middle of April aided by a good strong pair of crutches.[32]

For the next two months, Tully lay flat on his back in bed. The doctors at Beaufort were personal friends, and he was well cared for. He had enough books to last a month, and the hospital food was excellent. The wound in his right leg healed quickly, but an infection in his left leg was more resistant. Letters finally caught up to him, and

Sam Talbot included a copy of a letter from Alice, the first he had received in two years. She heard about Tully's wounds from a clipping sent to her from the *Philadelphia Inquirer* and invited her long-lost brother to come to Natchez so she could care for him. Tully's Uncle Wallace suggested that she visit Ohio instead and sent fifty dollars south to help her make the trip.[33]

Weeks soon turned into months and diminished Tully's hopes for an early release. Efforts to raise his spirits by his friends failed to alleviate his despair, and he grew more intolerant. Even Seymour's recommendation for brevet promotion to captain and the naming of one of the fortifications surrounding the federal encampment around Jacksonville as Battery McCrea failed to cheer him up. Regardless of the honors, Tully continually fretted that his injuries would not allow him to travel home to see Alice before she returned to Natchez. His future seemed very complicated.[34]

12

Sanderson, Semmes, and West at Pleasant Hill

West Point, January 1866. The math exams lasted two days. After the final section was tested, Professor Church informed the officers about several new resolutions just passed by Congress that affected West Point. The size of the Corps of Cadets was to be increased, and more veterans were to be allowed entrance. A new entrance exam would include history, geography, and English grammar. More important, there was a provision to allow other than engineer officers to be appointed as the superintendent. The Academic Board was in favor of most of the recommended changes, but Professor Mahan was on his way to Washington to argue against allowing officers from other branches to serve as Superintendent.

Outside the academic building, Tully negotiated the icy carriage road carefully to return to his quarters each day. The temperature dropped below zero a number of times, and the cadets complained that the new windows in the barracks didn't stop the drafts coming into their rooms. Additionally, the freezing weather caused the bath house next to the barracks to be temporarily closed, and bathing was restricted to once every two weeks.

Tully needed to negotiate the carriage road one more time that day. There was a band concert later that evening that he wanted to attend. The winter weather often isolated West Point, and the musical interludes helped break the monotony of the gray winter days. He looked forward to spring and warm weather again.

The persistently gray atmosphere dulled everyone's spirits and gave rise to the term "gloom period." It was not helped by attendance at funerals for recent graduates. The cemetery brought back memories of those lost in Tully's class who did not survive the war. One of those was

Fig. 12.1. Gunboats Attacking Federal Troops. *LOC*

James Sanderson, who was killed at Pleasant Hill, Louisiana, during the Red River campaign.

Department of the Gulf—March 1864

James Sanderson found himself along Bayou Teche in western Louisiana near the area where Sam Mansfield had earlier led the Twenty-fourth Connecticut volunteers during the battle of Irish Bend. He was now assigned to 1st Lt. Franck E. Taylor's Battery L, First US Artillery, which he joined in November 1863 after leaving the Army of the Potomac. Marching orders sent Sanderson's battery and Maj. Gen. William B. Franklin's Nineteenth Corps toward Alexandria to join the rest of General Banks's forces gathering for the Red River Campaign.[1]

Sanderson was a veteran of multiple campaigns, having served on "detached duty" in several units with the Army of the Potomac. His exploits during the Chancellorsville campaign had gained him respect. After Gettysburg, General Hunt shifted a number of artillery officers between the Artillery Reserve and the various corps to replace losses, and Sanderson was transferred to 1st Lt. Gulian V. Weir's Battery C, Fifth US Artillery. A week later, General Meade was ordered to send several regiments back to help quell the draft riots that had broken out in New York City. Sanderson helped load Weir's guns on railcars and headed north along with the Eighth US Infantry and several New York regiments.[2]

The regulars from Meade's army arrived in lower Manhattan on July 17, 1863. Still shaking the dust of Gettysburg off their uniforms, the infantry carried their ragged flags, shot full of holes on Cemetery Ridge, into the streets of New York. Martial law was declared, and New York City was placed under curfew. Within a matter of days, the riots ceased.[3] For three months Sanderson helped patrol various parts of the city before being transferred to his permanent unit in Louisiana.

He was the only one of his classmates assigned to General Banks's Department of the Gulf in 1864. Two of his former classmates, newly promoted Maj. Oliver Semmes and Capt. John West, were part of Maj. Gen. Richard Taylor's army opposing them. Semmes, having escaped from Union custody the previous year, was now the chief of artillery for Taylor's two cavalry divisions. Part of Semmes's horse artillery included West, who now commanded the Sixth Louisiana Light Artillery (also called the Grosse Tete Flying Artillery).[4]

The Red River Campaign

Banks's campaign along the Red River addressed part of President Lincoln's concerns over recent affairs in Mexico. It was designed to open a line of operations along the Red River, secure Shreveport,

Louisiana, and then place federal troops in Texas as a warning to France against setting up a puppet government in Mexico. Grant was opposed to the operation, but Halleck had already approved it before Grant took charge of all the Union armies in March 1864.[5]

Banks's expeditionary force of some seventeen thousand men came from Maj. Gen. Andrew J. Smith's Thirteenth and Maj. Gen. William Franklin's Nineteenth Corps. In addition, ten thousand men from the Army of the Tennessee and fifteen thousand from the Department of Arkansas joined them once the campaign began. By April 1, the various commands reached Alexandria and headed toward Shreveport.[6]

Franklin's Nineteenth Corps marched eighty miles from Alexandria to Natchitoches without any serious resistance from Taylor's gray horsemen. From that point forward, Banks saw the shortest road to Shreveport was the stage road through Pleasant Hill and Mansfield, a distance of over a hundred miles first through barren, sandy country where little water was available, followed by narrow roads through heavy, unbroken pine forests.[7]

On April 6, Banks put his army in motion toward Shreveport. Heavy rains hit the rear of the column, making the road almost impassable and delaying movement of his rear units. The delays stretched out the Union column well over twenty miles, creating an inviting target under any conditions. At the same time the cavalry and the Thirteenth Corps at the head of the column were unaffected by the rain and pressed ahead toward Mansfield.

Battle of Sabine Crossroads

On the morning of April 8, the cavalry and the Thirteenth Corps marched toward Mansfield where Taylor's three rebel divisions lay waiting on both sides of the road to Shreveport. Oliver Semmes and his horse artillery batteries supported Taylor's cavalry divisions. The Union cavalry was surprised by Taylor's skirmishers and infantry at Sabine Crossroads, three miles from Mansfield. Calls for reinforcements brought the Thirteenth Corps infantry forward.

Desultory exchanges took place during the day. Semmes's batteries of horse artillery, including West's battery, were used sparingly because the heavy forests made firing difficult. But at 4:30 P.M., one of Taylor's divisions suddenly charged across an open field toward the Union position. It precipitated a general advance that quickly overwhelmed both flanks of the small Thirteenth Corps, sending it rearward in confusion.[8]

When Franklin soon arrived, he sent word for the Nineteenth Corps to move forward in support. Sanderson's Battery L marched with Brig. Gen. William H. Emory's First Division to a sawmill on the Mansfield road eight miles from Pleasant Hill. When apprised of the engagement, Emory led his infantry regiments up the Mansfield Road. Battery L started moving forward, but Sanderson galloped up to deliver orders from Brig. Gen. Richard Arnold, the chief of artillery for Department of the Gulf, for it to remain near the sawmill. [9]

While assigned to Battery L, it is quite possible that Sanderson was temporarily assigned to General Arnold or possibly to Capt. Henry W. Closson, chief of artillery for the Nineteenth Corps. This was a typical assignment for junior artillery officers, who were then detailed to deliver orders and messages to various artillery units during movement or engagements. Sanderson was obviously not with Battery L near the sawmill on April 8.[10]

Meanwhile, Emory's infantry took up defensive positions along the crest of a hill astride the road about three miles from Sabine Crossroads. After the fleeing Union soldiers and wagons streaming down the road toward Pleasant Hill passed through, rebel units pressed up to Emory's defenses and were repulsed. Later that night, the infantry and artillery pulled back to Pleasant Hill. Semmes and West enjoyed their victory along with the rest of Taylor's rebels near Mansfield after capturing over twenty-five hundred Union soldiers and twenty-two guns.[11]

Battle of Pleasant Hill

The next morning, Taylor moved his cavalry forward along the Mansfield Road only to find that the Union forces had withdrawn dur-

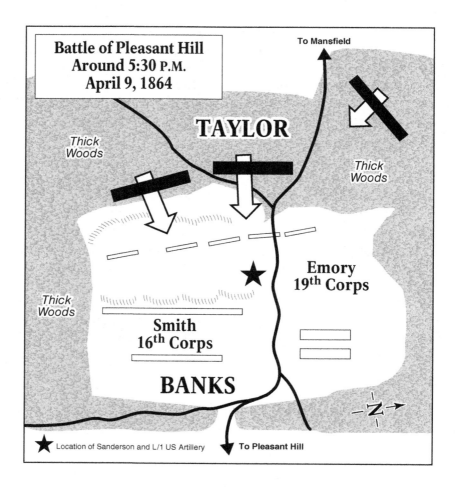

Battle of Pleasant Hill
Around 5:30 P.M.
April 9, 1864

To Mansfield

TAYLOR

Thick Woods

Thick Woods

Emory
19th Corps

Thick Woods

Smith
16th Corps

BANKS

★ Location of Sanderson and L/1 US Artillery

To Pleasant Hill

ing the night. Now reinforced with two more infantry divisions, he marched toward Pleasant Hill where he concentrated his infantry and cavalry divisions in the dense forests just north of the small hamlet. Semmes positioned West's Sixth Louisiana battery and the others to support the attacks and target the Union batteries positioned on a small hill mass north of the hamlet.[12]

Pleasant Hill consisted of a few old houses and a school on a slight rise. A half a mile along the Mansfield Road lay a second hill mass where the Union forces occupied defensive positions. The area surrounding the rise was heavily timbered with open fields only to the west.[13]

Anticipating Taylor's attack, Emory's First Division and a brigade from Smith's Sixteenth Corps occupied positions across the two roads that led to Pleasant Hill from the north. Two divisions from Sixteenth Corps had now joined Banks's Nineteenth Corps at Pleasant Hill and defended the left flank of the Nineteenth Corps.[14]

Around 5 P.M., Semmes's batteries opened fire on an advanced Union battery astride the Mansfield Road to divert attention from the main rebel attack. The rebel shelling scattered the battery. Taylor then launched his main attack with the two infantry divisions at the juncture between Emory's and Smith's Sixteenth Corps brigades. The rebel soldiers advanced almost at the charge, and hand-to-hand fighting in a ditch at the foot of the hill mass soon forced Emory's brigades to fall back. He needed artillery to stem the rebel attack and ordered Lieutenant Taylor's nearby battery to send four guns forward to support his failing first line.[15]

Soon after Battery L's guns unlimbered on the left of the Mansfield Road, it came under repeated attack from Semmes's artillery. The battery was located at a critical point of the rebel attack. The momentum of the attack forced the Union infantry support to fall away from Battery L. Canister fire failed to deter the rebel advance, and the battery was in danger of being overrun.

At some point during the engagement, Sanderson had rejoined Battery L. As he had at Chancellorsville, it is reasonable to assume that he tried to help extract his battery from impending loss. Lieutenant Taylor reported that his pieces were ordered to limber to the rear. Horse teams were brought up, but rebel musket fire killed or disabled almost all of them. The fast-approaching gray lines seemed ready to sweep over the battery before it could be moved. Only one or two horses could be hitched to a limber, and the crews helped pull one gun to the rear to help cover the withdrawal of the others. Musket balls whizzed by as enemy infantrymen came closer. Sanderson likely ordered, "Double canister," and his crews blasted away at the approaching enemy lines, but it was too late. More shells from Oliver

Semmes's artillery rained down on his position, and Sanderson was struck down. Three guns were lost as gray lines swept over the battery position.[16]

General Taylor's main attack had penetrated the right-center of the Nineteenth Corps position, and gray lines soon topped the rising hill mass and ran into a surprise. Waiting in position behind the hill were Smith's two divisions from the Sixteenth Corps along with their artillery batteries. Concentrated fire from the artillery and infantry staggered the rebel lines. Smith ordered his men to charge and broke the enemy advance. Emory's brigades rallied on his right and joined the Sixteenth Corps in pushing the rebel forces back into the forest. Elements of both corps chased them for some time before returning to Pleasant Hill. When the Union advance reached Battery L's position, they recovered the guns and found Sanderson lying between two of them, mortally wounded by a shell fragment, perhaps fired by one of his former classmates. He lived only a few hours and died early the next morning.[17]

Then, inexplicably and in the face of a Union victory, Banks ordered his army to withdraw to Grand Ecore that evening, leaving many of his wounded and some of his dead behind on the field. Sanderson's remains were hurriedly buried, but little information was kept on the location of his grave. The Confederate command reported Banks's withdrawal as a great victory. A year later, Sanderson's relatives were unsuccessful in finding his final resting place. The rapidity with which Banks's army left contributed to the uncertainty surrounding the location of his grave, and his remains still lie in an unknown grave near Pleasant Hill, Louisiana.[18]

Sanderson's loss was not mentioned in the official reports of his battery commander or the Nineteenth Corps chief of artillery. His name finally appeared in an endorsement to General Emory's official report several days later. Sanderson was the first in his class to die in combat.

13

Mackenzie, Gillespie, Calef, Egan, Dearing, and Schaff during the Overland and Petersburg Campaigns

West Point, January 1866. After returning to his quarters, Tully sought the warmth of the stove and thought about the results of the exams. Most of the plebes passed, but a second examination would be given to each cadet who failed or was judged to be deficient. If they failed again, a final "writ" would be given, which few cadets ever passed. Within a few days the names of the deficient cadets would be read in the mess hall, and they would pack their bags and head for home. As was often the case, the true reason for their dismissal carried with it a stigma that many families chose to hide.

On a different note, he thought about the news that a billiard parlor, created and used by the second class for several months, had only just been discovered in the basement of the sixth division. When the tactical officers finally found it, a note was propped up on the table transferring ownership of the room and table to them.[1]

Still chuckling about the incident, he put on his overcoat and limped down the carriage road to the officers' mess. As classmates often do, he would chastise John Egan and the Tactical Department for failing to find the billiard room sooner. He knew dinner would probably degenerate into more war stories.

Some of the stories about his classmates' exploits during the Overland and Petersburg Campaigns were exciting. Mackenzie took command of a volunteer regiment at Cold Harbor and launched a spectacular career. John Egan's assignment during the Wilson-Kautz raid to destroy

Fig. 13.1. Entrenchments Being Constructed (Edwin Forbes). *BLCW, vol. 4*

the Staunton River bridge led to his capture at Ream's Station west of Petersburg. Morris Schaff survived the battle in the Wilderness and then three months later had his ordnance depot destroyed at City Point, which left him under a cloud of suspicion not cleared up until after the war. The most interesting was George Gillespie's story about his narrow escape while delivering critical information between General Sheridan and General Meade just before the battle at Cold Harbor.

The Class and Grant's Overland Campaign

May 1864 was an auspicious time. Grant's plan to coordinate the efforts of the various Union armies began with a major attack by Meade's Army of the Potomac against Lee's Army of Northern Virginia. At the same time, Maj. Gen. William T. Sherman and three armies were to march on Atlanta, destroy Gen. Joseph Johnston's Army of Tennessee, and sweep away all Confederate forces east of the Mississippi. Supporting these operations were three smaller campaigns. Maj. Gen. Benjamin Butler and the Army of the James were to push up the James River, threaten Richmond, and destroy the railroads south of Petersburg. Maj. Gen. Nathaniel Banks was to finish

Table 13.1. Class Assignments, US Army, July 1864

Army of the Potomac	Other Commands	Atlanta Campaign
Engineer Bn.: **Gillespie,** *Mackenzie* Ordnance Dept.: **Schaff** 6th Corps: 2nd CT Heavy Arty.: *Mackenzie* 1st Horse Arty. Brigade B&L/2 US Arty.: Heaton (**McIntire**) M/2 US Arty.: Pennington (*Hamilton*) 2nd Horse Arty. Brigade A/2 US Arty.: Dennison (**Calef**) K/1 US Arty.: Maynard (*Egan*)	Dept. of the Gulf 19th Corps: L/4 US Arty.: Taylor (*Sanderson*) Dept. of the South Engineer Dept.: **Suter** Ordnance Dept.: **Myers** Defenses of Washington 22nd Corps, G/2 US Arty.: **Wilson** Dept. of Engineers: **Mansfield** (Rhode Island), **Smith** (Maine) Ordnance Bureau DC: **Rollins** Arsenals: **Arnold** (Springfield), **Chaffee** (Allegheny), **Comly** (Watertown) Mustering Officer: **Lord** (Boston) West Point: **Lancaster,** *Hamilton* Died: **Bolles** (April 1863) *Sanderson* (April 1864) Sick/Wounded/POW: **McCrea,** *Egan*	Army of the Cumberland Engineer Dept.: **Burroughs, Wharton** Ordnance Dept.: **Marye** H/4 US Arty.: Rodney (**Warner**) Army of the Tennessee 16th Corps F/4 US Arty.: **Murray** 3rd US Cav.: **James** Army of the Ohio Aide-de-camp: **Bartlett**

Note: Members of Class of 1862 shown in bold. Other names are commanders of their units at this time. Italicized names are shown in two different places because of transfer or death.

his Red River Campaign and push on to Mobile. Finally, Maj. Gen. Franz Sigel was to move up the Shenandoah Valley and then turn to destroy the rail hub and supply center at Lynchburg.[2]

The execution of Grant's plan found seven members of the Class of 1862 still assigned to the Army of the Potomac, and two members rode with Sherman's armies toward Atlanta. The rest of the class was scattered about eastern and western arsenals, engineer staffs, or garrison units in various departments. Changes and transfers between the Battle of Gettysburg and the middle of 1864 were myriad and made tracking the assignments of each member of the class somewhat difficult. A revised organization chart is shown at table 13.1, with assignments current as of the end of July 1864.

During the Overland Campaign, artillery could not be used properly in the close confines of the Wilderness and Spotsylvania. The concentrated and continuous conflict that Grant now waged required many replacements. Additionally, he sought to reduce his dependency on the large army supply trains. The Washington defenses were purged, and a number of artillery regiments converted to infantry to replace the losses suffered. At the same time, he ordered the artillery component of Meade's army reduced. General Hunt was reluctantly forced to conduct a major reorganization of the artillery at the end of May. Many Artillery Reserve batteries were sent back to Washington, while all other batteries in the Army of the Potomac were reduced to four guns with the horse artillery batteries utilizing a mixture of two 3-inch rifles and two 12-pounders.[3]

In Hunt's reorganization, the two horse artillery brigades were consolidated into a single brigade with a total of eight horse batteries directly attached to Maj. Gen. Philip H. Sheridan's Cavalry Corps. Horses and equipment to support the transfers came from the Second Horse Artillery Brigade. John Egan's Battery K, First US Artillery, and John Calef in 1st Lt. Clarke's Battery A, Second US Artillery, were transferred to Capt. James M. Robertson's First Horse Artillery Brigade with their units. Sam McIntire in 1st Lt. Edward Heaton's Battery B&L, Second US Artillery, was already there. John Calef was relieved of command of Battery A, Second US Artillery, in August 1863 but chose to remain in his old unit. Four other horse batteries in the Second Horse Artillery Brigade, including James Wilson in 1st Lt. William N. Dennison's Battery G, Second US Artillery, were dismounted and sent north to Washington with the other reserve batteries. Upon arrival, Wilson took command of Battery G and was assigned to the Washington defenses throughout the war. During that campaign and the subsequent siege of Petersburg, the engineers were actively employed in the construction of batteries and parapets as well as examining enemy fortifications to determine weaknesses. Ranald Mackenzie, George Gillespie, and Morris Schaff were part of Meade's engineer and ordnance staffs at the beginning of the Overland Campaign.[4]

After Gettysburg, Tully McCrea was transferred to the Department of the South in August 1863, losing command of Battery I. James Sanderson lay dead somewhere in western Louisiana in April 1864, and Charles Warner was transferred to the Department of the Cumberland at Nashville in December 1863. Frank Hamilton and James Lancaster were each ordered back to West Point as instructors before the end of 1863. Fred James made his way west to join the 3rd US Cavalry in the Sixteenth Corps near Memphis. During the same interval, the Ordnance Department assigned William Marye, Clifford Chaffee, Jasper Myers, Isaac Arnold, and James Rollins to various arsenals or field depots with the Department of Tennessee, the Department of North Carolina and Virginia, and the Department of the South in support of the various operations and campaigns.

On the opposing side, the Overland Campaign and subsequent movement to Petersburg again brought newly promoted Col. James Dearing and Maj. Joseph Blount in direct contact with their former classmates. Dearing had gained rapid promotion and now commanded a cavalry brigade in the defenses of Petersburg where Blount remained in Dearing's old artillery battalion with the Lynchburg battery. Dearing would later arrange a transfer of Richard Kinney into his brigade to command the dismounted troopers after Kinney recovered from wounds suffered at Spotsylvania. Henry Farley would move with Maj. Gen. Wade Hampton's cavalry to command the dismounted elements of Brig. Gen. Pierce Young's (ex-June '61) cavalry brigade around Richmond.

During the first few months of Grant's campaigns, the status of several members of the class changed. In May, George Gillespie returned from engineer recruiting duty and was almost captured while delivering extremely important information to General Meade, an incident that would later gain him the Medal of Honor. In June, John Egan was captured at Ream's Station while supporting Brig. Gen. James H. Wilson's ('60) cavalry division. Morris Schaff almost lost his life during the battle of the Wilderness delivering messages. Three months later, he commanded a major ordnance depot at City Point near Grant's headquarters where a great explosion took place.

Ranald Mackenzie was appointed to command a volunteer infantry regiment right after Cold Harbor. Their stories are the subject of this chapter.

Gillespie Rides to Cold Harbor

After the battle at Spotsylvania, the two opposing armies collided again on the banks of the North Anna River where Lee again successfully defended his position. Grant and Meade's army slipped sideways to the Pamunkey River and then to Totopotomoy Creek. Each time Lee's forces thwarted Grant's attempted envelopment. By the end of May, Grant shifted once more toward Bethesda Church and at the same time ordered the Eighteenth Corps, Army of the James, to join Meade's army. Maj. Gen. Gouverneur Warren, now in command of the Union Fifth Corps, had a furious fight with Maj. Gen. Jubal Early's Second Corps before moving into positions around Bethesda Church on the left flank of Meade's army.[5]

Lee, sensing another shift by Grant, began moving his divisions to block any further movements toward Richmond. He requested reinforcements, but it took pressure from Richmond before an infantry division and an artillery battalion were released from the Howlett Line near Petersburg. Both moved toward Cold Harbor, but they were twenty miles away, and it took time to get there. Joseph Blount's Lynchburg battery marched through Richmond on the night of May 31 and camped near Mechanicsville, east of the city.[6]

The area beyond Bethesda Church included the strategic intersection at Old Cold Harbor where roads led directly to Richmond, the James River, and the Union supply center at White House. Sheridan and two of his cavalry divisions were sent to secure that intersection and protect it for future operations. Lee also knew the importance of the Old Cold Harbor road junction and also sent his cavalry there while he tried to determine where Grant was headed next. New Cold Harbor was located about a mile closer along the road to Richmond. The battlefield lay between these two locations. It was into this area that Blount's battery and Maj. Gen. Robert

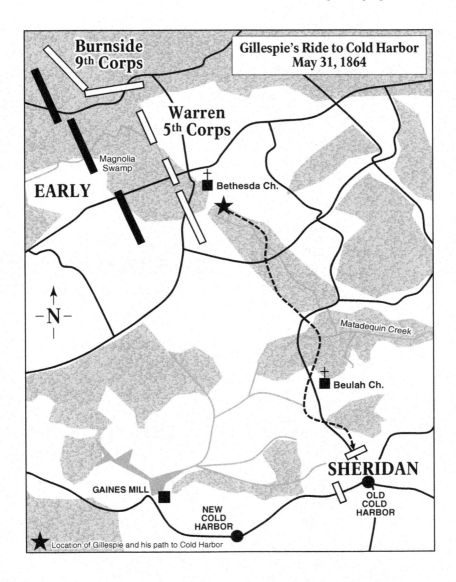

Hoke's infantry division from the Petersburg defenses arrived to bolster Maj. Gen. Fitzhugh Lee's cavalry during an early-morning engagement with Sheridan's troopers on June 1 before a concentrated Union attack began.[7]

On the morning of May 31, Capt. George Gillespie, just returned from a six-month assignment with the Recruiting Service, was sent to Warren's Fifth Corps on the left flank of Meade's army to ascertain when General Sheridan's cavalry made contact with the enemy at Cold Harbor. Upon arrival, he helped interrogate several prisoners at Warren's headquarters. Around noon, the muted thunder of cannon fire to the southwest indicated that Sheridan's cavalry was in contact. Sending messengers back to Meade, George decided to contact Sheridan directly. He pulled out his compass and started cross-country toward the strategic road junction.[8]

The cannon fire resulted from Sheridan's troopers engaging Fitzhugh Lee's cavalry waiting behind breastworks near the strategic road junction. Sheridan swung one of his brigades around Fitzhugh Lee's flanks and forced him to withdraw almost three-quarters of a mile along the road to New Cold Harbor. After the engagement ended, the Confederate breastworks were turned around. Calef's battery became part of a twelve-gun line of cannons located between Brig. Gen. Wesley Merritt's ('60) and Brig. Gen. George Armstrong Custer's defensive positions.[9]

Meanwhile, Gillespie rode through a dense forest, detoured around a swamp, crossed several streams, and ran into a rebel cavalry picket. His Tennessee accent and information gained from his earlier interrogations convinced the outpost that he was searching for Fitzhugh Lee's headquarters. They pointed him in the right direction, and he rode off. As soon as he reached the safety of a nearby forest, he turned toward the Old Cold Harbor road junction once more. Emerging from another patch of woods, he found himself in the middle of a rebel infantry regiment. This time musket rounds whizzed past as he rushed back into the protective cover of the trees. He circled wide around the rebel unit, picked up the road to Cold Harbor, and arrived around 7 P.M.

General Sheridan explained that his brigades were far from any Union support and that he had already ordered them to begin withdrawing that evening. Sensing this information to be of great importance to General Meade, Gillespie rode back to Bethesda

Church through enemy lines once more, this time without interference from rebel pickets. He arrived at Meade's tent around 9 P.M. and delivered Sheridan's message, outlining his intention to leave Cold Harbor.[10]

Meade immediately sent a messenger galloping to Sheridan to "hold Cold Harbor at all hazards" and then directed Maj. Gen. Horatio G. Wright's Sixth Corps and Maj. Gen. Andrew J. Smith's Eighteenth Corps to march there that evening. Around 1 A.M. on June 1, his messenger reached Sheridan on the road, causing him to turn his brigades around to reoccupy the breastworks near Old Cold Harbor. His troopers hunkered down and anxiously looked over their shoulders as they awaited the arrival of the Sixth Corps and the Eighteenth Corps.[11]

Back at Meade's headquarters, George probably thought he had experienced a good day. He had crossed enemy lines, escaped capture twice, and evaded musket fire. Most important, he had delivered critical information to Meade upon his return. He relaxed in his tent and thought about tomorrow. The chief engineer had just placed him in charge of constructing the entrenchments on the left at Cold Harbor.[12]

Many years later, Col. Gillespie claimed that it was his information about Sheridan's intention to withdraw from Cold Harbor that prompted the late-night shift of forces. His foray through enemy lines and return to Meade's headquarters with such critical information was considered important enough to warrant a belated award of the Medal of Honor thirty-one years after the event. His citation read: "First Lieutenant George L. Gillespie, Corps of Engineers, U.S. Army, near Bethesda Church, Virginia, 31 May 1864, exposed himself to danger by voluntarily making his way through the enemy's lines to communicate with General Sheridan. While rendering this service he was captured, but escaped; again came in contact with the enemy, was again ordered to surrender, but escaped by dashing away under fire."[13]

Later in his career, Gillespie believed that many patriotic organizations were issuing medals so similar to the Medal of Honor that it belittled its image. After he was appointed chief of engineers, Maj. Gen. Gillespie formed a committee to redesign the army's Medal of Honor. The new design was successfully patented and received congressional approval in 1904. Even now, the current army Medal of Honor is often called the Gillespie medal.[14]

Mackenzie Gets a Command

The next day, June 1, the Army of the Potomac launched a major attack at Cold Harbor with the Sixth and Eighteenth Corps. General Lee's divisions had rapidly shifted to that location, and a substantial defense was already present. One of the assaulting regiments in the Sixth Corps was the recently arrived Second Connecticut Volunteer Heavy Artillery, then a part of Brig. Gen. Emory Upton's brigade in Maj. Gen. David A. Russell's First Division. As it rushed forward, a sudden volley from rebel breastworks felled many in the regiment, including its commander. Two hours later the Union attack stalled, and Grant called it off. [15]

Unexpectedly, the second-in-command of the Second Connecticut Heavy Artillery refused to take charge. After some discussion a day later, Upton advised the second-in-command that Capt. Ranald Mackenzie, a regular engineer officer, should be recommended for the position. Earlier Mackenzie had assisted Upton and the Sixth Corps at Spotsylvania where he found a weakness in the enemy fortifications. That weakness was exploited by the then colonel Upton, who successfully assaulted and broke through the fortified lines just short of the Muleshoe Salient on May 10. He was not adequately supported and was forced to retreat but took numerous prisoners. Upton was promoted to brigadier general after that action, and Mackenzie's sharp eye was not forgotten.[16]

The regiment voted to accept Mackenzie as their commander, and the recommendation was quickly approved by Upton, Russell, Meade, Grant, and the state of Connecticut. Colonel Mackenzie, US Volunteers, rode into the camp of the dispirited Second Connecticut Heavy Artillery to take command on June 10.[17]

Gillespie Helps Bridge the James

After another extended battle at Cold Harbor, Grant moved Meade's army sideways once more to cross the James River and attack Petersburg, one of the Confederacy's major supply centers. When Meade's lead elements reached the crossing site near Charles City on June 14, construction of the pontoon bridge across the James River was just beginning. Ships, barges, and steamers were used to move the first units over the wide waterway until the bridge was completed.

George Gillespie and the regular engineers were instrumental in building the initial portion of the lengthy pontoon bridge over the James. When the rest of the engineer brigade arrived, his company moved to the far shore to construct approaches and build out to meet the continuing bridging operation. When completed, the 2,100-foot span was the longest pontoon bridge constructed in history to that date. After midnight on June 15, masses of soldiers, wagons, and supplies moved over the swaying span night and day until the entire army was across.[18]

Calef at St. Mary's Church

Sheridan's two cavalry divisions returned to the Army of the Potomac after their raid to Trevilian Station to find that Grant had moved the Army of the Potomac across the James River. When the troopers arrived at the Union supply base at White House on June 21, Sheridan was directed to guard the movement of nine hundred army supply wagons to the James. For the next week, his divisions guarded the lengthy columns as they slowly made their way toward Charles City and the crossing site on the river. Sam McIntire with Heaton's battery rode with Brig. Gen. Alfred Torbert's division guarding one column of wagons. They reached the crossing site without incident.[19]

Meanwhile, Hampton, now in command of General Lee's cavalry after the death of Stuart, was intent upon destroying Grant's wagon trains before they crossed the river. A cordon was spread across the area to find and halt the wagon trains. To protect against any such incursions, Brig. Gen. David M. Gregg's cavalry division was positioned at St. Mary's Church (also called Samaria Church) on June 24 as a barrier to halt Hampton's cavalry. Barricades and breastworks were thrown up. Calef and 1st Lt. William N. Dennison's battery were posted with another battery on a slight hill in the rear of the two brigades.[20]

Fitzhugh Lee's troopers soon located Gregg's division at St. Mary's Church and Hampton quickly gathered his widespread forces to attack. For over two hours, Gregg's two brigades fended off multiple charges by Hampton's and Fitzhugh Lee's divisions. When a large rebel force finally flanked Gregg's position, his other battery was ordered to withdraw. Similar orders were given to Dennison, but he replied, "Take my battery? They cannot take my battery. No rebels on that field can take my battery!" He continued to fire until his ammunition almost ran out, then pulled his guns off the field just before Hampton's troopers overran the site. Calef unlimbered his guns more than once to clear the road behind them as the battery leapfrogged between positions for close to six miles. The weary gunners and troopers finally reached the safety of Sheridan's camp at Charles City near 8 P.M.[21]

The Petersburg Campaign

Earlier the rest of Meade's army had crossed the James and moved into positions around the defenses of Petersburg. The rest of June was filled with multiple and unsuccessful attempts to breach the fortified lines around Petersburg after a siege of that city began. The subsequent arrival of Lee's army further bolstered the meager defenses around Petersburg and Richmond. The two armies settled down until June 22 when the battle heated up once more.

Egan, the Wilson-Kautz Raid, and First Ream's Station

Hoping to extend his lines south of Petersburg, Grant ordered the Second and Sixth Corps to make a fiercely resisted attack toward the

Weldon Railroad on June 22. While the attack was under way, Brig. Gen. James H. Wilson led his Third Cavalry Division, three horse artillery batteries, and Brig. Gen. August V. Kautz's cavalry division from the Army of the James across the Weldon Railroad on a raid to destroy the Staunton River Bridge, some eighty miles west. Egan and 1st Lt. William Maynadier's Battery K, First US Artillery, followed Wilson's division.

The raid began south of Ream's Station and initially destroyed sixty miles of tracks and a number of depots and facilities, with limited interference from rebel cavalry until Maj. Gen. William H. F. "Rooney" Lee's cavalry division blocked the road between Nottoway Court House and Blacks and Whites, a station on the railroad on June 23 and 24. Just before noon near the railway, Col. George H. Chapman's brigade from Wilson's division, with Maynadier's battery in support, ran into Dearing's cavalry brigade, now a part of Rooney Lee's division. In one of the few incidents where classmates directly confronted classmates, Egan's guns blasted away as Chapman's brigade pushed Dearing's troopers back across the tracks. Brig. Gen. Rufus Barringer's brigade from Rooney Lee's division soon arrived to reinforce Dearing's men. Around midnight, Wilson's troopers withdrew and circled west to rejoin Kautz's division. Dearing's brigade and an artillery battery were then sent back to guard the Weldon Railroad while Rooney Lee and Barringer's brigade followed Wilson's columns west.[22]

The next morning, the Union raiders continued breaking up the Richmond-Danville rail line until they reached the Staunton River Bridge (at present-day Randolph) late on June 25. The town's home guard, reserves, militia, a few cannons, and even boys from a local high school guarded the bridge on both sides of the river. An hour-long artillery duel resulted in one of Egan's guns being disabled and several casualties. Kautz's dismounted troopers then charged forward under cover of artillery fire while Wilson's men protected the rear. In the interim, Barringer's brigade came up and attacked Wilson's rear, causing him to call off the attack. The Union attempt to destroy the bridge had failed.[23]

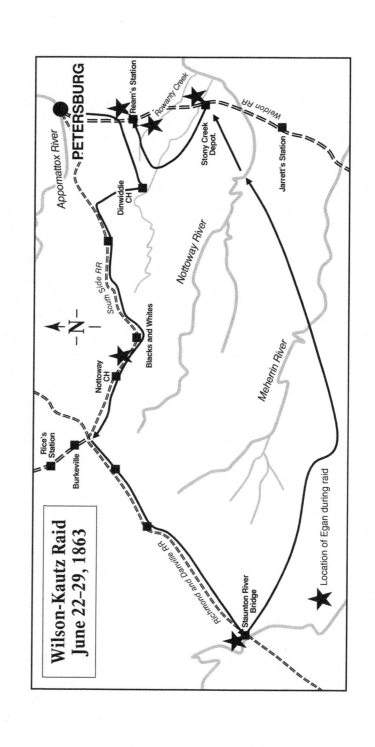

Wilson-Kautz Raid
June 22-29, 1863

Wilson was now short of supplies, and his horses and troopers were tired. After four days and eighty miles, he decided to end the raid and return to friendly lines. After midnight on June 25, his troopers headed southeast on a roundabout route that would first reach the Weldon Railroad and then Ream's Station, which they expected to be in friendly hands. They walked their horses at times and moved through the night to avoid skirmishes with rebel infantry and cavalry. Egan's guns supported the rear guard and frequently helped fend off Barringer's attacks as the long column headed east.

Two days later, Wilson's raiders reached the Nottoway River and turned north along the Weldon Railroad. After midnight on June 28, Kautz's division started north toward Ream's Station with Egan's battery following. Behind them, a spirited engagement took place at Stony Creek Depot (Sappony Church) where a number of blue troopers were captured before Wilson's men finally broke contact. As Wilson's raiders came closer to friendly lines, more rebel cavalry and infantry joined the hunt.[24]

When he arrived at Ream's Station, Wilson found Hampton's troopers and a rebel infantry division advancing through the woods from three different directions. Before any relief could be mounted from Meade's lines, Wilson was forced to move quickly to avoid capture.[25]

Wagons and caissons were destroyed, but a sudden rebel attack split the two cavalry divisions apart. Maynadier and Egan led Battery K away from Ream's Station to the southwest. When rebel cavalry and infantry suddenly appeared, Maynadier ordered the caissons blown in place and sent the rest of the battery galloping toward a nearby wood. Halfway through, the swampy bottomland surrounding Rowanty Creek brought them to an abrupt halt. The gunners frantically cut down tree branches and piled fence rails into the creek to get the guns across. Egan's horses strained in their harnesses; gunners lent their shoulders to the wheels, but only one gun made it across. It was swung around and opened fire on the approaching rebel infantry, but it only delayed the inevitable. The gunners chopped the spokes of each wheel and spiked the guns in the face of looming capture. Then a "general skedaddle" took place, as one trooper later put it, but it was too late. Maynadier, Egan, fourteen enlisted men, and their guns were captured. Egan joined a long column of Union prisoners trudging toward Richmond where, upon arrival, he was later transferred to an officers' prisoner-of-war camp at Columbia, South Carolina.[26]

Schaff at City Point

It was another sweltering summer day near Grant's headquarters at City Point on August 11, 1864. A line of soldiers stood in front of a barber's tent while others drank cool, lemon-flavored drinks on the grounds of a nearby plantation. After Meade's army reached City Point, Capt. Morris Schaff had taken charge of the ordnance depot supplying the Union armies before Richmond. Late that afternoon, he played cards with several staff officers in a tent near the headquarters. The atmosphere in the tent was pleasant although extremely hot. As they played cards, he and the other officers were likely telling stories about their war experiences.

Schaff had almost been captured during the Battle of the Wilderness when he unexpectedly rode into a line of rebel skirmishers emerging from the thick and tangled underbrush. Slipping to the side of his horse, he turned abruptly and rode off, musket balls whizzing around him. One struck his belt buckle, dislodging his pistol and holster. As he reached down to grab them from the ground, a low-hanging tree limb knocked his hat off. Later, when he arrived at the headquarters, he found out he had been reported as killed.[27]

As the officers continued their play, a massive explosion suddenly rocked the ground. Seconds later, a cannon ball crashed into a mess chest right next to Schaff. Everyone scattered to avoid the debris that rained down from the sky. As soon as it was safe to move about, Schaff ran to the bluff and looked down.

Ships in the James River slipped their anchors to get away from the fiery wharf where his six-hundred-foot-long ordnance building was ablaze. Grant's later message to Washington stated, "Every part

Fig. 13.2. Explosion at City Point (Alfred Waud). *LOC*

of the yard used as my headquarters is filled with splinters and fragments of shells." It became apparent during a subsequent investigation that a barge next to the wharf filled with a large quantity of artillery and small arms ammunition had exploded.

Schaff later reported that over two hundred men were lost, including half his ordnance detachment. Estimates of the damage reached over $2 million. A court of inquiry was convened, and he was investigated on charges that his soldiers caused the explosion.

He was exonerated, but orders soon arrived transferring him to the arsenal at Reading, Pennsylvania, and he left City Point on September 15, perhaps under a bit of suspicion.[28]

After the war ended, the cause of the explosion was finally solved. A Confederate war report was discovered in Richmond describing how a spy planted a mine on one of the ammunition barges in the river, then set it off with a timing device. Several years later, one of the saboteurs submitted a patent application for what was described as a "horological torpedo" that had worked well at City Point.[29]

Schaff was brevetted for gallantry at the Battle of the Wilderness and before the end of the war was assigned to the Watertown Arsenal in Massachusetts. Mackenzie and the Second Connecticut Heavies followed the Sixth Corps to Petersburg and went with it to join Sheridan's command in the Shenandoah Valley. Egan remained a prisoner of war until December 1864 when he was able to escape. Calef remained with his horse artillery battery in support of the cavalry divisions until late in the war.[30]

14

Murray at Atlanta

West Point, January 1866. The next morning, the reveille gun fired and the drums rumbled in the sally port, reminding Tully of the joyous celebrations that erupted when General Sherman captured Savannah. The cadets learned about it at noon and could not be controlled for the rest of the day. The officers finally gathered some cadets to fire a national salute from the battery on the Plain in honor of Sherman's action. The cannons crashed, and the reports echoed back from the mountains across the river. More celebrations were held when Richmond and Petersburg fell in the months ahead.

Tully limped closer to the warm stove in his quarters to finish reviewing his notes for today's classes. On the table, covered with textbooks, pipes, and tobacco tins, was his class album. He idly flipped the pages until Albert Murray's picture appeared. Below it was penned a note: "Died in a prisoner-of-war camp—August 1864."

Albert was one of those reassigned several times during the war. A number of stories had been told in the officers' mess about his actions at Antietam, Fredericksburg, Suffolk, and Chattanooga. But it was his battery's support of McPherson's Army of the Tennessee during the Atlanta campaign that Tully remembered most. He knew Albert was captured as Sherman's armies encircled the city, but it was not until after the war that his final status was determined. He was the last of the class to fall in battle.

The Atlanta Campaign—May 1864

Maj. Gen. William T. Sherman began his campaign to seize Atlanta on May 4, 1864, at the same time that Meade's Army of the Potomac advanced into the Wilderness. Roughly following the railway, Sher-

Fig. 14.1. Site of General McPherson's Death. *LOC*

man's three armies marched south from Chattanooga and Knoxville toward Atlanta.[1]

1st Lt. Albert M. Murray, commanding Battery F, Second US Artillery in the Fourth Division, Sixteenth Corps, was a part of Maj.

Gen. James B. McPherson's Army of the Tennessee. His battery moved along generally good mountain roads into the six-mile-long Snake Creek Gap south of Gen. Joseph Johnston's rebel positions at Resaca, Georgia. McPherson's army was sent to force Johnston's rebel army away from those fortifications blocking the road to Atlanta.[2]

Albert Murray was not the only member of his class to participate in the Atlanta campaign. Staff captain William Bartlett was an aide-de-camp to Maj. Gen. John M. Schofield, commanding the Army of the Ohio. 1st Lt. Henry Wharton was the chief engineer for Maj. Gen. George H. Thomas's Army of the Cumberland. For the time being, 1st Lt. George Burroughs remained in Chattanooga as the acting chief engineer for the Department of the Cumberland. Meanwhile, 1st Lt. Charles Warner remained with his battery in Nashville.[3]

A few former classmates were scattered across Johnston's opposing army. In Lt. Gen. William J. Hardee's corps, Maj. Frank Maney's Twenty-fourth Battalion, Tennessee Sharpshooters, had suffered many casualties and was now absorbed into the Fourth Tennessee Infantry in Maj. Gen. Benjamin Cheatham's division. Maney had had quite a stellar career so far. Initially dismissed from West Point before the South split away, he joined Garibaldi's army in Italy and then returned when Tennessee joined the Confederacy. His battery was overrun at Fort Donelson and he was captured and sent off to a Union prisoner-of-war camp from which he escaped. Returning to Tennessee, he formed the Twenty-fourth Sharpshooter Battalion. Another former classmate, Capt. Stephen Moreno, remained the assistant adjutant general in Brig. Gen. J. K. Jackson's brigade, a part of Maj. Gen. H. T. Walker's division in Hardee's Corps.[4]

Capt. Horace Twyman commanded Company A of the First Battalion, Georgia Sharpshooters, a part of Brig. Gen. C. H. Stevens's brigade in the same division. In Hood's corps, Maj. James Hamilton was one of the aides to the commander. He would be reassigned to Maj. Gen. Joseph Wheeler's cavalry corps as chief of artillery before the Atlanta campaign ended.[5]

Meanwhile, Murray was accustomed to action. He served with 1st Lt. Charles P. Muhlenberg's battery at Antietam and was brevet-

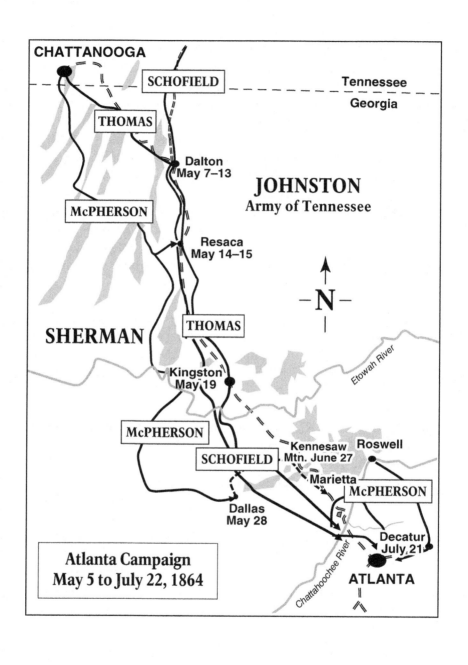

CHATTANOOGA

SCHOFIELD

Tennessee
Georgia

THOMAS

Dalton
May 7–13

JOHNSTON
Army of Tennessee

McPHERSON

Resaca
May 14–15

-N-

THOMAS

SHERMAN

Etowah River

Kingston
May 19

McPHERSON

Kennesaw Roswell
Mtn. June 27

SCHOFIELD

Marietta

McPHERSON

Dallas
May 28

Decatur
July 21

Atlanta Campaign
May 5 to July 22, 1864

Chattahoochee River

ATLANTA

ted for gallantry. At Fredericksburg, he and 1st Lt. James Gilliss's battery covered the middle crossing site and followed Maj. Gen. George W. Getty's division into the lower town. After Hooker took over the Army of the Potomac, Murray and Gilliss's battery were sent south to Fort Monroe with the Ninth Corps in February 1863. A short time later, his battery and Getty's division were sent to reinforce the Union Seventh Corps near Suffolk, Virginia, when the other two Ninth Corps divisions were transferred west.[6]

The appearance of the Ninth Corps near Fort Monroe in February and federal troops near Suffolk caused Richmond to detach Longstreet's First Corps from General Lee's army and send it to southern Virginia to contest the increased Union presence. Two former members of Murray's class, Capt. James Dearing and 1st Lt. Joseph Blount supported Maj. Gen. George Pickett's division when Longstreet launched an attack to the banks of the Nansemond River in mid-April 1863.[7]

When a rebel battery blocked passage of naval forces into the upper Nansemond River, Union forces executed an amphibious assault to capture it. Murray and his men were ferried over the next day to man the captured pieces. Only then did he learn that the battery had been part of Dearing's artillery battalion. Much to Dearing's dismay, the battery had been ordered away from his unit without proper support.[8]

Murray was later cited in official reports for his efforts in constructing and laying out fortifications along the river. By the beginning of May, Longstreet's command returned to Lee's army, and enemy activity around Suffolk gradually subsided. Subsequently, Murray's days were filled with lengthy periods of deadly inactivity. Longing for action, he applied for a transfer to Battery F in the Second US Artillery Regiment. Unlike Tully McCrea's requests, his was quickly granted, and he was soon on his way to Memphis.[9]

Battery F was battle tested and filled with veterans of campaigns in western Missouri and at Vicksburg. It supported Brig. Gen. John W. Fuller's Ohio Brigade with the Sixteenth Corps.[10] The rough-and-tumble Westerners were in stark contrast to the better-uniformed and -disciplined Easterners that Murray was used to. It was likely the men were equally skeptical of the young Eastern lieutenant who took command on July 28.

When General Sherman passed through Memphis in early October, he ordered the Sixteenth Corps to send as many men as possible to the relief of Maj. Gen. William S. Rosecrans at Chattanooga. General Fuller's Ohio Brigade and Murray's battery began a four-hundred-mile march that ended at Prospect, Tennessee, on November 2. The Sixteenth Corps's participation in the Chattanooga campaign was limited. Murray's battery was assigned to guarding several railroads and crossroads over the next four months, until it reached Decatur, Alabama, in March 1864 where it remained for a few weeks. When Fuller's brigade and Murray's battery were ordered to Chattanooga in preparation for the Atlanta Campaign, they arrived by train along with part of Brig. Gen. James C. Veatch's Fourth Division. The rest of the Sixteenth Corps joined them prior to the beginning of Sherman's attack.[11]

Resaca, Kingston, Dallas, and Kennesaw Mountain

While General Thomas's and General Schofield's armies pressed Johnston near Dalton and Rocky Face Gap, McPherson's army emerged from Snake Creek Gap and closed on Resaca. Johnston quickly realized that his line of retreat was in danger, and he shifted his forces back to Resaca where he was joined by Lt. Gen. Leonidas Polk's corps from Mississippi.[12]

The withdrawal to Resaca began a series of delays that characterized the Atlanta Campaign. Sherman would maneuver around Johnston's flank, and Johnston would fall back to the next fortified line to protect his force. Sherman would follow, halt, deploy, reconnoiter, and then maneuver against the new line. This cycle was repeated again and again during the campaign.[13]

McPherson's army, and the Sixteenth Corps in particular, was frequently used to lead Sherman's envelopments. Murray's battery and Fuller's brigade shifted across Sherman's entire front line as Sherman tried to bring Johnston to a decisive battle. Murray's battery was engaged in demonstrations and attacks at Resaca (May 8–16); at Dallas, New Hope Church, and Allatoona Hills (May 25–June 5); and then in operations around Kennesaw Mountain and Marietta (June 9–July 2).[14]

One of his former classmates, Captain Twyman, was seriously wounded when Johnston's army withdrew toward Kingston. A musket ball broke his right leg and lodged in his left. Evacuated from the field, he was first sent to a hospital in Marietta, then Atlanta, and finally was sent home to recover in Virginia in October. He would not rejoin the First Georgia Sharpshooters until April 1865 during the last days of the war.[15]

Despite deplorable weather conditions, Sherman's armies finally reached the base of Kennesaw Mountain. Murray's battery then participated in an hour-long, two-hundred-gun bombardment that tore up trees and enveloped the mountainside in flame and smoke before Sherman's armies began their assault. The men of the Fourth Division then crept up the sides of Little Kennesaw Mountain and occupied a tenuous position just below the summit as the attack progressed. But the steep, rocky face became a major obstacle that could not be crossed in the face of stiff rebel resistance.[16]

On June 1, McPherson's army was shifted from the right to the left flank in the midst of a torrential rainstorm that made the roads almost impassable. Murray's men had trouble getting footholds in the muck and mire, resulting in many tumbles on the slippery, muddy roadways. From that day forward, an almost continuous battle was waged along the entire line. The Fourth Division moved slowly around the base of Kennesaw Mountain with Murray's guns sporadically engaged on June 14, 15, and 17. McPherson's army was shifted to the right again and its emergence on Johnston's left flank forced him to withdraw, this time to fortified positions along the Chattahoochee River.[17]

Upon reaching the new fortified line, the Ohio Brigade and Murray's battery led the assault by General Veatch and the Fourth Division. His guns spoke again and again as the Fourth Division pushed across Nickajack Creek and then at Ruff's Mill against a strong line of rebel works on the hillside beyond. Johnston's defenders were surprised to find their flank turned so quickly, and by morning the entire Chattahoochee line was evacuated.[18]

The Sixteenth Corps was then ordered back to Sherman's left flank to secure a crossing point over the Chattahoochee River at Roswell. There the men of the Fourth Division carried their rifles and cartridge boxes above their heads as they crossed through waist-deep water under heavy fire. A footbridge was thrown across the river, and by July 12 a 710-foot-long double-track trestle bridge was erected by the Sixteenth Corps pioneers. Murray's battery suffered a number of casualties during a violent thunderstorm after crossing the river. When a lightning bolt struck his artillery park, the first sergeant, a private, and the bugler were killed.[19]

Meanwhile, Johnston's withdrawals had successfully delayed Sherman's three armies for seventy-four days, but Richmond was not pleased. His final movement across the Chattahoochee River prompted his dismissal, and Maj. Gen. John Bell Hood replaced him. Hood immediately sensed an opportunity to take the offensive when Sherman's armies were approaching Atlanta's outer defenses. He ordered a massive assault from carefully prepared positions along Peach Tree Creek into a gap between Thomas's and Schofield's armies on July 19 but was badly repulsed after a day-long battle. One day later, Hood withdrew his army into the defenses of Atlanta.[20]

While Sherman's other two armies crept up to the outer Atlanta defenses, McPherson's army was sent east to Decatur to prevent any rebel reinforcements from reaching Atlanta. McPherson's men got right to work. Sherman's orders were clear: "Keep every man . . . at work in destroying the railroad by tearing up track, burning the ties, and iron, and twisting the bars when hot. Officers should be instructed that bars simply bent may be used again, but if when red hot they are twisted out of line they cannot be used again. Pile the ties in to shape for a bonfire, put the rails across, and when red hot in the middle, let a man at each end twist the bar so that its surface becomes spiral."[21]

The Battle of Atlanta

After destroying the railroad at Decatur, General McPherson turned his army westward to rejoin Sherman's armies before Atlanta. His advance was only moderately contested, and soon two of his corps straddled the Augusta-Georgia railroad on the left flank of Sherman's lines facing the eastern side of the Atlanta defenses. An advance by all three armies toward the city took place the next morning.[22]

On July 21, McPherson sent Maj. Gen. John A. Logan's Seventeenth Corps forward to occupy a prominent bald hill from which

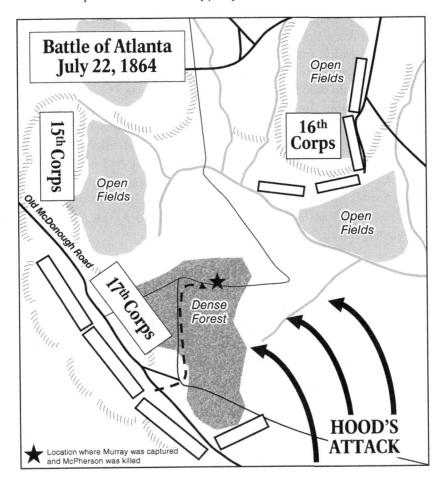

Battle of Atlanta
July 22, 1864

Open Fields

16th Corps

15th Corps

Open Fields

Open Fields

Old McDonough Road

17th Corps

Dense Forest

HOOD'S ATTACK

★ Location where Murray was captured and McPherson was killed

downtown Atlanta and its inner defenses could be seen. Attacks and counterattacks took place for several hours before Logan's men secured the hill mass from determined rebel defenders that evening. Meanwhile, Sherman wanted the railroad completely destroyed between Decatur and Atlanta. McPherson was ordered to send the Sixteenth Corps back to begin its destruction. General Fuller, now in command of the Fourth Division, was ordered to send his Second Brigade back to Decatur to guard the army's wagon trains and begin the process. His First Brigade, including Murray and Battery F, were attached to the Seventeenth Corps.[23]

The First Brigade occupied rising ground about five hundred yards behind the Seventeenth Corps's main line of battle. A wooded area and a ravine intervened between the two positions. Murray's Battery F occupied a position along the Old McDonough Road within the main defenses of the Seventeenth Corps.[24]

That evening, quiet reigned on the battlefield. From a bald hill in the Seventeenth Corps line, large rebel troop movements were observed moving within the Atlanta defenses. McPherson became apprehensive. The cavalry protecting his left flank had been ordered away, and the Sixteenth Corps was about to depart for Decatur. He was convinced that a flank attack was highly possible and sought relief from Sherman's order to send the Sixteenth Corps toward Decatur the next morning.[25]

Murray Is Captured

McPherson was correct to worry. After dark on July 21, Hood pulled Hardee's corps of four divisions out of the Atlanta defenses and sent them fifteen miles southeast to strike McPherson's left flank. When Hardee's assault began, Cheatham's corps was to attack the center of Sherman's line to prevent any reinforcements from shifting to the south.[26]

By morning on July 22, Sherman finally agreed to delay the Sixteenth Corps's movement. McPherson's general uneasiness caused him to immediately order Maj. Gen. Grenville Dodge, now in command of the Sixteenth Corps, to shift its Second Division into an open field behind Logan's Seventeenth Corps. The Second Division had barely reached its new area when its skirmishers came under fire from Hardee's advancing gray lines coming through the forest in the rear of the Seventeenth Corps.

Although a dawn attack was promised by Hardee, it was noon before all four of his divisions were in position. They had marched hard all night, and stragglers were everywhere. Just before 1 P.M., two divisions slammed into the rear and left flank of McPherson's army while his other two divisions attacked the Seventeenth Corps along the Old McDonough Road.[27]

Hearing the heavy firing, Dodge ordered the Second Division to form a line of battle facing south. Fuller's nearby First Brigade was added to form the base of an L-shaped defense with the Second Division. Needing more artillery, Dodge called for Murray's battery to be returned, and Capt. George Robinson, Fuller's chief of artillery, galloped off to find him.[28]

When Murray received the order, he limbered his guns and led the battery at a trot along the Old McDonough Road with his guns in front. He turned east through a heavily wooded area between the two corps positions. Soon after the battery entered the woods, the head of the column was overrun by rebel soldiers. It is conceivable that Murray cried out to unlimber and reverse the guns, but there was no time to do so. Officers yelled for the men to run. Men jumped from the gun carriages and ran to the rear. Others tried to escape in the underbrush but were quickly swept up by the rebel skirmishers.

Many of Murray's men escaped and returned to friendly lines where they were reassigned to other units. Two privates were wounded, and a corporal and another private were killed in the melee. The rebels captured Murray, another officer, a sergeant, a corporal, the bugler, and eleven privates. In addition, Hardee's forces captured over a hundred horses, as well as all the battery's guns, limbers, more than three hundred rounds of ammunition, and one caisson. Two days later the caisson was found between the skirmish lines during Sherman's advance toward Atlanta.[29]

A number of official reports described the events of July 22 in detail. General McPherson was killed earlier in the same woods where Murray's battery was captured. Sherman's report briefly mentioned the loss of the battery. Other reports included somewhat incriminating words about moving the battery without infantry support on the battlefield. General Dodge and his chief of artillery reported that Murray's movement was in accordance with orders and no fault was found. Battery F was soon reconstituted. However, its service record does not mention the loss of guns or men, and it was back in action again under a new commander within a few weeks.[30]

When Murray and the others reached Atlanta, the enlisted men were sent to Andersonville, while he and the other officer were sent to Camp Oglethorpe, an officers' prison at Macon, Georgia. That camp, located between the Ocmulgee River and the railroad tracks, consisted of fifteen to twenty acres surrounded by a stockade fence. The open areas were covered with a number of sheds and stalls, constructed from whatever materials were on hand within the stockade. A large building used as a hospital stood near the center of the area.

As many as nineteen hundred prisoners were crowded into the camp when Murray arrived. Treatment was harsh, rations were limited, and the death rate was high. Disease often swept the camp. In March 1865, a paroled officer sent a letter to the Adjutant General's Office in Washington detailing the fate of several Union officers held at Camp Oglethorpe. He wrote that 1st Lt. Albert Murray, the twenty-four-year-old West Pointer from the Class of 1862, had died of typhoid on or about August 12, 1864.[31] Thrice-brevetted Murray was the fourth member of his class to die during the war.

15

Mackenzie and McIntire
in the Shenandoah Valley

West Point, January 1866. The dull pain in Tully's leg still ached in the cold, and he knew it always would. He worried about his future, as he still needed a cane to walk to class. The medical review board forced a number of disabled instructors from the ranks of the army last year, and his own status with the Mathematics Department seemed predictable only through the end of the current academic year. A year ago, he could not stand in the classroom for any period of time. The doctors then told him that his leg was inflamed and sliced it open to allow the infection to drain, leaving him confined to his bed for several weeks. West Point was not Beaufort where lots of visitors stopped by to see him. Here it was limited to a few classmates who visited from time to time, and he was lonely.

Receiving letters became an important event during his long bedridden days in Quarters 3. He received letters from Belle, Alice, Sam Talbott, and Ranald Mackenzie's mother. One of her letters described how Mackenzie was wounded again during the battle at Cedar Creek in October with Sheridan's Army of the Shenandoah. Tully wrote home about Mackenzie's exploits: "He is the bravest man that I have ever seen, and I have seen a great many brave men. His bravery approaches rashness and foolhardiness and he too frequently exposed his life unnecessarily. This is the fourth battle that he had been wounded in, and it is miraculous how he is so well. He always gets well of his wounds and his mother writes that the doctors say that he will entirely recover from his present ones."[1]

Perhaps being at his mother's house helped Mackenzie more than any Union hospital. While he was recovering there, he was appointed a brigade commander with the Sixth Corps and then promoted to brigadier general by the end of the year. Before that happened, though, Mackenzie

Fig. 15.1. Belle Grove under Attack (J. E. Taylor). *LOC*

stopped by to see Tully in Quarters 3 and told him about his command and Sam McIntire before returning to the Shenandoah Valley.

The Shenandoah Valley Campaign—October 1864

Col. Ranald S. Mackenzie, USV, and the Second Connecticut Heavy Artillery Regiment were almost to Ashby's Gap on October 13 when they and the Sixth Corps were suddenly ordered to return to Cedar Creek. Mackenzie was baffled until it became clear that Maj. Gen. Jubal Early's command had reoccupied Fisher's Hill, just south of Strasburg.

Maj. Gen. Philip Sheridan's Army of the Shenandoah had followed Early's rebels up the valley after the Battle of Winchester in September 1864. Then, in early October as Sheridan's army slowly withdrew toward Winchester, his cavalry destroyed grain, mills, and

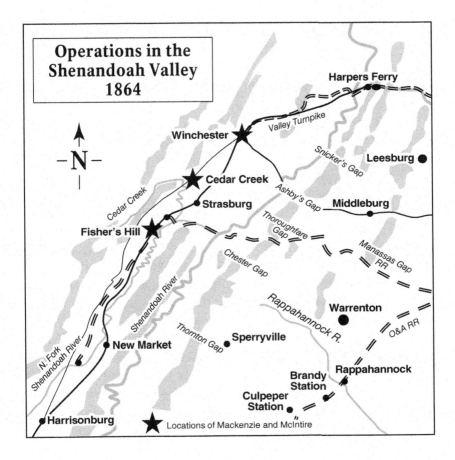

Operations in the Shenandoah Valley 1864

-N-

Harpers Ferry

Valley Turnpike

Winchester

Snicker's Gap

Leesburg

Cedar Creek

Ashby's Gap

Cedar Creek

Strasburg

Middleburg

Thoroughfare Gap

Fisher's Hill

Manassas Gap RR

Chester Gap

Shenandoah River

Rappahannock R.

Warrenton

O&A RR

Thornton Gap

Sperryville

N. Fork Shenandoah River

New Market

Rappahannock

Brandy Station

Culpeper Station

Harrisonburg

Locations of Mackenzie and McIntire

barns and left the valley ablaze. They eliminated a major source of supplies for Lee's army, but the citizens of the valley later called it "The Burning." Sheridan's three corps and two cavalry divisions halted and camped on both sides of the Valley Turnpike near Cedar Creek. With no rebel forces interfering with his actions, Sheridan had released Maj. Gen. Horatio Wright's Sixth Corps to return to the Army of the Potomac then located around Petersburg. When Early reoccupied Fisher's Hill, Sheridan revoked his order sending the Sixth Corps east.[2]

Upon its return, the Sixth Corps occupied a ridgeline above the

Meadow Brook ravine just north of Sheridan's headquarters at Belle Grove. Brig. Gen. Frank Wheaton's First Division was located on a flat area atop the ridge. Col. Joseph E. Hamlin's Second Brigade, with Mackenzie's "Second Connecticut Heavies," was located on the extreme right of the First Division area.[3]

Below the Sixth Corps and closer to Cedar Creek, Brig. Gen. William H. Emory's Nineteenth Corps occupied entrenched camps on the western side of the Valley Turnpike, and the camps of Brig. Gen. George Crook's Eighth camps lay on the east. Between them was Sheridan's headquarters at Belle Grove.

Mackenzie knew that only one other classmate, Sam McIntire with Capt. Charles H. Peirce's Battery B&L, Second US Artillery, was part of Sheridan's army. McIntire was camped some distance behind the Sixth Corps with Custer's cavalry division along the western flank of the army near Buffalo Run. Brig. Gen. Wesley Merritt's cavalry division covered the northern flank of the army.[4]

Sheridan, confident that Early would not attack, left Wright in charge and on October 16 rode off to Washington to attend a meeting. The camps were quiet, and most of the soldiers enjoyed the beautiful autumn weather. On October 18, Mackenzie's soldiers lined up at tables manned by electoral commissioners from Connecticut to vote for either Lincoln or McClellan. They identified their hometowns, placed their votes in envelopes, and handed them to one of the commissioners who carried their votes back to be duly counted in the state.[5]

The next morning, the camp was quiet, and Mackenzie, an early riser, listened and watched as his soldiers ate breakfast around him. A heavy fog lay in the ravine as he looked toward Belle Grove. He had been in command of this regiment for just four months. It was much better trained now than when he first took command just after Cold Harbor. He had spent a week listening and watching after he took command before deciding that the volunteers needed a stiff dose of discipline. The movement to Petersburg provided an excellent training opportunity before the regiment was thrown into combat again.

Washington and Winchester

Before his assignment to Sheridan's command, Mackenzie's Second Connecticut Heavy Artillery arrived at Petersburg with the Sixth Corps and occupied positions near Battery 27, the same position defended by James Dearing earlier that month. During an attack toward the Weldon Railroad on June 22, his regiment lost ten killed and nine wounded. His command tour was interrupted when a sharpshooter shot off the first two fingers of his right hand as he stood on top of one of the entrenchments. This time he recovered at his mother's new home near Newport, Rhode Island.[6]

When Early's rebels closed on Washington in early July, Mackenzie returned to his regiment "with a rag wrapped around his abbreviated fingers." His regiment was sent north with the Sixth Corps to help repel Early's soldiers near Washington. Late in the afternoon of July 11, the first units of the Sixth Corps reached the capital city and occupied Fort Stevens. Mackenzie's regiment arrived early the next morning, marched up Seventh Street, and camped at Fort Kearney that evening. The increased Union presence at Fort Stevens caused Early to break off the attack, and his raiders marched away that evening. The Sixth and Nineteenth Corps soon took up the hunt to find him. They crossed the Potomac, marched through Leesburg, and spent time in a fruitless search in the Shenandoah Valley before returning to Washington on July 23.[7]

Upon return to Washington, the Second Connecticut Heavies were detached from the Sixth Corps and sent to man the same forts it had defended sixty-six days before. The regiment's stay in garrison was not long. Early's defeat of Union forces in the Shenandoah Valley caused the Second Connecticut Heavies to be reassigned to the Sixth Corps twenty-four hours later. The long roll sounded and the men, cursing and complaining, fell in. It rejoined the Sixth Corps near Frederick, Maryland, on August 3.[8]

The new Army of the Shenandoah was organized under General Sheridan who soon put his three cavalry divisions and the Sixth and Nineteenth Corps to work. For several weeks, Mackenzie's regi-

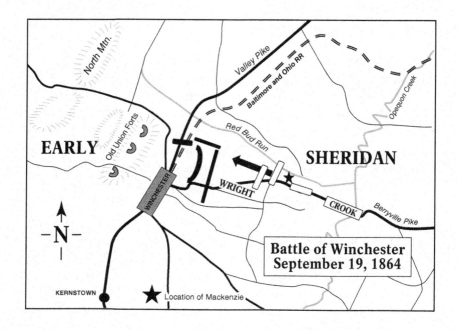

Battle of Winchester
September 19, 1864

ment marched up and down the Shenandoah Valley, something the historian of the regiment called "marching and counter-marching" and other historians called a "mimic war." Sheridan's final movement left his divisions in danger of having their supply lines severed. As he moved his army out of danger, he decided to attack Early at Winchester.[9]

Mackenzie continued his training as a regimental commander during the Third Battle of Winchester on September 19, 1864. The Second Connecticut Heavies and Upton's Second Brigade were part of General Wright's reserve during the initial assault. The Sixth Corps attack began well but sputtered to a halt on the far side of the Berryville Canyon. When a Confederate counterattack threatened to exploit a gap between the Sixth and Nineteenth Corps, Wright ordered his reserve to plug the gap.

Upton led his brigade along the right flank of the Sixth Corps into a grove of trees where he ordered his men to fix bayonets and await his order to fire. When the advancing rebel infantry was just two hundred yards away, he yelled out, "Ready, aim, fire!" then shouted, "Forward, charge!" Mackenzie's Second Connecticut Heavies and two other regiments rushed forward. The assault stunned the advancing rebel infantrymen and forced them to pull back, closing the gap between the two Corps. Twice more that day, Mackenzie's regiment led the Second Brigade in successful attacks against Early's infantry.

At one point, Mackenzie rode back and forth in plain sight of enemy riflemen. Musket balls whizzed around him, and he told the men on the ground around him, "I guess those fellows will get tired of firing at me by and by." He continued the practice in the afternoon, but was forced to halt when his horse was cut in half by a solid shot, toppling him to the ground. Undaunted by the tumble, he raised his hat on the tip of his saber and led the Second Connecticut Heavies forward against rebel breastworks near the town. He jokingly referred to the incident later as "dismounting without the numbers."[10]

Four days later Sheridan's army had pushed Early's men back to Fisher's Hill. During the next battle, the Second Connecticut Heavies overwhelmed the rebels' lower breastworks and climbed the steep hillside. The regimental historian later wrote they were the first to plant the Union flag on top that day. Mackenzie's actions in both battles were cited in Wright's official report, and he was soon recommended for another brevet promotion.[11]

The Battle of Cedar Creek

Over the next few weeks, Jubal Early looked for a good time and place to conduct a major attack against Sheridan's army. After a reconnaissance was made of the Union camps at Cedar Creek by some of Early's engineers, one of Early's division commanders suggested a plan during a late night meeting on October 18. He believed he could take much of the Second Corps along the North Fork of the Shenandoah River to attack the rear of Sheridan's army while the rest of the Second Corps attacked its left flank. After lengthy discussion, Early agreed to the plan and set it in motion.[12]

After crossing the river around 4 A.M. on October 19, the flank-ing force moved through a heavy fog toward the rear of the Eighth Corps camps. Their surprise attack an hour later sent Crook's sleepy and half-clothed soldiers reeling across the road toward Emory's Nineteenth Corps camps. Several units made determined stands, but within the hour both corps defenses were swept away. Fleeing horse teams, wagons, ambulances, and disorganized units soon filled the Valley Pike headed toward Winchester.[13]

When it became clear that the other two corps were falling back, Wright ordered the Sixth Corps into defensive positions above the Meadow Brook Ravine. Mackenzie's soldiers were already up and brewing coffee long before the drums beat assembly. The Second Brigade moved about a hundred yards away from their camp and went into position along the ridgeline overlooking Meadow Brook and the Hite Road.[14]

The heavy morning fog attenuated the sounds of the ongoing battle below the ridge. Nearby, Sixth Corps artillery batteries fired blindly at any noise in the mist. Confused and disorganized groups of soldiers from the Nineteenth Corps rushed up the ridge, often forc-ing Mackenzie's men and others to frequently open gaps in their lines to let them through. Without any warning, gray silhouettes began emerging from the mist at the base of the ridge.[15]

For the next thirty minutes, the sustained rifle fire from the First and Third Divisions atop the ridge halted the rebel advance. But the withdrawal of the Nineteenth Corps uncovered the Sixth Corps's right flank, and Wright finally ordered it to withdraw by battalions. When a messenger arrived with the order, Mackenzie was horrified, "My God, I cannot! This line will break if I do." Then a musket ball struck his right heel. Wounded and limping slightly, he mounted his horse, but a few seconds later it was struck in the head, spun around two or three times, and fell dead, sending Mackenzie head over heels to the ground.[16]

As he dusted himself off, a second messenger rode up. The Sec-ond Brigade commander was wounded, and he was directed to take command of the brigade. With Confederate battle flags not more

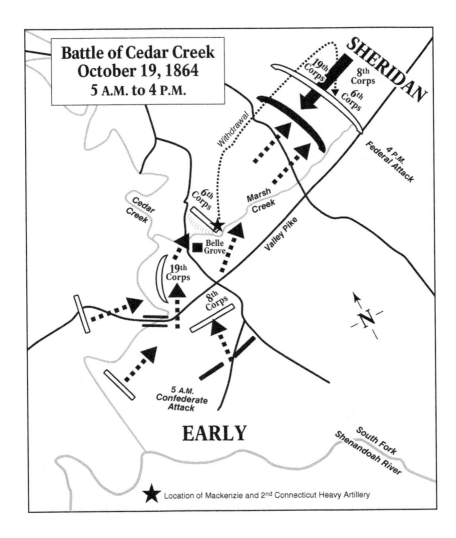

**Battle of Cedar Creek
October 19, 1864**
5 A.M. to 4 P.M.

SHERIDAN

19th Corps   8th Corps

6th Corps

4 P.M. Federal Attack

Withdrawal

6th Corps

Marsh Creek

Cedar Creek

Valley Pike

Belle Grove

19th Corps

8th Corps

N

5 A.M. Confederate Attack

EARLY

South Fork Shenandoah River

★ Location of Mackenzie and 2nd Connecticut Heavy Artillery

than three hundred yards away, he mounted another horse and yelled, "Rise up, retreat!" and the Second Brigade headed back to the next ridgeline. An hour later and almost a mile farther away, the First and Third Divisions gathered their wayward units on the western side of a hill mass near Middletown, and Mackenzie went to the rear to have his wound dressed.[17]

Near 9 A.M., General Wright made a major decision. He needed time to form a defense with his infantry and ordered both cavalry divisions forward to delay Early's advance up the Valley Pike to give him time to establish a new defensive line behind them. Custer's Third Cavalry Division and McIntire's battery trotted east and fell in on the left of Merritt's Second Cavalry Division across the Valley Pike. McIntire's gunners quickly joined four other horse batteries firing as fast as they could sponge and load. The blue troopers drew heavy fire from Early's artillery and infantry as they slowly pulled back, their rapid-firing carbines and cannons giving Wright the time he needed to build a new defensive line.[18]

Meanwhile, Sheridan left his hotel in Winchester unaware that his army was under attack. Mounted on his favorite horse, Rienzi, he began the twenty-mile ride to Belle Grove. Soon he ran into wagons and disorganized units moving to the rear. Issuing rapid-fire instructions to his staff to turn them back toward the fight, Sheridan galloped south toward Cedar Creek.[19]

As soon as he arrived at the new defensive line around 11 A.M., he met with Wright and the other corps commanders. When told they were ready to commence a retreat, Sheridan bristled and informed them they would be back in their camps that night. In expectation of an imminent attack, he ordered the rest of the Sixth and Nineteenth Corps to come up to the new defensive line and sent Custer's and Merritt's cavalry divisions to opposite flanks.[20]

Three hours later, bugles sounded, flags were raised, the cavalry drew sabers, and the Army of the Shenandoah stepped off. The Nineteenth and Sixth Corps began a great wheel to its left and pressed the rebel infantry back down the Pike. In the face of a determined rebel defense, Mackenzie led the first line of his Second Brigade forward but was momentarily halted by heavy fire. Riding out in front of his first line, he exhorted the soldiers to try again. Checked once more, the reserve was called up, and a final effort finally drove the enemy from their front.[21]

During that final effort, a shell or shot grazed Mackenzie's shoulder, knocking him off his horse again, and he suffered his fourth wound of the war. With his left arm temporarily paralyzed, he ordered his men to lift him into his saddle, and a sergeant led the horse forward. When Sheridan later noticed his wounds, he ordered him to the rear, but Mackenzie implored the general to let him stay until victory was certain.[22]

After some initial success, Sheridan's advance up the Valley Pike bogged down. Sensing an opportunity, the leftmost division on Early's defensive line launched a flank attack toward the Nineteenth Corps but was repulsed. The attack opened a gap in Early's lines, and Sheridan sent Custer's troopers to exploit it. Custer and his blue riders drew sabers and charged toward the unprotected left flank, with McIntire's battery following as fast as it could. The sight of the thundering troopers headed toward them proved too much for the gray defenders. Early's line wavered and then broke, his soldiers running wildly to the rear toward the safety of the bridge at Cedar Creek.[23]

Unable to keep up with the fast-moving Union cavalry divisions, McIntire's battery halted to guard the Cedar Creek Bridge after the blue troopers chased Early's men across. Following more slowly, Sheridan's infantry reoccupied their old camps and eagerly watched their foes retreat in great disorder. Remnants of Early's command limped up the Valley to New Market and ceased to be a serious threat.[24]

A few days after the battle, Capt. George Gillespie joined Sheridan's staff as his chief engineer. McIntire and Peirce's battery rode north to Pleasant Valley, Maryland, to recover and refit for the rest of the year. Mackenzie again traveled to Newport to recover. His actions at Cedar Creek were recognized in several reports, resulting in a fifth brevet for gallantry and promotion to brigadier general, US Volunteers. When he returned to active duty with the First Division a month later, he found himself still in command of the Second Brigade.[25]

16

Dearing at High Bridge

West Point, January 1866. That morning, Tully reached the officers' mess just as breakfast was being served. He and Frank Hamilton shared biscuits and coffee. Frank mentioned that he heard recently that James Dearing's body was moved from his family cemetery on his uncle's estate at Castle Craig and reburied in Lynchburg with other Confederate generals. Dearing had done well at West Point but resigned in April 1861 when Virginia seceded to join the Confederacy. He was initially assigned to the Washington Artillery and later appointed to command the Lynchburg Artillery. He participated in almost every major eastern campaign during the war as an artilleryman with Pickett's Division and later as a cavalry commander around Petersburg.

Of all their former classmates, Dearing was the one with whom Tully's classmates had the most frequent encounters during the war. Tully and John Egan were on the receiving end of part of his bombardment at Gettysburg. Egan exchanged fire with Dearing's cavalry near Nottoway Court House just a few days before he was captured at Ream's Station. Most of them knew that Dearing commanded a cavalry force around Petersburg later in the war and that he had gotten married. It was likely that Ranald Mackenzie's troopers crossed swords with some of Dearing's men near Amelia Court House during Lee's retreat to Appomattox. When he died just after the end of the war, he became the last Confederate general to die of wounds suffered during the war. Perhaps one day members of the class would pay their respects to his wife and daughter as they had with Henry Farley's wife in Winchester long ago. During one of his visits to West Point, Mackenzie had explained to Tully more of the story of Dearing's final days and the battle of High Bridge during Lee's retreat.

Fig. 16.1. High Bridge (Timothy O'Sullivan). *LOC*

Actions around Petersburg

Two months after Gettysburg, Maj. Gen. George Pickett and his much-reduced division were assigned to the Department of Virginia and North Carolina at Petersburg. When they arrived, James Dearing and his artillery battalion camped near a farmhouse outside the city. Close proximity to the farmhouse led him to meet Roxanna Birchett, the daughter of the wealthy Prince George County planter who lived there, and they soon fell in love.

By November 1863, Pickett, commanding the department, found himself in need of cavalry to help guard the Weldon Railroad and created a composite brigade of cavalry units from Georgia, North Carolina, and Virginia. He recommended that Major Dearing be placed in command with a temporary promotion to colonel. His task was to maintain watch along the Weldon Railroad, one of the key supply routes into Petersburg and Richmond.[1]

Undaunted by his new assignment, Dearing found time to marry Roxanna in Petersburg on January 27, 1864. He did not get much of a honeymoon. His cavalry brigade was ordered to immediately take part in a raid on New Bern, North Carolina. His troopers loaded aboard railcars with Pickett's infantry, his old artillery battalion (Read's Thirty-eighth Virginia Artillery) with Joseph Blount's Lynchburg battery, and Maj. Gen. Robert F. Hoke's infantry brigade.[2]

The New Bern raid to relieve the Union supply blockade on the Neuse River was unsuccessful, but two months later a similar attack at Plymouth cemented Dearing's role as a cavalryman. On April 29, 1864, he was promoted to brigadier general in the Provisional Army of the Confederate States. In early May, General Hoke's force moved to attack New Bern again, but the initial operations of Maj. Gen. Benjamin Butler's Army of the James against Petersburg prompted Gen. P. G. T. Beauregard, commanding the Department of Southern Virginia and North Carolina, to call Hoke's force back to bolster the defenses around Petersburg and Richmond. Upon their return, Hoke's infantry and Dearing's cavalry were sent to reinforce the Howlett Line opposite Bermuda Hundred, while Blount's Lynchburg battery remained near Swift Creek, closer to Petersburg.[3]

While Grant was contemplating shifting Meade's army across the James River at Cold Harbor in early June, an assault on Petersburg was already under way. An infantry force under Maj. Gen. Quincy Gillmore and Brig. Gen. August V. Kautz's cavalry division from the Army of the James attacked the outer line of defenses east of Petersburg on June 9. There were few defenders left in the city, mostly old men and young boys who made up the several militia companies of its home guard. Gillmore's infantry and Kautz's cavalry attempted to penetrate the thinly manned, horseshoe-shaped series of batteries, redoubts, and trenches called the Dimmock Line, which stretched around Petersburg for ten miles.[4]

"The Battle of Old Men and Young Boys"

Confederate brigadier general Henry Wise, in charge of the Petersburg defenses, sent word to Beauregard that the federals were attacking his outer defenses, and he needed reinforcements. By mid-morning, Beauregard released a few units from the Howlett Line to help. Dearing's cavalry brigade with one battery of horse artillery left Dunn's farm, seven miles north of the city, to rush to its defense.[5]

His troopers and guns entered the city around noon at the gallop. The battery's six-horse teams careened through the streets, their hoofs striking sparks on the cobblestones while the caissons bounced from side to side behind them. Citizens recognized Capt. Edward Graham's Petersburg battery as it passed by and cheered it on. The gunners called out to their wives to get inside, as the Yankees were coming.

Dearing led his column out the Jerusalem Plank Road toward Battery 27 on the Dimmock Line. Kautz's cavalry division had already pierced the line, forcing the home-guard militia back. Dashing up the Plank Road, Dearing ordered one gun section positioned on Reservoir Hill and the others on either side of the Cameron House. He then dismounted his cavalry regiments and spread them out along the crest of Reservoir Hill, just as the tattered militia unit fell back through his line.

Dearing's guns and cavalry arrived not a moment too soon. Union troopers and a section of artillery advanced toward them on the Jerusalem Plank Road. Graham's guns immediately opened fire, and Dearing ordered one regiment to charge the advancing blue column. The shock of the charge and cannon fire caused Kautz's force to halt and then rapidly withdraw. By 3 P.M., Dearing's men had reoccupied Battery 27, recovered a spiked Union gun, and captured several prisoners. Dearing swung his regiments across the road, threw up breastworks, and sent a message to Beauregard saying, "The enemy are repulsed and the city is safe. But should they attack again more troops will be necessary for its defense."[6]

With Lee's army finally flowing into the defenses of Richmond and Petersburg, his cavalry brigade was reassigned to Rooney Lee's cavalry division on June 19. Dearing liked his new assignment, as it kept him closer to home. When his daughter was born, he was ecstatic and presented her to his men during a brigade review much the same as Roman generals of old. His letters home were filled with his love for Roxanna and the baby and he constantly reminded them to stay healthy.[7]

The Great Cattle Raid

Actions by the Union army to cut off supplies to Petersburg greatly limited the city's access to beef. Hoping to alleviate the situation, Wade Hampton and his cavalry commanders concocted a plan to capture a large herd located behind Union lines near City Point. Dearing's brigade and the rest of Rooney Lee's division joined Brig. Gen. Tom Rosser's cavalry brigades on August 15 as the plan began to unfold. At midnight, Dearing's brigade rode to Cocke's Mill on the James River to halt any Union reinforcements coming from the east. The rest of Rooney Lee's division headed toward Prince George Court House to hold off any Union advance from that direction.

Before dawn on August 16, Hampton, Rosser's brigade, and another cavalry unit surprised the Union cavalry guarding the cattle herd at Coggins Point about five miles from City Point. The herd was rounded up and started toward Confederate lines. By noon, Union cavalry pounded along various routes trying to cut off the raiders and recover the cattle. Two hours later, Hampton had the herd over the Blackwater River. Dearing's and Rosser's brigades protected the crossing and then destroyed the bridge. For the rest of the day, Dearing's troopers repeatedly delayed any belated Union attempts to cut them off. The next morning over twenty-four hundred cattle, three hundred prisoners, wagons, and the cavalry passed through Confederate lines into Petersburg. General Grant was later asked by a reporter at City Point, "When do you expect to starve out Lee and capture Richmond?" He answered sharply, "Never, if our armies continue to supply him with beef-cattle."[8]

The Road to High Bridge

In the waning days of the Confederacy in March 1865, General Dearing rode with General Rosser's cavalry division. Gen. Robert E. Lee had finally approved Rosser's request to place Dearing in command of the Laurel Brigade in mid-March. When he left his old brigade, he took a small staff with him, including his former classmate, the now-recovered Richard Kinney, who was assigned to take charge of any dismounted troopers in Dearing's new command. In late March, Rosser led his troopers to camps on the Nottoway River on the extreme right of Lee's army around Petersburg. Within a few days, they moved again to cover a gap that existed between Lee's right flank and Pickett's few infantry brigades at Five Forks, protecting the South Side Railroad.[9]

Rosser's sadly reduced division reflected the losses sustained in its last battle with Sheridan's cavalry in the Shenandoah Valley. Supplies were short, and the lack of forage showed. Dearing described the condition of his horses in a letter to his wife: "My pony does not look like his former self," and "the ambulances and horses are in miserable shape." Supplies were increasingly difficult to find.[10]

In late March, Grant gathered his commanders together at City Point to discuss with President Lincoln the final stages of the war. A day or so later, Grant directed Sheridan to move his cavalry past his far left flank and be ready to strike Lee's right and rear. Sheridan's cavalry arrived near Dinwiddie Court House on March 29 and the next day advanced toward Five Forks.[11] Brig. Gen. MacKenzie, now a cavalry division commander, joined Sheridan's command.

Behind his breastworks at Five Forks, General Pickett directed his infantry and cavalry to push Sheridan's troopers away from the South Side Railroad. Near 2 P.M. on March 31, Rosser's and Rooney Lee's divisions attacked one of Sheridan's brigades occupying Fitzgerald's Ford while Pickett's infantry attacked the upper ford over Chamberlain's Bed, a mile north. Rosser sent Dearing's and Brig. Gen. John McCausland's dismounted troopers against the entrenched Union defenders at Fitzgerald's Ford, but they were forced back with a number of casualties. Meanwhile, Pickett's infantry successfully crossed the upper ford and pushed Sheridan's troopers away from Five Forks and back toward Dinwiddie Court House.[12]

Pickett soon realized that evening that his advanced position along the road to Dinwiddie Court House was vulnerable, and he withdrew to Five Forks. His elation at successfully halting Sheridan was dampened by General Lee's disappointment in not pushing Sheridan farther away from the railway. Lee directed him to "hold Five Forks at all hazards."[13]

Pickett's command was composed of a few infantry brigades from his and Maj. Gen. Bushrod Johnson's infantry divisions and Fitzhugh Lee's three cavalry divisions. They occupied prepared defenses around the intersection at Five Forks. Rooney Lee's cavalrymen were sent to the right flank, and Maj. Gen. Tom Munford's to the left. Rosser's division with Dearing's and McCausland's brigades was Pickett's reserve and was located north of Hatcher's Run protecting the wagon trains. That location had major implications before the sun went down. Confident that Sheridan would not attack on April 1, Pickett and Fitzhugh Lee joined Rosser near Hatcher's Run for an afternoon shad bake.[14]

When Sheridan's late afternoon attack began, messengers did not find the two generals relaxing at Hatcher's Run until it was almost too late. The Union assault by Sheridan's cavalry and Maj. Gen. Gouverneur Warren's Fifth Corps overwhelmed Pickett's defenses and almost trapped Pickett as he galloped down the road to Five Forks. Rosser's brigades remained north of Hatcher's Run until the next day.[15]

Sheridan's successful attack captured thousands of Pickett's soldiers. His success prompted Grant to order a general advance by his entire force around Petersburg. The loss of Five Forks unraveled Gen. Robert E. Lee's defenses, and he ordered his forces to begin withdrawing from Richmond and Petersburg. His forces were closely followed by Sheridan's cavalry and Meade's infantry. As Lee's columns left the two cities on multiple routes, Dearing's Laurel Brigade skirmished with Sheridan's cavalry several times along the Namozine Road on the way to Amelia Court House, the consolidation point for Lee's army.

Dearing and his brigade arrived at Amelia Court House tired and hungry on April 5. He started a search for food and forage, but there was none remaining. A day later, Rosser's division was sent to halt the capture of part of Lee's wagon trains as the army moved farther south. Meanwhile, Mackenzie reported that large numbers of rebel cavalry, artillery, and infantry were present near Amelia Court House. Sheridan ordered him "to feel the enemy frequently and make constant demonstrations without pushing them too hard."[16]

At roughly the same time, Rosser rode along the road to Amelia Springs and saw a line of Union troopers with the captured wagons passing on a ridgeline ahead of them. He turned in his saddle and called out to Dearing's brigade to "ride over them!" With Dearing in the lead, the Laurel Brigade spurred to a gallop and slammed into the blue column with sabers swinging left and right. The violent charge sent the Union cavalry fleeing into nearby woods. Dearing was slightly wounded in the arm, and several of his officers were lost. His gallantry was later cited in Fitzhugh Lee's official report.[17]

Dearing and his tired and hungry troopers arrived in Longstreet's camp near Farmville the next day. Again, they unsuccessfully sought forage and rations. When Rosser reported to General Longstreet, he was informed about a Union task force headed toward High Bridge. Longstreet made it clear that it was imperative that the bridge be kept open to allow Lee's infantry and trains to cross. He ordered Rosser and Munford to take their cavalry divisions and capture or destroy the Union task force "*if it took the last man of his command to do it*" (italics in the original). Bugles rent the air, and Dearing's weary troopers climbed back into their saddles.[18]

Battle at High Bridge

The small Union task force from the Army of the James left Burkesville before dawn on April 6. When Maj. Gen. Edward Ord, now commanding the Army of the James, received word that Longstreet's First Corps was close to the bridge, he sent his chief of staff, Brig. Gen. Theodore Read, to recall it. After Read caught up to the task force, Col. Francis Washburn assured him that he could destroy the bridge. Solidly built and 160 feet high, the High Bridge was almost a half mile long with a wagon bridge alongside it. The Union task force reached the area first, but Washburn's first attempt was turned back

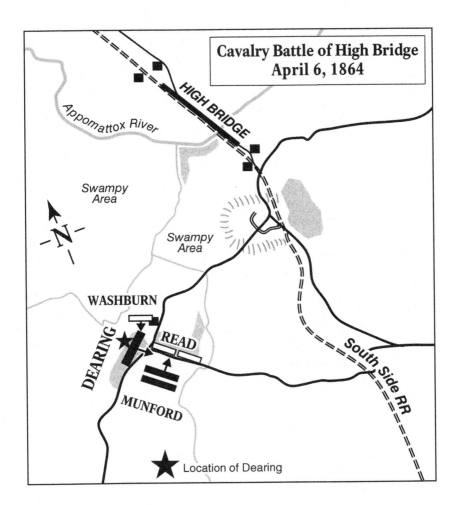

**Cavalry Battle of High Bridge
April 6, 1864**

HIGH BRIDGE

Appomattox River

Swampy Area

Swampy Area

WASHBURN

DEARING

READ

MUNFORD

South Side RR

-N-

★ Location of Dearing

by the home guards protecting the bridge. While Washburn prepared a flanking attack, Read moved the rest of the small task force behind a rail fence near Watson's farm.[19]

Around 1 P.M., Dearing's lead regiment approached a wooded area and ran into the Union infantry. When Washburn heard the scattered shots, he turned his cavalry and infantry around and headed back to Read's support. At the same time, Munford dismounted his brigades and advanced across an open field toward the fence line. The rest of Rosser's division began to swing through the woods to attack the right flank of the Union line.

Munford's men came under heavy fire from the Union infantry behind the rail fence. Just as Dearing's troopers began their charge, Washburn's small force slammed into its flank. For several minutes, blue and gray horsemen swirled about in a saber-swinging, hand-to-hand battle. According to most accounts, Dearing engaged Washburn in a saber fight with orderlies and officers from both staffs surrounding them. Washburn's head was slashed, and he fell to the ground. Moments later, a pistol shot knocked Dearing off his horse just as he shot and killed Read with his pistol. Despite the heroics, the Union task force was overwhelmed and captured.

Dearing was carried to a nearby farmhouse where Rosser found him lying in bed, shot through the lungs. When Col. E. V. "Lige" White, the commander of the Thirty-fifth Virginia Cavalry, came in, Dearing said to Rosser, "I want these [stars] to be put on his coat." The High Bridge was saved but at high cost. Dearing and several of his officers were either killed or wounded. Within a few days, the badly wounded Dearing was carried to the Ladies Relief Hospital in Lynchburg where he was well cared for.[20]

17

Mackenzie, Lord, and Dearing at Appomattox

West Point, January 1866. It was Sunday morning, and Tully had just returned from chapel. He relaxed in his comfortable chair by the stove and reflected upon more recent events. The new year was beginning on a positive note. Peace had come to the land but at great cost. All the Lincoln conspirators had been captured, tried, and hanged. With few exceptions, the Thirteenth Amendment was ratified by twenty-seven states and was now the law of the land, although some Southern provisional governments had not yet adopted all the required changes to their constitutions. In Washington, President Andrew Johnson and Congress were at odds over imposing more restrictions on reluctant Southern governments.

Tully remembered cadets frequently manning the batteries on the river, the Plain, and Fort Putnam six months before, as the war drew to a close. They fired two-hundred- and three-hundred-gun salutes in honor of the fall of Richmond and the surrender of Lee, respectively. How the mountains rang from those booming reports.

Then came that awful day when Lincoln was assassinated. Tully felt as if the whole world had stopped. He listened, disbelievingly, as a description of his death was read in the cadet area. Less than two weeks later, the entire Corps of Cadets crossed the river with the regulars to form an honor guard at the train station at Garrison's Landing when the train bearing Lincoln's body slowly passed through. Gloom descended over West Point for weeks, and little laughter was heard until almost graduation. Even now, almost a year later, the loss of Lincoln still evoked strong emotions.

Returning to his newspaper, Tully read that Ranald Mackenzie's cavalry division was recently mustered out of volunteer service. It had done well with Sheridan's cavalry during the last month of the war.

Fig. 17.1. On the Way Home (Edwin Forbes). *Calkins*

His troopers and James Lord and his battery helped block the road to Lynchburg, leading to the surrender of the Army of Northern Virginia at Appomattox. A few days later, Mackenzie found James Dearing lying in a hospital in Lynchburg.

The War Draws to a Close—April 1865

Brig. Gen. Ranald Mackenzie's small cavalry division from the Army of the James was bivouacked along Plain Run about a mile south of the intersection of the Lynchburg and Oakville roads. It was April 8, and Mackenzie's troopers were part of the final thrust by Sheridan's cavalry to bring Lee's army to a halt. The twinkling campfires of Meade's Army of the Potomac and Ord's Army of the James almost surrounded Lee's army, camped between them near Appomattox Court House. All was quiet in the early evening hours. It was possible that history was in the making.

His classmates, for the most part, had all left the Army of the Potomac except for 1st Lt. James Lord commanding Battery A, Second US Artillery (John Calef's old battery), with Maj. Gen. George Crook's cavalry division. Mackenzie had seen Lord several times during the past week as his battery clattered past with either Custer's or Crook's division as they approached Appomattox. Capt. George Gillespie was now the chief engineer of Sheridan's Army of the Shenandoah. 1st Lt. John Egan had escaped from a Confederate prison camp in December 1864 and returned to active duty. He was now a battery commander in the Twenty-fifth Corps, Army of the James, occupying Richmond. The rest of the class was scattered far and wide as the war ground to a halt. Months earlier, Mackenzie commanded the Second Brigade, First Division, when the Sixth Corps returned from the Shenandoah Valley to the Army of the Potomac at Petersburg. Now he was a cavalry commander.[1]

For some time, General Ord had argued with Brig. Gen. August Kautz over the performance of his cavalry division in the Army of the James. Ord wanted someone new. In March 1865, Grant sought the advice of Ord and Meade about who might replace him. When Kautz returned from leave in late March, he found that he had been relieved by Ord. With Grant's approval, Brig. Gen. Ranald Mackenzie, USV, took command of the cavalry division on March 20. He immediately began remounting the regiments, resupplying ammunition and rations, and turning it into a more disciplined unit.[2]

After a coordination meeting with President Lincoln, Sherman, and Adm. David D. Porter on March 28, Grant issued orders to begin what he hoped was the final offensive. He planned to shift part of Ord's Army of the James thirty miles west from Bermuda Hundred to the south of Petersburg to replace the Second and Fifth Corps in Meade's defenses. The two corps would then strike across Hatcher's Run to cut the South Side Railroad, breaking Lee's main supply route, and force an end to hostilities.[3]

Mackenzie's cavalry division left its camp along the New Market Road twenty-four hours after Ord's infantry divisions departed. As did the rest of the Army of the James, it left a detachment behind to keep campfires burning as a deception. His troopers reached Varina Station early in the morning of March 29 and later crossed the James River at Aikens. They rode to Point of Rocks, crossed the Appomattox River, and arrived behind the Second Corps near daybreak on March 30. Mackenzie then received orders to guard the Army of the Potomac's wagon trains. His horsemen escorted the heavily laden supply wagons to a supply depot near Ream's Station and then rested behind the new positions of Ord's Army of the James.[4]

Meanwhile, Sheridan's three cavalry divisions along with Lord's battery rode west in the pouring rain over horribly muddy roads to Dinwiddie Court House. Sheridan had been turned loose by Grant to turn Lee's right flank and rear to destroy the South Side Railroad. On March 31, Pickett's few cavalry and infantry brigades halted his advance toward Five Forks and drove his cavalry back to Dinwiddie Court House where Custer's troopers and Lord's battery finally halted Pickett's advance.

Sheridan saw an opportunity to attack Pickett's extended lines but needed reinforcements. He had previously asked Grant to send him the Sixth Corps, but Grant directed Meade to send Warren's Fifth Corps to support him. Around 9:45 P.M. on March 31, Grant also ordered Mackenzie's cavalry division to join Sheridan's command. Mackenzie had his troopers on the road by 3:30 A.M. on April 1, and, when he arrived at Dinwiddie Court House a few hours later, Sheridan ordered him to bivouac nearby until called for.[5]

Later that morning, Sheridan sent Mackenzie's division north along the Crump Road to its intersection with the White Oak Road. Sheridan's instructions were clear: turn on the White Oak Road, attack anything in sight, and block any reinforcements from reaching Pickett's infantry at Five Forks.[6]

About 1 P.M., Mackenzie's lead elements found a strong rebel force posted in rifle pits blocking their way along the White Oak Road. He dismounted one of his regiments and then led a charge with a second regiment up and over the rebel works. The ensuing melee ended with the rebel troopers scattering into the adjoining fields. Sheridan was elated with his success and sent him on toward Five Forks.

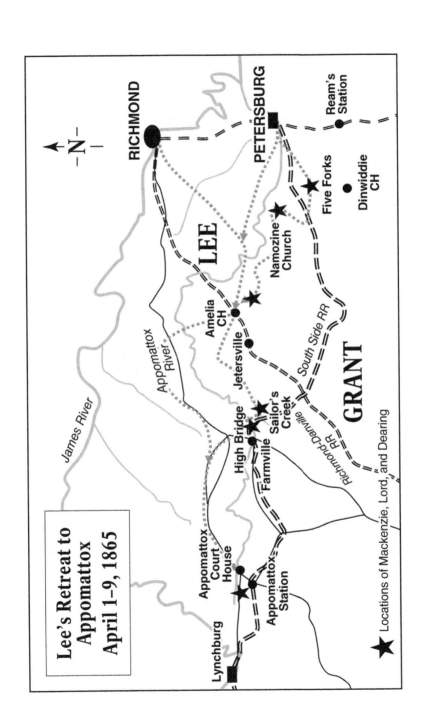

Lee's Retreat to
Appomattox
April 1–9, 1865

RICHMOND

PETERSBURG

Ream's
Station

Five Forks

Dinwiddie
CH

Namozine
Church

LEE

Amelia
CH

Jetersville

South Side RR

GRANT

Sailor's
Creek

High Bridge

Farmville

Richmond-Danville RR

Appomattox
River

James River

Appomattox
Court
House

Appomattox
Station

Lynchburg

Locations of Mackenzie, Lord, and Dearing

–N–

His lead elements soon ran into Warren's infantry crossing the road ahead. Mackenzie then swung his brigades north to guard the right flank of the Fifth Corps as Sheridan's attack began. When one of Warren's infantry divisions joined Sheridan's troopers, they overwhelmed Pickett's left flank, and the rest of his defenses at Five Forks quickly broke. Parts of his command escaped, but thousands of rebel soldiers were captured.

After capturing a number of Pickett's men, Mackenzie's men camped that evening near Five Forks along the road to Hatcher's Run. Sheridan's success at Five Forks prompted Grant to realize that Lee's defenses were stretched too thin, and he immediately ordered a frontal assault along the entire Union line. The next day the Army of the Potomac and the Army of the James crashed through the thinly held Petersburg defenses and streamed into the city. Within hours, Lee's army began to withdraw from Richmond and Petersburg on multiple routes.

The next week saw Sheridan's cavalry continually harass the movement of Lee's forces and his lengthy wagon trains. Mackenzie's division supported Sheridan's cavalry engagements along the Namozine Road. On April 5 at Deep Creek, his division crossed to the north bank and became the only Federal force to reconnoiter rebel positions near Amelia Court House. Two days later, his division was at Burkeville when new orders arrived to rejoin Sheridan's cavalry at Prince Edward Court House.[7]

The Battle at Appomattox Court House

When Sheridan received a report that four supply trains were seen at Appomattox Station, he sent his cavalry divisions after them at dawn on April 8 with Lord's battery trotting along with Crook's division. Upon Mackenzie's arrival at Prince Edward Court House, his smaller division was assigned to Crook's division as a fourth brigade. At the same time, Sheridan urged General Ord to bring the Army of the James up to Appomattox Station as quickly as possible to finally bring Lee's army to a halt.[8]

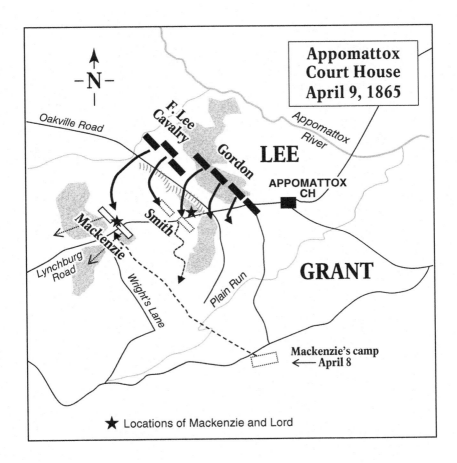

Appomattox
Court House
April 9, 1865

Oakville Road

F. Lee
Cavalry

Gordon

LEE

Appomattox
River

APPOMATTOX
CH

Smith

Mackenzie

Lynchburg
Road

Wright's Lane

Plain Run

GRANT

Mackenzie's camp
← April 8

★ Locations of Mackenzie and Lord

With Custer's division in the lead, Sheridan's horsemen rode twenty-eight miles to Appomattox Station at a fast pace. When Custer's troopers arrived around 4 P.M., they immediately engaged advance elements of Lee's army, capturing twenty-five cannons, two hundred wagons, and a thousand prisoners. Brig. Gen. Thomas C. Devin's and Crook's divisions arrived before nightfall. Devin's troopers fell into line of battle on the right of Custer's division near Appomattox Station, while Crook's division moved to Custer's left flank. Sheridan's troopers had effectively blocked Lee's routes to the south.[9]

Crook sent Col. Charles H. Smith's Third Brigade to a ridgeline overlooking the village of Appomattox Court House to block the Lynchburg Road and retained his other two brigades in reserve. Mackenzie's division camped south of Plain Run that night. At some point during the last two days, a section of two guns from Battery M, First US Artillery (Tully McCrea's old Florida battery), joined his division from the Army of the James.[10]

By midnight Smith had dismounted his four regiments and thrown up breastworks across the road to Lynchburg on a commanding ridgeline a quarter mile west of Appomattox Court House. Lord took two guns from his battery forward to join Smith's picket line.[11]

Meanwhile, Ord's Army of the James arrived before the sun came up on April 9 after an exhausting forced march of thirty-eight miles. His tired soldiers halted two to three miles away from Appomattox Station with Meade's Fifth Corps right behind them. At the same time, Meade's Second and Sixth Corps arrived on the road from Farmville and bivouacked on the other side of Appomattox Court House.[12]

What was left of Lee's Army of Northern Virginia lay camped in a broad, shallow valley around Appomattox Court House, some three to four miles north of the railroad station. With Meade's army at his rear, Ord's army on the west, and Sheridan's cavalry to the south, his army was nearly boxed in. Grant sensed that this was a final moment in the war and sent another letter through the lines to Lee, urging him to surrender. Lee was now forced to make a momentous decision: attack or surrender.[13]

The End Is Near

Before midnight on April 8, General Lee met with his commanders and decided to sweep aside Sheridan's cavalry and continue his march south. He ordered Fitzhugh Lee's sadly reduced cavalry divisions and what was left of Lt. Gen. John B. Gordon's three infantry divisions to open the Lynchburg Road. A little after dawn, the cavalry advanced towards Smith's positions. When Fitzhugh Lee's troopers made contact with Smith's picket line, Gordon's infantry began a giant wheeling movement toward the Lynchburg Road.[14]

Smith's pickets fired their rifles as fast as they could, and Lord's two guns blasted gaps in the advancing gray lines, but they were forced to withdraw to the ridgeline behind them. In one account, two North Carolina cavalry regiments recorded they captured four brass cannons. The First Maine Cavalry on the line of vedettes wrote later that the artillery horses were killed, and one of Lord's guns was pulled to the rear. No official record shows the loss of Lord's guns.[15]

The sound of heavy firing sent Mackenzie's troopers into their saddles. They galloped west to Smith's assistance with Col. Samuel B. Young's brigade from Crook's division right behind. When Mackenzie and his troopers arrived near 8 A.M., they found Smith's brigade already forced away from the road. Unable to link up, Mackenzie's regiments blocked the Lynchburg Road about one mile west of Smith's old position with two guns placed in a field to the right of the road. There was no time to prepare breastworks. Within minutes, his troopers were trading shots with Fitzhugh Lee's cavalry. Rebel horsemen soon overlapped his left flank, forcing him to withdraw into a wooded area to his rear. The artillery section was sent to the rear, but one gun was captured in a nearby wooded area.

Meanwhile, Gordon's infantry continued their wheeling movement and crossed the Lynchburg Road. As the gray lines advanced, Custer's and Devin's cavalry divisions backed slowly up a hillside. Believing the way south was still open, Gordon's infantry pushed forward, only to be suddenly confronted by a line of blue battle flags from the Army of the James coming toward them up the Lynchburg Road and two divisions of Union cavalry poised on a hillside ready to attack. The lead brigades of Maj. Gen. John Gibbon's Twenty-fourth Corps had arrived, with Brig. Gen. Charles Griffin's Fifth Corps from Meade's Army of the Potomac right behind them. Lee's escape route south was completely blocked.[16]

Sheridan, anxious to finish the task, ordered Custer's and Devin's divisions to advance. Sabers were drawn, and the line began to move forward. Suddenly an officer carrying a white flag galloped across the field in front of Custer's cavalry. Reining up in front of Custer, he excitedly explained that General Lee was meeting with General Grant and a temporary truce was in effect.[17]

Meanwhile, Mackenzie's division was delayed in remounting its men and arrived too late to join Crook's other two brigades confronting Brig. Gen. Thomas T. Munford's cavalry division along the Lynchburg Road. Mackenzie's troopers arrived just as Crook's men began moving forward in the attack. Again an officer carrying a white flag galloped across the front of the line, bringing news of a truce. Within minutes a white flag approached from Munford's division. Mackenzie intercepted the small escort and escorted Munford to a meeting with Crook, Brig. Gen. Henry F. Davies, and Young. It soon became apparent that none of these officers could tell Munford much about the conditions of the truce, and he turned to leave. One of the Union officers asked him if a spring was nearby to quench his thirst. Munford turned back and offered him a canteen filled with peach brandy and shared it with all those present.[18]

The Surrender Takes Place

That afternoon at the McLean house, General Grant and General Lee agreed upon the terms of surrender for the Army of Northern Virginia. The next day, designated Union and Confederate officers decided the mechanics of how the surrender would actually take place. The Fifth Corps and Twenty-fourth Corps were ordered to conduct the actual surrender of all arms and to issue paroles to Lee's soldiers. The rest of the Union army started returning north. Mackenzie received orders to conduct the surrender of the remaining Confederate cavalry on April 10. On that day, some fifteen hundred troopers—the remnants of Lee's cavalry still at Appomattox—turned over their arms, cartridge belts, sabers, flags, and ammunition to his troopers in accordance with the terms of surrender. Parts of Lee's cavalry slipped away prior to that time and were not included in the surrender.[19]

The remaining artillery units in Lee's army were formally surrendered on April 11. Maj. Joseph Blount stood with all that remained of his battalion—twenty-four soldiers—to receive his parole. It is likely his guns were destroyed prior to the surrender, as such actions were common. The final act took place when Lee's infantrymen surrendered their arms on April 12 near Appomattox Court House in a well-recorded ceremony.[20]

The Occupation of Lynchburg

After accepting the surrender of the Confederate cavalry, Mackenzie was then ordered to occupy Lynchburg, a major Confederate supply center, several miles south of Appomattox. He had learned much from watching Custer's theatrics in the Shenandoah Valley. One of Mackenzie's regimental bands playing "Hail Columbia" led his column as they rode into the town to accept the surrender. A few Union flags hung from balconies, but for the most part the citizens stood silent. Lynchburg's warehouses and factories contained great amounts of supplies and munitions. After a rapid inventory established that some warehouses were plundered prior to his arrival, Mackenzie directed that only needy civilians and paroled rebel soldiers had access to the food.[21]

As his regiments took charge of the town, Mackenzie learned that James Dearing lay in the Ladies Relief Hospital. He immediately sent guards to ensure that no harm would come to him. When his official duties permitted, he rode to the hospital to visit. One account related that he dropped to his knees by Dearing's bed and burst into tears.[22] It is highly unlikely that Mackenzie, the staunch disciplinarian, actually did that, but it made good copy in later Southern accounts, Dearing's family records, and magazine articles.

Mackenzie made sure that Dearing was covered under the terms of the surrender at Appomattox and placed a signed parole in his hand. Morris Schaff wrote many years later that Mackenzie told him after the war that "Dearing greeted him with all of his old-time cordiality, and inquired affectionately for us all."[23]

Mackenzie was not present when Dearing passed away on April 23, 1865, the last Confederate general to die of combat wounds.

Mackenzie's division was ordered to return to Richmond on April 16 where it was assigned to administer the release and parole of Confederate prisoners in camps near the city. The last of his regiments was finally mustered out of volunteer service in August 1865. During the war, Mackenzie was wounded six times and received seven brevet promotions, the last to major general of US Volunteers. He remained on active duty until August 1866, when he reverted to his regular army rank of captain in the Corps of Engineers. It was not long before he resumed his career as a cavalry officer on the southwestern frontier, but that is another story.[24]

18

Warner, Bartlett, and the Last Battles

West Point, January 1866. Tully McCrea continued to read the newspaper. Maj. Gen. Oliver Howard, his old mathematics professor, was back in the news again. Southern owners were petitioning for return of their confiscated lands, essentially overturning the "forty acres and a mule" rule General Sherman had promulgated. Howard's Freedman's Bureau contested the petitions in several states, but President Andrew Johnson seemed to back Southern efforts to overturn it. Another troubling occurrence was the issuance of thousands of presidential pardons that allowed ex-Confederate officers to seek political offices as representatives of their states. So far, the US Congress was not convinced that Southern states were abiding by agreements to revise their constitutions and refused to accept or seat the former Confederates when they arrived in Washington to begin their duties.

Another article pointed out that "bushwhackers" were still present in the mountains of eastern Tennessee and western North Carolina. Tully knew that the war did not end with the surrender of Lee and Johnston in April 1865. Officially the end of the war took place when Gen. Edmund Kirby Smith surrendered the last Confederate units in Texas in early June. In the interim, the eastern mountains were filled with paroled soldiers, isolated Confederate units, and "bushwhackers" who preyed upon the population. Two classmates, William Bartlett and Charles Warner, were the last of the class to actively pursue Confederate forces in the East. Stories about Bartlett and his regiment enforcing the terms of Johnston's surrender in the North Carolina mountains were frequently heard in the officers' mess. At the same time, Warner and his battery actively pursued organized Confederate forces with Maj. Gen. James H. Wilson's cavalry before and after Johnston's surrender. After the war, Warner's

Fig. 18.1. Feeling the Last of the Enemy (Winslow Homer). *BLCW, vol. 3*

battery was kept in Atlanta to enforce the peace, protect property, and help process paroled soldiers long after the guns stopped firing.

Warner and Wilson's Cavalry Corps—April 1865

Charles N. Warner spent his birthday on the march to Macon, Georgia, with 1st Lt. George B. Rodney's Battery I, Fourth US Artillery. His battery supported Maj. Gen. Emory Upton's Fourth Division in Maj. Gen. James H. Wilson's ('60) cavalry corps. When Wilson's cavalry arrived on the outskirts of Macon on April 21, the lead elements were met by a Confederate messenger carrying a white flag. The messenger announced that a truce was in effect after General Johnston's surrender in North Carolina. Declining to accept the messenger's announcement, Wilson's cavalry swept into the town and captured the entire garrison. For the next two weeks, Warner and his battery remained in Macon where he heard the terrible news of Lincoln's assassination and was elated with the surrender of Johnston's army. The war in the East was finally over.[1]

The time spent in Macon was relatively uneventful. Camp Oglethorpe, the prisoner-of-war camp on the outskirts of town where Albert Murray had been imprisoned, was now being used to process paroled rebel soldiers. There was a constant stream of information

Fig. 18.2. First Horse Artillery Brigade Officers. *LOC*

about the surrender of Lee's and Johnston's armies, and a search for Jefferson Davis was begun. With lots of time on his hands, Warner thought about what had happened since he left the Sixth Corps after the Battle of Gettysburg.

When Warner's battery was transferred to one of the horse artillery brigades after Gettysburg, he was reassigned to Horse Battery A, Fourth US Artillery. After the Army of the Potomac reached the Rappahannock River a photograph was taken of the officers of Capt. James M. Robertson's First Horse Artillery Brigade in Culpeper. Warner is seated on the ground in the right front. Frank Hamilton is standing, second from left, and Sam McIntire is pictured standing on the far right.[2]

Warner's battery supported Brig. Gen. David Gregg's Second Cavalry Division at Bristoe Station in October and at Mine Run in December. It was his last action with the Army of the Potomac. Orders arrived transferring him to 1st Lt. G. B. Rodney's Battery H, Fourth US Artillery, in Tennessee. After a short leave at home in Montrose, Pennsylvania, he joined his new battery near Chattanooga.[3]

His new battery supported the First Division, Fourth Corps, and Warner participated in various forays away from Chattanooga until March 1864, when his battery was sent to join the Artillery Reserve at Nashville. He found duty there very uneventful and boring. The days were long and, according to his diary, "Nothing New" was a frequent notation. One entry stood out when he was notified of his promotion to first lieutenant in May.[4]

Warner took command of Battery H several times when Rodney was ordered away on recruiting duty. In October and November, mass transfers of ordnance and men took place. He was transferred into 1st Lt. Frank G. Smith's Battery I, Fourth US Artillery. A month later, his new battery was assigned to the Sixth Cavalry Division in Wilson's cavalry corps just before General Hood attacked Nashville. Maj. Gen. George Thomas, commanding the Army of the Cumberland, launched a counterattack against Hood on December 15, the first day horses could stand without skidding on the icy, muddy roads around Nashville.[5]

Warner's first action in support of the Sixth Cavalry Division was at Bell's Landing on the Cumberland River where Smith's battery helped a Union gunboat drive off a rebel battery. The combination of Wilson's cavalry engagements on Hood's flank and assaults by Thomas's infantry divisions in the center soon forced Hood to withdraw, and the battle for Nashville was over.[6]

From then on, Wilson's cavalry divisions sparred with Maj. Gen. Nathan B. Forrest's rebel horsemen. Warner's guns engaged Hood's rear guard sporadically as it withdrew. The long daily movements (most over twenty-five miles per day) quickly depleted Battery I's supplies and forage. On December 19, Smith sent Warner back to Nashville with three teams to find replacement horses and bring the battery wagons and more supplies forward.[7]

Warner later described an almost deadly brush with Mother Nature during his trip back to Nashville. When his small group was within ten miles of the city, he rode ahead. Here is how he described in a letter what happened during that ride:

I kept up a nearly constant short gallop or trot until within a few miles of town. Now the roads were so bad that I had to walk him. When about 2 miles from there I came to a large creek where the bridge had been broken and a wagon fallen through. I dismounted and tried to lead my horse, when he went through falling about 10 feet into the water. He jerked me down but I put out my hands and caught on the beams. My cap went off and that was the last of Mr Cap. My horse recovered himself and came back out of the creek to the road. I caught him and was going to mount when I found the saddle was gone. Fortunately, the girth had broke [sic] and instead of falling into the creek it fell on the bank close to the water's edge. When I went for the saddle my horse walked away. After going some distance, the mud was about half way up to my knees I caught him. I put on the saddle without any girth and mounted. Tried to ford the creek. It was dark as tar, I could scarcely see the opposite bank, which seemed vertical. Went along trying to find a place to ascend, my horse commenced floundering, his foot stuck in the mud, the water nearly covering him. Finally got turned around and went up the creek the other way till I found an inclined bank.[8]

On December 23, he drew rations, harnessed twenty-five replacement horses to the battery wagons, had several of his men released from the stockade, and started south. It took more than a week before he caught up to Battery I near Lexington, Georgia. He pressed forward with some of the replacement horses to rejoin the battery, but the battery wagons were delayed and did not arrive until much later. Along the way, Warner patriotically described his feelings after seeing the soldiers marching south in the pouring rain:

You ought to see our stout men marching through the rain, and mud, wet to the skin, perhaps with nothing to eat, day after day, and without a word of complaint. In fact, in the highest spirits. . . . What care they for hardships when the strong and defiant enemy they have been fighting for nearly four years, is flying in confusion before them. Do you think that wet, or cold, or hunger, or want of sleep or fatigue or discomfort of any kind can extinguish the fire that such a thought kindles within them? . . . They have their victory and look forward to the time when the last rebel shall have been brought to terms, and they can return to their friends and families. Such men deserve a country and they will have one—a great, free, and happy country.[9]

Warner's battery ended the first phase of Wilson's campaign at Gravelly Springs, Alabama, at the end of January 1865. The men began gathering construction material to construct winter quarters but were interrupted when new orders arrived transferring the battery to Brig. Gen. Emory Upton's Fourth Cavalry Division.[10]

The second phase of Wilson's campaign began on March 22, 1865. Grant had earlier ordered Thomas to prepare a cavalry expedition of about ten thousand troopers to penetrate northern Alabama. Thomas subsequently directed Wilson to take his cavalry and capture Tuscaloosa, Selma, and Montgomery. Afterward he was to operate against any enemy forces in the direction of Mobile and then head for Macon, Georgia.

There was little rebel interference as the blue columns rode south toward Selma. On April 2, Upton's division arrived north of its fortifications. An attack was planned to begin the next day when Warner's guns were to fire a signal round, but another cavalry division attacked before the appointed time. In the initial confusion, Upton's men charged forward in the attack, and overwhelmed the fortifications before them.

Selma was quickly captured, and twenty-seven hundred prisoners were taken. Warner and his men relaxed for the first time since they left Chickasaw. Meanwhile, Wilson's troopers burned much of the facilities in Selma; the arsenal, the naval foundry, and various warehouses were all systematically destroyed. His men were not kind to the city before they left. Warner recorded the events in his diary as a "splendid conflagration." Next Upton's troopers rode east to Montgomery, where the city surrendered on April 12. There Warner heard of the capture of Richmond for the first time.[11]

A few days later on April 16, Upton's division reached Columbus, Georgia. The city and the bridges were well defended. During the initial attack, Rodney's battery suffered several casualties. A subsequent attack across one of the upper bridges brought Upton's troopers into the town.[12]

Warner later wrote: "Marched out at daylight 24 miles to the Chattahoochee [River] opposite Columbus. Were shelled by the enemy and had 2 men wounded in my section. Afterwards marched 4 miles across the country on horrible roads following the First Brigade to get into position. The Command attacked soon after dark, drove the enemy, and captured the town about 11 P.M. The Battery did not participate but remained in harness all night—we have been gloriously successful."[13]

Three days later, Warner and Battery I marched to Macon, occupied the city, and camped for almost two weeks. There he received final word of the surrenders in the East and the death of President Lincoln. Upton's division was then ordered to Atlanta and Augusta to secure military stores and process paroles for all prisoners passing through those cities. Warner and Battery I fired two hundred rounds to celebrate a day honoring peace and victory on May 4. Afterward Rodney and the rest of the battery marched away to Atlanta. Warner was left behind in Macon because of the worn-out condition of the battery horses. He and a few men arranged to transport the guns and three horses by rail to Atlanta.[14]

After a lengthy rail trip on May 5, Warner and his small detachment arrived in Atlanta late in the afternoon. They unloaded the guns and horses and established a temporary camp near the rail yard until the rest of the battery arrived. The next day, he walked about Atlanta's ruined business district feeling that he was the object of much curiosity. After attending church, he passed one young lady on the street who "elevated her nasal organ as if she smelt something bad" as she brushed past him.[15]

When Rodney and the rest of the battery arrived on May 8, the guns were limbered up, and the battery marched to a new camp on the grounds of a ruined and once elegant mansion along Peach Tree Creek Road. Warner was amazed by the extent of the abandoned fortifications, breastworks, rifle pits, and such that surrounded them for miles in every direction. He later noted in a letter, "It would not be necessary for us to fight any more, and gave us hope that we will see our friends again before a great while, but do not know when my desires will be granted." He was to remain there for some time.[16]

"Last Shot Fired in the East"

Lt. Col. William C. Bartlett, USV, arrived in Boone, North Carolina, on April 5 from the Cumberland Gap. His mission was to capture all rebel units or bandits passing through the area, ensure that rebel soldiers adhered to their paroles, and collect all surrendered military equipment. Bartlett took command of the Second North Carolina Mounted Infantry (Second NCMI) in November 1864 after its first commander resigned. He was no stranger to action, having been brevetted three times for gallantry at Antietam, Campbell's Station, and during the Atlanta Campaign.

For the first few months, his regiment operated near the Cumberland Gap as part of the Twenty-third Corps, Department of the Cumberland. Made up of men recruited from western North Carolina and eastern Tennessee, the Second NCMI was one of two Union mounted infantry units to be mustered into service in North Carolina. Both units were soon accorded the nickname of "Home Yankees," attesting to the derision heaped upon them by the local populace.

Bartlett's tour near the Cumberland Gap only involved several small skirmishes as his unit tried to protect the local populace from poaching, thefts from outlaws, and attacks by "bushwhackers," the local term for guerrilla forces that plagued the mountain communities of eastern Tennessee and western North Carolina during and after the war. At the end of March 1865, Bartlett and the Second NCMI were ordered to Greenville, Tennessee, with the First Brigade of Brig. Gen. Davis Tillson's Fourth Division. The regiment then continued to Boone, North Carolina, with General Tillson's division when it became part of Maj. Gen. George Stoneman's District of East Tennessee.[17]

Bartlett had seen much combat before commanding the Second NMCI. After graduation from West Point, he was assigned to Battery L&M, Third US Artillery and fought at Antietam and Fredericksburg with the Ninth Corps. He then moved west to Lexington, Kentucky, with the Ninth Corps. Sickness caused him to miss the Ninth Corps's involvement at Vicksburg in June 1863. He returned home to West Point to recover and was subsequently assigned as a mustering officer at Brattleboro, Vermont, until his unit returned to Kentucky. He rejoined the Ninth Corps and Battery L&M, now under command of 1st Lt. Erskine Gittings (May '61), as it moved toward Chattanooga in October, just before Longstreet's command pushed up the valley toward Knoxville.

Maj. Gen. John G. Parke, commander of US forces in the field, worried that Longstreet's command would cut off his line of retreat to Knoxville. A small cavalry detachment and Bartlett's two guns from Gittings's battery was dispatched to protect the withdrawal of his command. The small task force galloped off to reach Campbell's Station and successfully secured the key intersection before Longstreet's advance arrived. Bartlett's guns subsequently conducted frequent rear-guard actions to help delay Longstreet's advance toward Knoxville. After the battle of Knoxville in late November, he was assigned to the staff of the Ninth Corps and then in March 1864 appointed aide-de-camp to Maj. Gen. John M. Schofield, commanding the Army of the Ohio.[18]

Now, a little over a year later, Bartlett's regiment and Col. George Kirby's Third North Carolina Mounted Infantry (NMCI) were located at Boone, North Carolina. Both regiments were then ordered to capture Asheville in the mountains of western North Carolina. Kirby's regiment had tried to capture it earlier in the month but found the roads blocked and Bartlett's former classmate, Col. George Clayton, and the Sixty-second North Carolina Infantry (Palmer's brigade,

Brig. Gen. James C. Martin's command) waiting to ambush them. Kirby's assault was repulsed, and he withdrew to Boone. Now the Second NCMI was to assault the area south of the city, and Kirby's Third NCMI was sent to the north. This time Asheville was success-fully occupied.[19]

Meanwhile, General Martin's rebel command was fast dissolv-ing. After the loss of Asheville, he shifted his headquarters to the mountains near Waynesville with Thomas's Legion (aka the Sixty-ninth North Carolina Infantry). Brig. Gen. Joseph B. Palmer's units had already slipped away into the mountains in early April. George Clayton refused to surrender the Sixty-second North Carolina Infan-try. Asheville was his hometown, and after the attack Clayton's unit melted away into the mountains, disbanded, and never accepted parole or pledged allegiance to the new government.

The Second NCMI was then sent to Waynesville, a twenty-eight-mile march through the Smoky Mountains on May 4. The small vil-lage consisted of about twenty houses that lay in a valley surrounded by high mountains. On May 5, Bartlett's regiment occupied the vil-lage without any resistance. His arrival set the stage for what some historians call the last battle fought between organized units in the East.[20]

According to one account, Thomas's Legion included some four hundred Cherokees. Seeking to intimidate Bartlett's defenders in Waynesville, they built multiple campfires on the hillsides around the town and began drumming and dancing. Kirby's Third NCMI was somewhere nearby. Bartlett requested that he come to Waynesville as soon as possible, but the Third NCMI never arrived.

A flag of truce appeared in the village on May 6. It is not clear which side initiated the parley, but local lore accords that to Bartlett. General Martin and Col. William Thomas soon arrived. Thomas, sur-rounded by a bodyguard of Cherokees in full war paint, immedi-ately began to berate him over the destruction and thefts performed by the Third NCMI. It had achieved a reputation for destruction that exceeded Grant's and Sherman's vision of total war. In this case, cooler heads prevailed, and the trio headed for the local stagecoach inn, the Battle House, where Bartlett made his headquarters. Supposedly during this second meeting, he attempted to convince General Martin of the futility of continuing to fight, stressing that if his regiment was overrun, the Union response would be massive and relentless. The trio agreed to meet again.

Sometime that same day, an event known as the "last shot fired in the East" took place a mile northeast of Waynesville near a resort at White Sulphur Springs. Local histories describe it as the Battle of Waynesville and a Confederate victory. The accounts state that part of Thomas's Legion ran into Bartlett's regiment and sent it flying, with one Union soldier killed.[21]

Robert Conley, author of *A Cherokee Encyclopedia*, recorded that his ancestor 1st Lt. Robert L. Conley led a small detachment of sharpshooters (likely twenty to twenty-five men) around Waynesville to make contact with another rebel regiment near Franklin. His mission was to encourage it to join Martin's command around Waynesville. His account, written in the *Atlanta Constitution* and later in *Confederate Veteran*, is the basis for the belief that an engagement took place at Waynesville. The description stated that Conley "charged with [his] skirmishers, driving them from the spring and killing one of them named Arwood."[22]

Not surprisingly, a letter written later in life by James Pickens, who had been a member of Company B, Second NCMI, stated that he was present during the so-called engagement and that nothing more than a few shots were fired at four privates, one of whom was named Arwood, and all escaped and none were killed.[23]

This incident has since become lodged in Southern history as the last battle in the East. It was not recorded in official Union reports, something that Bartlett frequently did when his unit operated in the Cumberland Gap, and it did not affect the pending surrender of General Martin's command. Again, accounts differ. One Southern account recorded that Thomas's Legion captured Waynesville and adamantly refused to give up its arms. What is clear is that General Martin and a much subdued Colonel Thomas came to the Battle House on May 9 to meet with Colonel Bartlett. General Johnston's surrender of

Confederate forces in North Carolina was finally acknowledged, and General Martin agreed to negotiate the surrender of the Confederate District of Western North Carolina and Thomas's Legion.

As part of the negotiations, Bartlett allowed the Cherokee Indians in Thomas's Legion to retain their weapons. That part of the surrender was later overruled by his superiors. Bartlett later explained that they needed arms to ward off bandits and robbers who infested the region. His superiors ordered the collection of their arms in order to meet the terms of Johnston's surrender.

A few days later, Bartlett's regiment was ordered to Asheville where it remained until mustered out of federal service in August 1865. For his actions during the war, he received four brevet promotions, being brevetted one final time to brigadier general, USV, in June 1865. He then doffed his volunteer rank and returned to the regular army.[24]

Standing Guard in Atlanta

After the war ended in the East, many of Wilson's cavalry divisions were released or mustered out as the Union Army rapidly reduced in size. However, Warner and Battery I were ordered to remain in Atlanta as part of roughly four thousand men scattered across the state to enforce the peace. He was not anywhere near the prolific letter writer that Tully McCrea was, but his diary contained many tidbits of information about daily life during and just after the war. Even after mail to the South resumed, it took almost two weeks before he received letters from his family.

One of Warner's letters sent home described the plight of civilians struggling to make ends meet after the war ended:

> I will say a word about the common class of people in this vicinity . . . they wear but one garment, and that one in tatters and reeking with filth from constant use for an unknown period. Hirds [*sic*] of them come to sell Berries, and draw supplies from the Commissary, some of them traveling a dis-

tance of 60 miles for the purpose. There is a Commissary in town appointed for the sole purpose of issuing rations to these destitute people. The office is thronged by thousands every day. The crowd is so great that several women and children have been pressed to death and suffocated in the midst of it. They encamp about the building every night, and sleep on the floor near the door of the office, in order to be first served in the morning. I passed by the place the other evening, and the poor miserable half-starved women (and some children) sitting about their camp-fires, reminds me of Gypsies—and this is the result of Jeff Davis' 4 years reign and pious endeavor to rid the chivalrie [*sic*] and long-suffering South from Northern tyranny and oppression—and to establish a government of which the Slave holding aristocracy with himself at the head, should have the entire control, while the Black and poor whites were merely slaves and vassals, one having about as much liberty as the other.[25]

Regardless of the devastated surroundings in Atlanta, life in camp after the war was much preferred to the long days on the march. But chores became more of a drudgery as the threat of combat no longer faced the men of Battery I. While Warner maintained order near Atlanta, rebel generals Braxton Bragg, P. G. T. Beauregard, Joseph Wheeler, and politicians Clement Clay and Gov. Joseph E. Brown of Georgia were captured elsewhere. On May 13, Jefferson Davis was captured near Irwinsville, Georgia, about eighty-five miles south of Macon.[26]

Warner sent one letter home describing the unhappiness of some of the volunteer units being kept in the service after the war was over. He had no use for mutineers and was very much in favor of the strong measures used to oppose them. He wrote twice about incidents involving the imposition of discipline and direct disobedience of orders:

There have been some prospects of trouble in our camp. We have some volunteers attached to the battery who have been in the habit of running away to their regiments. They were treated leniently at first, but after repeatedly offending, we tied a man up on the wheel and kept him there nearly all day. In the evening, a brother of the culprit brought a letter to Lt. Smith from a number of men in his regiment, threatening harsh measures if the prisoner was not released. Smith did not flinch a particle, but told the man that his brother would be punished exactly according to the orders which had already been given. A few moments afterwards it was reported that two or three hundred cavalry men were with a short distance from camp. Lt. Smith ordered one of the guns to be got in readiness for action, and if they had attempted a rescue, there would have been a few of them stretched out certain. They finally concluded that they had undertaken a job that would not pay, and wisely withdrew from the contest.[27]

Charles Warner had "seen the elephant" many times during the war. He received two brevet promotions for gallantry—one for actions at Gettysburg and the second for Selma. He wanted to return home just as much as anyone else and awaited approval of his leave request. Until then, he stood guard in Atlanta far away from home, long after the guns stopped firing.[28]

19

Remembrances

West Point, January 1866. Tully's legs were better now, although he needed to use a cane to walk and probably would forever. The cold weather still made them ache, but the warmth of the fire helped ease the pain. Outside his window, the sounds of a sleigh passing and the shouts of cadets reminded him of some of the more enjoyable aspects of living and working at West Point. He was also reminded that he might lose that window on the Plain when a new group of officers arrived. The idea that he might be "bumped" out of his comfortable quarters by a more senior officer did not sit well with him. Most of his fellow officers laughed off the practice, but those who were married treated it more seriously as their wives were more sensitive to status changes.

Financially Tully was better off this year. His first lieutenant's salary was now over $150 per month. It allowed him to send a monthly stipend to his sister in Natchez and some additional money to his uncle in Ohio to help pay for his brother's upkeep. He eagerly looked forward to the time when he could go home to Ohio and perhaps then visit Natchez. As far as he knew, Alice's fiancé returned to Natchez after the war and she planned an early wedding, but the doctors still refused to let him travel.

He leaned back in his chair and puffed on his new pipe, having lost the one he carried during the war. The newspapers were beginning to publish letters and articles about various incidents and battles. Here at West Point, the senior professors were engaged in a detailed review of the war to determine its lessons and impact on how cadets should be trained and educated.

The sound of drums and bugles meant the cadets were forming to march to supper. The long lines of cadets marching to the mess hall reminded him of the Grand Review held in Washington last year. The

Fig. 19.1. West Point circa 1867. *1867 CA, SCAD*

triumphant armies marched down Pennsylvania Avenue through lines of cheering people. That well-received military gathering brought to mind that he and his classmates might someday gather once more at West Point to renew friendships and exchange more stories about the Class of 1862.

The Grand Review—May 1865

Washington was draped in patriotic colors as the city prepared itself for a grand military review near the end of May. General Meade's Army of the Potomac and General Sherman's two armies were camped near the city. Their camps were filled with soldiers cleaning their uniforms and polishing their gear. Small groups gathered around sergeants who explained what would happen the next day. The evening before the first parade, one of Meade's corps crossed the Long Bridge and camped in a field east of the Capitol. The others left their camps in Alexandria early the next morning in plenty of time to take up their positions on the parade route.

On May 23, the sun shone brightly. The recent rains had damp-

Fig. 19.2. The Grand Review. *LOC*

ened the dust in the streets. Cheering crowds lined the streets from the Capitol to the White House. National flags flew from almost every house, building, and window. Patriotic music from regimental bands filled the air. President Johnson, General Grant, Secretary Stanton, the diplomatic corps, and many dignitaries packed a reviewing stand set up in front of the White House.

Precisely at 9 A.M., a signal gun fired and the parade began. Roughly seventy-five thousand soldiers of the Army of the Potomac marched down Pennsylvania Avenue behind General Meade and his staff. The engineer brigade and provost marshal came next, then the cavalry under the command of General Merritt. The crowds cheered General Custer as he passed. One young lady threw a bouquet of flowers at him that he caught on his arm, but it scared his horse so badly that it galloped out of control down the street until Custer was able to bring it back to its proper place in front of his division.[1]

The parade lasted for most of the day. The various corps marched behind the cavalry. Divisions with bullet-ridden flags held high carried banners inscribed with victories such as "Gettysburg," "Petersburg," or "Richmond." Unit after unit marched down the street in close columns. Rows upon rows of uniformly spaced soldiers, all in step, saluted their commander in chief and General Grant on the reviewing stand. For close to six hours, the tread of thousands of soldiers echoed off the stately buildings along the avenue. Unseen were the ghosts of many more thousands who marched beside them.

None of the Class of 1862 participated in the Grand Review, although a few might have been spectators. Capt. George Gillespie was with General Sheridan and his staff on their way to New Orleans to take command of all troops west of the Mississippi. Battery A, Second US Artillery, paraded with Col. James M. Robertson's Horse Artillery Brigade. Its rifled cannons, adorned with bouquets of flowers, shone in the sunlight as the horse teams clattered down the avenue toward the White House. But Lord, the last member of the class assigned to the Army of the Potomac, was not present. He had turned his battery over to another officer and was now an aide to General Crook. He and most of the Second Cavalry Division were deployed elsewhere.[2]

Overcrowded trains from New York and other cities brought more spectators to the Capitol City. Early the next morning, General Sherman's Army of Tennessee, followed by the Army of Georgia, crossed the Long Bridge and were massed east of the Capitol ready to begin their parade. Lines of people, four and five deep, swelled by officers and soldiers from the Army of the Potomac, arrived early to stand along Pennsylvania Avenue. Sherman and his staff rode to the front of the column, and at 9 A.M., the signal gun fired and their parade began. When Sherman reached the Treasury Building, he turned in his saddle and looked back at a truly magnificent sight. The bayonets of the long column glittered in the sunlight and swayed from side to side as tens of thousands of soldiers moved in perfect cadence along the entire avenue.[3]

The western theater units carried flags and banners with the names of battles such as Shiloh, Franklin, and Chickamauga embroidered on them. The strange symbols of unfamiliar corps created comments and cheers from the people. Pioneers armed with picks and axes marched in front of most units while Sherman's famous foragers walked in the rear of various divisions along with a few cows, goats, and pack mules. The president and his cabinet, General Grant and his staff, and many dignitaries stood in the reviewing stand for another six and a half hours as the storied units passed by.[4]

A month later, a final day of pageantry was accorded the Sixth Corps when it returned to Washington. Its citizens looked upon the men of the Maltese Cross as their saviors, and once again turned out in droves to line Pennsylvania Avenue to witness their parade. After General Wright and the Sixth Corps turned the corner on Fifteenth Street to pass in front of the White House, the crowds began to thin and the streets emptied as Washington quieted.

With this last military ceremony, the hundreds of thousands of soldiers who had taken up arms in defense of the Union began the process of mustering out of federal service. In a few days, the government clerks began tallying their mustering-out pay. By the end of June, the Army of the Potomac, home to so many members of the Class of 1862, ceased to exist.[5]

Returning Home

There were no such celebrations in the South. After hostilities ended, roads were filled with rebel soldiers in tattered gray uniforms returning to their homes. They walked along dirt roads to Staunton, Richmond, Columbia, Charleston, Mobile, and Atlanta, uncertain what future lay in store for them. They returned to lands devastated by four years of war. Most carried in their haversacks written paroles issued when they were released. Most kept those documents safe over the coming years, proof that they had served the cause to the end. Most walked with Gen. Robert E. Lee's eloquently phrased parting words to the Army of Northern Virginia echoing in their heads: "You will take with you the satisfaction that proceeds from the consciousness of duty faithfully performed."[6]

In Richmond, the Twentieth New York Cavalry, a part of Ranald Mackenzie's division, was assigned duties issuing paroles to rebel prisoners released from various detention camps around the city. On May 12, Richard Kinney received his parole and headed home to Staunton. He was released in advance of a general release of Confederate prisoners that took place after May 27, when President Johnson granted amnesty and pardon to all persons who participated in the rebellion.[7] Why he received his release early will never be known. Perhaps Mackenzie found his name on the list of prisoners in Richmond and arranged an early parole.

West Point—June 1865

In early June, the senior Union commanders visited West Point. General Sherman came on June 5, General Grant on June 8, and General Thomas on June 9, but the focus was clearly on General Grant. A large crowd thronged the grounds of the hotel and the Plain, eager to catch sight of him after he arrived on the steamer *Henry Burden* from New York City. The superintendent whisked him off to the West Point Hotel for lunch before visiting several classrooms to talk to cadets. Late that afternoon, the drums beat "Assembly," and the Corps of Cadets paraded in his honor, their precise movements applauded by all present. Afterward General Grant took time to shake hands and speak with each graduating cadet.[8]

At one point during the general's visit, Tully McCrea stood in the crowd with a young lady who expressed a desire to obtain a memento to remember the general. He walked over to the general's aide and asked him if General Grant would trade a new cigar for his old one. The general nodded, and the young lady walked away with her souvenir, a half-smoked stub.[9]

Life at West Point was pleasant now that the war was over. The newspapers no longer carried news of far-off battles, and Tully no longer searched the casualty lists for names of classmates and friends. His medical condition continued to improve, but the doctors still refused to let him travel.[10]

He was particularly glad to see John "Dad" Egan return to begin duties in the Tactical Department. They had served together through some harrowing times. It was quite likely that Egan, Frank Hamilton, and he sat down one evening, packed their pipes with tobacco and exchanged stories about their classmates, much the same as they had in Warrenton two years before. Most of their information was now based on updated biographical descriptions requested by Col. George W. Cullum, the new superintendent, who was preparing a first-ever register of graduates.[11]

At the end of the war, the members of the Class of 1862 were scattered across the country. Those in the Ordnance Department—Bill Marye, Cliff Comly, Morris Schaff, Jasper Myers, Clement Chaffee, James Rollins, and Isaac Arnold—were assigned to various arsenals or military departments. Engineers Jared Smith and Sam Mansfield were managing projects in the Northeast, while George Burroughs and Charles Suter filled chief engineer positions at Nashville and Hilton Head, respectively. Henry Wharton was en route to a new assignment in California after mustering out of his volunteer engineer regiment in Tennessee. George Gillespie was the chief engineer for Sheridan's new Military Division of the Southwest in New Orleans. Ranald Mackenzie was still awaiting orders in Richmond.

Two of their artillery classmates—Sam McIntire and James Lancaster—were temporarily assigned to recruiting service. John Calef and James Wilson were located at Fort McHenry, Maryland, as the adjutant and quartermaster of the Second US Artillery regiment, respectively. James Lord was now the aide-de-camp to General Crook in the Second Cavalry Division. William Bartlett had left North Carolina when his unit was mustered out of service and was now in garrison at Fort Richardson, Virginia. Charles Warner still remained on guard in Atlanta with his battery. The remaining artillerymen in the class (McCrea, Hamilton, and Egan) were at West Point.

In the wee hours of the morning, Tully likely limped over to his bookshelf and returned with three glasses and a bottle of whiskey. He poured the amber liquid into the glasses and, raising his, said, "Gentlemen, I give you a toast to our departed classmates—Bolles, James, Murray, and Sanderson." They sipped slowly, quietly remembering the faces and voices of their late comrades and classmates. Setting the glasses down, they each returned to their rooms. Reveille still came early at West Point.

West Point, May 1866. Several months later, Tully picked up his class album and idly turned its pages. Dates of death were now marked under the four classmates who had failed to make it through the "late unpleasantness." Many of the rest, like himself, still needed time to recover from wounds suffered during the war. He lit his pipe and relaxed by the grate as the sweet aroma filled the room. Thoughts of what lay in store for him came to mind. He would be leaving West Point when his tour as an instructor ended in June. His new assignment as quartermaster for the First Artillery Regiment would take him to Fort Hamilton on New York Harbor. His classmates who held higher ranks during the war had all reverted to their regular army grade after mustering out of volunteer service. It would be some time before they and the rest of the class were promoted in the regular army.

Congress now seemed amenable to increasing the size of the Corps of Cadets to four hundred cadets. The regular engineer company had returned, but the old West Point battery never did. The senior professors had completed their review of the war and strongly believed that the institution's core principles were validated by the war. They agreed that the Thayer system built regular habits and needed no adjustment. Teaching math and science built mental discipline, and training all cadets as generalists ensured a similar standard of proficiency. There was a strong belief that the training the cadets received at the academy carried over into the regular army.

Although the institution had regained the respect of the nation and again stood tall in the eyes of its citizens, West Point did not escape unscathed from its earlier battles with Congress. There were no more cries to abolish the academy, but the superintendent no longer came from just the ranks of engineers. As much as it believed otherwise, other colleges and universities had become more specialized, and West Point lost its prewar academic eminence in engineering.[12]

Perhaps the best metric to gauge the worth of a West Point education lay in the demonstrated battlefield performance of its graduates. By the end of the war, both Union and Confederate armies were commanded by graduates of West Point. Most of the corps, a majority of the divisions and brigades, as well as both logistics commands were also led by West Pointers. Tully thought his classmates could take some credit for what the army had accomplished. The brotherhood forged at West Point at the outset of war had been tested in combat, and no member was found wanting. He was convinced they had served their country well and executed their duty honorably.

With a sigh, Tully returned to the late-night routine begun so many years before and started a letter to Belle. Their relationship had changed drastically since he returned to West Point to teach, and he missed her frequent letters and her teasing. He reached for a blank sheet of paper, dipped his pen into the inkwell and paused. West Point, his classmates, and the war brought back all-too-poignant memories—remembrances of times past—and he began to write.

Epilogue
Class Assessment

The accomplishments of West Point classes are often measured by collecting statistics, such as the number of members promoted to general officer, the number of awards for gallantry, and how many held high-level offices or commands. Such information about the twenty-eight members of the Class of 1862 was found in the *Biographical Register of the Officers and Graduates of the U.S. Military Academy* by George W. Cullum, the *Annual Reports,* and the *Annual Reunions* published over time by the Association of Graduates of the United States Military Academy.

It is easy to collect statistics but much more difficult to measure the value of a class to West Point or the country. The numbers of those who achieved higher rank and the number of merit or gallantry awards all provide some insight. For example, one member of the class was brevetted seven times during the war and rose in rank equivalent to several of those in the preceding two classes (May '61, June '61) that many stories and histories about West Point during the Civil War focus upon.

Research for this book showed that the Class of 1862 thrived in the military during and after the war. The education and training they received at West Point helped them mold men into formidable soldiers. They served as second and third officers on staffs or in units in the regular army during the war where their days were often filled with long periods of deadly inactivity followed by short periods of absolute terror during intense combat.

One area uncovered during research seemed inconsistent with the behavior exhibited by the two preceding West Point classes. There were only a limited number of transfers to volunteer service by members of the Class of 1862, which raises the question of why

Fig. 20.1. Cadets at Rest. *1868 CA, SCAD*

didn't more members join volunteer units to seek faster promotion during the war? Aspects such as the pace of regular promotions, any perceived inadequacies in volunteer units or service, and several others may have affected any affinity this class might have had for volunteer service. The following sections examine some of these aspects.

Civil War Promotions

Twenty-three members of this class were brevetted for gallantry, some multiple times, and a few served in higher ranks with volunteer units (Mansfield, Mackenzie, Wharton, and Bartlett). Despite these facts, the members of this class were not treated equally in regular army promotions during the war.

The first member of the class to be promoted to first lieutenant was a cavalryman (Comly in July 1862) when the cavalry regiments were expanded, who later transferred to ordnance in May 1863. All four graduating ordnance officers were promoted to first lieutenant by April 1863. A few artillerymen (Arnold, Rollins) transferred to the Ordnance Department and were immediately promoted to first lieutenant in 1863. McCrea briefly considered transferring also but came to believe that ordnance duty would be highly inactive and decided not to. All seven graduating engineer officers were promoted to first lieutenant by April 1863, and five of them were promoted to captain by mid-June 1864, with the other two promoted before the end of that year. Only three artillerymen (McCrea, Calef, and Wilson) were promoted to first lieutenant in 1863. It took until the end of October 1864 for the remaining artillerymen in the class to all be promoted to first lieutenant. No others were promoted before the end of the war. Overall the pace of promotion in the regular army was slow as openings in the various regiments only occurred because of death, resignation, or retirement.

Volunteer Service

Only four members of the class served in volunteer units, a number somewhat less than those in the preceding classes. At the beginning of the war, General-in-Chief Winfield Scott made it clear that he did not want regulars mixed with volunteer units. He issued directives that limited their ability to transfer to volunteer units unless they resigned their regular commissions. Eventually that policy was canceled and regulars were allowed to return to their previous grades in the regular army after serving with volunteers.

Other factors may have inhibited transfers as well. Wayne Hsieh's recent book *West Pointers and the Civil War* identified several factors that affected graduates and their relationship to volunteer service. Of particular note were the following:

(1) *Old army animosity toward citizen soldiers:* Almost ingrained in cadets and graduates was a distrust of volunteers or citizen soldiers. This lack of trust stemmed from the US-Mexican War and still existed at the beginning of the Civil War. As an example, Henry du Pont in the May Class of 1861 was outraged when the secre-

338 FOR BROTHERHOOD AND DUTY

tary of war expanded the ranks of the regular army and began giving appointments to volunteers in early 1861. There were drawbacks to accepting volunteer appointments: citizen soldiers also held ingrained prejudice against regulars, a long-term animosity that stretched back in history.[1]

(2) *Army manpower policy:* By 1862, Army manpower was primarily driven by state replacement of entire units. An individual replacement policy to fill existing units was not practiced by the army during the war. Maj. Gen. William T. Sherman, in his report at the end of the war, identified this as one of the key failures of the army manpower program. Battle-experienced volunteer units were allowed to be drawn down by casualties, and the units were not given replacements. In their stead came units filled with untrained recruits and officers with limited knowledge of tactics and drills as a result of patronage given freely at the state level. Short-term enlistments of nine and twelve months continually caused personnel shortages prior to major campaigns until late in the war when the practice was terminated. McCrea, assigned to muster out a number of volunteer units during the war, commented on their lack of records and the states' failure to supply and support their units over time. All this likely tempered the view of members of the Class of 1862 that joining volunteer units was not a pathway to higher promotions.[2]

(3) *Congressional attitude:* The early years of the war were filled with congressional attacks on graduates and the Military Academy after cadets and officers trained by the army left the defense of the nation in its time of need. Historical arguments against standing armies were continually raised by congressmen. They praised the introduction of citizen soldiers into the army who would soon learn to fight and bring victories to the Union.[3] With West Point and the army under constant attack, it is not hard to imagine that the members of the Class of 1862 would be reluctant to join volunteer service.

(4) *Battlefield experience:* The army, to its credit, established a limited process of evaluating officers through boards and examinations during the war, hoping to eliminate those who did not, by deed

or examination, meet the basic requirements for leadership positions. Within two years of combat, it was quite clear who could handle troops under pressure at regiment and brigade level. Trained volunteer units were limited during the early days in 1861. The May and June classes immediately became the drillmasters for the volunteer units as the army began forming around Washington. Their proximity to these units may have allowed some of them to be more easily appointed to command volunteer units. A year later, members of the Class of 1862 were not involved in similar training programs in the Washington area.[4]

My research provided a few additional aspects affecting volunteer service:

(5) *Actions of members of preceding classes:* The Class of 1862 joined existing corps, department staffs, or regular units as second and third officers. Their detachments or units were often commanded by officers who had graduated just ahead of them. Some in those classes did join volunteers very early in the conflict. For example, in the Class of 1861, Ames and Kilpatrick (both May graduates) went quickly into volunteer service (cavalry), and Upton (May) and Custer (June) joined volunteer infantry and cavalry units, respectively, much later. Du Pont (May) did not seek volunteer service, and his classmate, Kirby (artillery), refused to make the switch although he was offered the opportunity. Arriving during the second year of the war, the Class of 1862 did not see many of their immediate leaders seeking transfer to volunteer units as a means of gaining faster promotions. Consequently they seemed more prone to remain with the regulars and accept slow promotion in their regiments.

(6) *Initial assignments:* Many of their initial assignments placed them in a "detached service" in other units that caused them to be geographically separated from their permanent units (see table 20.1 for actual assignments after graduation). This by itself may have affected later promotions. Personnel policy during the war required officers not serving in their assigned units (e.g., on "detached service") to notify their regiments monthly of their location and status. Regimental records sometimes showed that the locations of some

members of the class were unknown, and they were recorded as being absent without authorization. It is possible that geographic separation prevented any close relationships from forming in their permanent units that would have led to earlier promotions. Again, promotions in the regular army were limited to death, resignations, or promotions to higher ranks within the various regiments.

(7) *Promotions after the war:* In 1866 the size of the army was reduced to roughly fifty-seven thousand, and three members of the class (McCrea, Hamilton, and Egan) took promotion to captain in regular infantry regiments and then later transferred back to their artillery regiments. McIntire shifted to the cavalry to accept promotion to captain in 1867. In addition, Mackenzie received a promotion to colonel in 1867 and took command of the Forty-first Infantry, US Colored Troops, before being appointed to command the Fourth US Cavalry in Texas and later advancing to brigadier general in the regular army.

The four who served with volunteer units during the war (Mansfield, Mackenzie, Wharton, and Bartlett) appeared to do so by being in the right place at the right time. Mansfield was appointed to command his hometown regiment after his father (Maj. Gen. J. K. F. Mansfield) was killed at Antietam. Mackenzie's efforts to identify weaknesses in Confederate entrenchments at Spotsylvania led Brig. Gen. Emory Upton to remember his aid and to offer his name to command the Second Connecticut Heavy Artillery regiment after Cold Harbor. Wharton managed many of the engineering projects in the Pioneer Brigade in the Department of the Cumberland before being offered command of one of its engineer battalions. Finally, Bartlett was aide-de-camp to Maj. Gen. John M. Schofield and acquitted himself gallantly during the Atlanta Campaign. General Schofield likely offered his name to take command of the Second North Carolina Mounted Infantry in Schofield's old Twenty-third Corps when that position became available.

These four individuals did not seek continued service in the volunteer ranks after their own units were mustered out. Instead, they each reverted to their regular army rank. Even Mackenzie, whom Grant described as "the most promising young officer in the Army," reverted to his regular army rank of engineer captain in January 1866. His later climb to prominence would not begin for another year when he gained command of a regular infantry regiment in the Southwest.

Class Statistics

They began their cadet careers as the Class of 1863, but graduation of two classes in 1861 advanced them one full year to become the Class of 1862. Over one hundred candidates were offered appointments, and eighty-four arrived at West Point during the month of June 1858 to be examined. Only sixty-six passed the medical and academic exams and were officially recorded as new cadets on July 1, 1858. Nine more joined the class—eight appointments and one turn-back—bringing the class strength to seventy-five members on September 1, 1858. They came from twenty-four states and the Nebraska Territory, with twenty-four Southerners in the class. To be consistent, the reader is again advised that in this book the term "Southerner" is only applied to those who came from the eleven states that formed the Confederacy.

The academic departments dealt harshly with the class during its first two years. Twenty-one were dismissed because of academic failures or discipline matters. The chaotic period beginning with Lincoln's election through mid-1861 was described in part 1. During that period, eighteen Southerners resigned to return to their states. Several of the original seventy-five were turned back to join the next class, and a few resigned to join Union regiments. Four turn-backs from earlier classes (Rollins, Warner, Lancaster, and Lord) later joined this class and graduated with them. Only twenty-eight (including one Southerner) made it to graduation on June 17, 1862, just over a third of the size of the group that first entered in 1858.

Assignments upon Graduation

The initial graduation assignments for almost half the class were modified by Maj. Gen. George B. McClellan in July 1862. He ordered all

Table 20.1

		Class of 1862 Graduation Order and First Assignments		
Rank	Name	Branch	Graduation Assignment	Actual Assignment
1	Ranald S. Mackenzie	Engineers	Engineer Officer, Corps of Engineers	Engineer Officer, 9th Corps, Army of the Potomac (AOP)
2	George L. Gillespie	Engineers	Engineer Officer, Corps of Engineers	West Point; by end Sept., Co. C, Engineer Bn., AOP
3	George Burroughs	Engineers	Engineer Officer, Corps of Engineers	Engineer Officer, Army of the Ohio, Defenses of Cumberland Gap
4	Charles R. Suter	Engineers	Engineer Officer, Corps of Engineers	Engineer Officer, McDowell's 3rd Corps, Army of Virginia; then Co. D, Engineer Bn., AOP
5	Jared M. Smith	Engineers	Engineer Officer, Corps of Engineers	Engineer Officer, Bank's 2nd Corps, Army of Virginia by Nov., West Point
6	Samuel M. Mansfield	Engineers	Maj. Gen. J. F. K. Mansfield's staff	7th Corps; by Oct., CO, 24th Connecticut Infantry0
7	Henry C. Wharton	Engineers	Engineer Officer, Corps of Engineers	West Point; by end Oct., asst. engineer, Dept. of the Cumberland
8	Clemens C. Chaffee	Ordnance	Ordnance Department	Watervliet Arsenal, NY
9	Morris Schaff	Ordnance	Ordnance Department	Fort Monroe Arsenal, VA
10	Jasper Myers	Ordnance	Ordnance Department	Allegheny Arsenal, PA
11	William A. Marye	Ordnance	Ordnance Department	St. Louis Arsenal, MO
12	Frank B. Hamilton	Artillery	3rd US Arty.	Battery M, 2nd US Arty., Cavalry Div., AOP
13	Isaac Arnold Jr.	Artillery	2nd US Arty.	Battery K, 4th US Arty., 3rd Corps, AOP
14	Tully McCrea	Artillery	Battery M, 1st US Arty., Dept. of the South	Battery I, 1st US Arty., 2nd Corps, AOP

15	James M. Lancaster	Artillery	3rd US Arty.	Battery C, 3rd US Arty., 6th Corps, AOP
16	John Egan	Artillery	Battery G, 1st US Arty.	Battery I, 1st US Arty., 2nd Corps, AOP
17	Asa Bolles	Artillery	3rd US Arty.	Recruiting Service, CA
18	James A. Sanderson	Artillery	Battery L, 1st US Arty.	Battery H, 1st US Arty., 3rd Corps, AOP
19	Clifton Comly	Cavalry	1st US Cav.	Regiment Adjutant, 1st Cav, AOP
20	William C. Bartlett	Artillery	3rd US Arty.	Battery L&M, 3rd US Arty., Arty. Reserve, AOP
21	J. Eveleth Wilson	Artillery	5th US Arty.	Battery G, 2nd US Arty., 6th Corps, AOP
22	John H. Calef	Artillery	Battery K, 5th US Arty.	Battery C, 5th US Arty., Arty. Reserve, AOP
23	Samuel B. McIntire	Artillery	5th US Arty.	Battery I, 5th US Arty., 5th Corps, AOP
24	Albert M. Murray	Artillery	5th US Arty.	Battery F, 2nd US Arty., Arty. Reserve, AOP
25	James H. Rollins	Artillery	4th US Arty.	Tactical Officer, West Point
26	James H. Lord	Artillery	2nd US Arty.	Battery E, 2nd US Arty.; Arty. Reserve, AOP
27	Frederick J. James	Cavalry	3rd US Cav.	Company C, 1st US Cav., AOP
28	Charles N. Warner	Artillery	2nd US Arty.	Battery D, 2nd US Arty., 6th Corps, AOP

REF: Assignments shown are based on "Monthly Returns for Artillery, Engineer and Cavalry Regiments," RG 94, M727, rolls 3, 5, and 21, and M851, roll 2, National Archives, Washington DC; *Cullum's 1891*, 863–64; *BLCW*, vol. 2, 313–15; *OR* 11:2, 33–34; GO 73, July 4, 1862, Adjutant General's Office, Headquarters, Washington, DC; and engineer assignments taken from *OR* Series 3, vol. 2:1, 762.

artillerymen, except those on summer duty, to report to the Army of the Potomac. Additionally, James was placed on "detached service" with the First US Cavalry in the Army of the Potomac because his own unit (the Third US Cavalry) had been paroled, and he could not join it in the West. The graduation order, graduation assignments, and actual assignments for the twenty-eight who finally graduated are shown in table 20.1.

Those Who Left before Graduation

No summary of a West Point class during the Civil War is complete without identifying those who resigned and took up arms against their comrades. Review of Confederate service records and muster rolls, articles in Southern magazines, Confederate histories, and official records helped find various former members of the class in specific units and various campaigns.

Dearing was promoted to brigadier general in the Confederate Army on April 29, 1864. He commanded an artillery battalion (the Thirty-eighth Virginia Artillery Regiment), a composite cavalry brigade, and the Laurel Brigade. A few commanded regiments (Clayton the Sixty-second North Carolina Infantry, Maney the Twenty-fourth Tennessee Sharpshooter Battalion, Barrow the Sixty-fourth Georgia Infantry, Lovejoy the Fourteenth North Carolina Infantry, and Blount Dearing's old battalion and Mosley's artillery battalion).

Five died or were killed during the war. Dearing was mortally wounded in action at High Bridge, Virginia, just before Appomattox, while Lovejoy, Noonan, Barrow, and Blakistone died or were killed while serving with their regiments earlier in the war. Three former classmates participated in the beginning of the war at Fort Sumter (Farley, J. Hamilton, and Blocker), and Farley fired the first signal round initiating the bombardment.

Table 20.2 details information found about the Southerners who resigned. This same information was provided to the West Point Association of Graduates and is currently included in its 2010 *Register of Graduates*.

Table 20.2	
Confederate Members of the Class of 1862	
Brig. Gen. James Dearing (VA)	Washington Arty.; Lynchburg Arty.; 38th Arty. Bn., Pickett's div.; cavalry bde., W. H. F. Lee's cavalry div.; wounded at High Bridge with Rosser's Laurel bde. April 7, 1865; died April 23, 1865
Maj. Joseph Blount (GA)	Lynchburg Arty.; 38th Arty. Bn., Pickett's div.; Mosley's arty. bn.; paroled at Appomattox
Maj. James Hamilton (VA)	1st SC Arty.; ADC to Hood; chief of arty., Wheeler's cavalry; paroled with Johnston's army in NC
Maj. Richard Kinney (VA)	52nd VA Inf.; Dearing's cavalry bde., Rosser's cavalry div.; paroled in Richmond in May 1865
Pvt. Joseph Alexander (GA)	Deserted CSA and went to New York City in 1863
Maj. Henry Farley (SC)	1st SC Arty.; commanded dismounted cavalry, Young's cavalry bde.; paroled with Johnston's army in NC
Maj. Frank Maney (TN)	POW after Ft. Donelson; Maney's 24th TN Sharpshooter Bn., Army of TN
Capt. Ebenezer Ross (TN)	Recruiting command, Richmond, regular Confederate army
Col. George Clayton (NC)	Bn. commander, 62nd NC Inf.; never surrendered
Maj. Oliver Semmes (AL)	1st Regular Arty. Btry.; captured during Red River Campaign and escaped; chief of arty., Wheeler's cavalry corps
Maj. John West (GA)	1st Regular Arty. Btry.; 6th LA Light Arty.; Taylor's cavalry
Maj. Stephen Moreno (FL)	Jackson's bde., Walker's div., Hardee's corps; District of FL
Lt. Col. James Barrow (GA)	64th GA Inf.; killed at Olustee, FL, February 19, 1864
Lt. Col. George Lovejoy (NC)	14th NC Inf.; died of illness July 23, 1862
Maj. John Blocker (SC)	1st SC Arty.; 59th VA Inf.; captured on Roanoke Island and exchanged; 1st SC Arty.; Butler's cavalry bde. in the West
2nd Lt. George Marchbanks (TN)	16th TN Inf., Johnson's bde.; Wheeler's corps
2nd Lt. Robert Noonan (MD)	42nd VA Inf.; killed near Winchester 1862
Maj. Joseph K. Dixon (MS); listed with June '61	Asst. inspector general, Cleburne's div., Hardee's corps, Army of TN
John McNab (AL)	Unknown unit, regular Confederate army
Capt. Horace Twyman (VA)	1st GA Sharpshooter bn., Walker's div., Hardee's corps; wounded at Calhoun May 1864; paroled with Johnston's army April 1865
1st Sgt. William Blakistone (MD)	Co. A, 2nd MD Inf.; wounded at Gettysburg; died August 1863
Sources: Confederate Compiled Service Records (CSR), *OR,* and various articles in Evans's *Confederate Military History.*	

Union Volunteers from the Class of 1862

A few members of the Class of 1862 elected to resign and join the Union army in 1861. Their names and units are shown in table 20.3. Two were promoted to brigadier general (Kress and Spurgin).

Members Dismissed before the War

Those who were dismissed from West Point prior to the summer of 1860 are shown in table 20.4. Their possible participation in the Civil War is not included in research for this book. Some of those shown as turned back to other classes did not graduate.

Leadership Positions Held

Only a few members of the class rose to lead major units during the war. Mackenzie commanded a regiment and a brigade and rose to the grade of brevet major general, USV, just two years after graduation to command the cavalry division of the Army of the James. He was not the first in the class to command a volunteer unit. Mansfield commanded the Twenty-fourth Connecticut Volunteer Infantry at Port Hudson between 1862 and 1863. Wharton commanded an engineer battalion in the Pioneer Brigade with the Army of the Cumberland in 1864. McCrea, Egan, Sanderson, Calef, McIntire, Wilson, and Warner each commanded regular artillery batteries as second lieutenants. However, each of them lost those commands after being relieved by more senior artillerymen within a few months. Lord commanded a horse artillery battery with Sheridan's cavalry corps at the end of the war.

Several members of the class became general officers later in their military careers. Six were promoted to brigadier general (Smith, Suter, Mansfield, McCrea, Mackenzie, and Schaff, the latter in the Connecticut Militia). One was brevetted to that rank (Bartlett) at the end of the war but never served in that position. Only Mackenzie, Schaff, and Gillespie actually served as general officers. Mackenzie, as a brigadier general in the regular army, commanded the Fourth US

Table 20.3

Union Volunteers from the Class of 1862

Lt. Col. John Kress (NY)	Commanded 94th NY Inf., 1st Corps; transferred to ordnance; retired as brigadier general, US Army, in 1903; inducted into Ordnance Hall of Fame
Maj. Edmund K. Russell	65th NY Inf.
Capt. Henry S. Wetmore	9th OH Arty.
1st Lt. Benjamin King	Killed in action at Shiloh 1862
1st Lt. William Spurgin	38th US Inf.; retired as brigadier general, US Army, in 1902
Lt. Col. Robert Merritt	NY Inf.
Capt. John Hampden Porter	Assistant surgeon, US Volunteers
1st Lt. William Barnard	Believed to have joined the 3rd NJ Inf.

Table 20.4

Members Dismissed before the War

Name	State
William C. Barnard	NJ
Charles H. Barron	NC
William S. Beebe	NY – Turned back to Class of 1863
Ozias A. Blanchard	ME – Turned back to Class of 1863
William Eratus Cannady	NC
William B. Chapman	MA
Vancleve Coonrod	OH
James Piper Cox	VA
Hervey B. Denny	OH
Henry C. Dodge	NY – Turned back to Class of 1863
James Perry Drake	IN
Bartholomew Dupuy	KY
John B. Johnson	GA
George McKee	KY – Turned back to Class of 1863
John M. McNab	AL – See table 20.2
Arthur F. Reed	IN
James Riddle	PA
Kenell Robbins	MA –Turned back to Class of 1863
Armand Selby	LA
John Woodburn Shrewsbury	IN
Charles W. Smith	PA – Turned back to Class of 1863
Singleton Van Buren	SC
Joseph W. Vance	IL

Cavalry in the Southwest. As a brigadier general, Gillespie served as the chief of engineers, acted temporarily as the secretary of war, and upon promotion to major general served as assistant chief of staff before he retired. The others (McCrea, Mansfield, Suter, and Smith) were promoted and then retired the next day.

After leaving the service following the Civil War, a few members of the class launched successful civilian careers. Schaff became a respected businessman in Connecticut, a writer of Civil War books, president of the USMA Association of Graduates, and eventually the oldest surviving member of this class. McIntire, Warner, and Myers followed careers as lawyers after they resigned. Most of the engineers followed careers as members of various state engineer boards after they retired.

North-versus-South Animosity

The Military Academy fiercely opposed any recognition of former Confederate graduates until the centennial celebrations in 1902. Members of the Class of 1862, on the other hand, did not appear to have any long-term animosity against their former classmates. Specific incidents of friendship among the members of the various classes present at West Point during the Civil War are abundantly recorded in history. Custer (June '61), Merritt ('60), and Du Pont (May '61) remained at the bedside of Maj. Gen. Stephen Ramseur ('60) in the Shenandoah Valley in 1864 until he passed away. In this class, Mackenzie's care for the mortally wounded Dearing (ex-'62) in Lynchburg took place without any animosity even though his and Dearing's troopers likely traded shots more than a few times during the war.

Schaff fondly noted in his book that he ran into many former classmates in later years. One historian succinctly put the topic of friendships and relationships among cadets during that difficult time:

> At the Academy, the common experience of all cadets, regardless of social or sectional background, together with a feeling of solidarity they shared as a member of a neglected and even despised profession, strengthened the bonds of college

classmates. West Point was small enough to allow everyone to know everyone else and to know the names and reputations of many of those who had earlier attended the Academy. In the Army and even more at West Point, the graduate or cadet was isolated from the rest of the world. His friends and acquaintances were men who shared the same experiences, and the result was a feeling of comradeship stronger, for example, than that in most college fraternities.[5]

Length of Service

The length of time members of the class served in the army is a unique measure of their service. Some did not serve until retirement—six members were honorably discharged or retired at their own request. A few succumbed to disease or accidents shortly after the war ended, and a total of seven died before the turn of the century. The rest remained on active duty until they retired medically or at their own request after almost forty years in uniform.

Thirty-three years after the Civil War, four members of this class served in various capacities in support of the Spanish-American War. General Gillespie commanded the Department of the East during the war and headed a board adjudicating acquired Spanish territory afterward. Colonel Lancaster fought at Coamo, Puerto Rico, and Colonel Tully McCrea commanded an installation in Manila. Colonel Arnold was cited for the manner in which the Springfield Arsenal increased its production of arms and ammunition during the war. Others remaining in the army were assigned to arsenals, engineer boards, or duty in Western territories. The last to serve on active duty was General Suter, who retired in 1906 after forty-four years of service to his country.

Summary

On balance, the Class of 1862 was a gallant bunch—courageous and dedicated to restoring the Union. The brotherhood was strengthened by shared experiences at West Point in terms of respect for authority and obedience to orders, which carried over into the army. Although most had their hopes for early promotion dashed during the war, their performance and that of the army helped restore confidence in West Point. Throughout the long conflict, they adhered to their class motto, *In Causam Communem Conjuncti*—"Joined in a Common Cause." The brotherhood that was born at the outset of war truly served their country well and in a manner that made them more than worthy of the current motto of the US Military Academy: "Duty, Honor, Country."

Acknowledgments

What began as a West Point class-reunion project turned into a multi-year effort. None of this would have happened without support from the late historian Mary Elizabeth Sergent, my mentor and adopted aunt. As one of her "nephews," I was accorded special consideration and assistance in taking on this effort.

In the process of preparing this book, I was helped by many people. I particularly want to express my sincere appreciation to Suzanne Christoff and members of the Special Collections and Archives Division at the West Point Library. They helped guide me through the musty old cadet records and Tully McCrea's letters and supported many requests for information about the Class of 1862 and cadet life at Civil War West Point.

I am a firm believer in walking the battlefields to better understand the official reports and letters. Along the way, I had the opportunity to discuss the battles and campaigns with a number of interesting and insightful people who made my research that much sounder. Individuals such as D. P. Newton at the White Oak Museum near Fredericksburg, Donald Pfanz at the Fredericksburg and Spotsylvania National Military Park, Chris Calkins at the Petersburg National Battlefield (now at Sailor's Creek Battlefield Historical State Park), John Heiser at Gettysburg National Military Park, Patrick Schroeder at Appomattox Court House, and Dr. Richard Sommers and his staff at the Military History Institute, US Army Heritage and Education Center, all took time to discuss and pull together material for me. The maps shown in the book were created by myself and edited by Robert McDonough.

I frequently used the resources of the National Archives in Washington, DC, and the Virginia Room at the Fairfax County Regional Library in Fairfax, Virginia. Ms. Betty Smith and her staff greatly assisted with my review of Charles Warner's papers and letters at the Susquehanna Historical Society in Montrose, Pennsylvania. Jim Lafferty, Charles Warner's great-great-grandson, and I exchanged information that was most helpful. The staff of the Virginia Historical Society in Richmond was equally helpful in allowing me access to James Dearing's family files.

Editing has been long and tedious. My daughter, Anne, made excellent comments about various chapters that kept me on track. I am very thankful for the assistance of my longtime friends and classmates, the late Jim Worthington and Richard Helmuth, who read my early chapters for content and style, as did Ben Rapaport, a colleague from my days with Science Applications International Corporation. My mentor and friend from the Bull Run Civil War Roundtable, E. B. Vandiver III, former director of the US Army Center for Analysis and an avid student of the Civil War, read my war chapters and made many suggestions that I have since incorporated into the various stories.

Finally, I am blessed with having one of the most wonderful women in the world, Lillian, as my wife and best friend. Without her support, the long hours in my office, writing, revising, and editing would not have been possible.

Appendix
Biographical Sketches of the Class of 1862

The assignment and service information presented in each biographical sketch is limited to their cadet and Civil War service periods. Most information was found in Francis B. Heitman's *Historical Register and Dictionary of the United States Army, Cullum's 1891*, pension records, muster rolls, and regimental records at the National Archives. Some information and photographs were found in obituaries and cadet files at the USMA Library at West Point as well as in the various volumes of the Military Order of the Loyal Legion of the United States (MOLLUS) collection held by the Military History Institute at Carlisle, Pennsylvania. Some postwar information is included, such as family and personal information taken from the federal census and attained through the genealogical research website Ancestry.com. Additional information about the class members' postwar assignments and service was found in the *Annual Reports* and the *Historical Register and Dictionary*.

Isaac Arnold Jr. (1840–1901)

Born in Haddam, Connecticut, on March 20, 1840, Arnold attended Wilbraham Academy in Massachusetts before he was appointed to West Point from the Sixth Congressional District of Connecticut. He entered with the Class of 1862 on July 1, 1858, graduated thirteenth in his class, and was commissioned in the Fourth US Artillery. His battery supported the Third Corps at Fredericksburg, and he was conspicuous in action at Fairview during

Cadet Isaac Arnold. *SCAD*

the Battle of Chancellorsville, where he was wounded. After Gettysburg, Arnold transferred to the Ordnance Department and was immediately promoted to first lieutenant and was brevetted to captain for meritorious service at the end of the war. Over the years, he became a recognized expert on the manufacture of heavy cannons. He commanded numerous arsenals and managed the construction of the Columbia Arsenal in Tennessee. During the Spanish-American War, he com-

Maj. Isaac Arnold. *AR 1902*

manded the Springfield Arsenal, where he was credited with greatly increasing its production of small arms and ammunition to outfit the deploying troops. In 1864, he met and married Lucetta Apgar at Hartford, Connecticut, and they had five children. Known as a great hunter and fisherman as well as a congenial and well-respected officer, Arnold died at age sixty-one on October 15, 1901, at the Allegheny Arsenal in Pittsburgh, and is buried at West Point.

Civil War Assignments: **Army of the Potomac:** Battery K, Fourth US Artillery, in the Third Corps during the Rappahannock Campaign and engaged in the Battle of Fredericksburg and the Battle of Chancellorsville. **Ordnance Department:** Assistant ordnance officer at **Washington Arsenal**, June 17, 1863, to January 1, 1864; at **St. Louis Arsenal** January 1, 1864, to May 1, 1864, and at Springfield, IL, arming volunteers, May 1 to September 29, 1864. **Department of the South:** Chief of ordnance, Hilton Head, SC, October 19, 1864, to September 11, 1865.

Williams Chambers Bartlett (1839–1908)

Born at West Point, New York, on June 2, 1839, to Prof. William H. C. Bartlett and his wife, Harriet. William was appointed as an at-large candidate by the president and entered West Point with the Class

Cadet William C. Bartlett.
SCAD

of 1862 on July 1, 1858. He graduated twentieth in his class and was commissioned in the Third US Artillery. Brevetted three times for gallantry while serving with the Army of the Potomac, Lt. Col. William C. Bartlett, USV, ended his war service in command of the Second North Carolina Mounted Infantry and participated in the last combat action in the eastern theater in late May 1865. At the end of the war, he was brevetted to brigadier general for meritorious service. Bartlett married Josephine Warren in 1878 in Helena, Montana. He retired from active service in 1892 and passed away at Larrabee's Point, Vermont, on July 27, 1908, at the age of sixty-nine. He is buried in the cemetery at West Point.

Lt. Col. William C. Bartlett, US Volunteers. *MHI*

Civil War Assignments: **Army of the Potomac:** Battery L&M, Third US Artillery, with the Ninth Corps in the Peninsula Campaign; participated in the Battle of Antietam and the skirmish at Black Ford, the Rappahannock Campaign, and the Battle of Fredericksburg. In garrison at Newport News, VA, February 15 to March 19, 1863. **Department of Ohio, Ninth Corps:** With Battery L&M, Third US Artillery, March 30 to April 8, 1863; at Camp Dick Robinson, KY, April 9–30, 1863; sick leave, April 30 to July 4, 1863; at draft rendezvous at Brattleboro, VT, July 4 to September 20, 1863. East Tennessee Campaign: Engaged at Lenore Station, Campbell's Station, the Battle of Knoxville, and the skirmish at Strawberry Plains. Assigned as commissary of musters, Ninth Corps, December 28, 1863, to March 19, 1864. **Army of the Ohio:** Aide-de-camp to Maj. Gen. John M.

Schofield, March 19 to November 17, 1864. Participated in the invasion of Georgia at Buzzard's Roost, Resaca, Dallas, Lost Mountain, Kennesaw Mountain, and operations before and during the siege of Atlanta. Became volunteer aide-de-camp to Maj. Gen. Judson Kilpatrick on raid around Atlanta to Jonesboro and Lovejoy's Station. **District of East Tennessee:** Commissioned as lieutenant colonel, USV, in command of Second North Carolina Mounted Infantry Regiment, Fourth Division, Twenty-third Corps, November 17, 1864. At Cumberland Gap, TN, November 30, 1864, to March 8, 1865. Transferred with Second NC Mounted Infantry Regiment to Boone and Asheville, NC, where he served from March 8 to August 16, 1865. At Waynesville, NC, he accepted the surrender of Brig. Gen. J. G. Martin and the last Confederate units in East. Honorably mustered out of volunteer service on August 16, 1865.

Asa Bolles (1840–1863)

Born in Athens, Ohio, on June 20, 1840, to David C. Bolles and the former Frances Mather. Asa Bolles was appointed from the Seventeenth Congressional District of Ohio and entered West Point on July 1, 1858, with the Class of 1862. He graduated seventeenth in his class and was commissioned in the Third US Artillery. Morris Schaff remembered listening to his tenor voice in the chapel choir during services on Sundays. Bolles became ill during

Cadet Asa Bolles. *SCAD*

his initial assignment and was transferred to the Recruiting Service. Sent west for health reasons, he died from consumption on April 21, 1863, shortly after his arrival in California and is buried in the Old City Cemetery in Sacramento. He was twenty-three years of age.

Civil War Assignments: **Army of the Potomac:** Battery L, Third US Artillery, July 1862. **Recruiting Service:** November 14, 1862, to

February 9, 1863. Taken sick on voyage to California, February to April 1863, and died April 21, 1863, in Sacramento, California.

George Burroughs (1841–1870)

Born in Camden, New Jersey, on December 11, 1841, to Rev. Henry Burroughs and the former Sarah Tilden. After his family moved to Boston, Massachusetts, in 1852, Burroughs attended the Latin School and then Harvard for one year before accepting a nomination to West Point from the Fourth Congressional District of Massachusetts. During his first-class year, he was appointed an acting assistant professor in the French Department. He graduated third in the class

Cadet George Burroughs. *SCAD*

and was commissioned in the Corps of Engineers. After graduation he served with distinction in Kentucky and Tennessee where, at one point, he was the acting chief engineer for the Department of the Cumberland. While on the staff of Maj. Gen. William S. Rosecrans, Burroughs was temporarily assigned to the Twenty-

1st Lt. George Burroughs. *MHI*

second Corps and brevetted to captain for gallantry in rallying its troops during the Battle of Chickamauga. In 1866 he married the former Carrie Bryson in Cincinnati, Ohio, and they had two children. Brevet Major Burroughs was in charge of the Sixth Light House District in South Carolina when he was taken ill with "congestion of the brain" and died near Charleston on January 22, 1870, at age twenty-eight. He is buried in Forest Hill Cemetery in Boston.

Civil War Assignments: **Department of the Ohio:** Assistant engineer of Brig. Gen. G. W. Morgan's Division (Army of the Ohio), July 30 to October 4, 1862. Defense of Cumberland Gap, East Tennessee, July 30 to September 17, 1862. Acting aide-de-camp to the commanding general on the retreat to the Ohio River, September 17 to October 4, 1862. On staff at Louisville, KY, prepared drawings of the Defenses of Cumberland Gap, October 4 to December 11, 1862, and was involved in constructing the defenses of Louisville and Nashville Railroad, November 8 to December 11, 1862. **Department of the Cumberland:** Assistant engineer, December 12, 1862, to November 19, 1864. Involved in construction of the defenses of Nashville, December 15, 1862, to November 19, 1864 (except while on sick leave of absence, March 15 to May 15, 1864), and was detached for duty at Gallatin, Fort Donelson, Fort Henry, Clarksville, and Murfreesboro. Participated in General Rosecrans's Tennessee Campaign and in the Battle of Chickamauga followed by duty at Chattanooga, TN, Bridgeport, AL, and Resaca and Kingston, GA. Participated in the investment and Battle of Nashville. Served as assistant engineer at Engineer Agency, Cincinnati, OH, June 28 to September 21, 1865, when he became engineer in charge.

John Haskell Calef (1841–1912)

John Haskell Calef was born September 24, 1841, in Gloucester, Massachusetts, to John C. Calef and the former Eliza Baldwin Haskell. He was appointed from the Twenty-second District of Massachusetts and joined the Class of 1862 on July 1, 1858. Initially assigned to B Company, he roomed with Morris Schaff in the fourth division during their first year at West Point. He graduated twenty-second in the class and was commissioned in the Fifth US Artillery. He

Cadet John H. Calef.
SCAD

soon became a veteran of the war's major campaigns, including the first day at Gettysburg when, in support of Brig. Gen. John Buford's cavalry division, his battery fired the first artillery rounds in that opening battle. During the war, he came under fire twenty-five times, had two horses shot from under him, and suffered but two slight wounds the whole time. He was brevetted to captain for gallantry at Gettysburg and again to major at the end of the war. The barrels of two of his guns at Gettysburg now adorn the base of General Buford's statue on McPherson

Ridge. His wife, Mary, and he were married on September 15, 1870, in Stockton, California. Over the years, Colonel Calef wrote several obituaries for his classmates, authored several articles, and a textbook used at the artillery school. He retired as a colonel on April 23, 1904, after forty-two years of service. He died in St. Louis, Missouri, on January 14, 1912, at age seventy and is buried at West Point. There was difficulty in awarding his pension until a private bill sponsored it in Congress.

Col. John H. Calef. *AR 1912*

Civil War Assignments: **Army of the Potomac:** Battery K, Fifth US Artillery during the Peninsula Campaign. Fought at Harrison's Landing and at Malvern Hill. Participated in the Second Battle of Manassas and the Maryland Campaign, including the Battle of Antietam and action at Sharpsburg. **Second US Artillery Regiment:** Battery A, Second US Artillery, on October 6, 1862. Participated in the Rappahannock Campaign, Stoneman's Raid, Battle of Chancellorsville. During the Pennsylvania Campaign, while in command of Horse Battery A, Second US Artillery from June to July 1863, engaged in the skirmish at Upperville, VA, and the Battle of Gettysburg, followed by the engagements at Williamsport, PA, Boonsboro, MD, Funkstown, MD, and the pursuit to Warrenton, VA. During the Rapidan Campaign, he was wounded at Raccoon Ford. Leave of absence, February 14 to April 1864. Overland Campaign: Engaged at Cold Harbor, Bottom's Bridge, Trevilian Station, and the action at St. Mary's Church. Sick leave, August 5 to September 1, 1864. Saw action at the siege of Petersburg, Boynton Plank Road, Stony Creek Station, and Bellefield. At the beginning of 1865, he became the adjutant, Second US Artillery, at Fort McHenry, MD, where he served until the end of the war.

Clemens Clifford Chaffee (1841–1867)

Born in Rochester, New York, on June 28, 1841, to Calvin C. Chaffee and the former Clara Nourse. The family moved to Massachusetts, and he was appointed from its Tenth Congressional District to join the Class of 1862 on July 1, 1858. A bright student, he was assigned as an assistant professor during his last year, teaching English to the plebe class. Chafee graduated eighth in his class and was commissioned in the Ordnance Department.

Cadet Clifford Chaffee. *SCAD*

After graduation, he served at various arsenals and depots. Ordered on temporary duty from St. Louis Arsenal to the Vicksburg area, he gathered arms and munitions for distribution to Grant's army through a field depot. Unexpectedly, all West Point graduates were ordered to act as engineer officers during the siege of Vicksburg. Chaffee supervised tunnel and entrenchment construction in the Fifteenth Corps's sector. His actions during the campaign resulted in being brevetted to captain for gallantry. After the battle, he joined Grant's staff at the Department of the Tennessee until he was transferred to the Alleghany Arsenal. His last assignment was to the Springfield Armory where he died on July 5, 1867, at the age of twenty-five. He is buried in Springfield, Massachusetts.

Civil War Assignments: **Watervliet Arsenal:** Assistant ordnance officer, July 1 to August 28, 1862. **Frankford Arsenal**: September 1,

1862, to April 21, 1863. **Department of the Tennessee:** As chief of ordnance from May 16 to October 1, 1863, participated in the campaign and siege of Vicksburg followed by temporary engineer duty, May 30 to June 29, 1863, then commanded Vicksburg Ordnance Depot, October 1, 1863, to March 18, 1864. **Allegheny Arsenal:** Assistant ordnance officer, March 22, 1864, to June 1865. His final actions during the war were to receive arms from Connecticut Volunteers mustering out of federal service, June–July 1865.

Clifton Comly (1841–1894)

Born in Dayton, Ohio, on May 31, 1841, to Richard N. Comly and the former Julia Sanders. He was appointed to West Point from the Third Congressional District of Ohio and entered on July 1, 1858. He graduated nineteenth in his class and was commissioned in the First US Cavalry. He served as its adjutant until 1863 and was the first officer in his class to be promoted to first lieutenant before later transferring to the Ordnance Department. His service

Cadet Clifton Comly.
SCAD

during the war resulted in being brevetted to captain for meritorious service. He married Sarah Garrard in April 1868, and they had four children. From 1881 to 1886, he served as an assistant professor in the Military Academy's Ordnance and Gunnery Department. A distinguished ordnance officer during his career, Major Comly participated in many of the major gun and artillery trials conducted at Sandy Hook, New Jersey, during his tenure as inspector of ordnance and member of the Ordnance and Fortifications Board. Among his accomplishments was his appointment by the president to represent the War Department on the board of governors for the World's Fair in 1890. He suffered a stroke and passed away at Governors Island, New York, on April 17, 1894, at age fifty-two and is buried at West Point.

Civil War Assignments: **Army of the Potomac:** Adjutant, First US Cavalry, July 19, 1862, to May 26, 1863; at Yorktown, VA, July–August 1862. During the Maryland Campaign, his troop was assigned on quartermaster duty. Participated during the Rappahannock Campaign in the actions at Kelly's Ford, and Stoneman's Raid. **Ordnance Department:** May 26, 1863. **Watertown Arsenal:** Assistant ordnance officer, June 11, 1863 to June 1, 1864. **Ordnance Bureau**, Washington, DC, June 10 to December 1, 1864. **Fort Pitt Foundry:** Assistant constructor of ordnance, December 1, 1864, to June 4, 1867.

John Egan (1837–1918)

John "Dad" Egan was born in Vermont on July 23, 1837, making him the oldest in the Class of 1862. He entered the academy as an alternate from the Sixteenth Congressional District of New York, graduated sixteenth in his class, and was commissioned in the First US Artillery Regiment. He served in the Army of the Potomac and received three brevet promotions for gallantry. Captured at First Ream's Station in late June 1864, he

Cadet John Egan. *SCAD*

spent six months in a Confederate prison camp before escaping. After

Capt. John Egan. *SCAD*

a short recovery, he took command of a battery in the Army of the James. Egan returned to West Point and the Tactical Department twice (1865–1869, 1871–1873). In January 1868, he married Diantha Gilbert in New York City. Later he commanded both artillery and infantry units in Washington Territory and participated in Indian campaigns on the West Coast. Major Egan retired in 1896 and died in New York City in 1918 as a result of a trolley car accident at age sixty-nine. He is buried in Plattsburgh, New York.

Civil War Assignments: **Army of the Potomac:** Battery I, First US Artillery. Participated in the Peninsula Campaign, the Northern Virginia Campaign, the skirmish at Fairfax Court House, and the Maryland Campaign, including the Battle of Antietam. **Battery E, Fourth US Artillery:** Participated in the march to Falmouth, VA, the skirmishes at Jefferson and Sulphur Springs, the Rappahannock Campaign, the Battle of Fredericksburg, the action at Kelly's Ford, and Stoneman's Raid. **Battery I, First US Artillery:** In the Pennsylvania Campaign, including the Battle of Gettysburg and the pursuit of enemy to Warrenton, VA, and in the Rapidan Campaign. **Horse Battery K, First US Artillery:** Movement to Centreville, VA, in October 1863, in support of cavalry actions at Mine Run (November 26 to December 3, 1863), and raid to Front Royal (January 1–6, 1864). In the Richmond Campaign, involved in cavalry actions and skirmishes at Cold Harbor, Barker's Mill, Bottom's Bridge, Yellow Tavern, Seminary Church (aka St. Mary's Church), Charles City Court House, and with Wilson's cavalry raid to the Staunton River Bridge, where he was captured at Ream's Station. **Prisoner of War:** Columbia Military Prison, June 29 to December 8, 1864, when he escaped. **Army of the James:** Commanded Horse Battery D, First US Artillery. With the Twenty-fifth Corps in the siege of Petersburg. **US Military Academy:** Assistant instructor of infantry tactics (March 3, 1865, to February 6, 1869).

George Lewis Gillespie Jr. (1841–1913)

Born in Kingston, Tennessee, on October 7, 1841, to George and Margaret McEwen Gillespie. Gillespie began his education at Western Military Institute in Nashville with Frank Maney. He was appointed from the Third Congressional District of Tennessee and entered West Point on July 1, 1858. He graduated second in his class and was commissioned in the Corps of Engineers. After serving at West

Point for two months after graduation, he then joined the Army of the Potomac and built fortifications and pontoon bridges at various sites (at Fredericksburg, and across the Potomac, Occoquan, Rappahannock, Rapidan, and James Rivers). He later became the chief engineer for Maj. Gen. Philip Sheridan's Army of the Shenandoah, the Middle Division of the Southwest, and the Military Division of the Gulf. His actions as an engineer led to being brevetted twice for gallantry during

Cadet George L. Gillespie. *SCAD*

the war. In particular, his actions at Cold Harbor resulted in award of the Medal of Honor, but not until 1897. After the war, he served on several engineer boards, commanded various engineer districts, and was part of the War College Board. He married Rhobie McMaster of Ballston, New York, on October 29, 1868. In 1898 he was appointed a brigadier general of US Volunteers and took command of the Department of the East and its defenses during the Spanish-American

War. General Gillespie was appointed the chief of engineers in 1903. While in that position, he was instrumental in redesigning and patenting the design of the current US Army Medal of Honor. Upon promotion to major general, Gillespie served as assistant chief of staff and temporarily as secretary of war. He retired from the army on June 15, 1904. General Gillespie died on September 27, 1913, at Saratoga, New York, at age seventy-two and is buried at West Point.

Maj. Gen. George L. Gillespie. *MHI*

Civil War Assignments: Assigned at **West Point** (June 17 to August 31, 1862) as tactical officer and instructor of artillery. **Army of the Potomac:** US Engineer Bn., in command of engineer company.

Involved in the building of fortifications and pontoon bridges during the Maryland Campaign, including Antietam, Harpers Ferry, and
Berlin. Rappahannock Campaign: Fredericksburg (Middle Bridge),
Mud March, and Chancellorsville (Franklin's Crossing). During the
Pennsylvania Campaign, his company built bridges over the Rappahannock, Potomac, and Occoquan Rivers. Rapidan Campaign (August
to November 1865). **Recruiting Service:** November 26, 1863, to
May 29, 1864. **Army of the Potomac:** Multiple bridging operations
during the Richmond Campaign. Engaged at Battle of Cold Harbor
and constructed bridge over James River; siege of Petersburg. **Army
of the Shenandoah:** Assistant engineer on General Sheridan's staff;
chief engineer on Sheridan's staff (February 28, 1865, to June 1,
1865). Participated in actions at Dinwiddie Court House, Five Forks,
Sailor's Creek, and Appomattox. **Military Division of the Southwest:** Chief engineer (June 3, 1865, to July 17, 1865).

Frank Brown Hamilton (1838–1891)

Born in Monroeville, Ohio, on August
31, 1838, to James and Emily Hamilton, he began his higher education at
Western Reserve College. Hamilton was
appointed from the Thirteenth Congressional District of Ohio and entered West
Point on July 1, 1858. After graduating
twelfth in his class, he was commissioned
in the Third US Artillery. He served with
the Army of the Potomac in horse artillery and was brevetted twice for gallantry
(Antietam and Gettysburg). After serving

Cadet Frank B. Hamilton.
SCAD

in the Army of the Potomac, he returned to West Point as an instructor from 1863 to 1868. He later received a belated AM degree from
Western Reserve College in 1865. In the postwar period, he was
assigned to multiple artillery units. He was married in 1888, just prior
to being assigned military attaché to the US embassy in Spain, but

1st Lt. Frank B. Hamilton.
SCAD

his wife died two years later. Major Hamilton passed away after an illness at Fort Adams, Rhode Island, on May 29, 1891, at the age of fifty-three. A wartime picture of Lieutenant Hamilton, standing second from left, is shown in figure 18.2—First Horse Artillery Brigade Officers.

Civil War Assignments: Commissioned as second lieutenant in Battery A, Third US Artillery Regiment; **Army of the Potomac:** Battery M, Second US Artillery, he served in the Horse Artillery Brigade in support of cavalry actions during the Peninsula Campaign; in the Maryland Campaign including the battle of Antietam; and in skirmishes at Williamsport, Martinsburg, Nolan's Ford, Philomont, Upperville, Barber's Crossroads, Amisville; Rappahannock Campaign, the Battle of Fredericksburg and Stoneman's Raid. During the Pennsylvania Campaign, he was involved in actions at Beverly Ford (June 9, 1863), Hanover, Hunterstown, and the Battle of Gettysburg. Following Gettysburg his battery was in support of cavalry skirmishes at Monterey, Williamsport, Boonsboro, Hagerstown, Falling Waters, and Battle Mountain (July 4 to July 24, 1863); Rapidan Campaign: Brandy Station (October 11, 1863). **US Military Academy:** Assistant professor of chemistry, mineralogy, and geology (October 20, 1863, to July 17, 1868), assistant professor of geography, history, and ethics (September 1 to October 10, 1864, and April 4 to May 3, 1865), and assistant professor of drawing (January 17 to March 22, 1865).

Frederick Joseph James (1841–1864)

Born in Cold Springs, New York, August 24, 1841, to Frederick James and the former Julia Safford. He was appointed from the Ninth Congressional District of New York and entered West Point on July 1, 1858. After graduating twenty-seventh in the class, he was commissioned in the Third US Cavalry. His unit was initially paroled during the first year of the war, and Lieutenant James was assigned on "detached service with the First US Cavalry" with the Army of the Potomac. A year later, he joined Maj. Gen. William T. Sherman's Army of the Tennessee and his own Third US Cavalry. He was seriously wounded in an engagement at Colliersville, Tennessee, on October 11,

Cadet Frederick J. James. *SCAD*

1863, when General Sherman's train was attacked. Lieutenant James returned home to recuperate and was subsequently reassigned to light duty in the Department of the East at Governors Island in New York City. While on leave and riding near his parents' home at Cold Springs one afternoon, James was thrown from his horse and accidently killed on August 4, 1864, at age twenty-three.

Civil War Assignments: Commissioned as second lieutenant in Company F, Third US Cavalry. **Army of the Potomac:** Assigned on "detached service" with the First US Cavalry (July 1862, to February 1863) where he participated in the Peninsula, Maryland, and Rappahannock Campaigns: covering the movement of the army from Harrison's Landing, the Battle of South Mountain, the Battle of Antietam, the march to Falmouth, VA, and the Battle of Fredericksburg. **Army of the Tennessee:** Third US Cavalry at Columbus, KY (February 8 to March 12, 1863) on expedition up the Tennessee River to Pittsburg Landing, TN (March 12–19, 1863); in garrison at Columbus, KY (March 19 to April 13, 1863); assistant commissary of musters, Sixth Division, Sixteenth Army Corps (March 13 to August 10, 1863); and in command of company, and acting ordnance officer, at Camp McRae near Memphis (September 4 to October 8, 1863). During movement by train to Chattanooga with General Sherman was engaged in action at Colliersville, TN (October 11, 1863) where he was severely wounded. On sick leave of absence October 12, 1863, to February 10, 1864. **Headquarters, Department of the East:** Placed on light duty at Governors Island, NY (February 10 to August 4, 1864) until fit for service in the field. Accidently killed August 4, 1864.

James Madison Lancaster (1840–1900)

Cadet James M. Lancaster. *SCAD*

Born October 13, 1840, at Bardstown, Kentucky, to Judge William Lancaster and the former Malvina Churchill. The Lancasters came from a long line of colonial settlers (Maryland), and it was his grandfather who immigrated to Kentucky. Lancaster was appointed from the Fifth Congressional District of Kentucky and initially entered the academy in July 1857. A turn-back from the preceding class, he joined the Class of 1862 in September 1860. Although members of his family urged him to resign and fight for the South, Lancaster remained true to his oath and graduated with his classmates. He remained assigned at West Point for several

Maj. James Lancaster. *AR 1901*

months after graduation and then joined the Army of the Potomac. Initially he was assigned to a horse artillery battery in Brig. Gen. Henry Hunt's artillery reserve, his unit supporting various cavalry brigades or cavalry divisions in the major battles of Antietam, Fredericksburg, and Chancellorsville, and the engagements at Brandy Station and along the road to Gettysburg, Monterey Pass, and the pursuit of the enemy to Virginia. He was reassigned to West Point as a tactical officer and instructor in August 1863 and served there four years. Lancaster married Cleffee Burke in 1873 and had no children. He was one of the few in the class to serve over forty years in the army and in two wars. In 1898, he commanded an artillery battalion during the Spanish American War in Cuba and Puerto Rico (actions at Coamo and Asomanto). He returned to the United States on disability leave from Puerto Rico in 1898. After two years of illness, Colonel Lancaster died at age sixty-one on October 5, 1900, at Fort Monroe, Virginia. He is buried in Arlington National Cemetery.

Civil War Assignments: **Army of the Potomac:** Battery C, Third US Artillery (September 1862). Engaged in a skirmish near Warrenton (November 6, 1862), in the Rappahannock Campaign, the Battle of Fredericksburg, and several raids and skirmishes (December 1862 to June 1863). In the Pennsylvania Campaign in the pursuit of the enemy, he supported cavalry skirmishes at Cavetown, Boonsboro, Antietam Creek, and near St. James College, MD. **Military Academy:** Assistant instructor of artillery, infantry, and cavalry tactics (August 29, 1863, to September 13, 1865) and as assistant professor of geography, history, and ethics (September 1, 1863, to March 17, 1865). On leave of absence, September 13 to November 7, 1865.

James Henry Lord (1840–1896)

Born in Honesdale, Pennsylvania, on February 27, 1840, to Russell F. Lord and his wife. He attended military school in New Haven before applying to West Point. Appointed from the Thirteenth Congressional District of Pennsylvania, he initially entered the Military Academy on July 1, 1857, and was turned back one year in June 1859 to join the Class of 1862. Lord also came perilously close to being kicked out several times for disciplinary prob-

Cadet James H. Lord. *SCAD*

lems. He graduated twenty-sixth in his class and was commissioned in the Second US Artillery. Serving almost entirely with the same battery in the Ninth Corps during the war, he was brevetted three times for gallantry. His battery commander, 1st Lt. Samuel Benjamin, stated that Lord "was one of the coolest men under fire he had ever

seen." An early widower with two children, he married again in 1872 to Fannie Eaton in California. Having an inventive mind, Major Lord held several patents for inventions he designed during tours with the Quartermaster Department later in his career. Medically retired in 1893 as a result of his service during the Civil War, he passed away on February 21, 1896, in San Francisco at the age of fifty-six and is buried in the Presidio National Cemetery.

Maj. James H. Lord. *AR 1896*

Civil War Assignments: **Army of the Potomac:** Battery E, Second US Artillery in the Peninsula Campaign, the Northern Virginia Campaign, the Second Battle of Manassas, the Battle of Chantilly, the Maryland Campaign (including the Battle of South Mountain and the Battle of Antietam), the march to Falmouth, VA, the Rappahannock Campaign, and the Battle of Fredericksburg. **Department of Ohio:** Transferred with the Ninth Corps and Battery E, Second US Artillery. At Covington, KY, April 1863, and Lexington, KY, April 24 to June 4, 1863. In movement of Ninth Corps to Young's Point, LA, June 4–17, 1863. **Army of Tennessee:** Transferred with the Ninth Corps and Battery E, Second US Artillery, during the Vicksburg Campaign, including the siege of Vicksburg (June 17 to July 4, 1863), and the capture of Jackson, MS. On sick leave of absence August 10 to September 26, 1863. Believed to be present with Ninth Corps in East Tennessee at the siege of Knoxville through December 1863. Assigned as mustering and disbursing officer at Cincinnati, OH, March 15 to May 2, 1864, and at Boston, MA, May 2 to December 25, 1864. **Army of the Potomac:** Involved in operations about Petersburg with General Sheridan's cavalry corps. In command of Horse Battery A, Second US Artillery (February to April 1865) at Battle of Dinwiddie Court House, the Battle of Five Forks, and in pursuit of the enemy in support of cavalry at Lisbon Centre, High Bridge, Farmville, and Appomattox Court House. At headquarters of Second Division, Cavalry Corps, April 22 to June 22, 1865. Aide-de-camp to Brig. Gen. George Crook, June 22 to August 25, 1865.

Ranald Slidell Mackenzie (1840–1889)

Cadet Ranald S. Mackenzie. *SCAD*

Born in New York City on June 27, 1840, to Commodore Alexander Mackenzie and the former Catherine Robinson, whose family lived in Mount Pleasant, New York, for several years. After his father's untimely death, Mackenzie's mother moved the family to Morristown, New Jersey, in 1849 to be near her family. Mackenzie was educated first at the Mount Pleasant Academy, New York, and later at Williams College in Massachusetts. In 1858 his mother sought an appointment to West Point through his uncle, Louisiana senator John Slidell, who secured an at-large presidential appointment for him to join the Class of 1862 on July 1, 1858. He contested for the top slot in the class each year. Appointed a cadet lieutenant his final year, he endured one final scrape with the Tactical Department, which brought a reduction to "high private." Mackenzie graduated first in his class and was commissioned in the Corps of Engineers. His gallantry in action as an engineer officer and later in command of infantry and cavalry units brought multiple brevet promotions. He was appointed brigadier general in the regular army within two years of graduation and brevetted to major general, USV, in command of a cavalry division before the war was over. He was wounded six times during the war and once during later cavalry campaigns in the Southwest. After the war, he served as an engineer and then took command of an infantry regiment of US Colored Troops. Three years later, he was appointed to command the Fourth US Cavalry in Texas where he had an illustrious career. General Mackenzie was medically retired in 1884 as a result of a combination of wounds and mental instability. He spent the remainder of

his days in New Brighton, Staten Island, with his sister. He died on January 19, 1889, at age forty-eight and is buried at West Point. There are at least five books and multiple articles written about his exploits while in command of the Fourth US Cavalry in the Southwest. A television program titled *Mackenzie's Raiders* was popular during the 1950s, and actor John Wayne depicted Mackenzie as "Colonel Brittles" in the movie *Rio Grande*.

Brig. Gen. R. S. Mackenzie. *MHI*

Civil War Assignments: **Army of the Potomac:** US Engineer Battalion. As assistant engineer, served with Ninth Corps during the Battle of Second Manassas and in the Maryland Campaign. During the Rappahannock Campaign with the Grand Right Division staff during the Battle of Fredericksburg and on the Army of the Potomac engineer staff at the Battle of Chancellorsville. In the Pennsylvania Campaign, in command of the engineer company laying bridges over the Potomac and the Occoquan, and during the Battle of Gettysburg was an aide to Brig. Gen. Gouverneur Warren. Served in the Rapidan Campaign. In the Richmond Campaign, in command of the engineer company laying bridges and building defensive works and roads during the Battles of Wilderness, Spotsylvania, and Cold Harbor. **Second Connecticut Heavy Artillery:** At Cold Harbor, appointed colonel, USV, in command (June 10, 1864). At Petersburg with Sixth Corps and Second Connecticut Heavy Artillery (June–July 1864). Participated in the repulse of Early's Raid on Washington. **Army of the Shenandoah with Sixth Corps:** Actions with Second Connecticut Heavy Artillery at Winchester, Fisher's Hill, and Cedar Creek (August 15 to October

19, 1864). **Army of the Potomac:** At Petersburg, with Sixth Corps, in command of Second Brigade, Upton's division (December 1864 to March 1865). **Army of the James:** Commanded cavalry division attached to Sheridan's cavalry corps (March–April 1865) and participated in actions at Five Forks, the pursuit of enemy to Appomattox Court House, and final surrender. In Richmond, commanded cavalry division (April to August 1865).

Samuel Bates McIntire (1839–1917)

Cadet Samuel B. McIntire. *SCAD*

Born in Massachusetts, McIntire was appointed to the Military Academy from that state and entered West Point on July 1, 1858. He graduated twenty-third in his class and was commissioned in the Fifth US Artillery. He began his military career at Harrison's Landing with the Army of the Potomac and almost immediately was sent north with the Fifth Corps to participate in the Second Battle of Manassas, actions for which he was brevetted for gallantry. McIntire participated in the initial engagement at Chancellorsville with the Fifth Corps and was then transferred with his unit into the horse artillery in support of

Samuel B. McIntire. *AR 1918*

the cavalry corps where he participated in most of the remaining major campaigns and cavalry raids during the war. When General Jubal Early threatened Washington, he was sent with his battery to join Maj. Gen. Philip Sheridan's Army of the Shenandoah and participated in the battles of Winchester and Cedar Creek. Before the end of the war, he was sent off to recruiting duty. Discharged October 1, 1870, at his own request, he moved to Houston,

Minnesota, where he spent the rest of his life. He died June 17, 1917, at age seventy-eight. In a wartime picture taken with the First Horse Artillery Brigade officers at Culpeper in September 1863 (figure 18.2 in chapter 18), Lieutenant McIntire appears standing on the far right.

Civil War Assignments: **Army of the Potomac:** Battery C, Fifth US Artillery during the Peninsula Campaign; the Second Battle of Manassas; the Maryland Campaign, including the Battle of Antietam, the skirmish at Shepherdstown, and the march to Falmouth, VA. Transferred to Battery B&L, Second US Artillery (October 6, 1862), in which he served in the Rappahannock Campaign and the Battle of Chancellorsville, the Pennsylvania Campaign, the pursuit of the enemy to Warrenton, VA, and the Rapidan Campaign in support of actions at Morton's Ford, Culpeper, and Bealton Station. On leave of absence (January–February 1864). Served in the Richmond Campaign in support of cavalry actions at Todd's Tavern, Sheridan's Raid to Haxall's Landing, Yellow Tavern, Hawes's Shop, Trevilian Station, and at Deep Bottom. **Army of the Shenandoah:** With Battery B/L, Second US Artillery, during the Shenandoah Campaign in support of cavalry actions at White Post, Front Royal, Luray, Mount Jackson, Waynesboro, and the Battles of Winchester and Cedar Creek. **Recruiting Service:** April 1 to July 1865.

Samuel Mather Mansfield (1839–1928)

Born September 23, 1839, to Capt. J. K. F. and Mary Mansfield in Middletown, Connecticut. Samuel received an at-large appointment and entered the Military Academy on July 1, 1858. An excellent student and a cadet captain during his last year, Mansfield graduated sixth in his class and was commissioned in the Corps of Engineers. After graduation, he joined the staff of his father (then a major gen-

Cadet Samuel M. Mansfield. *SCAD*

eral) as a staff captain. When his father was killed at Antietam, Mansfield returned to his hometown and helped raise the Twenty-fourth Connecticut Volunteer Infantry, of which he took command. The Twenty-fourth became part of Maj. Gen. Nathaniel Banks's expedition to open the Mississippi River and took part in the campaign to capture Port Hudson. The regiment returned to Connecticut in September 1863 and was mustered out of federal service. Mansfield then reverted to his permanent rank in the Engineer Department. He was brevetted three times for gallantry during the war. His subsequent career spanned the continent and included command of various engineer districts, lighthouse divisions, and depots. He also headed

the Yosemite National Park Commission and a presidential commission to set the boundaries between Indian Territory and Texas. He met and married Anna Baldwin Wright in Michigan in 1874, and they had three children. He was promoted to brigadier general in 1903 and retired from active service the same year. He died at Fort Leavenworth, Kansas, on February 18, 1928, at age eighty-eight and is buried at the Indian Hills Cemetery, Middletown, Connecticut.

Brig. Gen. Samuel M. Mansfield (Ret.). *MHI*

Civil War Assignments: Commissioned as second lieutenant in the Corps of Engineers. **Seventh Corps (Suffolk, VA):** Staff of Maj. Gen. J. K. F. Mansfield (July 1 to September 1862). **Twenty-fourth Connecticut Infantry Regiment:** Appointed colonel, USV, in command of unit (October 1862). **Department of the Gulf:** With Nineteenth Corps (December 17, 1862, to August 3, 1862). Participated in the action at Irish Bend, LA, the march to Alexandria, and the siege of Port Hudson, including the assaults of May 27 and June 14, 1863. Mustered out of volunteer service, October 1863. **Engineer Department:** Assistant engineer during the construction of the fort at Sandy Hook, NJ (November 6, 1863, to March 19, 1864). Superintending engineer for defenses of West Pass into Narragansett Bay, RI (March 19, 1864, to November 7, 1865) and construction of batteries at New Haven, CT (May 20, 1864, to September 17, 1866). In charge of Fort Trumbull and Battery Griswold, CT (June 8, 1864, to September 17, 1866) and repair of Fort Adams, RI (June 8, 1864, to November 7, 1865). Temporarily detached as assistant engineer in the construction of the defenses at Point Lookout, MD (July 16–26, 1864). **Engineer Recruiting Service:** November 2, 1864, to September 25, 1866. Also a member of the special board considering the defenses of Willet's Point, NY (April 7 to June 20, 1865).

William Augustus Marye (1840–1903)

Born in Baltimore, Maryland, to George T. Marye and the former Helen Tucker on April 21, 1840. His father moved to California during the gold rush in 1849. William Marye stayed behind and later attended Georgetown University for one year before he was appointed to West Point from the newly created First Congressional District of California. He served as first captain during his last year at West Point, graduated eleventh in his class (became first cadet to graduate from California), and was commissioned in the Ordnance Department. A skillful horseman, he loved to ride the unruly animals not generally popular with his classmates. He did not marry until stationed in California, where he met Madie Mae Marye of Port Gibson, Mississippi, and married her on January 28, 1879. Unfortunately, she passed away in Augusta, Georgia, on November 28, 1885, leaving him a widower while in command of the arsenal. He contributed greatly to various research projects during his career and particularly on new and improved gun carriages at the Watertown Arsenal. While assigned to Fort Monroe, he met Marie Alice Doyle, mar-

Cadet William A. Marye. *SCAD*

ried her on April 9, 1895, and took leave of absence to tour England, France, and Switzerland. The loss of their only child in 1896 took its toll on Colonel Marye, then in command of the arsenal at Fort Monroe. Changes in his general health and eyes forced him to seek retirement in 1902 in Washington, DC, where he lived until his death on May 13, 1903, at age sixty-three. He is buried in Greenmont Cemetery in Baltimore, Maryland.

Col. William A. Marye. *AR 1905*

Civil War Assignments: Commissioned as second lieutenant in the Ordnance Department. **St. Louis Arsenal:** Assistant ordnance officer (July 23, 1862, to June 13, 1863), being detached at various times for duty at Cairo, IL, Helena, AR, and near Vicksburg, MS. **Department of the Cumberland:** July 16, 1863, to July 15, 1864. In charge of ordnance depots at Murfreesboro, TN, Stevenson and Bridgeport, AL, and Chattanooga, TN. **Watervliet Arsenal, NY:** Assistant ordnance officer (June 28, 1864, to July 1865).

Tully McCrea (1839–1918)

Born in Natchez, Mississippi, July 23, 1839, to John and Mary McCrea. McCrea was orphaned as a child and sent north to live with an uncle in Ohio. Appointed to West Point from the Eighth District of Ohio, he became a cadet on July 1, 1858. During his first-class year, he served as a cadet lieutenant, during summer camp, was broken to high private, then was reappointed as a lieutenant during the academic year. He graduated fourteenth in his class and was commissioned in the

Cadet Tully McCrea. *WPAOG*

First US Artillery. Initially assigned to the Army of the Potomac on the Peninsula, he participated in three major battles (Antietam, Chancellorsville, and Gettysburg) before he was transferred to his permanent unit in the Department of the South. After he was severely wounded at Olustee, Florida, it took several months for him to recover before assignment to West Point as an instructor. During the war, he was brevetted for gallantry three times. He left West Point in 1866, met and married Harriet Hale Camp in 1868, and they had one daughter, Alice. He returned to West Point as its quartermaster and then served as deputy commander at the Soldiers' Home in Washington.

His lengthy career included service with and command of several artillery units and forts, including command of the garrison at Cartel de Espagne in Manila after the Spanish-American War. After forty-one years of service, he retired from the army on February 22, 1903, as a brigadier general. The last years of his life were spent at West Point where he died on September 5, 1918, at age seventy-nine. He is buried in the cemetery at West Point.

Brig. Gen. Tully McCrea (Ret.). *AR 1925, WPAOG*

Civil War Assignments: Commissioned as a second lieutenant in Battery M, First US Artillery Regiment. **Army of the Potomac:** Battery I, First US Artillery (on detached service) with the Second Corps. Saw action at Harrison's Landing, the Battle of Antietam, the Battle of Fredericksburg, the Battle of Chancellorsville, the Pennsylvania Campaign (including the Battle of Gettysburg), and the pursuit to Warrenton. **Department of the South:** Battery M, First US Artillery at Beaufort, SC (September 7, 1863); Battle of Olustee, FL (wounded February 21, 1864). **Hospital and Sick Leave:** Beaufort, SC; New York City; and Morristown, NJ (March to May 1864). Home leave at Dayton, OH (June to August 1864). General Hospital, Cincinnati, OH (August to September 1864). **US Military Academy:** Assistant professor of geography, history, and ethics (August 31, 1864, to

August 31, 1865) and assistant professor of mathematics (August 31, 1865, to June 23, 1866).

Albert Morse Murray (1840–1864)

Murray was born in Canandaigua, New York, to Albert G. Murray and the former Emily A. Morse on July 11, 1840. He was appointed to the Military Academy from the Twenty-sixth District of New York and entered with the Class of 1862 on July 1, 1858, one month short of his eighteenth birthday. Appointed as a cadet lieutenant in the last year at West Point, he graduated twenty-fourth in his class and was commissioned in the artillery. He served initially with the Army of

Cadet Albert M. Murray. *SCAD*

the Potomac and fought in most of its major campaigns through the Battle of Fredericksburg. His battery, a part of the Ninth Corps, was then transferred to Suffolk, Virginia, where he participated in several engagements. Before the end of the year, Murray found that a battery in the Second US Artillery Regiment had no regular officers, received

a transfer to join it in Memphis, and took command. His new battery, a part of Maj. Gen. James B. McPherson's Army of the Tennessee, participated in most of the early battles of Gen. Sherman's Atlanta Campaign. While under attack near Atlanta on July 22, 1864, his battery was captured by Confederate forces. Murray was sent to Camp Oglethorpe, a Confederate military prison near Macon, where he contracted typhoid fever and died a month later at age twenty-four. He is buried in the West Avenue Cemetery, Canandaigua, NY.

1st Lt. Albert M. Murray. *OCHS*

Civil War Assignments: **Army of the Potomac:** Battery A, Fifth US Artillery, Ninth Corps. Served in the Virginia Campaign, the Maryland Campaign (including the Battle of Antietam), the march to Falmouth, VA, the Rappahannock Campaign, the Battle of Fredericksburg, and in operations about Suffolk, VA (April to June 1863). **Army of Tennessee:** In command of Battery F, Second US Artillery, Sixteenth Corps at Memphis, TN (July 18 to October 18, 1863), and march to Chattanooga (October 18, 1863, to May 4, 1864). In the Atlanta Campaign, participating in the Battles of Resaca, Dallas, Kennesaw Mountain, Ruff's Station, and Atlanta (July 22, 1864), when he was captured. **Prisoner of War:** Macon, GA (July 22 to August 12, 1864). Died in captivity from typhoid fever, August 12, 1864.

Jasper Myers (1838–1918)

Born in Anderson, Indiana, on December 25, 1838, to Samuel and Elizabeth Myers. He was appointed to the Military Academy from the Eleventh Congressional District of Indiana and entered West Point on July 1, 1858. Jasper was a good student, graduated tenth in his class, and was commissioned in the Ordnance Department. Upon graduation, he was assigned to Allegheny Arsenal and was present during the horrendous explosion that took

Cadet Jasper Myers. *SCAD*

over a hundred lives on September 19, 1862. Shortly thereafter, Myers was reassigned to the Department of Virginia and North Carolina, a position he returned to several times as chief ordnance officer during his career. Late in the war, he was responsible for establishing field depots at Wilmington and along Sherman's route north into North Carolina. At Raleigh, North Carolina, he collected all Confederate arms turned in after the surrender of Gen. Joseph Johnston's army. At the end of the war, he was brevetted to captain for meritorious service. During the next five years, Myers studied the law as a judge advocate in the army. When stationed at Benicia Arsenal, California, he was honorably discharged and became an attorney in San Francisco for a short period. Injuries suffered in the army limited his ability to act in his chosen profession. Upon advice of his physician in 1872, he abandoned his

new career and became a rancher near Bakersfield, California. He married late in life to the former Martha Cather, and they had three children. Myers, known for being succinct, pointed out in his last letter to the Association of Graduates, "I have some thoughts of preparing my own obituary which I think can easily be condensed into one page with some spare space left." His death in Bakersfield, on December 13, 1918, at age seventy-nine was the result of a stroke.

Jasper Myers. *AR 1919*

Civil War Assignments: **Allegheny Arsenal, PA:** Assistant ordnance officer (July 27 to December 24, 1862). **Department of North Carolina:** Chief of ordnance (January 1 to July 15, 1863). **Department of Virginia and North Carolina:** Chief of ordnance (July 15, 1863, to January 1864). **Watervliet Arsenal:** Assistant ordnance officer (February 6 to June 6, 1864). **Watertown Arsenal:** Assistant ordnance officer (June 6, 1864, to February 1865). **Field Depot, Wilmington, NC:** March to June 1865. Presided over collection of surrendered arms from General Johnston's army at Goldsboro, NC, May 1865.

James Hickman Rollins (1841–1898)

James Rollins was born in Columbia, Missouri, on September 29, 1841, to James S. Rollins and the former Mary Elizabeth Hickman. He was appointed to the Military Academy from the Second District of Missouri and initially entered West Point on July 5, 1857. A turn-back from the preceding class, he joined the Class of 1862 in September 1859. His father was a prominent legislator in Missouri who was a congressional representative from 1861 to 1865. During his last year at West Point, Rollins was appointed a cadet captain and the adjutant of the Corps of Cadets. He graduated twenty-fifth in his class and chose the artillery. He was retained at West Point after graduation as an instructor in artillery and tactics. In April 1863, he transferred to the Ordnance Department where he served in various assignments. He was brevetted to captain for meritorious service during the war. Rollins married Eulalie Bowman of Wilkes-Barre, PA, the daughter of former West Point superintendent Col. Alexander H. Bowman, and they had four children. He retired from active service, March 15, 1883, for disability incurred in line of duty and returned to Columbia. Although he was in declining health, his death on February 5, 1898, was not expected. Major Rollins is buried in Columbia, Missouri.

Cadet James H. Rollins. *SCAD*

Civil War Assignments: Commissioned in the Second US Artillery Regiment as a brevet second lieutenant. **US Military Academy:** Assistant instructor of artillery and infantry tactics (June 16, 1862, to June 25, 1863). **Watervliet Arsenal:** Assistant ordnance officer (July 2, 1863, to February 28, 1864). **Ordnance Bureau, Washington, DC:** February 29 to October 31, 1864. **St. Louis Arsenal:** November 14, 1864, to October 18, 1865.

James A. Sanderson (1841–1864)

Born in Athens, Ohio, in 1841 to Robert Sanderson and the former Margaret Fraser. Soon after it became known that an earlier appointee did not pass his examination, residents of Athens signed a petition recommending that Rep. Valentine Horton of Ohio's Eleventh District appoint James Sanderson to replace him. "Sep" Sanderson arrived in August 1858 to undergo examination and joined the Class of 1862 on September 1, 1858. He was no stranger to punishments imposed by the Tactical Department. Appointed a cadet lieutenant during his last year, Sanderson graduated eighteenth in his class and was commissioned in the First US Artillery Regiment. He joined the Army of the Potomac and participated in a number of major campaigns and in suppressing the New York City draft riots. He was cited for bravery during the Battle of Chancellorsville when he galloped forward with a limber to extract a gun and his mortally wounded battery commander. In late 1863 he transferred to the Department of the Gulf to join his own battery and participated in the Red River Campaign. Sanderson was wounded when his battery was overrun at Pleasant Hill on April 9, 1864. He was found between his guns when the battery was retaken and died the next day. His body was hastily buried on the battlefield, the location of his gravesite unknown. He was twenty-three.

Cadet James A. Sanderson. *SCAD*

Civil War Assignments: **Army of the Potomac:** Battery H, First US Artillery. In the Peninsula Campaign and in the defenses of Washington near Alexandria, VA (August to October 1862). On the march to Falmouth, VA. In the Rappahannock Campaign, the Battle of Fredericksburg, and the Battle of Chancellorsville. In the Pennsylvania Campaign and the Battle of Gettysburg. **New York City Draft Riots:** With Battery C, Fifth US Artillery (July 19 to October 13, 1863). **Department of the Gulf:** With Battery L, First US Artillery, Nineteenth Corps (November 7, 1863, to April 11, 1864), participated in actions at New Iberia and Franklin, LA, as well as the Red River Campaign. During the Battle of Pleasant Hill, he died of wounds received on the battlefield.

Jared Augustine Smith (1840–1910)

Cadet Jared A. Smith.
SCAD

Born in Wilton, Maine, on July 6, 1840, to Jared Smith and the former Sarah Dakin. He was appointed from the Second Congressional District of Maine and entered West Point on July 1, 1858. A good student as a cadet, he was appointed a cadet lieutenant during his first-class year and served temporarily as an assistant instructor. Graduating fifth in his class, he was commissioned in the Corps of Engineers. Smith initially served with Pope's Army of Virginia's Second Corps in the early days of the war but was seriously wounded at Cedar Mountain. After hospitalization, a medical board limited any active duty, and he was sent to West Point, where he served as an assistant professor and command of the engineer detachment from late 1862 to 1863. He was brevetted for gallantry once and received a second brevet to major for meritorious service at the end of the war. He married Emily G. Reed in 1864 and had two sons. Assigned to various projects, boards, and districts

Brig. Gen. Jared A. Smith.
AR 1911

across the country during his career, he was recognized as one of America's highest authorities on military engineering, and coast and harbor defenses. As a brigadier general, Smith retired from active service April 14, 1903, at his own request after over forty years' service. After retirement, General Smith resided in Cleveland until he passed away there on December 10, 1910, at age seventy-one. He is buried in the Lake View Cemetery, Cleveland, Ohio.

Civil War Assignments: **Army of Virginia:** Assistant engineer on the staff of Maj. Gen. Nathaniel Banks (July 10 to November 24, 1862).

In the Northern Virginia Campaign and at the Battle of Cedar Mountain (wounded on August 9, 1862). On sick leave of absence August 28 to November 22, 1862. **US Military Academy:** Assistant professor of geography, history, and ethics (November 26, 1862, to August 19, 1863). **Engineer Department:** Assistant engineer in the construction of the defenses of Portland, ME, and of the northeastern coast (August 11, 1863, to August 9, 1864). **Engineer Recruiting Service:** December 1, 1863, to August 9, 1864. **Project Engineer:** Defenses of Baltimore, MD (August 10 to September 22, 1864); Fort Montgomery, NY (September 28, 1864, to March 2, 1865); and Fort Ontario, NY (March 3, 1865, to November 1866).

Morris Schaff (1838–1927)

Cadet Morris Schaff. *SCAD*

Brig. Gen. Morris Schaff, MA Militia. *AR 1933, WPAOG*

Born in Etna Township, Ohio, on December 28, 1838, to John and the former Charlotte Hartzell. He was appointed from the Twelfth District of Ohio and entered West Point on July 1, 1858. He graduated ninth in his class and was commissioned in the Ordnance Department. He served on the staff of the Army of the Potomac and at several arsenals during his career. His depot at City Point supplied the powder for the Petersburg crater and was destroyed by Confederate saboteurs in August 1864. Schaff was brevetted to captain for gallantry before the end of the war. After City Point, he was transferred to Watertown Arsenal, where he married Alice Page on August 8, 1868. After resigning from the army in 1871, Schaff became a successful businessman and was the author of several books about the

Civil War. His book *The Spirit of Old West Point* is a primary reference for this period. He later served as a member of the Board of Visitors to West Point, was appointed a brigadier general in the Massachusetts militia, and served as president of the USMA Association of Graduates from 1913 to 1914. He passed away at Southborough, Massachusetts, on October 19, 1929, at the age of eighty-nine, the last surviving member of his class. He is buried in Pittsfield, Massachusetts.

Civil War Assignments: **Army of the Potomac:** Ordnance officer at Fort Monroe and Aquia Harbor. Served in the Rappahannock Campaign, the Pennsylvania Campaign (during which he was on the staff of Maj. Gen. George Meade; collected arms at Gettysburg June–August 1863), the Rapidan Campaign, and the Richmond Campaign (as acting aide-de-camp to General Warren in May 1864). Participated in the Battles of the Wilderness and Spotsylvania. In charge of the ordnance depot at City Point supplying the armies before Richmond (May 19 to September 15, 1864). Assistant inspector of ordnance at Reading, PA (September 13 to December 31, 1864). **Watertown Arsenal:** Assistant ordnance officer (January 3, 1865, to September 1, 1866).

Charles Russell Suter (1842–1920)

Born in Brooklyn, New York, on May 5, 1842, to Capt. Alexander Suter (an army surgeon) and the former Grace Degen. After his father's death during the US-Mexican War in 1847, he was sent off by his uncle for schooling in Europe and soon became fluent in French, having to relearn his native tongue before attending West Point. He received an at-large appointment and entered West Point on July 1, 1858. "Ole Sute" graduated fourth in his class and was commissioned in the

Cadet Charles R. Suter.
SCAD

Corps of Engineers. He initially served with Pope's Army of Virginia, then with the Army of the Potomac, and finally with the Department of the South during the Civil War. He received one brevet to captain for gallantry and another to major for meritorious service during the war. Suter's lengthy career spanned multiple engineering assignments across the country. During the Spanish-American War, he was in charge of the fortifications at San Francisco. Colonel Suter became one of the longest-serving officers associated with

projects and commissions concerning the Mississippi River. Known and admired by many of the great pilots on the river, he designed a snag boat that carried his name and dredges that helped clear the river for many years. His first wife passed away in Minnesota in 1867, some six months after they were married. Eight years later, he married Martha Winkley in Massachusetts, and they had seven children. As a brigadier general, Suter retired from the army in 1906 and moved to Brookline, Massachusetts, where he passed away on August 7, 1920, at age seventy-eight.

Brig. Gen. Charles R. Suter.
AR 1921

Civil War Assignments: **Army of Virginia:** Assistant engineer, Third Corps, in the Northern Virginia Campaign. Participated in the Battle of Cedar Mountain and skirmishes on the Rappahannock in August 1862. **Army of the Potomac:** Assistant engineer, First Corps (September 6–20, 1862), and with the US Engineer Battalion (September 22 to November 16, 1862). In the Maryland Campaign, he fought at the Battle of South Mountain and was wounded during the Battle of Antietam. Engaged in the building, guarding, and repairing of pontoon bridges across the Potomac and Shenandoah Rivers at Harpers Ferry, and constructing defenses on Maryland Heights (September 21 to November 3, 1862). In the Rappahannock Campaign, he was assistant engineer of Center Grand Division (November 16, 1862, to

February 25, 1863) and participated in the Battle of Fredericksburg, commanding an engineer company, constructing fieldworks, making surveys, guarding bridges, etc. **Department of the South:** As assistant engineer (March 1863 to March 31, 1864), in charge of covering batteries on Folly Island (July 10, 1863) and the construction of batteries to bombard Fort Wagner and Fort Sumter (August 17–23 and November 1–10, 1863). Participated in the siege of Fort Wagner and in charge of engineer operations at Hilton Head and Port Royal Island (December 5, 1863, to March 31, 1864). **District of Florida:** Chief engineer (March 31 to May 3, 1864) and assistant engineer (May 3–28, 1864). **Department of the South:** Chief engineer (May 28, 1864, to October 2, 1865).

Charles Nelson Warner (1839–1920)

Charles Nelson Warner was born April 19, 1839, in Bridgewater Township, Pennsylvania, to Nelson C. Warner and Eliza Baldwin Warner. Appointed from the Fourteenth District of Pennsylvania, he initially entered the Military Academy on July 1, 1857. A turn-back from the preceding class, he joined the Class of 1862 in September 1981. He graduated twenty-eighth in the class (last) and was commissioned in the Second US Artillery. During the war, Warner participated in most of the major campaigns and was brevetted for gallantry twice. He married Eliza Houston in Leavenworth, Kansas, in October 1868 and had six children. Hon-

Cadet Charles N. Warner. *SCAD*

Charles N. Warner. *James Lafferty Collection*

orably mustered out in 1871, he returned to Montrose, Pennsylvania, to study law, which he practiced for over fifty years. At the time of his death on September 5, 1920, he was the senior member of the bar at age eighty-one. He is buried in Montrose.

Civil War Assignments: **Army of the Potomac:** Battery D, Second US Artillery (on detached service), with the Sixth Corps. During the Peninsula Campaign, he participated in the Second Battle of Manassas. In the Maryland Campaign, his unit supported the Sixth Corps during the Battle of South Mountain and the Battle of Antietam. Served on the march to Falmouth, VA. In the Rappahannock Campaign, fought at the Battle of Fredericksburg and Battle of Chancellorsville, and in the Pennsylvania Campaign at the Battle of Gettysburg. Transferred to Battery A, Fourth US Artillery, First Horse Artillery Brigade in August 1863. In the Rapidan Campaign, he supported cavalry actions at White Sulphur Springs and Bristoe Station as well as the Mine Run Expedition. **Department of the Cumberland:** Battery H, Fourth US Artillery, in Nashville, TN, as part of the Artillery Reserve conducting operations about Chattanooga, TN, Dalton, GA, and Nashville, TN (March to December 1864). His service with Horse Battery I, Fourth US Artillery (November 1864 to August 1865) included the Battle of Nashville and support of the cavalry division in pursuit of Maj. Gen. John Bell Hood's rebel forces (December 1864 to January 1865). **Wilson's Cavalry Corps:** With Horse Battery I, Fourth US Artillery, during Maj. Gen. J. H. Wilson's cavalry campaign in Alabama and Georgia (January to May 1865), and in camp near Atlanta, GA (May to August 1865).

Henry Clifton Wharton (1842–1872)

Born in Arkansas in November 1842 to Maj. Henry W. Wharton and the former Ellen G. Nugent. He was appointed from Nebraska Territory and entered the Military Academy on July 1, 1858. He graduated seventh in his class and was commissioned in the Corps of Engineers. After graduation he served on temporary duty at West

Point for several months before joining the engineer staff of the Department of the Cumberland as assistant engineer. He traveled with the staffs of Maj. Gen. William S. Rosecrans and Maj. Gen. George H. Thomas during the Battle of Chattanooga, the Battle of Nashville, and the Atlanta Campaign. In August 1864, he took command of one of the Pioneer Engineer Regiments serving General Thomas's army. Wharton was brevetted once for meritorious service with the

Cadet Henry C. Wharton. *SCAD*

Department of the Cumberland. He resigned his commission in January 1870 and moved to Baltimore where he died on April 8, 1872, at age twenty-nine. He is buried in the St. John Episcopal Church Cemetery in Norristown, Pennsylvania.

Civil War Assignments: **US Military Academy:** On temporary duty (June 17 to October 27, 1862). **Department of the Cumberland:** Assistant engineer engaged in inspecting and superintending the construction of fortifications at Franklin, Nashville, and other points (November 7, 1862, to August 27, 1864). **Veteran Volunteer Engineer Regiment:** In command of regiment at Nashville, TN, constructing defensive works and guarding the Nashville and Chattanooga Railroad (August 27, 1864, to March 10, 1865). Mustered out of volunteer service March 10, 1865. **Corps of Engineers:** Assistant engineer in the construction of defenses at San Francisco harbor (August 17, 1865, to August 1, 1866).

James Eveleth Wilson (1842–1887)

Born in Georgetown, District of Columbia, to James C. and Alice E. B. Wilson in September 1842. He was appointed by President Buchanan as an at-large candidate and entered West Point on September 1, 1858. He graduated twenty-first in his class and was initially commissioned in the Fifth US Artillery. Four months later, he transferred to the Second US Artillery where he remained assigned throughout the war. He served with the Army of the Potomac during some of its major campaigns and in the defenses of Washington and guarded rebel prisoners at Point Lookout before he was appointed quartermaster of the Second US Artillery Regiment at Fort McHenry. He married Violet Pickrell around 1870, and they had four children. Captain Wilson passed

Cadet James E. Wilson. *SCAD*

away after an illness in Washington, DC, on November 20, 1887, at age forty-five and is buried in Arlington National Cemetery.

Civil War Assignments: **Army of the Potomac:** Battery C, Fifth US Artillery (on detached service) with the Sixth Corps. Participated in the Peninsula Campaign, the Northern Virginia Campaign, the Maryland Campaign (including the Battle of Antietam, followed by a skirmish at Williamsport), and the march to Falmouth, VA. Transferred to the Second US Artillery on October 6, 1862, and served in the Rappahannock Campaign with the Sixth Corps at the Battle of Fredericksburg. On sick leave of absence February 20 to April 1, 1863. **Fort McHenry:** Served as quartermaster, Second US Artillery, and with Battery I, Second US Artillery (December 10, 1863, to July 1, 1866). **Army of the Potomac:** With Battery I, Second US Artillery near Mitchell's Station, VA, and at the skirmish at Barnett's Ford. In the Richmond Campaign, served with his battery at the Battle of Cold Harbor. **Dept. of Washington:** In command of Battery G, Second US Artillery, in the defenses of Washington, DC (June 1864 to June 1865) and at Point Lookout, MD, guarding rebel prisoners. **Fort McHenry:** On regimental staff (June to August 1865).

Notes

Abbreviations

AGO	Adjutant General's Office, War Department, Washington, DC.
Annual Report (date)	*Annual Reunion/Report of the Association of Graduates of the United States Military Academy* (Saginaw, MI: Seeman & Peters, for years 1870–1925).
BLCW	*Battles and Leaders of the Civil War,* 4 vols. Secaucus, NJ: Castle Books, 1991.
Cadet Applications (date)	"US Military Academy Cadet Application Papers (1805–1866)," record group 94, microfilm publication M668, 242 rolls, National Archives, Washington, DC.
Cadet Register (date)	*Official Register of the Officers and Cadets of the U.S. Military Academy* (1833–1866). Special Collections and Archives Division, USMA Library, West Point, NY.
CSR	Compiled Service Records of Confederate Soldiers, RG 109, National Archives, Washington, DC.
Cullum's 1891	George W. Cullum, *Biographical Register of the Officers and Graduates of the U.S. Military Academy, Volume II,* 3rd ed. (Cambridge, MA: Riverside Press / Houghton Mifflin, 1891).
CWD	Everette Beach Long, *The Civil War Day by Day: An Almanac 1861–1865* (New York: Da Capo, 1985; originally 1971 by Doubleday).
Davis Report	US Congress, Senate, *Report of the Committee to Examine the Organization, System of Discipline, and Course of Instruction of the United States Military Academy,* report prepared by Sen. Jefferson Davis, 36th Congress, 2nd Session, Senate Misc. Doc. No. 3 (December 13, 1860).

EDLR	Letters received by the Engineer Department related to the USMA (1819–1866), RG 94, microfilms M91 and M2047, National Archives, Washington, DC.
GNMP	Gettysburg National Military Park.
GO	General Order, Headquarters (HQ), Adjutant General's Office, Washington, DC.
MOLLUS	Military Order of the Loyal Legion of the United States: Commandery Series (1882), US Army Heritage and Education Center, Carlisle, PA.
OR	US War Department, *The War of the Rebellion: A Compilation of the Official Records of the Union and Confederate Armies* (Washington: Government Printing Office, 1880–1901).
OR Atlas	George B. Davis, *Official Military Atlas of the Civil War* (New York, NY: Barnes and Noble Books, 2003).
NA	National Archives, Washington, DC.
Post Orders (No.)	"Post Orders (1837–1877)," 16 volumes, Special Collections and Archives Division (SCAD), USMA Library. Daily records of orders, messages, and disciplinary actions at West Point.
RG	Record Group, National Archives, Washington, DC.
SCAD	Special Collections and Archives Division, USMA Library.
SO	Special Order.
Warner Diary	Charles N. Warner, unpublished diaries and letters for 1859 to 1865, Susquehanna Historical Society, 2 Monument Square, Montrose, PA, 18801.
WP Atlas	Vincent J. Esposito, ed., *The West Point Atlas of American Wars* (New York: Holt, 1995).

1. Aspirations

1. An abbreviated history of this class, written by Brian McEnany and Mary Elizabeth Sergent, "Remembrances: An Abbreviated History of the Class of 1862," was given to each graduate of the Class of 1962 attending their fortieth West Point reunion in June 2002.

2. Tully McCrea to Belle McCrea, October 5, 1864. McCrea file of 256 letters is held by the Special Collections and Archives Division of the

US Military Academy Library (hereafter referred to as SCAD). In this letter, Tully wrote about how much he remembered about the academy from his cadet days, and therein lays the genesis of the title "Remembrances." Further references to McCrea letters will take the form: McCrea and the date. All letters were written to Belle McCrea unless otherwise indicated.

3. Catherine S. Crary, *Dear Belle: Letters from a Cadet and Officer to His Sweetheart* (Middletown, CT: Wesleyan University Press, 1965), 241. The McCreas actually had six children, but two daughters died during childbirth or from yellow fever.

4. Ibid., 5–7.

5. Ibid., 6–9.

6. Ibid., 9–10.

7. Ibid., 11–12.

8. Joshua Antrim, *History of Champaign and Logan Counties* (Bellefontaine, 1872), 427, and Crary, *Dear Belle,* 112. One Champaign County history records Henry Weaver as one of the richest men in the county. He built or acquired several stores and buildings in Urbana and in 1859 became the president of the Champaign County Bank.

9. Crary, *Dear Belle,* 13; Stephen E. Ambrose, *Duty, Honor, Country: A History of West Point* (Baltimore: Johns Hopkins University Press, 1966), 130; and "Cadet Applications," 1858 item 182. Location is McCrea's application papers.

10. W. Asbury Christian, *Lynchburg and Its People* (Lynchburg, VA: J. P. Bell, 1967), 235–36.

11. Ambrose, *Duty,* 128.

12. Michael D. Pierce, *The Most Promising Young Officer* (Norman: University of Oklahoma Press, 1993), 16–21, and James L. Morrison Jr., *The Best School: West Point, 1833–1866* (Kent, OH: Kent State University Press, 1986, 1998), 63.

13. Ambrose, *Duty,* 43–44. The superintendent was brevetted to the local rank of colonel while stationed at West Point.

14. "Engineer Department Records Related to the U.S. Military Academy," RG 94 (RG94), microfilm publication 91 (M91), roll 22 (January 1857 to December 1858), NA.

15. "Cadet Applications," 1858 item 182, and Ambrose, *Duty,* 128. Congress passed legislation in 1843 authorizing each member of Congress one appointment and ten at-large appointments for the president.

16. EDR, RG 94, M91, roll 22 (January 1857 to December 1858). Items included in package based on material received from the Library of Congress (May 13, 2002) and appointment files of William C. Bartlett and Tully McCrea found in "Cadet Applications." The final at-large appoint-

ments were sent from the Engineer Department to the applicants on March 12, 1858, as shown in RG 94, M91.

17. Description of contents of the package and quote from circular was signed by John B. Floyd, secretary of war, sent to William C. Bartlett, March 16, 1858, RG 94, M688, 1858/17.

18. Morrison, *Best School,* 63; Ambrose, *Duty,* 128; and *Centennial History of the United States Military Academy at West Point, New York 1802–1902,* vol. 1 (Washington, Government Printing Office, 1904), 228–29.

19. "Cadet Applications," 1858 item 182.

20. Gerald L. Gutek, *Historical and Philosophical Foundations of Education* (Chicago: Merrill Prentice Hall, 1991), 165, 199–201; Mary Dearing Ward, "The Last Hero," unknown publisher (March–April 1982), 45; and Pierce, *Most Promising,* 20.

21. Edward C. Boynton, *History of West Point* (North Stratford, NH: Ayers Company 1863, reprinted in 2000), 54–55, 207.

22. "Annual Report of the Secretary of War," *Message of the President to both Houses of Congress, Second Session, 35th Congress,* vol. 2, part 2, House Executive Document, US Congress, 769.

23. Description of passage up the Hudson River based on Mary Elizabeth Sergent's *Growing up in Alabama* (Middletown, NY: Prior King Press, 1988), 55–64; Carl Carmer's *The Hudson* (New York: Farrar & Reinhart, 1939); and Boynton, *History of West Point.*

2. The Beginnings of Strife

1. Description of Quarters No. 3 taken from "Headquarters, USMA Quartermaster Office records, Letterbook 1889 Description of Buildings," provided by Alan Aimone, Special Collections, USMA Library, January 2002.

2. "New Cadet Book 1858," SCAD; Mary Elizabeth Sergent, *They Lie Forgotten* (Middletown, NY: Prior King Press, 1986), 15; Boynton, *History of West Point,* 262; and Morrison, *Best School,* 64.

3. Morris Schaff, *The Spirit of Old West Point* (New York: Houghton, Mifflin, 1907), 19–21 (Schaff and Ritchey arrived at West Point on June 2, 1858), and Boynton, *History of West Point,* 257–64.

4. Ambrose, *Duty,* 43, 126; "Report of the Working Committee on Historical Aspects of the Curriculum for the Period 1802—1945," West Point, Special Collections and Archives Division, 31; George S. Pappas, *To the Point* (Westport, CT: Praeger, 1993), 123; Morrison, *Best School,* 72–73, 114–15; and Boynton, *History of West Point,* 250, 252.

5. Theodore Crackel, *West Point: A Bicentennial History* (Lawrence: University of Kansas Press, 2002), 113, and Boynton, *History of West Point,* 259–60.

6. "Table of Candidates of 1858," *Descriptive Lists of New Cadets,* SCAD; *Official Register of the Officers and Cadets of the U.S. Military Academy, June 1858* (hereafter cited as the "Cadet Register"); "Circular to Persons Receiving Cadet Appointments" for admittance to USMA sent to William C. Bartlett, RG 94, M688, 1858/17; Boynton, *History of West Point,* 268; Alan Aimone and Barbara Aimone, "The Civil War Years at West Point," *Blue & Gray Magazine,* December 1991, 12; and Sergent, *They Lie Forgotten,* 22–23.

7. Boynton, *History of West Point,* 261.

8. Sergent, *They Lie Forgotten,* 22–23.

9. G. C. Strong and Bernard Lossing, *Cadet Life at West Point* (La Crosse, WI: Brookhaven Press, 2002), 52, originally published in Boston by TOHP Burnham, 1862.

10. Dwight L. Smith, "Cadet Life in the 1860's," *Assembly* 34, no. 1 (June 1975), 11, and McCrea, October 5, 1864. Cliff Comly and Joseph Alexander were members of the class. Tully apparently left out a comma between the two names in his letter leading some accounts to surmise there were two roommates rather than three.

11. Schaff, *Spirit of Old West Point,* 24–26.

12. Ibid., 40–41.

13. Smith, "Cadet Life," 35–37; Aimone and Aimone, "Civil War Years," 12; Hugh T. Reed, *Cadet Life at West Point,* 3rd ed. (La Crosse, WI: Brookhaven, Press, 2002; originally published 1896 by Irvin Reed & Son), 40; and Strong and Lossing, *Cadet Life,* 57.

14. Charles King, "Cadet Life at West Point," *Harper's Monthly Magazine,* July 1887, 200; Schaff, *Spirit of Old West Point,* 31; and Aimone and Aimone, "Civil War Years," 12.

15. Reed, *Cadet Life,* 67; *The School of the Soldier* is outlined in US Army Tactic Handbook, 1863; Schaff, *Spirit of Old West Point,* 31–32; and Davis Report, 184.

16. Sergent, *They Lie Forgotten,* 26; Morrison, *Best School,* 65; and "Proceedings of Medical Board," June 1856 to August 1862, SCAD. Eighty-three members were examined; sixteen were given probation or were rejected. Tully's probation is listed in note 12 of the Medical Board Proceedings.

17. Schaff, *Spirit of Old West Point,* 37–38, 40.

18. Edward Harz, letters to his father, as quoted in Ambrose, *Duty,* 129. Vulgar fractions are also termed complex fractions.

19. Schaff, *Spirit of Old West Point,* 43. Kinney was listed in VMI records as part of VMI class of 1862.

20. Schaff, *Spirit of Old West Point,* 38; "Cadet Register," the "New Cadet Book," and results of the Medical Board detail the losses in the entering

class; and "U.S. Military Academy Cadet Application Papers (1805–1866)," RG 94, microfilm publication M668 (see Sanderson's application in 1858).

21. Aimone and Aimone, "Civil War Years," 13.

22. Thomas Rowland, "Letters of a Virginia Cadet at West Point, 1859–1861," *South Atlantic Quarterly* 15, no. 1 (January 1916). See letter dated May 27, 1860.

23. Ezra M. Hunt, "West Point and Cadet Life," *Putnam's Monthly* 4, August 1854, 195.

24. Ibid., 195, and King, "Cadet Life at West Point," 199.

25. Strong and Lossing, *Cadet Life,* 120–23, and King, "Cadet Life at West Point," 206. Tully identified Robert Noonan as his tent mate in a letter after he graduated. His assignment to A Company was likely based on his height.

26. Rowland, "Letters of a Virginia Cadet," to mother, June 25, 1860; Edward Anderson to mother, July 3, 1860, in Edward Anderson, "Letters of a West Pointer, 1860–1861," *American Historical Review* 33 (October 1927 to July 1928): 604; and McCrea, June 30, 1858.

27. McCrea, June 30, 1858. There are some discrepancies in time in this letter, but for the most part it depicts an average day in the life of a cadet during summer camp.

28. McCrea, June 30, 1858.

29. Sergent, *They Lie Forgotten,* 30; McCrea, October 29, 1858; and Anderson, "Letters of a West Pointer," letter to uncle dated June 24, 1860.

30. Schaff, *Spirit of Old West Point,* 19.

31. Boynton, 277–80, and Stephen Ambrose, "Letters of Henry A. Du Pont," *Civil War History* 10 (September 1964), letter dated July 22, 1856.

32. McCrea, June 30, 1858.

33. Joseph Pearson Farley, *West Point in the Early Sixties* (Troy, NY: Pafraets Book Co., 1902) 49–50; Ambrose, "Letters of Henry A. Du Pont," July 22, 1856; and Sergent, *They Lie Forgotten,* 33.

34. Farley, *West Point in the Early Sixties,* 48; Schaff, *Spirit of Old West Point,* 63–64; and Rowland, "Letters of a Virginia Cadet," *South Atlantic Quarterly,* July 1915, letter dated July 10, 1859.

35. Anderson, "Letters of a West Pointer," 603, and Morrison, *Best School,* 68–69.

36. William H. French, Henry J. Hunt, and William Barry, *Instruction of Field Artillery* (New York: Van Nostrand, 1864), 73–79.

37. Ambrose, "Letters of Henry A. Du Pont," June 23, 1856, and McCrea, June 30, 1858.

38. "Table of Candidates of 1858."

39. Ibid.; summary charts found in "Cadet Applications" files at NA and

SCAD; "Military Academy Letters," vol. 22 (October 8, 1857, to November 19, 1858), RG 94, roll 22; "Cadet Applications" (see applications for 1858); and Dearing family files, Virginia Historical Society, Richmond, VA.

40. McCrea, October 5, 1864, described him living in the second division where A Company was located. Others were assigned based on their heights and states. It was assumed that each company received an equal number of fifth classmen.

41. Pappas, *To the Point*, 245, and Hunt, "West Point and Cadet Life," 197.

42. Based on room arrangement belonging to Brig. Gen. Aldelbert Buffington (May '61), held by SCAD.

43. McCrea, January 19, 1861.

44. Schaff, *Spirit of Old West Point*, 66–67.

45. Ibid. Assignments to C Company based on heights from the medical board and home states shown in "Table of Candidates of 1858."

46. Boynton, *History of West Point*, 261, and Pappas, *To the Point*, 241.

47. Mary Elizabeth Sergent, *An Unremaining Glory* (Middletown, NY: Prior King Press, 1997), 40.

48. McCrea, December 3, 1858, as quoted in Crary, *Dear Belle*, 22.

49. John C. Waugh, *The Class of 1846 from West Point to Appomattox: Stonewall Jackson, George McClellan and Their Brothers* (New York: Warner Books, 1994), 30.

50. Composite schedule shown in table 2.1 was created from the following articles: Harold Hammond, "West Point: Its Glamour and Grind," http://www.west-point.org/publications/glamour-grind.html; King, "Cadet Life at West Point," 217; Strong and Lossing, *Cadet Life*, 181–84; Morrison, *Best School*, 73; and Reed, *Cadet Life*, 89–90.

51. Names were found in multiple cadet registers for years 1858–1862; Ambrose, *Duty*, 152; and Schaff, *Spirit of Old West Point*, 68–71.

52. Morrison, *Best School*, 51–52, and Schaff, *Spirit of Old West Point*, 68.

53. Reed, *Cadet Life*, 92–95, and Strong and Lossing, *Cadet Life*, 185–86.

54. Morrison, *Best School*, 166. A complete academic schedule for each class can be found in the cadet register each year.

55. Morrison, *Best School*, 87–88, 91–92, and Boynton, *History of West Point*, 272.

56. Morrison, *Best School*, 115, 122–23, and Boynton, *History of West Point*, 248, 250.

57. William J. Hardee, *Rifle and Light Infantry Tactics* (Philadelphia: J. B. Lippincott, 1860).

58. Du Pont to mother, September 9, 1856, in Ambrose, "Letters of Henry Du Pont," 291–308.

59. McCrea, October 29, 1858, and October 9, 1859.

60. Boynton, *History of West Point,* 270, and McCrea, October 29, 1858.

61. Crary, *Dear Belle,* 23–24, and "Register of Punishments, Volume 3, October 1857 to February 1865," SCAD, for J. R. Blocker, January 31, 1860.

62. Schaff, *Spirit of Old West Point,* 114; Pappas, *To the Point,* 269; Ambrose, *Duty,* 15; and Sergent, *They Lie Forgotten,* 33.

63. Crackel, *West Point,* 121–22; Robert Crowley and Thomas Guinzburg, eds., *West Point: Two Centuries of Honor and Tradition* (New York: Warner Books, 2002), 42; and Davis Report, 304–7.

64. Crackel, *West Point,* 89–90, 113, and Reed, *Cadet Life,* 180.

65. Rowland, "Letters of a Virginia Cadet," *South Atlantic Quarterly,* July 1915, letters to mother December 27, 1859, and January 1, 1860; James Dearing, letter to his uncle, George Lynch, 1859, Dearing family files held by the Virginia Historical Society, folder MSS 1D3475a 65–66, Richmond, Virginia; and McCrea, January 5, 1860.

66. Schaff, *Spirit of Old West Point,* 103–4, and Morrison, *Best School,* 54.

67. Sergent, *They Lie Forgotten,* 46–47; Morrison, *Best School,* 79; and McCrea, December 8, 1860.

68. Horace Porter ('60) read "West Point Life" at the Dialectic Society during this time. See Farley, *West Point in the Early Sixties,* 181–94.

69. McCrea, February 6, 1859, and *Newburgh Tribune* article identifying river closings due to ice from 1858 to 1861, February 4, 1870.

70. McCrea, January 23, 1859.

71. Post Orders No. 5, No. 42, December 31, 1860, and Davis Report, 254–55, 284.

72. Strong and Lossing, *Cadet Life,* 195, and "Report of the Academic Board."

73. "Cadet Register," January 1859; "Secretary of War, Letters Sent," January 15, 1859, RG 94, M91, roll 22; and "New Cadet Roster, 1858."

74. Sergent, *They Lie Forgotten,* 59; Boynton, *History of West Point,* 273; and Davis Report, 255.

75. Text copied from McCrea warrant found in cadet application papers for year 1858 "Cadet Applications."

76. Pappas, *To the Point,* 304–5, and Boynton, *History of West Point,* 250.

77. King, "Cadet Life at West Point," 210.

78. McCrea, April 30, 1859.

79. Davis Report, 255.

80. Warner to family, May 29, 1859, Warner Diary.

81. "Cadet Register," June 1859.

82. Post Order No. 5, SO 89, June 14, 1859, and SO 97, June 21, 1859, and McCrea, June 16, 1859.

83. McCrea, June 16, 1859, and October 5, 1864.

84. Strong and Lossing, *Cadet Life*, 224–26, 235.

85. McCrea, September 12, 1859.

86. Schaff, *Spirit of Old West Point*, 67, 85, 208, 216; McCrea, December 31, 1859, and October 5, 1864; and "Cadet Register," June 1859.

87. Boynton, *History of West Point*, 269, and Morrison, *Best School*, 72–73.

88. Crary, *Dear Belle*, 15n, and "Cadet Register," June 1859.

89. McCrea, September 12, 1859.

90. Morrison, *Best School*, 56; Davis Report, 31; and "Cadet Register," June 1860.

91. Schaff, *Spirit of Old West Point*, 68.

92. McCrea, September 16, 1860.

93. Sergent, *They Lie Forgotten*, 81; McCrea, September 16, 1860; and Schaff, multiple pages in *Spirit of Old West Point*.

94. Morrison, *Best School*, 130–31; Pappas, *To the Point*, 311; and Brian R. McEnany, "John Brown's Raid and West Point," *Assembly* 48, no. 1 (October–December 2009), 36.

95. Clifford Dowdy, *The Land They Fought For* (Garden City, NY: Doubleday, 1955), 63–64; Robert E. Lee's report to AGO concerning the attack at Harpers Ferry, available at http://www.law.umkc.edu/faculty/projects/FTrials/johnbrown/; and Samuel E. Morison, *The Oxford History of the American People* (New York: Oxford University Press, 1965), 601–2.

96. Rowland, "Letters of a Virginia Cadet," letter dated October 23, 1859, *South Atlantic Quarterly*, July 1915, 219.

97. Du Pont as quoted in Pappas, *To the Point*, 310.

98. Schaff, *Spirit of Old West Point*, 149.

99. Ibid., 149, and Sergent, *Unremaining Glory*, 70.

100. Schaff, *Spirit of Old West Point*, 143; McCrea, December 3, 1859; and Pappas, *To the Point*, 310–11.

101. Pappas, *To the Point*, 311.

102. Schaff, *Spirit of Old West Point*, 147, and Pappas, *To the Point*, 311.

103. Schaff, *Spirit of Old West Point*, 151, and Pappas, *To the Point*, 310.

104. Pappas, *To the Point*, 314.

105. Morison, *Oxford History*, 603–4.

106. As quoted in Pappas, *To the Point*, 315.

107. Crary, *Dear Belle*, 30–31, and McCrea, November 8, 1859.

108. Isaac Arnold, letter to father, March 11, 1860, SCAD.

109. SO 37, February 28, 1860, AGO.

110. Schaff, *Spirit of Old West Point*, 216.

111. Larry J. Daniel, *Cannoneers in Gray: Field Artillery of the Army of Tennessee* (Tuscaloosa: University of Alabama Press, 2005), 222; James Lord,

letter to father, October 28, 1860, SCAD; "Cadet Register," June 1860; Davis Report, 157–60; and Ambrose, *Duty*, 142.

112. McCrea, June 19, 1860.

113. McCrea, June 1, 1860, and "Register of Punishments."

3. Crises of Conscience

1. Strong and Lossing, *Cadet Life*, 229; and Sergent, *They Lie Forgotten*, 71–72.

2. Hometowns were found in letters sent to the superintendent in 1861 from various parents as shown in RG 94, M2047, roll 40, Engineer Department letters received (EDLR) related to USMA, November 1860 to May 1861.

3. Sergent, *They Lie Forgotten*, 72, and Strong and Lossing, *Cadet Life*, 282.

4. Post Orders (1856–1861), SO 81, 82, and 88, June 1860.

5. McCrea, July 3, 1861, August 26 and 30 and September 8, 1860, and Crary, *Dear Belle*, 12n.

6. Crary, *Dear Belle*, 65; Strong and Lossing, *Cadet Life*, 291; and Reed, *Cadet Life*, 155.

7. Post Orders, SO 120, August 28, 1860, and McCrea, August 30, 1860.

8. Schaff, *Spirit of Old West Point*, 85, 236–37; McCrea, August 30, 1860, September 16, 1860; and *Richmond Dispatch*, March 19, 1893, as quoted at http://www.civilwarhome.com/dixieorigin.htm (accessed May 14, 2007).

9. James Lord, letter to father, July 16, 1860, SCAD, and "Cadet Register," June 1860.

10. Davis Report, 1.

11. Pappas, *To the Point*, 315–16.

12. Schaff, *Spirit of Old West Point*, 156.

13. Morrison, *Best School*, 50, and Ambrose, *Duty*, 95–97.

14. McCrea, September 8 and 16, 1860.

15. Pappas, *To the Point*, 300–1; Ambrose, *Duty*, 100–2; Pappas, *To the Point*, 250–51; and Crackel, *West Point*, 125–26.

16. McCrea, September 9, 1860; Ambrose, *Duty*, 94; and Pappas, *To the Point*, 250, 265.

17. McCrea, September 16, 1860.

18. Sergent, *They Lie Forgotten*, 49.

19. McCrea, October 6, 1860.

20. Pappas, *To the Point*, 316–17; Sergent, *They Lie Forgotten*, 87; and McCrea, October 20, 1860.

21. McCrea, October 6 and 27, 1860.

22. McCrea, October 27, 1860.

23. Schaff, *Spirit of Old West Point,* 164.

24. Ibid., 164–65; Ambrose, *Duty,* 169; McCrea, October 27, 1860; and Pappas, *To the Point,* 318.

25. Pappas, *To the Point,* 319–21; McCrea, November 10, 1860; and David Detzer, *Allegiance: Fort Sumter, Charleston, and the Beginning of the Civil War* (San Diego: Harcourt, 2001), 11–12, 69.

26. McCrea, November 18, 1860.

27. Boynton, *History of West Point,* 252; McCrea, November 10, 1861; Pappas, *To the Point,* 321; EDLR, RG 94, M2047, roll 40, items BB101 and MA 2345 (Resignation of John Blocker and James Hamilton); and Post Orders, No. 5, SO 18, 19, 25, and 29.

28. Crary, *Dear Belle,* 72, and EDLR, RG 94, M2047, items MA2349 and MA2365.

29. Crackel, *West Point,* 131.

30. McCrea, November 10, 1860, and December 8 and 15, 1860.

31. Detzer, *Allegiance,* 90–92, and Henry Hendrickson, *Sumter: The First Day of the Civil War* (Chelsea, MI: Scarborough House, 1990), 61–62.

32. Houston to Rosser, December 1860, as quoted in Pappas, *To the Point,* 320.

33. Sergent, *They Lie Forgotten,* 94; Pappas, *To the Point,* 320; and Rowland, "Letters of a Virginia Cadet," letter to mother dated November 11, 1860, *South Atlantic Quarterly* 15, no. 2 (April 1916): 148.

34. Mrs. Anderson to Edward, December 31, 1860, in Anderson, "Letters of a West Pointer," 603.

35. McCrea, December 15, 1860, March 1861, and Sergent, *They Lie Forgotten,* 92.

36. McCrea, December 29, 1860.

37. Pappas, *To the Point,* 321, and Schaff, *Spirit of Old West Point,* 178. Dixon, a turn-back to Tully's class, is recorded against the Class of June 1861 in Cullum's register—the class with whom he originally entered the Corps.

38. McCrea, December 29, 1860.

39. Hendrickson, *Sumter,* 51–52, 80–82, and William Marvel, *Five Flags over Fort Sumter,* National Parks Civil War Series (Fort Washington, PA: Eastern National, 1998), 6–7.

40. Hendrickson, *Sumter,* 71, 75–77, and Abner Doubleday, *Reminiscences of Forts Sumter and Moultrie in 1860–'61* (Charleston, SC: Nautical and Aviation Publishing Company, 1998), 59–64.

41. Detzer, *Allegiance,* 72–73; William G. Bell, *Secretaries of War and*

Secretaries of the Army (Washington, DC: US Army Center for Military History, 1992), 66–69; and Hendrickson, *Sumter,* 84–86.

42. Morison, *Oxford History,* 607, 610, and *CWD,* 27–31. The cotton states were Alabama, Georgia, Florida, Mississippi, Louisiana, South Carolina, and Texas.

43. EDLR, based on review of resignations sent by cadets as shown in RG 94, M2047, rolls 40 and 41.

44. EDLR, RG 94, M2047, roll 40, items SW2918, SW2954, MA2381, MA2404; David J. Coles, *Men and Arms: Sketches of the Commanders and Units of the Olustee Campaign, Vol. II* (Gainesville, FL: Renaissance Printing, 1995), 26; and William C. Barnard, lieutenant, Third New Jersey Infantry, at http://www.ancestry.com, taken from M550, roll 1 (accessed January 31, 2009).

45. Crackel, West Point, 131, and Mark M. Boatner III, *The Civil War Dictionary* (New York: David McKay, 1959, 1988), 55.

46. Post Orders No. 6, SO 3, January 7, 1861; Donald M. Buchwald, "Chronological Listing of Significant Changes to Troop Units at West Point, New York from 1775 to 1978," USMA Library, 1978, 42–44; and McCrea, January 19, 1861.

47. "Enlistment Records of the U.S Army (1798–1914)," microfilm publication M233, NA; *Returns from Regular Army Engineer Battalions, Sept. 1846–June 1916* (NA microfilm M690, roll 27); Records of the AGO, 1780s–1917, RG 94, NA; Margaret Leech, *Reveille in Washington (1860–1865)* (New York: Harper and Brothers, 1941), 29; and Buchwald, "Chronological Listing," 41–42.

48. Sergent, *They Lie Forgotten,* 95.

49. Ibid., 94, and Ambrose, *Duty,* 174.

50. A portion of Washington's Farewell Address given in Washington in 1796 as quoted in Schaff, *Spirit of Old West Point,* 204. Segment is taken from that portion of the address dealing with unity of government.

51. Schaff, *Spirit of Old West Point,* 206–7.

52. Crackel, *West Point,* 132.

53. Schaff, *Spirit of Old West Point,* 215–16.

54. "Federal Union Extra" *New York Herald,* February 24, 1861, and Letter from Delafield to Totten, forwarding resignations of Blount, Alexander, and West, as shown in RG 94, MA2047, roll 40, item MA2412, NA. Affirmation letters from West and Alexander are shown at MA2416 on roll 40.

55. Post Orders, SOs 34, 36–39, March 1861, and Warren F. Spencer, *Raphael Semmes: The Philosophical Mariner* (Tuscaloosa: University of Alabama, 1997), 13, 103. See RG 94, M2047, roll 40.

56. Leech, *Reveille*, 43–44; Ernest B. Furgurson, *Freedom Rising* (New York: Knopf, 2004), 59; Buchwald, "Chronological Listing," 42; and Maureen Harrison and Steve Gilbert eds., *Abraham Lincoln Word for Word* (San Diego: Excellent Books, 1994), 304.

57. Anderson, "Letters of a West Pointer," letter dated April 12, 1861, 610.

58. Du Pont to Mother, April 10, 1861, as quoted by Virginia T. Lake, "A Crisis of Conscience: West Point Letters of Henry A. Du Pont," *Civil War History* 25, no. 1: 60.

59. EDLR, RG 94, M2047, roll 40, April 4, 1861, and EDLR, M91, roll 23, April 9, 1861.

60. Message from Steward to Chew, April 6, 1861, Abraham Lincoln Papers, Series 1, General Correspondence, 1833–1912, Library of Congress, available at www.loc.gov; *New York Times*, April 13, 1861, 1; Hendrickson, *Sumter*, 168, 176, 180, 183; and James M. McPherson, *Ordeal by Fire: The Civil War and Reconstruction* (New York: McGraw-Hill, 2001), 154–57.

61. H. S. Farley, letter to Dr. Robert Lebby circa 1893, as quoted in Robert J. Trout, *They Followed the Plume* (Mechanicsburg: Stackpole, 1993), 102–5 (original source Robert Lebby, "The First Shot on Fort Sumter," *South Carolina Historical and Genealogical Magazine*, July 1911, 144), and Yates Snowden, *History of South Carolina, Volume II* (Chicago: The Lewis Publishing Company, 1930).

62. Articles in the *New York Times* dated April 16 and 17, 1861; Detzer, *Allegiance*, 269–70; Doubleday, *Reminiscences*, 182, 184; and *OR* 1:1, 43.

63. Doubleday, *Reminiscences*, 171–74, and *BLCW*, vol. 1, 48–49.

64. Pappas, *To the Point*, 330; McCrea, April 18, 1861; *New York Times*, April 13, 1861, 1; and Schaff, *Spirit of Old West Point*, 219–20.

65. Maurice Matloff, ed., Office of the Chief of Military History, US Army, *American Military History* (Washington, DC: Government Printing Office, 1969), 189–90.

66. Rowland, "Letters of a Virginia Cadet," *South Atlantic Quarterly* 15, no. 3, letter dated April 16, 1861. The border states of concern to the Union were Delaware, Maryland, Kentucky, and Missouri.

67. T. Harry Williams, "The Attack on West Point during the Civil War," *Mississippi Historical Review* 25 (March 1939), and Schaff, *Spirit of Old West Point*, 257.

68. Post Orders, SO 45, April 18, 1861, and McCrea, April 20, 1861.

69. Anderson to Mrs. J. W. Anderson, April 18, 1861, in Anderson, "Letters of a West Pointer."

70. EDLR, RG 94, M2047, roll 40, April 19, 1861, and EDLR, RG 94, M91, roll 23, April 20, 1861.

71. EDLR, RG 94, M2047, roll 40; Post Orders, No. 6, SO 42, 44, 46; Pappas, *To the Point,* 333; and McCrea, April 27, 1861.

72. McCrea, April 27, 1861.

73. Boynton, *History of West Point,* 252, and McCrea, April 27, 1861.

74. Ambrose, *Duty,* 171; Pappas, *To the Point,* 331, 340; and McCrea, April 20, 1861.

75. McCrea, April 20, 1861.

76. Schaff, *Spirit of Old West Point,* 249.

77. McCrea, April 27, 1861.

78. Pappas, *To the Point,* 332, 335; Du Pont to father, April 14, 1861, as quoted in Lake, "Crisis of Conscience," 61; and EDLR, Totten to Bowman, April 29, 1861.

79. McCrea, May 11, 1861, and Pappas, *To the Point,* 337.

80. EDLR, General Totten to Colonel Bowman, RG 94, M91, roll 23, May 4, 1861; Ralph Kirshner, *The Class of 1861* (Carbondale: Southern Illinois Press, 1999), 13–14; and Pappas, *To the Point,* 336. There are differences in where the class was arrested. Pappas states it was in Washington, while Kirshner, quoting from a letter from one member of the May class (Barlow), states it was Philadelphia. I have chosen to use Barlow's account.

81. EDLR, letter from Totten to Bowman, RG 94, M91, roll 23, May 22, 1861; Pappas, *To the Point,* 337–38; and McCrea, May 4, 1861.

82. Post Orders, SO 60, May 6, 1861.

83. McCrea, May 11, 1861.

84. Ibid.

85. McCrea, May 26 and June 1, 1861.

86. Pappas, *To the Point,* 336.

87. McCrea, June 1, 1861.

88. McCrea, May 19, 1861.

89. McCrea, June 24, 1861; Ambrose, *Duty,* 176; Post Orders, SO 80, June 7, 1861; and "Cadet Register," June 1861.

4. "When Shall We Meet Again?"

1. Post Orders No. 6, SO 84, June 14, 1861; EDLR, June 14, 1861; and McCrea, June 24, 1861.

2. Sergent, *Unremaining Glory,* 12; Kirshner, *Class of 1861,* 17; and Frances B. Heitman, *Historical Register and Dictionary of the United States Army, from Its Organization, September 29, 1789, to March 2, 1903,* vol. 1 (Washington: Government Printing Office, 1903).

3. Pappas, *To the Point,* 337; Boynton, *History of West Point,* 252; McCrea, May 11, 1861; EDLR, RG 94, M2047, roll 41, item SW3480, June 17, 1861, and roll 40, item MA2495, June 13, 1861; and Post Orders

No. 6, SO 48, June 22, 1861. (The "Cadet Register" strengths and Pappas's text show that 65 Southerners resigned or left, leaving 179 cadets present at the end of May.) After the June class and the furlough class left, only 70 cadets remained. Russell was commissioned a second lieutenant in the Sixty-seventh New York Infantry Regiment two days later.

4. Post Orders No. 6, SO 101, June 30, 1861.

5. "Cadet Register," June 1861, and Post Orders No. 6, No. 52, August 21, 1861.

6. Post Orders No. 6, SO 111, July 15, 1861, and EDLR, Frank James letter to the superintendent requesting leave of absence, RG 94, M2047, roll 48, July 1861.

7. McCrea, July 7, 1861, and Schaff, *Spirit of Old West Point*, 113–14.

8. McCrea, July 12, 1861.

9. McCrea, July 3 and 7, 1861.

10. McCrea, July 12, 1861.

11. McCrea, July 20, 1861, and Post Orders No. 6, SO 113, July 15, 1861.

12. McCrea, July 12 and 20, 1861.

13. Ibid. John Russell was the clerk of the Ohio Court at this time.

14. McCrea, July 25, 1861, and Crary, *Dear Belle*, 114n.

15. McCrea, July 25, 1861.

16. Schaff, *Spirit of Old West Point*, 261, 264.

17. McCrea, July 25, 1861. Captain Griffin was not killed and would eventually be promoted to general and command a Corps.

18. Sergent, *They Lie Forgotten*, 109; Matloff, *American Military History*, 200; William C. Davis, *Battle at Bull Run* (Mechanicsburg, PA: Stackpole, 1977), 211–13; William L. Haskin, *The History of the First Regiment of Artillery* (Portland, ME: B. Thurston, 1879), 148–49; Bruce Catton, *The Civil War* (Boston, MA: Houghton Mifflin, 1987), 49–50; and Shelby Foote, *The Civil War*, vol. 1 (New York: Vintage Books, 1986; originally 1958), 82.

19. William Parker, "Brigadier General James Dearing, CSA," thesis, master of arts in history, Virginia Polytechnic Institute, 1969, located with Dearing family files, Southern Historical Society, Richmond, VA, 14–15; *OR* 1:2, 517; and muster rolls of the Washington Artillery for July 1861.

20. Russel H. Beatie, *The Army of the Potomac*, vol. 1 (Cambridge, MA: Da Capo Press, 2002), 380, and Jeffrey D. Wert, *Sword of Lincoln* (New York: Simon & Schuster, 2005), 32–37.

21. McCrea, July 25, 1861, and Post Orders No. 6, SO 25, July 27, 1861, SCAD.

22. McCrea, July 31, 1861.

23. Ibid.

24. Ibid.

25. Schaff, *Spirit of Old West Point*, 267, and Post Orders, SO 136, August 23, 1861.

26. "Report of the Secretary of War," Thirty-seventh Congress, Senate Executive Documents, First Session, vol. 1, no. 1, 27–28; and Williams, "Attack on West Point," 491–504.

27. Boynton, *History of West Point*, 357–58.

28. Ibid., 360. The last change to the oath of allegiance was enacted by Congress on July 2, 1862, after the Class of 1862 graduated.

29. McCrea, August 25, 1861.

30. Ibid.

31. Post Orders No. 6, SO 138, August 29, 1861, and SO 147, September 6, 1861, and McCrea, September 7, 1861.

32. McCrea, September 7, 1861, and Morrison, *Best School*, 122.

33. "Cadet Register," June 1862; Boynton, *History of West Point*, 274; Davis Report, 31, 274–75; Morrison, *Best School*, 135; McCrea, September 14, 21, and November 15, 1861; and EDLR, RG 94, M2047, SW3542, July 27, 1861

34. McCrea, September 21, 1861.

35. Post Orders No. 6, SO 142, August 31, 1861, and SO 146, September 3, 1861; "Cadet Register," June 1862; Pappas, *To the Point*, 106–7; and Boynton, *History of West Point*, 221–22.

36. Boynton, *History of West Point*, 315, and Crackel, *West Point*, 151.

37. EDLR, RG 91, M2047, roll 41, March 18, 1861; Buchwald, "Chronological Listing," 43; and McCrea, September 28, 1861.

38. McCrea, October 5, 12, 14, and 26, 1861, and "Post Order No. 6," SO 167, October 5, 1861.

39. McCrea, September 28, 1861, October 26, 1861, and November 10, 1861.

40. RG 94, M2047, roll 41, items SW 3622 and SW3678, September 6 and 16, 1861; Post Order No. 6, SO 175, October 12, 1861, and SO 176, October 14, 1961; and HQ, War Department SO 274, October 9, 1861, AGO, Washington, DC.

41. Morrison, *Best School*, 72; Post Orders No. 6, SO 138, August 29 and SO 176, October 14, 1861, SCAD; and Robert J. Nicholson, "West Point's First Captains," *Assembly* 27, no. 4: 2.

42. *Centennial History*, vol. 1, 519; Sergent, *They Lie Forgotten*, 47–49; and McCrea letters, September 7, 14, 21, and 28, 1861.

43. McCrea, September 14, 1861, and Brian R. McEnany, "A History of the McEnany Family," unpublished manuscript.

44. McCrea, October 26, 1861.

45. McCrea, December 14, 1861.

46. McCrea, November 1, 1861; Post Orders No. 6, October 25, 1861; handwritten description of courts-martial results held by SCAD; Farley, *West Point in the Early Sixties*, 78–79; SO 81, May 29, 1861, SCAD; and experience of author during his cadetship.

47. McCrea, October 26, 1861.

48. McCrea, November 30, 1861.

49. Morison, *Oxford History*, 633–34; Foote, *Civil War*, 156–57; and *New York Times*, November 17 and December 9, 1861, 1.

50. McCrea, November 30, 1861, and Boynton, *History of West Point*, 316.

51. McCrea, December 29, 1861.

52. McCrea, January 4, 1862.

53. Post Orders No. 6, SO 58, December 21, 1861, and "Cadet Register."

54. Schaff, *Spirit of Old West Point*, 107–8.

55. McCrea, February 1, 1862.

56. McCrea, December 21, 1861.

57. McCrea, February 28 and March 14, 1862; Boynton, *History of West Point*, 268; Schaff, *Spirit of Old West Point*, 269; and *Register of Officer and Agents Civil, Military and Naval in the Service of the United States* (Washington, DC: Government Printing Office, 1862), 146.

58. Schaff, *Spirit of Old West Point*, 278.

59. McCrea, January 25, 1862, and McCrea, March 27, 1861.

60. Egan obituary, *Annual Report*, June 12, 1908, 45–46.

61. McCrea, February 9, 1862.

62. McCrea, February 23, 1862.

63. McCrea, January 25, 1862.

64. General War Order No. 1, January 27, 1862, as quoted in Wert, *Sword of Lincoln*, 58–59. The Confederacy decided to shorten its extended lines in March and withdrew from Centreville.

65. *CWD*, 168; Foote, *Civil War*, vol. 1, 225–30; and GO No. 118, AGO, names of prisoners paroled, August 27, 1862.

66. *OR* 1:7, 358–63, 868–69; McCrea, February 28 and March 7, 1862; *BLCW*, vol. 1, 410–12, 429; Clement A. Evans, ed., *Confederate Military History*, extended ed., 19 vols. (Wilmington, NC: Broadfoot Publishing, 1987), 10:24–25; and K. D. Gott, "Gateway to the Heartland," *North and South* 7, no. 2 (March 2004): 46–59.

67. McCrea, March 7, 1862.

68. Typed notes about Gillespie found in Mary Elizabeth Sergent's Class of 1862 records, and *Annual Report*, 1913, 73–88.

69. McCrea, April 7, 1863, and *OR* 12:1, 401, 403.

70. Warner Diary, May 21, 1862.

71. McCrea, February 28, 1862, and February 1, 1863.

72. McCrea, March 21, 1863.

73. McCrea, May 10, 1862; Index to CSR, microfilm M231; and War Department Collection of Confederate Records (RG 109), M268 (Tennessee), roll 221, NA. The Tennessee Confederate service records show that Maney escaped during transfer to Johnson Island prison on April 26, 1862.

74. Schaff's and Warner's class albums are part of SCAD holdings at West Point; McCrea, May 23, 1862; and Schaff, *Spirit of Old West Point,* 51.

75. McCrea, May 17, 1862.

76. "Cadet Register," June 1862.

77. McCrea, June 9, 1862.

78. McCrea, May 5, 1861; Schaff, *Spirit of Old West Point,* 278; and Sergent, *They Lie Forgotten,* 100.

79. Schaff, *Spirit of Old West Point,* 278.

80. *Centennial History,* vol. 1, 519. Warner's tale was based on Schaff's experience (Schaff, *Spirit of Old West Point,* 278–83).

81. Schaff, *Spirit of Old West Point,* 278–82, and Pappas, *To the Point,* 245–46, 360. This description is based on graduation parades described in Schaff and Pappas from that period of time and the author's personal experience.

82. McCrea, June 9, 1862.

83. Schaff, *Spirit of Old West Point,* 282. Records of an actual ceremony for the Class of 1862 could not be found. This description is based on the ceremony conducted for the Class of June 1861.

84. James S. Robbins, *Last in Their Class* (New York: Encounter Books, 2006), 221–22, and *Cullum's 1891,* 865.

85. Post Orders No. 6, SO 71, June 10, 1862, and SO 75, June 14, 1862.

5. McCrea Joins the Army of the Potomac

1. McCrea, June 29, 1862. Appointments were confirmed on July 4. See General Order 73, War Department, July 4, 1862, AGO.

2. McCrea, June 29, 1862.

3. *New York Times,* July 7, 1862, 5, column 1.

4. Crary, *Dear Belle,* 133.

5. Crary, *Dear Belle,* 134–35, and James E. Barber, *Alexandria in the Civil War* (Lynchburg, VA: H. E. Howard, 1988).

6. McCrea, July 28, 1862; Thomas P. Lowry, ed., *Swamp Doctor: Diary of a Union Surgeon in the Virginia and North Carolina Marshes* (Mechanicsburg, PA: Stackpole, 2001), 16; and Steven J. Shepard, "Reaching for

the Channel," *Alexandria Chronicle*, Alexandria Historical Society (Spring 2006), 8.

7. Lowry, *Swamp Doctor*, 25; Crary, *Dear Belle*, 133; John M. Coski, *The Army of the Potomac at Berkeley Plantation* (Richmond, VA: John M. Coski, 1989), 17 and map inside rear cover; and *OR Atlas*, plate 13–3.

8. *BLCW*, vol. 2, 427.

9. Coski, *Army of the Potomac*, 17, and Matloff, *American Military History*, 223–24.

10. Crary, *Dear Belle*, 135, and Philip Van Doren Stern, *Soldier Life in the Union and Confederate Armies* (New York: Gramercy Books, 2001), 46.

11. Warner Diary, September 22, 1862.

12. McCrea, July 20, 1862, as quoted in Crary, *Dear Belle*, 135–36.

13. Sergent, *They Lie Forgotten*, 158–59.

14. *OR* 2:1, 407; Sergent, *They Lie Forgotten*, 158–59; and Schaff, *Spirit of Old West Point*, 71–73.

15. Sergent, *They Lie Forgotten*, 157–59, and Sergent, *Unremaining Glory*, 67.

16. Coski, *Army of the Potomac*, 19.

17. Stern, *Soldier Life*, 83–88, 114–18.

18. Jay Luvaas and Harold W. Nelson, *The U.S. Army War College Guide to the Battle of Antietam* (New York: Harper & Row, 1987, 1988), 264, and Curt Johnson and Richard C. Anderson Jr., *Artillery Hell: The Employment of Artillery at Antietam* (College Station: Texas A&M University Press, 1995), 27–28. An additional 128 rounds were carried in the corps and army ammunition wagons, making 256 rounds the basic load for each twelve-pounder battery.

19. Johnson and Anderson, *Artillery Hell*, 27–28.

20. William H. French, William F. Barry, and Henry J. Hunt, *Instruction for Field Artillery* (New York, D. Van Nostrand, 1864), 15, republished by Stackpole Books, 2005; Johnson and Anderson, *Artillery Hell*, 27–29, 122; and *Horse Power Moves the Guns*, found at www.batteryb.com/horsepower.html. A light artillery battery had 146 horses and 125 men.

21. McCrea, July 28, 1862, and Coski, *Army of the Potomac*, 22–23.

22. Coski, *Army of the Potomac*, 22, and McCrea, July 28 and August 3, 1862.

23. McCrea, July 28, 1862.

24. McCrea, August 11, 1862. Supplements to the *OR*s for Massachusetts, Connecticut, Michigan, Pennsylvania, and Ohio volunteer regiments show McCrea as mustering officer.

25. *OR* 11:1, 78–79; the Ninth Corps history found at http://www.civilwararchive.com/CORPS/9thcorp.htm; and McCrea, August 31, 1862.

26. McCrea, August 23, 1862.

27. McCrea, August 23 and 31, 1862.

6. McCrea, Egan, and the Maryland Campaign

1. Morrison, *Best School,* 137.

2. Stephen Sears, *Landscape Turned Red* (New York: Houghton Mifflin, 2003), 72–73, 77; A. L. Long, *Memoirs of Robert E. Lee* (Secaucus, NJ: Blue & Gray Press, 1983), 203–5; and Wert, *Sword of Lincoln,* 142–43.

3. Leech, *Reveille,* 190–93; Sears, *Landscape Turned Red,* 78; and Wert, *Sword of Lincoln,* 139.

4. Leech, *Reveille,* 197; Bruce Catton, *Mr. Lincoln's Army* (Garden City, NY: Doubleday, 1951), 164–65; Sears, *Landscape Turned Red,* 80; Wert, *Sword of Lincoln,* 144–47; and George B. McClellan, *Report on the Organization and Campaigns of the Army of the Potomac* (New York: Sheldon, 1864), 208.

5. Assignments shown in chart are based on a review of muster reports for artillery, engineers, and cavalry regiments found at NA, graduation assignments shown in the epilogue, some obituaries, and letters and diaries of McCrea and Warner.

6. Leech, *Reveille,* 191, 197–99.

7. Warner Diary, September 7, 1862.

8. Lowry, *Swamp Doctor,* 16, 22. Tully's travels to rejoin his battery are based on trip taken by Dr. Willliam Smith of the Eighty-fifth New York Infantry Regiment.

9. McCrea, September 8, 1862, and *OR* 3:2, 762–64.

10. *Annual Report 1889,* 71–74, appendix 1–19. He returned to duty on October 9, 1862.

11. Francis A. Walker, *History of the 2d Corps in the Army of the Potomac* (Gaithersburg, MD: Olde Soldier Books, 1987; originally published 1887), 89, 93; McCrea, September 8, 1862; McClellan, *Report on the Organization,* 336; *OR* 19:2, 174–75; Description of Fort Reno listed at http://www.nps.gov/cwdw/historyculture/fort-reno.htm; and Sergent, *Unremaining Glory,* 67.

12. McCrea, September 8, 1862.

13. *OR* 19:1, 25–27, 39–41; McClellan, *Report on the Organization,* 347–49; and *OR* 19:1, 169–80.

14. Warner, September 11, 1862.

15. Luvaas and Nelson, *Guide to the Battlefield of Antietam,* 269–70; Stern, *Soldier Life,* 123, 235; and address by Edwin C. Bearss, January 13, 2004, to the Civil War Roundtable of the District of Columbia.

16. McCrea, September 8, 1862.

17. Sears, *Landscape Turned Red*, 108–9, and Catton, *Mr. Lincoln's Army*, 178, 187.

18. Catton, *Mr. Lincoln's Army*, 167, and author's road trip following the Second Corps up Rockville Pike in 2005.

19. Sears, *Landscape Turned Red*, 112–13; *WP Atlas*, map 65b; and National Park Service ranger lecture at the Antietam battlefield, September 1, 2003.

20. McCrea, September 20, 1862.

21. *OR* 19:1, 53, and McCrea, September 20, 1862.

22. McCrea, September 20, 1862.

23. McCrea, September 20, 1862; "Morning Phase," Antietam National Battlefield map series National Park Service; E. B. Cope and H. W. Mattern, *Atlas of the Battlefield of Antietam* (Washington, DC: AGO, 1904), 0830; and *OR* 19:1, 55–56. The other battery was Tompkins's Battery A, First Rhode Island Artillery. Lt. Col. E. B. Cope prepared the atlas for the Antietam Battlefield Commission as a series of fourteen maps depicting various time periods of the fighting on September 17. Available online at the Library of Congress. Hereafter referred to as the Cope Maps (time).

24. Cope Maps, 0900 series, and *WP Atlas*, map 68.

25. Sears, *Landscape Turned Red*, 218, and Armstrong, *Disaster in the West Woods*, 3–5.

26. Frederick Tilberg, *Antietam* (Washington, DC: National Park Service, 1960), 30.

27. *OR* 19:1, 309; Cope Maps 0900, 1030, 1215; and L. VanLoan Naisawald, *Grape and Canister* (Mechanicsburg, PA: Stackpole, 1999): 160–61.

28. John M. Priest, *Antietam: The Soldier's Battle* (New York: Oxford University Press, 2003), 79; McCrea, September 20, 1862; and Walker, *History of the 2d Corps*, 101–8.

29. *OR* 19:1, 309–10, and McCrea, September 20, 1862.

30. Priest, *Antietam*, 123–24.

31. Cope Maps 0830, 0900, 1030, 1215 hours, September 17, 1862; *OR* 19:1, 228, 309–10; McCrea, September 20, 1862; Priest, *Antietam*, 122–24; and Naisawald, *Grape and Canister*, 160–61. There are some differences in the time Woodruff's battery reached the East Woods. From all reports, Company I likely arrived after 10 o'clock rather than earlier.

32. Naisawald, *Grape and Canister*, 161–62; Haskin, *History of the First Regiment of Artillery*, 158–59, 540–41; Priest, *Antietam*, 127; and McCrea, September 20, 1862.

33. *OR* 19:1, 309–10, and "The Antietam Manuscript of Ezra Ayres Carman," 36, available at http://kperlotto3.home.comcast.net/~kperlotto3/carman/EzraCarman.pdf (accessed on 11/16/2010).

34. McCrea, September 20, 1862.

35. Haskin, *History of the First Regiment of Artillery*, 542.

36. Ibid., 158–59.

7. Egan at Fredericksburg

1. Warner Diary, October 31 to November 16, 1862, and Augustus Woodbury, *Ambrose E. Burnside and the Ninth Army Corps* (Providence, RI: Sidney S. Rider & Brother, 1867), 168–69.

2. See class order of battle for Antietam shown previously.

3. Woodbury, *Burnside and the Ninth Army Corps,* 169.

4. McPherson, *Ordeal by Fire,* 324; Wert, *Sword of Lincoln,* 174; *OR* 19:2, 545–46; and *OR* 21:1, 82.

5. *OR* 21:1, 49–60; Edward J. Stackpole, *The Fredericksburg Campaign,* 2nd ed. (Mechanicsburg, PA: Stackpole Books, 1991), 65–66; and *WP Atlas,* map 72.

6. Francis A. O'Reilly, *The Fredericksburg Campaign: Winter War on the Rappahannock* (Baton Rouge: Louisiana State University Press, 2003), 25–27.

7. McCrea, December 24, 1863; *OR Supplement* 1:3, 735; O'Reilly, *Fredericksburg,* 32–33; and *OR* 21:1, 3–4.

8. Charles Seigel, *The Army of the Potomac in Stafford County 1862–1863 Driving Tour* (Stafford, VA: Rappahannock Valley Civil War Roundtable).

9. *OR* 21:1, 87, and *WP Atlas,* map 72.

10. *OR* 21:1, 88–89, 167–68, 180–81.

11. Naisawald, *Grape and Canister,* 187; Jennings C. Wise, *The Long Arm of Lee* (New York: Oxford University Press, 1959; originally published 1915 by W. P. Bell), 374–75; and *The Army of the Potomac in Stafford County* brochure.

12. *OR* 51:1, 956 (Supplement); and O'Reilly, *Fredericksburg,* 58, 61–62, 65.

13. *OR* 21:1, 175–76, 182, 191–92.

14. *OR* 21:1, 183, 221–22; O'Reilly, *Fredericksburg,* 78, 81–86; and *OR Supplement* 1:3, 747–48.

15. *OR* 21:1, 315, and Library of Congress photographs of Stafford Heights show little vegetation. Description of crossing based on McCrea's letter, December 18, 1862.

16. McCrea, December 18, 1862.

17. Events based on *Harper's Weekly,* December 22, 1862, vol. 6, 830–31; and Fredericksburg Visitors' Center movie.

18. Donald C. Pfanz, "The Sacking of Fredericksburg," part 12 of Behind the Lines Series (2005), available at http://www.fredericksburg.com/civilwar/battle/0414CW.htm, and O'Reilly, *Fredericksburg,* 127.

19. William K. Goolrick, *Rebels Resurgent: Fredericksburg to Chancellorsville* (Alexandria, VA: Time-Life Books, 1985), 72; O'Reilly, *Fredericksburg*, 250; and *OR* 21:1, 569–70.

20. O'Reilly, *Fredericksburg*, 88, 108–9, and *OR* 21:1, 311, 315, 317, 319, 325.

21. *OR* 21:1, 315, 325.

22. Naisawald, *Grape and Canister*, 206–7, and *OR* 21:1, 318.

23. *OR* 21:1, 318–19.

24. Ibid.

25. O'Reilly, *Fredericksburg*, 447, 450, and *OR* 21:1, 316.

8. Sanderson, Arnold, McIntire, and Warner at Chancellorsville

1. Pappas, *To the Point*, 348.

2. *OR* 25:1, 309–10, 483.

3. Stephen Sears, *Chancellorsville* (New York: Houghton Mifflin, 1996), 122, 139–40, and Naisawald, *Grape and Canister*, 217.

4. Sears, *Chancellorsville*, 61–68; O'Reilly, *Fredericksburg*, 504–5; *Cullum's 1891*, 858, 862, 863; *OR* 25:2, 12–13, 52; Pierce, *Most Promising*, 30; and see table 6.1.

5. *Cullum's 1891*, and Crary, *Dear Belle*, 219.

6. *OR* 25:1, 246–53; Stackpole, *Chancellorsville*, 116, 90–94, 124–26, and information contained on maps 7 and 8; and McCrea, May 10, 1863.

7. *OR* 25:1, 205–12, 563.

8. Warner Diary, letter to sister, April 30, 1863.

9. *OR Atlas*, map 39:2.

10. Frank A. O'Reilly, "'The Battle of Chancellorsville Was Lost Right Here': McLaws versus Sykes on the Orange Turnpike May 1, 1863," in *Fredericksburg History and Biography*, vol. 1 (Fredericksburg, VA: Central Virginia Battlefields Trust, 2002), 7, 13–15; Stackpole, *Chancellorsville*, 186–87; and Naisawald, *Grape and Canister*, 220.

11. Sears, *Chancellorsville*, 205, 211–12; O'Reilly, "Battle of Chancellorsville," 17–19; *OR* 25:1, 307, 526, 544–45; Ernest B. Furgurson, *Chancellorsville 1863: The Soul of the Brave* (New York: Knopf, 1992), 127; *BLCW*, vol. 3:159, 161; Stackpole, *Chancellorsville*, 128; and William Swinton, *The Army of the Potomac* (New York: W. S. Konecky Associates, 1995; originally published 1866), 282–83.

12. Gary Gallagher, *Chancellorsville* (Fort Washington, PA: Eastern National, 1995), 22–23; McCrea, May 10, 1863; and Haskin, *History of the First Regiment of Artillery*, 163, 542.

13. Gallagher, *Chancellorsville*, 27.

14. Walker, *History of the 2d Corps*, 229; Haskin, *History of the First Regiment of Artillery*, 542; Frank A. O'Reilly, *Battle of Chancellorsville Map Set*, 12 maps, produced by John Dove, 1998, map 6; Naisawald, *Grape and Canister*, 229; *OR* 25:1, 309–10; and Sears, *Chancellorsville*, 363.

15. Stackpole, *Chancellorsville*, 245, and Sears, *Chancellorsville*, 285.

16. Naisawald, *Grape and Canister*, 230–36.

17. *OR* 25:1, 483.

18. The position of Dimick's battery (Sanderson) is shown differently on maps and by historians. Most show the battery as the rightmost element of the gun line at Fairview. O'Reilly's maps show it as second in line. Naisawald shows it as first. The official reports seem to indicate that one or more guns were unlimbered on the left of the road. I have chosen to have Sanderson's two sections occupy both the road and the first two positions at Fairview.

19. William Powell, *The Fifth Army Corps (Army of the Potomac): A Record of Operations during the Civil War in the United States of America, 1861–1865* (Dayton, OH: Morningside Bookshop, 1984), 445; Furgurson, *Chancellorsville*, 216–17; Haskin, *History of the First Regiment of Artillery*, 163; and Naisawald, *Grape and Canister*, 230–31.

20. Fredericksburg and Spotsylvania National Military Park handout, *Hazel Grove and Fairview: A Walking Tour* (Chancellorsville, VA: Chancellorsville Battlefield Visitor Center, n.d.); Haskin, *History of the First Regiment of Artillery*, 163; *OR* 25:1, 249–50; Naisawald, *Grape and Canister*, 232–35; Sears, *Chancellorsville*, 290; and Stackpole, *Chancellorsville*, 250. The number of guns at Hazel Grove and Fairview are recorded differently in these references. I have chosen to use Hunt's report as the basis for the numbers cited in the text.

21. Author's visit to Fairview, March 22, 2005; *OR* 25:1, 674–76; and Stackpole, *Chancellorsville*, 246–48. The lunettes around the gun positions are still visible at Fairview.

22. Douglas Southall Freeman, *Robert E. Lee* (New York: Scribner & Sons, 1934), 550–51, and Naisawald, *Grape and Canister*, 236.

23. *OR* 25:1, 489; O'Reilly, *Chancellorsville*, map nos. 7 and 8; Naisawald, *Grape and Canister*, 239; and Sears, *Chancellorsville*, 344.

24. Stackpole, *Chancellorsville*, 287–88.

25. *OR* 25:1, 484.

26. Based on *OR* 25:1, 395, 484; and Naisawald, *Grape and Canister*, 240.

27. Wise, *Long Arm of Lee*, 509, and Gary W. Gallagher, ed., *Fighting for the Confederacy: The Personal Reflections of General Edward P. Alexander* (Chapel Hill: University of North Carolina Press, 1989), 209–10.

28. *OR* 25:1, 390, 489; Naisawald, *Grape and Canister*, 244; and

Steven W. Sears, *Chancellorsville* (New York: Houghton Mifflin, 1996), 344, 346.

29. Wise, *Long Arm of Lee*, 509, and Edward G. Longacre, *The Man behind the Guns: A Military biography of General Henry J. Hunt, Chief of Artillery, Army Of The Potomac* (Cambridge, MA: Da Capo, 2003), 138–40, 147.

30. Capt. Charles Morse, letter of May 7, 1863, Library of Congress, as quoted in Sears, *Chancellorsville*, 346.

31. *OR* 25:1, 675–76, and Naisawald, *Grape and Canister*, 244.

32. *OR* 25:1, 392–93, 484, 489–90; *New York Times*, May 7, 1863, 1; and Naisawald, *Grape and Canister*, 246–47.

33. Stackpole, *Chancellorsville*, 333–34.

34. Warner Diary, May 6, 1863.

35. Naisawald, *Grape and Canister*, 253–54, and *OR* 25:1, 564–65, 598.

36. Warner Diary, May 6, 1863.

37. Wise, *Long Arm of Lee*, 528–29, and *OR* 25:1, 210–12, 563–65, 597–98.

38. Warner Diary, May 6, 1863.

39. Ibid.

40. Powell, *Fifth Army Corps*, 472; Sears, *Chancellorsville*, 431; and McCrea, May 10, 1863.

41. *OR* 25:1, 565, 579–83.

42. Naisawald, *Grape and Canister*, 240; Sears, *Chancellorsville*, 323; and *OR* 25:1, 395, 450, 484–85.

9. Calef, Mackenzie, McCrea, Egan, Dearing, and Blount at Gettysburg

1. Harry W. Pfanz, *Gettysburg: The First Day* (Chapel Hill: University of North Carolina Press, 2001), 39; Noah A. Trudeau, *The Last Citadel: Petersburg, Virginia, June 1864–April 1865* (Baton Rouge: Louisiana State University Press, 1993), 141; and *OR* 27:1, 144, 926.

2. *OR* 27:1, 167, and *Cullum's 1891*.

3. *Cullum's 1891*, multiple entries.

4. Pfanz, *Gettysburg: First Day*, 39; John Calef, "Gettysburg Notes: The Opening Gun," *Journal of Military Service Institute of the United States* 40 (January–June 1907): 47; Stephen Sears, *Gettysburg* (New York: Houghton Mifflin, 2004), 143; Richard S. Shue, *Morning at Willoughby Run* (Gettysburg, PA: Thomas Publications, 1998), 35; and Trudeau, *Gettysburg*, 128.

5. Calef, "Gettysburg Notes," 44–47; Pfanz, *Gettysburg: First Day*, 42, 59; and *OR* 27:1, 228.

6. G. J. Fiebeger, *The Campaign and Battle of Gettysburg* (Hagerstown, MD: Barnwood Books, 1980; originally published 1915), 33–35.

7. Calef, "Gettysburg Notes," 40–58; Shue, *Morning at Willoughby Run*, 57–58; Trudeau, *Gettysburg,*159; and Douglas Southall Freeman, *Lee's Lieutenants: A Study in Command*, abridged by Stephen Sears (New York: Simon & Schuster, 1998), 562–63.

8. Trudeau, *Gettysburg*, 165–66; and Sears, *Gettysburg*, 163.

9. Pfanz, *Gettysburg: First Day*, 59, and Calef, "Gettysburg Notes," 42–44, 47. See cover of E. J. Coates, Michael J. McAffee, and Don Troiani, *Don Troiani's Civil War Series: Cavalry and Artillery*, 3rd ed. (Mechanicsburg, PA: Stackpole, 2006). Buford is pointing out positions to John Calef near the McPherson barn.

10. Calef, "Gettysburg Notes," 48, and *OR* 27:1, 1031. A monument identifying A Battery, Second US Artillery, is placed at approximately the position of Sergeant Newman's section on the left of the Chambersburg Pike.

11. Naisawald, *Grape and Canister*, 267; Fairfax Downey, *The Guns at Gettysburg* (New York: David McKay, 1955, 1956), 16; Pfanz, *Gettysburg: First Day*, 60; *OR* 27:1, 1031; Calef, "Gettysburg Notes," 48; Shue, *Morning at Willoughby Run*, 82–84; and Sears, *Gettysburg*, 163–64.

12. Pfanz, *Gettysburg: First Day*, 58.

13. Ibid., 62–65, and Calef, "Gettysburg Notes," 48. Words in quotes by Calef in "Gettysburg Notes."

14. *OR* 27:1, 1029–34, and Calef, "Gettysburg Notes," 48.

15. Sears, *Gettysburg*, 158, and Trudeau, *Gettysburg*, 172.

16. Pfanz, *Gettysburg: First Day*, 74–75; Trudeau, *Gettysburg*, 172; and Sears, *Gettysburg*, 166, 168.

17. Pfanz, *Gettysburg: First Day*, 75.

18. Ibid., 68; *OR* 27:1, 1029–34; and Calef, "Gettysburg Notes," 48–49.

19. Calef, "Gettysburg Notes," 49. There is no clear evidence in any of the diaries or letters as to the time this event took place. I have described it occurring prior to the arrival of the First Corps regiments sent to replace Devin's troopers.

20. Trudeau, *Gettysburg*, 182–83.

21. *OR* 27:1, 1031, and Pfanz, *Gettysburg: First Day*, 122.

22. There was some controversy among Buford, Wainwright, and Wadsworth over the use of Calef's battery instead of First Corps artillery units as reported by Grant Healy at http://wildcatbatterya2usarty.wordpress.com, a history site about Battery A, Second US Artillery. Healy states that Wainwright noted the controversy about arrest in his diary. And Calef, "Gettysburg Notes," 50.

23. Calef, "Gettysburg Notes," 50–51.

24. *OR* 27:1, 1028–34; Calef, "Gettysburg Notes," 50–51; Pfanz, *Gettys-*

burg: First Day, 157; Shue, *Morning at Willoughby Run*, 180; and Feibeger, *Campaign and Battle*, 44.

25. *OR* 27:1, 927, 934; Calef, "Gettysburg Notes," 51; and Pfanz, *Gettysburg: First Day*, 296, 303.

26. Trudeau, *Gettysburg*, 239–40, 243; Pfanz, *Gettysburg: First Day*, 294; *OR* 27:1, 231–32, 1032; Stackpole, *Gettysburg*, 140–41; Harry W. Pfanz, *Culp's Hill and Cemetery Hill* (Chapel Hill: University of North Carolina Press, 1993), 88; John B. Bachelder, *Maps of the Battlefield of Gettysburg: July 1st, 2nd, 3rd, 1863*, 3 maps (New York: Endicott, 1876), July 3, 1863, map; Calef, "Gettysburg Notes," 51; and J. David Petruzzi, "Cemetery Hill's Forgotten Savior," *Civil War Times*, October 2010, 50–51.

27. *OR* 27:1, 1030–32; Eric Wittenburg, "The Truth about the Withdrawal of Brig. Gen. John Buford's Cavalry," Gettysburg Discussion Group website, http://www.gdg.org/Research, 1–15; Trudeau, *Gettysburg*, 306; Calef, "Gettysburg Notes," 52; and *BLCW*, vol. 3, 276.

28. Frank A. Haskell, *The Battle of Gettysburg* (Cambridge, MA: Riverside Press, 1957), 35–37, and Edward J. Stackpole, *They Met at Gettysburg*, 3rd ed. (Harrisburg, PA: Stackpole Books, 1982), 208.

29. Trudeau, *Gettysburg*, 292, 294, and *OR* 27:1, 235.

30. Testimony by General Warren to the Joint Committee on Conduct of War as cited in *BLCW*, vol. 3, 307.

31. *OR* 27:1, 138, and Sears, *Gettysburg*, 269–70.

32. *OR* 27:1, 138, 600, and Harry W. Pfanz, *Gettysburg: The Second Day* (Chapel Hill: University of North Carolina Press, 1987), 206, 208, 212.

33. Pfanz, *Gettysburg: Second Day*, 63–64; Trudeau, *Gettysburg*, 283; *OR* 27:1, 369; and Haskell, *Battle of Gettysburg*, 18, 21–22.

34. Pfanz, *Gettysburg: Second Day*, 64; Haskin, *History of the First Regiment of Artillery*, 170, 545; *OR* 27:1, 478; Bachelder, *Maps*, July 2, 1863; McCrea, "Reminiscences of Gettysburg"; and Earl J. Hess, *Pickett's Charge at Gettysburg* (Chapel Hill, University of North Carolina Press, 2001), 199.

35. Jeffrey D. Wert, *Gettysburg: Day Three* (New York: Touchstone, 2001), 115, 117–18; Freeman, *Lee*, vol. 3, 108; Sears, *Gettysburg*, 358–60; and James Longstreet, *From Manassas to Appomattox: Memoirs of the Civil War in America* (New York: DaCapo Press, 1992), 386, 388–89.

36. George R. Stewart, *Pickett's Charge: A Microhistory of the Final Attack at Gettysburg, July 3, 1863* (Dayton, OH: Morningside Books, 1983), 35, 44–45; *OR* 27:2, 388–389; Wert, *Gettysburg: Day Three*, 123–24; and David Ladd and Audrey Ladd, eds., *John Bachelder's History of the Battle of Gettysburg*, Dayton, OH: Morningside House, 1997, see Third Day maps, sections IV and V. There are differences in various accounts where Dearing's

battalion was positioned. Priest places him on the northeastern corner of Spangler's Woods. Stewart's book places his rightmost battery almost touching the Emmitsburg Road near the Rogers's house. Bachelder's Third Day maps support Stewart's location. Gettysburg National Military Park (hereafter referred to as GNMP) historians believe that Stewart's account was correct.

37. Ladd and Ladd, *Bachelder's History of Battle of Gettysburg,* Third Day map, section V; Wert, *Gettysburg: Day Three,* 123–24; and Trudeau, *Gettysburg,* 452.

38. *BLCW,* vol. 3, 372.

39. Haskell, *Battle of Gettysburg,* 70, 77–80.

40. Freeman, *Lee,* vol. 3, 110.

41. Gallagher, *Fighting for the Confederacy,* 246, 257; Stewart, *Pickett's Charge,* 120; *OR* 27:2, 388; and Trudeau, *Gettysburg,* 467.

42. Haskell, *Battle of Gettysburg,* 81–84; Wert, *Gettysburg: Day Three,* 167–73, 175; Naisawald, *Grape and Canister,* 332; Haskin, *History of the First Regiment of Artillery,* 168–69; Downey, *Guns at Gettysburg,* 131–32; Stewart, *Pickett's Charge,* 129–30; Downey, *Guns at Gettysburg,* 136–37; Winfield Scott, "Pickett's Charge," paper presented before the California Commandery of the Military Order of the Loyal Legion of the United States, February 8, 1888, available at http://www.gdg.org/Research/MOLLUS/ mollus.html; and *BLCW,* vol. 3, 385–87.

43. Haskin, *History of the First Regiment of Artillery,* 169; Downey, *Guns at Gettysburg,* 129; *OR* 27: 238–39; and Gallagher, *Fighting for the Confederacy,* 248–49. The number of guns initially firing varies in the histories and official records.

44. Haskell, *Battle of Gettysburg,* 85.

45. Trudeau, *Gettysburg,* 467, and Wert, *Gettysburg: Day Three,* 178.

46. Hess, *Pickett's Charge,* 128, and Haskin, *History of the First Regiment of Artillery,* 170.

47. *OR* 27:1, 239; McCrea, "Reminiscences," 4; and *BLCW,* vol. 3, 374.

48. *OR* 27:1, 238–40, 480; see Hancock–Hunt letters in Hunt Papers at the GNMP and in *BLCW,* vol. 3, 385–87; George T. Fleming, ed., *Life and Letters of Alexander Hays* (Philadelphia: N.p., 1919), 442–43; and McCrea, "Reminiscences," 4.

49. *OR* 27:1, 250, 480–81.

50. *OR* 27:1, 239–40; Kent Masterson Brown, *Cushing of Gettysburg* (Lexington: University Press of Kentucky, 1983), 239–40; Stewart, *Pickett's Charge,* 179; and Naisawald, *Grape and Canister,* 339–40.

51. Gallagher, *Fighting for the Confederacy,* 259, and Longstreet, *From Manassas,* 392.

52. Stewart, *Pickett's Charge,* 169–73; Sears, *Gettysburg,* 419; and Wert,

Gettysburg: Day Three, 188–94. Size of the assault varies greatly. I have accepted Sears's view in his *Gettysburg* that the charge comprised thirteen thousand men. Many historians and participants estimated the length of the bombardment at two hours and some as short as one hour. General Hancock recorded the time as one hour and three-quarters, which is the view I have taken here.

53. McCrea, "Reminiscences," 5.

54. Trudeau, *Gettysburg,* 485; Gallagher, *Fighting for the Confederacy,* 262–64; and Wise, *Long Arm of Lee,* 684.

55. Haskin, *History of the First Regiment of Artillery,* 544–45.

56. Haskell, *Battle of Gettysburg,* 97–98; John M. Archer, "Remembering the 14th Connecticut Volunteers," *Gettysburg,* no. 9 (July 1993), 75; Wert, *Gettysburg: Day Three,* 195–96; and *OR* 27:1, 428.

57. Haskin, *History of the First Regiment of Artillery,* 544–45.

58. Stewart, *Pickett's Charge,* 198; McCrea, "Reminiscences," 5–6; and Wert, *Gettysburg: Day Three,* 202.

59. Haskell, *Battle of Gettysburg,* 101–2, and Stewart, *Pickett's Charge,* 208.

60. *BLCW,* vol. 3, 391–92; Hess, *Pickett's Charge,* 210; and Sears, *Gettysburg,* 429–32.

61. Stewart, *Pickett's Charge,* map on 229, 233; *BLCW,* vol. 3, 391–92; and Hess, *Pickett's Charge,* 208.

62. David Schultz, *Double Canister at Ten Yards* (Redondo Beach, CA: Rank and File Publications, 1995), 49, 54; Sergent, *Unremaining Glory,* 69; Haskin, *History of the First Regiment of Artillery,* 170.

63. David L. Ladd and Audrey J. Ladd, *The Bachelder Papers: Gettysburg in Their Own Words,* vol. 1 (Dayton, OH: Morningside House, 1994), 389, and vol. 2, 852–57, and Haskin, *History of the First Regiment of Artillery,* 170.

64. Stewart, *Pickett's Charge,* 253, and John Egan, letter to George Meade Jr., February 8, 1870, Peter F. Rothermal collection, GNMP. Egan's later letter clearly identifies his location and response to General Meade.

65. Haskin, *History of the First Regiment of Artillery,* 544–45.

66. McCrea, "Reminiscences," 7; Sergent, *Unremaining Glory,* 69; and Haskin, *History of the First Regiment of Artillery,* 171.

67. *OR* 27:1, 480, and *BLCW,* vol. 3, 375.

68. Sergent, *Unremaining Glory,* 70.

69. McCrea, July 5, 1863.

10. Mansfield, Semmes, and West at Port Hudson

1. John M. Gould, *Joseph K. F. Mansfield, Brigadier General of the U.S. Army,* a Project Gutenburg e-book, www.gutenberg.org/

files/32258/32258-h/32258-h.htm (accessed on October 6, 2010), 15–17, 27; Augustus H. Conklin, "History of Twenty-fourth Regiment Connecticut Volunteer Infantry," available at http://archiver.rootsweb .ancestry.com/th/read/CTNEWHAV/2001-07/0994054785(accessed on September 10, 2014); and Frederick H. Dyer, *A Compendium of the War of the Rebellion* (Des Moines, IA: Dyer Publishing Co, 1908), 1015. Digital copy is part of "The Civil War CD-ROM", Oliver Computing LLC, Indianapolis, IN, 2006.

2. *OR* 26:1, 530; *BLCW,* vol. 3, 599.

3. *BLCW,* vol. 3, 586–88; William C. Davis and Bell L. Wiley, eds., *Civil War Album: Complete Photographic History of the Civil War* (New York: Tess Press, 2000), 460–61; Clement A. Evans, ed., *Confederate Military History,* extended ed., vol. 8, *Alabama* (Wilmington, NC: Broadfoot Publishing, 1987), 794–95; and Richard P. Weinert Jr., *The Confederate Regular Army* (Shippensburg, PA: White Mane, 1991), 68.

4. *BLCW,* vol. 3, 586–88.

5. *OR* 15:1, 251–56, 714; Conklin, "History of the Twenty-fourth Regiment"; and Edward Longacre, "The Port Hudson Campaign," *Civil War Times* 10, no. 2 (February 1972): 20–34.

6. Longacre, "Port Hudson," 20–34, and *BLCW,* vol. 3, 588–89.

7. *OR* 15:1, 358.

8. *OR* 15:1, 390, 393, and Weinert, *Confederate Regular Army,* 68.

9. *OR* 15:1, 360–61, and "American Battlefield Protection Program Civil War Site Advisory Commission Battle Summary (CWSAC) Report on the Nation's Civil War Battlefields," technical vol. 2, Battle Summaries: Irish Bend, available at www.nps.gov/hps/abpp/battles/la007.htm (accessed September 21, 2009).

10. *Confederate Military History: Vol. VIII, Alabama,* 794–95; *OR* 15, 359–61; and Weinert, *Confederate Regular Army,* 68–70.

11. Conklin, "History of the Twenty-Fourth Regiment"; *OR* 26:1, 3–18; and *OR* 15, 357–62.

12. See *Harper's Weekly,* June 27, 1863, 410 and 412, and Foote, *Civil War,* vol. 2, 400–1.

13. Conklin, "History of the Twenty-fourth Regiment," and *OR* 26:1, 14–15.

14. Conklin, "History of the Twenty-fourth Regiment."

15. Longacre, "Port Hudson," 34.

16. Letter from Lincoln to Hon. James C. Conkling, August 26, 1863 available at http://www.abrahamlincolnonline.org/lincoln/speeches/conkling.htm, and *OR* 26:1, 14–15.

17. Conklin, "History of the Twenty-Fourth Regiment."

18. Dyer, *Compendium*, 1015; Conklin, "History of Twenty-fourth Regiment"; and *Cullum's 1891*, 849.

11. McCrea and the Battle of Olustee

1. McCrea, January 9, 1864.

2. *Cullum's 1891*, 854.

3. McCrea, November 25, 1863.

4. David J. Coles, "Far from the Fields of Glory: Military Operations in Florida during the Civil War," PhD diss., Florida State University, 1996, http://fulltext10.fcla.edupart 14–17, 24–25; Robert J. Broadwater, *The Battle of Olustee, 1864* (Jefferson, NC: McFarland, 2006), 16; and Paul Taylor, *Discovering the Civil War in Florida* (Sarasota, FL: Pineapple Press, 2001), 112.

5. *OR* 35:1, 275–80, 292. Units were taken from Fort Pulaski, St. Helena, Hilton Head Island, and the garrisons occupying St. Augustine and Fernandina in Florida to form the task force.

6. *Cullum's 1891*, 847.

7. Returns for First Regiment of Artillery, January 1864, in "Returns for Regular Army Artillery Regiments: June 1821–Jan. 1901," M727, roll 5, NA; Haskin, *History of the First Regiment of Artillery*, 404; McCrea, February 5, 1864 as quoted in Crary, *Dear Belle*, 227; and Lewis G. Schmidt, *The Civil War in Florida: A Military History Vol. 2; The Battle of Olustee* (Allentown, PA: Lewis G. Schmidt, 1989), 2. Note that there is a discrepancy between the official returns, Haskin, and Schmidt regarding the names of the vessels used to transport Company M. I have chosen to use the names listed in Haskin here.

8. Coles, "Far from the Fields," 40, and Crary, *Dear Belle*, 227–28.

9. Coles, "Far from the Fields," 46, and Schmidt, *Civil War in Florida*, 15.

10. *OR* 35:1, 298, and Haskin, *History of the First Regiment of Artillery*, 404.

11. *OR* 35:1, 295–96, and Schmidt, *Civil War in Florida*, 42–43.

12. McCrea, February 12, 1864, as quoted in Crary, *Dear Belle*, 228; Haskin, *History of the First Regiment of Artillery*, 404; and Schmidt, *Civil War in Florida*, 74.

13. *OR* 35:1, 277–78, 296; Coles, "Far from the Fields," 72–74, 77; and Schmidt, *Civil War in Florida*, 72–75.

14. Mark Boyd, "The Federal Campaign of 1864 in East Florida," *Florida Historical Quarterly* 29 (July 1950): 7–12, 15; Schmidt, *Civil War in Florida*, 96, 109; Coles, "Far from the Fields," 63; *OR* 35:1, 277, 285–86; and *BLCW*, vol. 4, 76.

15. Boyd, "Federal Campaign," 8, 13–14; Coles, "Far from the Fields," 77, 91; and Schmidt, *Civil War in Florida,* 83.

16. Coles, *Men and Arms,* 26.

17. Boyd, "Federal Campaign," 10–11; Schmidt, *Civil War in Florida,* 85; and *OR* 35:1, 288.

18. Richard J. Ferry, "The Battle of Olustee," *Blue & Gray Magazine,* February/March 1986, 44; Boyd, "Federal Campaign," 17–18; and Coles, "Far from the Fields," 113–16.

19. *OR Atlas,* plate 53; Boyd, "Federal Campaign," 2, 19–22; *BLCW,* vol. 4, 77; and *OR* 35:1, 301, 303–4. Boyd's maps are more descriptive than the single official map in *OR Atlas.*

20. *OR* 35:1, 316.

21. *OR* 35:1, 316; Ferry, "Battle of Olustee," 47; Coles, "Far from the Fields," 128, 135–36; *OR* 35:1, 332, 349–51; and Schmidt, *Civil War in Florida,* 222. See map on page 223 in the latter for the location of McCrea's guns.

22. Schmidt, *Civil War in Florida,* 222. The Seventh New Hampshire had disintegrated and was regrouping behind the lines. See page 208.

23. Boyd, "Federal Campaign," 21; Coles, "Far from the Fields," 135; and Schmidt, *Civil War in Florida,* 222. Barton's regiments filled the gap caused by the disintegration of the Seventh New Hampshire.

24. *OR* 35:1, 318, and terrain observed during author's visit to battlefield in 2008.

25. *OR* 35:1, 318.

26. Schmidt, *Civil War in Florida,* 290, and *OR* 35:1, 316–17.

27. Michael Morgan, "Surprise at Ocean Pond," *America's Civil War,* March 2000, 52, and Ferry, "Battle of Olustee," 47.

28. Boyd, "Federal Campaign," 29, and Haskin, *History of the First Regiment,* 406.

29. Schmidt, *Civil War in Florida,* 326, 331, and Haskin, *History of the First Regiment,* 406.

30. Letter from Peter S. Michie to S. Talbot, February 21, 1863, McCrea files, SCAD.

31. *OR* 35:1, 300–1; E. Swift, *Medical History of the War of the Rebellion* (Washington, DC: Government Printing Office, 1870), part first, appendix, 243–45; and Haskin, *History of the First Regiment,* 406.

32. McCrea, March 1, 1864, as quoted in Crary, *Dear Belle,* 232. Hospital No. 7 was located at Little C and First Street in Beaufort.

33. McCrea, April 2 and 10, 1864; Alice McCrea to Belle and Sam Talbot, March 21, 1864; and McCrea, April 2, 1864.

34. Letter from General Seymour to Brig. Gen. Lorenzo Thomas, July

26, 1864, and General Hunt's recommendation to increase McCrea's bre-vet promotion to major, August 8, 1865, M1064 (Letters Received by the Commission Branch of the Adjutant General's Office, 1863–1870), RG 94, M1064 , roll 217, item S1066.

12. Sanderson, Semmes, and West at Pleasant Hill

1. *OR* 34:1, 197, and *OR* 34:2, 358.

2. Walker, *History of the 2d Corps,* 312; *OR* 27:2, 878–85; *OR* 27:3, 817–18; and Herbert Asbury, *The Gangs of New York* (New York: Thunder Month Press, 1927, 1928, 1998), 111–112, 123, http://www.civilwarhome .com/draftriots.htm (accessed March 20, 2006).

3. Ashbury, 151–52.

4. *BLCW,* vol. 4, 349; *Confederate Military History: Vol. III, Alabama,* 794–95; "Mansfield" article found at Civil War Trust website at http:// www.civilwar.org/mansfield.htm (accessed 2014); Oliver J. Semmes, "First Confederate Battery an Orphan," *Confederate Veteran* 21 (1913): 58; CSR, M258, roll 47; Weinert, *Confederate Regular Army,* 71–72; and *Cullum's 1891,* 857.

5. McPherson, *Ordeal by Fire,* 446; *BLCW,* vol. 4, 108, 347; and Mat-loff, *American Military History,* 263.

6. *OR* 34:1, 170, 196, 420; *OR* 34:2, 357–58; and *Cullum's 1891,* 857.

7. *OR* 34:1, 198. Sanderson's probable assignment based on comments in official reports.

8. *OR* 34:1, 563–64, and article by Susan G. M. Bannerman, *The Shreveport Journal,* April 8, 1937. Other reports state that Mouton's division initiated the attack without orders from General Taylor—see General Kirby Smith's report in *OR* 34:1.

9. *OR* 34:1, 358, 409–10, and *OR* 34:2, 358.

10. This is conjecture on the part of the author and is based on events that took place the next day.

11. *OR* 34:1, 257–58, 392–93, 409, 414, 421.

12. Peter Cozzens, ed., *Battles and Leaders of the Civil War,* vol. 5 (Urbana, IL: University of Illinois Press, 2002), 581, and *OR* 34:1, 257–58, 392–93, 563–64. Batteries mentioned were all part of Semmes's artillery command.

13. Cozzens, *Battles and Leaders of the Civil War,* 581.

14. *OR* 34:1, 409–10; Dyer, *Compendium,* 696–97; and see map accom-panying General Franklin and General Emory's report in *OR* 34:1, 230–31, 391–92.

15. *OR* 34:1, 411.

16. *OR* 34:1, 392–93.

17. Haskin, *History of the First Regiment*, 236–37.

18. *BLCW*, vol. 4, 360; *OR* 34:1, 476; Ulysses S. Grant, *Personal Memoirs of U.S. Grant* (New York: Dover Publications, 1995), 281; William F. Fox, *Regimental Losses in the American Civil War* (Albany, NY: Randow Printing Company, 1889), 102 (the Joint Committee on the Conduct of the War took testimony later); *OR* 34:1, 413; and review of brigade and division reports, maps in General Emory's report, and Lieutenant Taylor's and Lieutenant Appleton's reports.

13. Mackenzie, Gillespie, Calef, Egan, Dearing, and Schaff during the Overland and Petersburg Campaigns

1. Pappas, *To the Point*, 357–58.

2. Matloff, *American Military History*, 264–66.

3. *OR* 36:1, 208, 287–89, 904; *OR* 40:2, 48; Calef, "Gettysburg Notes," 53; Edward G. Longacre, *The Man behind the Guns* (Cambridge, MA: Da Capo, 2003), 196; and Bruce Catton, *A Stillness at Appomattox* (Garden City, NY: Doubleday, 1953), 47.

4. *Annual Report, 1888,* 47; *OR* 37:1, 700; *OR* 43:1, 849; *OR* 46:2, 757; "Returns of the Second Artillery Regiment (January 1861–December)," RG 94, M727, roll 13, NA. Battery G, Second US Artillery, moved first to Fort Cass, Virginia, in June 1864 and then remained throughout the war at Fort Strong, Virginia (1870); and *OR* 36:1, 286–90, 301.

5. Grant, *Memoirs*, 336–38; *OR* 36:1, 854; and *WP Atlas,* map 134.

6. Robert H. Moore, *The Richmond Fayette, Hampden, Thomas, and Blount's Lynchburg Artillery* (Lynchburg, VA: H. E. Howard, 1991), 107–9; Freeman, *Lee,* vol. 3, 373–75; CSR, M324 (Virginia), roll 254; *OR* 36:3, 857–58; and Ernest B. Furgurson, *Not War but Murder: Cold Harbor, 1864* (New York: Knopf, 2000), 59.

7. Furgurson, *Not War but Murder*, 78, and Philip H. Sheridan, *Personal Memoirs of P. H. Sheridan* (New York: Da Capo, 1992), 219.

8. *Annual Report, 1913,* 78–88; AGO briefing paper 63212 found in Gillespie file at SCAD (background information related to the application of George L. Gillespie for a Medal of Honor, dated September 1897, provided basis for Gillespie's ride to Cold Harbor described in this section); *OR* 40:1, 300; and Grant, *Memoirs,* 338.

9. *OR* 36:1, 851. Dennison, named in Merritt's report, took command of Company A five days later. The scheduled rotation from the Second Horse Artillery Brigade on May 31 brought Calef's battery to Cold Harbor just prior to the reorganization of the army's artillery.

10. AGO briefing paper 63212; *OR* 36:1, 806; *OR* 36:3, 411; and *Annual Report, 1913,* 78–88.

11. Grant, *Memoirs,* 338; *OR* 36:1, 194, 806; and *OR* 36:3, 404, 469–70.

12. *Annual Report,* 1913, 78–88.

13. Medal of Honor Society web page, and Gillespie personnel file, NA.

14. In 1897 when assigned as the chief of engineers, Gillespie was instrumental in redesigning the army's Medal of Honor. He patented it as Design No. 37,236 on November 22, 1904; it was approved by the War Department and Congress in 1904. The current version of the army Medal of Honor is often called the Gillespie Medal. See US Army Corps of Engineers, chief of engineers' history; Medal of Honor Society web page; and US Patent Office files.

15. Theodore F. Vail, *History of the Second Connecticut Volunteer Heavy Artillery Regiment* (Winsted, CT: Winsted Printing Co., 1868; reprinted LaVerne, TN: BiblioLife, 2010), 50, 57–63, and Furgurson, *Not War but Murder,* 100–2.

16. *OR* 36:1, 295–97, 667; Pierce, *Most Promising,* 33; Catton, *Stillness at Appomattox,* 112–16; Gordon C. Rhea, *The Battles of Wilderness and Spotsylvania,* Civil War Series (Fort Washington, PA: Eastern National, 1995), 36–37; and Wert, *Sword of Lincoln,* 349–50.

17. Pierce, *Most Promising,* 34–35; *OR* 36:3, 729; SO 158, HQ Army of the Potomac, June 10, 1864; Vail, *History of the Second Connecticut,* 67–68; and Grant, *Memoirs,* 344. Vail notes that Mackenzie arrived on June 6 to take command.

18. *WP Atlas,* map 137, and Grant, *Memoirs,* 351.

19. *OR* 36:1, 798.

20. Henry A. Pyne, *Ride to War: A History of the First New Jersey Cavalry* (Brunswick, NJ: Rutgers University Press, 1961; originally published 1871, J. A. Beecher), 270–75, found at http://books.google.com (accessed November 19, 2009); and Eric Wittenberg, *Glory Enough for All* (Washington, DC: Brassey's, 2001), 266–67, 271–72.

21. Pyne, *Ride to War,* 270–75; *OR* 36:1, 186–87, 855–56; *BLCW,* vol. 4, 236; and Sheridan, *Personal Memoirs,* 236–37, 244.

22. Greg Eanes, *Destroy the Junction: The Wilson-Kautz Raid and the Battle for the Staunton River Bridge, June 21, 1864 to July 1, 1865* (Lynchburg, VA: H. E. Howard, 1999), 29–31, 37, map 116, task organization 185; *OR* 40:1, 621; and *OR* 40:2, 669, SO 26, HQ, Department of North Carolina and Southern Virginia, June 19, 1964.

23. Eanes, *Destroy the Junction,* 60, 63–64, 81, maps 117–118, and *OR* 40:1, 620–21, 635–36, 645–46.

24. *OR* 40:1, 622, 636–37, 646, and Eanes, *Destroy the Junction,* 80, 90–92, 123–25.

25. Parker, "Brigadier General James Dearing," 62; Trudeau, *Last Citadel,* 87–90; Eanes, *Destroy the Junction,* 132, 135–36; and *OR* 40:1, 623.

26. Eanes, *Destroy the Junction,* 139–41, 205n39; *OR* 40:3, 68; and list of prisoners held at Columbia Military prison, http://www.geocities.com/cmp_csa/index.html (accessed February 13, 2007).

27. Morris Schaff, *The Battle of the Wilderness* (Boston: Houghton Mifflin, 1910), 233–35.

28. Schaff, "The Explosion at City Point," *MOLLUS* (Massachusetts), vol. 53, 478–79; *Cullum's 1891,* 851; *OR* 42:2, 98, 112, 130–31, 295; *New York Times,* August 13, 1864, 2; and Farley, *West Point in the Early Sixties,* 147. Description of City Point area based on "City Point," a web page (part of the Petersburg NMP web site) found at http://www.nps.gov/pete/historyculture/city-point.htm and Schaff's article.

29. Schaff, "Explosion at City Point," 477–85; *Annual Report, 1933,* 51–53; Foote, *Civil War,* vol. 3, 543–44; *OR* 42:1, 956; and Bruce L. Brager, "The City Point Explosion" found at http://www.militaryhistoryonline.com/civilwar/articles/citypoint.aspx (accessed May 21, 2008).

30. Research of assignments through *Cullum's 1891* and muster reports.

14. Murray at Atlanta

1. Sherman, *Memoirs,* vol. II, 30–32, and Smith, *Fuller's Ohio Brigade,* 144.

2. *OR* 38:3, 17–18; Steven E. Woodworth, *Nothing but Victory: The Army of the Tennessee, 1861–1865* (New York: Vintage Books, 2005), 493, 497; and Smith, *Fuller's Ohio Brigade,* 145–46.

3. *Cullum's 1891,* 846, 850, 865; Foote, *Civil War,* vol. 3, 16–17; *OR* 38:4, 640; *OR* 38:1, 128; and *OR* 38:5, 419, 794.

4. CSR, M268 (Tennessee), roll 221; *OR* 38:3, 639, 648; and *Confederate Veteran,* vol. 32, 25, and vol. 26, 274.

5. CSR, M266 (Georgia), rolls 148 and 150; *OR* 32:3, 576; *OR* 38:4, 710, 744; *OR* 38:5, 932, 948; and *BLCW,* vol. 4, 290.

6. *OR* 18:1, 274, 562, 575; *OR* 24:3, 256; and Steven A. Cormier, *The Siege of Suffolk* (Lynchburg, VA: H. E. Howard, Inc., 1989), 121.

7. *OR* 18:1, 306, and Moore, *Richmond Fayette,* 68.

8. *OR* 18:1, 304–7, 334–37.

9. Michael N. Ingrisano Jr., *An Artilleryman's War: Gus Dey and the 2nd United States Artillery* (Shippensburg, PA: White Mane Books, 1998), 281n11.

10. Ingrisano, *Artilleryman's War,* 131–33, and *OR* 30:3, 320.

11. Smith, *Fuller's Ohio Brigade,* 144; *OR* 38:1, 108; *OR* 38:3, 483; and Ingrisano, *Artilleryman's War,* 180. General Veatch commanded the Fourth Division until early July when General Fuller took command.

12. *WP Atlas,* map 145.

13. Matloff, *American Military History*, 171–73.

14. Dyer, *Compendium*, 1699.

15. Russell K. Brown, *Our Connection with Savannah: A History of the 1st Battalion Georgia Sharpshooters, 1862–1865* (Macon, GA: Mercer University Press, 2004), 128.

16. *OR* 38:3, 484, and Ingrisano, *Artilleryman's War*, 180.

17. Sherman, *Memoirs*, vol. 2, 50–51; *OR* 38:1, 67; *OR* 38:3, 484; Smith, *Fuller's Ohio Brigade*, 152, 154; *WP Atlas*, map 146; Ingrisano, *Artilleryman's War*, 180; and *OR Atlas*, plate 59-1.

18. *OR* 38:3, 383, 485; *OR Atlas*, plate 59-2, plate 88-1; Foote, *Civil War*, vol. 4, 395; and Smith, *Fuller's Ohio Brigade*, 159–60.

19. *OR Atlas*, plate 49-3; Smith, *Fuller's Ohio Brigade*, 160–61; and Ingrisano, *Artilleryman's War*, 139–40.

20. *OR* 38:5, 891; *OR* 38:3, 383, 631; Sherman, *Memoirs*, vol. 2, 72–75; and Matloff, *American Military History*, 271.

21. *OR* 38:3, 383–84; *OR* 38:5, 179; and *WP Atlas*, map 147a.

22. Woodworth, *Nothing but Victory*, 540.

23. Sherman, *Memoirs*, vol. 2, 74–75.

24. *OR Atlas*, plate 131-3 (Murray's battery location along the Old McDonough Road), and *OR* 38:3, 474.

25. Woodworth, *Nothing but Victory*, 542–43.

26. *OR* 38:3, 631–32.

27. *OR Atlas*, plates 61-3, 131-3; *OR* 38:3, 474–88, 536–39; Woodworth, *Nothing but Victory*, 538; and Foote, *Civil War*, vol. 4, 475–76.

28. *OR* 38:3, 371, 475, 536.

29. *OR* 38:3, 539, and Ingrisano, *Artilleryman's War*, 140.

30. *OR* 38:1, 234; *OR* 38:3, 385, 539; *OR Atlas*, plates 62-3 and 62-8 for locations of Company F; and Ingrisano, *Artilleryman's War*, 140–42.

31. Description of Camp Oglethorpe found at www.Georgiastatefair/campolgethorpe.htm and *New Georgia Encyclopedia*, and copy of letter found in Mary Elizabeth Sergent's files (now the author's), detailing the loss of Murray.

15. Mackenzie and McIntire in the Shenandoah Valley

1. McCrea, October 30, 1864.

2. Vail, *History of the Second Connecticut*, 108–113, and Jeffrey D. Wert, *From Winchester to Cedar Creek* (New York: Simon & Schuster, 1987), 158–59.

3. *OR Atlas*, plate 99-2. Upton was wounded at Winchester and had not returned to duty.

4. *BLCW*, vol. 4, map on page 517; *OR* 43:1, 523–524; Wert, *From Winchester*, 170–72; and Sheridan, *Personal Memoirs*, 335.

5. Vail, *History of the Second Connecticut,* 119–20.

6. Ibid., 71–72, 77; *WP Atlas,* map 138; Pierce, *Most Promising,* 37; and Charles M. Robinson III, *Bad Hand: A Biography of General Ranald S. Mackenzie* (Abilene, TX: State House Press, 2005, 1993), 20.

7. Vail, *History of the Second Connecticut,* 77, 82, 84–86.

8. Ibid., 88–89.

9. Wert, *From Winchester,* 29, and Fred L. Ray, "Mimic War No More," *Civil War Times* 49, no. 1 (February 2010): 53.

10. *OR* 43:1, 47, 162–63, 173–74, 177, 179, 518; Wert, *From Winchester,* 91, 98; and Vail, *History of the Second Connecticut,* 94–98.

11. Vail, *History of the Second Connecticut,* 106–7; *OR* 43:2, 199–200; and Pierce, *Most Promising,* 43.

12. Ray, "Mimic War No More," 53–58; *BLCW,* vol. 4, 526; and Wert, *From Winchester,* 37–38, 175; and Sheridan, *Personal Memoirs,* 271.

13. Richard N. Griffin, ed., *Three Years a Soldier* (Knoxville: University of Tennessee Press, 2006), 299; Wert, *From Winchester,* 185–87, 194–95; and Thomas A. Lewis, *The Guns of Cedar Creek* (New York: Dell, 1988), 232–33.

14. Vail, *History of the Second Connecticut,* 120; Wert, *From Winchester,* 198; Isaac Oliver Best, *The History of the 121st New York State Infantry* (Chicago: Lt. J. A. Smith, 1921), 193; and Lewis, *Guns of Cedar Creek,* 231–32.

15. Wert, *From Winchester,* 202; Lewis, *Guns of Cedar Creek,* 233–35; and Vail, *History of the Second Connecticut,* 121.

16. Vail, *History of the Second Connecticut,* 122; Best, *121st New York State Infantry,* 195; and Wert, *From Winchester,* 202.

17. Vail, *History of the Second Connecticut,* 123; Best, *121st New York State Infantry,* 195–96; *OR Atlas,* plate 99-2; Joseph W. A. Whitehorne, *Battle of Cedar Creek,* 3rd ed. (Middletown, VA: Cedar Creek Battlefield Foundation, 2006), 21–22; Wert, *From Winchester,* 204–5; and *OR* 43:1, 174–75.

18. *OR* 43:1, 433–34, 522–23; Gregory J. W. Urwin, *Custer Victorious* (Lincoln: University of Nebraska Press, 1983), 207–8; and Wert, *From Winchester,* 214–15.

19. Wert, *From Winchester,* 221–22; Sheridan, *Personal Memoirs,* 322–23; and *OR* 43:1, 53.

20. *OR* 43:1, 53, 522–23; *OR Atlas,* plate 99-2; and Lewis, *Guns of Cedar Creek,* 283–84.

21. *OR* 43:1, 175–76; Vail, *History of the Second Connecticut,* 126; and Wert, *From Winchester,* 230.

22. Sheridan, *Personal Memoirs,* 332, and Vail, *History of the Second Connecticut,* 126.

23. *OR* 43:1, 53, 524, and Urwin, *Custer Victorious,* 212.

24. Wert, *From Winchester,* 234; Lewis, *Guns of Cedar Creek,* 301–3; and *OR* 43:1, 435, 532.

25. *Annual Report, 1914,* 79; *OR* 43: 2, 478; and Heitman, *Historical Register,* 672.

16. Dearing at High Bridge

1. Parker, "Brigadier General James Dearing," 41, and *OR* 33:1, 1083, 1103, 1202–3. Dearing's assignment to the cavalry brigade precluded General Lee from transferring him to command the horse artillery brigade in the Army of Northern Virginia where some authors place him in various organizational charts.

2. Wise, *Long Arm of Lee,* 814–15; *OR Atlas,* plate 67-3; Moore, *Richmond Fayette,* 94–95; and Parker, "Brigadier General James Dearing," 42.

3. Moore, *Richmond Fayette,* 98, 104, 106, and *BLCW,* vol. 4, 195–96.

4. William Robertson, *The Battle of Old Men and Young Boys* (Lynchburg, VA: H. E. Howard, 1989), 72–81.

5. Robertson, *Battle of Old Men,* 73. Dearing's promotion to general took place on April 29, 1864.

6. *WP Atlas,* map 138; Robertson, *Battle of Old Men,* 75–77, 81; and Parker, "Brigadier General James Dearing," 58–61.

7. SO 26, HQ, Department of North Carolina and Southern Virginia, June 19, 1986, www.nwinfin.net/~jagriffin/62nd.htm (accessed November 26, 2006); Edward G. Longacre, *Lee's Cavalrymen* (Mechanicsburg, PA: Stackpole, 2002), 308; *OR* 42:2, 1310; and Dearing to Roxanna, family letters, Virginia Historical Society, Richmond, Virginia.

8. William N. McDonald, *A History of the Laurel Brigade,* B. B. Washington, ed. (Baltimore: Johns Hopkins University Press, 2002), 285–95; Trudeau, *Last Citadel,* 196–201; and as quoted in Trudeau, *Last Citadel,* 201.

9. Edward Bearss and Chris Calkins, *The Battle of Five Forks* (Lynchburg, VA: H. E. Howard, 1985), 8–9; Parker, "Brigadier General James Dearing," 71–72, 75; CSR, M324 (Virginia), roll 254; CSR, M331 (General Officers and Staff), roll 150; McDonald, *History of the Laurel Brigade,* 364–65; Freeman, *Lee's Lieutenants,* 776; and Chris Calkins, *The Appomattox Campaign* (Conshohocken, PA: Combined Books, 1997) 17–20.

10. Dearing to Roxanna, March 28, 1865. This was his last letter to his wife found at Virginia Historical Society.

11. *OR* 46:1, 53–54, 119–20.

12. Bearss and Calkins, *Battle of Five Forks,* 36–42, and *OR* 46:1, 1154–55.

13. Freeman, *Lee's Lieutenants*, 778.

14. *BLCW*, vol. 4, 712–13; McDonald, *History of the Laurel Brigade*, 366–67; and Freeman, *Lee's Lieutenants*, 779–80.

15. McDonald, *History of the Laurel Brigade*, 367; *OR* 46:1, 1299–1300; and Bearss and Calkins, *Battle of Five Forks*, 102.

16. *OR* 46:1, 1119–20, 1245, and *OR* 46:3, 560–62.

17. *OR* 46:1, 1107, 1145, 1301; *New York Times*, April 14, 1865, 8; Richard L. Armstrong, *7th Virginia Cavalry* (Lynchburg, VA: H. E. Howard, 1992), 86; Richard L. Armstrong, *11th Virginia Cavalry* (Lynchburg, VA: H. E. Howard, 1989), 99; McDonald, *History of the Laurel Brigade*, 371–73; and Mary Dearing Ward, "Maj. Gen. James Dearing: The Last Hero," magazine article found in M. E. Sergent's records of ex-cadets in the Class of 1862, labeled March/April 1982, 44–49, unknown publication.

18. Longstreet, *From Manassas*, 612, and McDonald, *History of the Laurel Brigade*, 375.

19. *OR* 46:1, 1162, and Chris M. Calkins, *Thirty-Six Hours before Appomattox* (Farmville, VA: Farmville Herald, 1980), 37–40. According to National Park Service historian Patrick Schroeder (Appomattox National Historical Park) the current owner of the property stated that it was a rail fence, not a stone fence.

20. Calkins, *Thirty-Six Hours*, 40; Dennis E. Frye, *12th Virginia Cavalry* (Lynchburg, VA: H. E. Howard, 1988), 81–82; *OR* 46:1, 1302; McDonald, *History of the Laurel Brigade*, 376–77; and Calkins, *Thirty-Six Hours*, 40. Dearing's words quoted in Calkins were originally reported in Frank Meyer, *The Comanches: A History of White's Battalion, Virginia Cavalry* (Baltimore: Kelly Pret, 1871), 380. I have relied upon Parke's manuscript, Calkin's *Thirty-Six Hours*, and McDonald's *History of the Laurel Brigade* to describe the battle at High Bridge.

17. Mackenzie, Lord, and Dearing at Appomattox

1. Heitman, *Historical Register*, 672, and *OR* 43:2, 460.

2. *OR* 46:1, 148–49, and *OR* 46:2, 967.

3. Grant, *Memoirs*, 409–10; Catton, *Stillness at Appomattox*, 342; and Sherman, *Memoirs*, vol. 2, 325–31.

4. Grant, *Memoirs*, 409, and *OR* 46:1, 148–49.

5. *OR* 46:1, 1104, 1244–45; *OR* 46:3, 378; Bearss and Calkins, *Battle of Five Forks*, 86, 90–91; and Edward G. Longacre, *Army of Amateurs: General Benjamin F. Butler and the Army of the James, 1893–1865* (Mechanicsburg, PA: Stackpole, 1997), 292.

6. *OR* 46:1, 1244–45, and Bearss and Calkins, *Battle of Five Forks*, 90–91.

7. *OR* 46:1, 1109, 1245, 1120.

8. *OR* 46:12, 1142, 1245, and Sheridan, *Personal Memoirs,* 391–95.

9. *OR* 46:12, 1142, 1245; Sheridan, *Personal Memoirs,* 391–95; Longstreet, *From Manassas,* 622; and Edward P. Tobie, *History of the First Maine Cavalry* (Boston, MA: Emery & Hughes, 1887), 423.

10. Calkins, *Appomattox Campaign,* 156; Chris Calkins, *The Battle at Appomattox Station and Appomattox Court House* (Lynchburg, VA: H. E. Howard, 1987), 66; and Dyer, *Compendium,* 1693. Company M was transferred north with the Tenth Corps in 1864 and subsequently absorbed into the Twenty-fourth Corps artillery brigade when the latter was created.

11. Calkins, *Appomattox Campaign,* 57; *OR* 46:1, 1159–60; *OR* 46:1, 1246; and Sheridan, *Personal Memoirs,* 390.

12. Longacre, *Army of Amateurs,* 307; Sheridan, *Personal Memoirs,* 391–95; and Catton, *Stillness at Appomattox,* 376–77.

13. Freeman, *Lee's Lieutenants,* 803–4.

14. Calkins, *Appomattox Campaign,* 160–61, and Catton, *Stillness at Appomattox,* 376–78.

15. *OR* 46:1, 1159; Sheridan, *Personal Memoirs,* 391–95; Armstrong, *11th Virginia Cavalry,* 110–1; Frye, *12th Virginia Cavalry,* 82–83; Calkins, *Battle of Appomattox Station,* 62; and Henry E. Tremain, *Sailor's Creek to Appomattox Courthouse* (New York: Charles H. Ludwig, 1885), 37. Tremain indicates they were pulled to the rear. Calkins stated in *The Appomattox Campaign* on page 161 and in *The Battle of Appomattox Station and Appomattox Court House,* page 62, that they were captured; *Five Points in the Record of North Carolina* (Raleigh: North Carolina Literary and Historical Association, 1904), 64–72. The Appomattox Court House Historic Battlefield Park has erected a sign indicating the location of the capture of A Battery, Second US Artillery.

16. *OR* 46:1, 1109–10, 1159–60, 1245–46; Calkins, *Battle of Appomattox Station,* 66, 69, 78–84 (see maps on pages 65 and 67); Sheridan, *Personal Memoirs,* 391–92; Catton, *Stillness at Appomattox,* 377–78; and Freeman, *Lee,* vol. 4, 120.

17. Sheridan, *Personal Memoirs,* 392, and Catton, *Stillness at Appomattox,* 379.

18. *OR* 46:1, 1246, 1253; Frank P. Cauble, *The Surrender Proceedings: April 9, 1865, Appomattox Court House* (Lynchburg: H. E. Howard, 1987), 37; and Calkins, *Battle at Appomattox Station,* 121–23.

19. Freeman, *Lee,* vol. 4, 125–44; *OR* 46:1, 1266–67; Grant, *Memoirs,* 435–40; Calkins, *Appomattox Campaign,* 186; and Chris Calkins, *The Final Bivouac* (Lynchburg, VA: H. E. Howard, 1988), 9.

20. *BLCW,* vol. 4, 753; Wise, *Long Arm of Lee,* 952; and Joshua L.

Chamberlain, *The Passing of the Armies* (New York: Bantam, 1993), 186, 194–206.

21. *OR* 46:1, 1246, and Calkins, *Final Bivouac,* 58–61.

22. Ward, Mary D., "Maj. Gen. James Dearing," 44–49.

23. Schaff, *Spirit of Old West Point,* 237.

24. *OR* 46:1, 1163; Calkins, *Appomattox Campaign,* 143; and *Cullum's 1891,* 841.

18. Warner, Bartlett, and the Last Battles

1. Warner Diary, April 19–20, 1865. Diary held by Susquehanna County Historical Society, Montrose, PA. Subsequent endnotes: Warner Diary, (date). *OR* 49:1, 370–72, 475.

2. *OR* 27:1, 877, 1022; *OR* 27:3, 794; and "Returns from Regular Army Artillery Regiments, June 1821–Jan. 1901"; RG 94, M727, roll 29, NA. The photograph of the officers in Robertson's horse artillery brigade was taken on September 22, 1863.

3. Warner Diary, December 7, 1863, and January 5–19, 1964.

4. Numerous entries in Warner Diary; and his promotion to first lieutenant took place on May 11, 1864.

5. *OR* 45:1, 38, 96, and "Returns for Regular Army Artillery Regiments," RG 94, M727, roll 29.

6. *MOLLUS* (Pennsylvania), vol. 58, no. 1: 351–69; *Cullum's 1891,* 865; *OR* 45:1, 37–38; and *OR Atlas,* plates 112-4, 113-4.

7. Warner Diary, December 21, 1864, and *OR* 45:1, 90, 599–602.

8. Warner Diary, December 21, 1864.

9. Ibid.

10. *OR* 45:1, 90; *OR* 49:1, 586, 691; Warner Diary, December 15–27, 1864; and Warner Diary, December 21, 1864.

11. *OR* 49:1, 342, 473; *New York Times,* May 4, 1865, 1; and Warner Diary, April 2 and 13, 1865.

12. *OR* 49:1, 475.

13. Warner Diary, April 16, 1865.

14. *OR* 49:1, 372; Warner Diary, April–May and May 4–6, 1865; and Warner Diary, May 12, 1865.

15. Warner Diary, May 8–12, 1865, and Warner Diary, May 12, 1865.

16. Warner letter, May 12, 1865, and *OR* 49:1, 377–78, 472–75.

17. *OR* 45:2, 462, and Dyer, *Compendium,* 1472.

18. *OR* 31:1, 332–34, and *Cullum's 1891,* 858–59. Brig. Gen. Robert B. Potter was in command of the Ninth Corps during the withdrawal to Knoxville. Maj. Gen. Parke commanded all US forces in the field under General Burnside.

19. B. G. McDowell, "62nd North Carolina Infantry," a summary history of the regiment found at www.jcncgs.com/civilwar/62ncinf.htm (accessed August 25, 2012). Originally published in Walter Clark, ed., *Histories of the Several Regiments and Battalions from North Carolina in the Great War 1861–'65*, vol. 3 (Goldsboro, NC: Nash Brothers Printers, 1901); *OR* 49:1, 31–33; and *OR* 49:2, 407–8. Clayton's unit was unwillingly included in a previous surrender in the Cumberland Gap (1864) and refused to accede to a second surrender.

20. See summary history of William H. Thomas's Legion (aka the 69th North Carolina Infantry) during 1864–1865 found at http://thomaslegion .net/conclusion.htm, and *OR* 49:2, 407, 690, 754–55.

21. See summary history of Thomas's Legion.

22. Robert J. Conley, *A Cherokee Encyclopedia* (Albuquerque: University of New Mexico Press, 2007), 72–73.

23. James C. Pickens, "Reminiscences," North Carolina Mounted Infantry website, www.2ncmi.org/rem.html (accessed March 8, 2010).

24. *OR* 49:1, 339, 1048; *OR* 49:2, 669–70, 689–90, 754–55; *Cullum's 1891*, 858–59; *Annual Report, 1909*, 159–60; and William R. Trotter, *The Civil War in the Mountains of North Carolina* (Winston Salem, NC: John F. Blair, 1988), 295, 298–300. The date of General Martin's surrender is incorrect in some official Union reports. It took place on May 9, 1865.

25. Warner Diary, June 22, 1865. Lieutenant Smith had returned to the battery in May 1865 after an absence of four months. Rodney and he were both assigned to Company I.

26. Warner Diary, May 12–13, 1865, and *OR* 49:1, 375–78.

27. Warner, June 14, 1865.

28. Warner Diary, July 13 and 31, 1865, and Warner Diary, June 22 and 26, 1865.

19. Remembrances

1. *New York Times*, May 24, 1965.

2. *New York Times*, May 22, 23, and 24, 1865; Leech, *Reveille*, 415; Dyer, *Compendium*, 1697; and *Cullum's 1891*. Lord was now aide to General Crook who was on leave during the review. And see Henry Tremain, *Last Hours of Sheridan's Cavalry* (New York: Bonnell, Silvers, and Bowers, 1904), 501–3, digital copy available through Google Books. Lord's battery (A Battery, Second US Artillery) service record states it participated in the Grand Review, but it was not included in the *New York Times* list of units marching. In a later *Times* article on June 7, 1865, there was mention that all artillery of the Army of the Potomac that did not march in the Grand Review marched in the Sixth Corps review a month later.

3. Sherman, *Memoirs,* vol. 2, 376–77.

4. Woodworth, *Nothing but Victory,* 638–41; *New York Times,* May 22, 23, and 24, 1865; Sherman, *Memoirs,* vol. 2, 376–78; Leech, *Reveille,* 415–17; and Bruce Catton, *Grant Takes Command* (Boston: Little, Brown, 1968), 490–91.

5. *New York Times,* June 9, 1865, 1; Leech, *Reveille,* 418; and Furgurson, *Sword of Lincoln,* 413.

6. *OR* 46:1, 1267.

7. Dyer, *Compendium,* 1381; printed parole issued to Richard Kinney, CSR, M331 (Generals and Staff Officers), roll 154; author's discussion with Robert Krick, National Park Service historian, concerning paroles; and *CWD,* 690–91.

8. *New York Times,* June 9, 1865, 5.

9. McCrea, June 9, 1865.

10. Pappas, *To the Point,* 341.

11. Letter from McCrea to Cullum, dated March 15, 1865, found in McCrea files, SCAD. It outlined his assignments since graduation. Cullum requested information from graduates for the first edition of the Register of Graduates.

12. Crackel, *West Point,* 134–37; Pappas, *To the Point,* 350; and Ambrose, *Duty,* 196–97.

Epilogue

1. Ambrose, *Duty,* 174, and Wayne W. Hsieh, *West Pointers and the Civil War* (Chapel Hill: University of North Carolina Press, 2009), 72–73.

2. Sherman, *Memoirs,* vol. 2, 387–88, and Hsieh, *West Pointers and the Civil War,* 161–62.

3. Ambrose, *Duty,* 183–85, and Williams, "Attack on West Point," 497–500.

4. Hsieh, *West Pointers and the Civil War,* 144; *Cullum's 1891,* 840–65; and see table 20.1.

5. Ambrose, *Duty,* 168.

Bibliography

Books

Ambrose, Stephen E. *Duty, Honor, Country: A History of West Point*. Baltimore: Johns Hopkins University Press, 1966.

Annual Reunion/Report of the Association of Graduates of the United States Military Academy. Saginaw, MI: Seeman & Peters, for years 1870–1925.

Antrim, Joshua. *History of Champaign and Logan Counties, Ohio*. Bellafontaine, OH: Press Printing Co., 1872.

Armstrong, Marion V. *Disaster in the West Woods*. Sharpsburg, MD: Western Maryland Interpretative Association, Antietam National Battlefield, 1996, 2002.

Armstrong, Richard L. *7th Virginia Cavalry*. Lynchburg, VA: H. E. Howard, 1992.

———. *11th Virginia Cavalry*. Lynchburg, VA: H. E. Howard 1989.

Asbury, Herbert. *The Gangs of New York*. New York: Thunder Month Press, 1927, 1928, 1998. http://www.civilwarhome.com/draftriots.htm.

Baker, Levi. *History of the Ninth Mass. Battery*. South Framingham, MA: J. C. Clark Printing, 1888.

Barber, James E. *Alexandria in the Civil War*. Lynchburg,VA: H. E. Howard, 1988.

Basler, Roy P., ed. *The Collected Works of Abraham Lincoln*. 8 vols. New Brunswick, NJ: Rutgers University Press, 1953.

Battles and Leaders of the Civil War. 4 vols. New York: Century Co., 1884, 1888; Secaucus, NJ: Castle Books, 1991.

Battles and Leaders of the Civil War. 4 vols. New York: Century Co. and DeVinne Press, 1884, 1888.

Battles and Leaders of the Civil War: People's Pictorial Edition. New York: Century Co. and De Vinne Press, 1894.

Bearss, Edward, and Chris Calkins. *The Battle of Five Forks*. 2nd ed. Lynchburg, VA: H. E. Howard, 1985.

Beatie, Russel H. *The Army of the Potomac*. Vol. 1. Cambridge, MA: Da Capo, 2002.

Bell, William G. *Secretaries of War and Secretaries of the Army*. Washington, DC: US Army Center for Military History, 1992.

Best, Isaac Oliver. *The History of the 121st New York State Infantry*. Chicago: Lt. J. A. Smith, 1921.

Black, Robert W. *Cavalry Raids of the Civil War.* Mechanicsburg, PA: Stackpole, 2004.

Boatner, Mark A. III. *The Civil War Dictionary: Revised Edition.* New York: David McKay, 1988.

Bowers, John. *Chickamauga and Chattanooga.* New York: HarperCollins, 1994.

Boynton, Edward C. *History of West Point.* North Stratford, NH: Ayer Company, 2000. Originally published 1863.

Broadwater, Robert J. *The Battle of Olustee, 1864.* Jefferson, NC: McFarland, 2006.

Brown, Kent M. *Cushing of Gettysburg: The Story of a Union Artillery Commander.* Lexington: University Press of Kentucky, 1993.

———. *Retreat from Gettysburg.* Chapel Hill: University of North Carolina Press, 2005.

Brown, Russell K. *Our Connection with Savannah: A History of the 1st Battalion Georgia Sharpshooters, 1862–1865.* Macon, GA: Mercer University Press, 2004.

Calkins, Chris M. *The Appomattox Campaign.* Conshohocken, PA: Combined Books, 1997.

———. *The Battle of Appomattox Station and Appomattox Court House.* Lynchburg, VA: H. E. Howard, 1987.

———. *The Final Bivouac.* Lynchburg, VA: H. E. Howard, 1988.

———. *History and Tour Guide of Five Forks.* Columbus, OH: Blue & Gray Magazine, 2003.

———. *Thirty-Six Hours before Appomattox.* Farmville, VA: Farmville Herald, 1998.

Carmer, Carl. *The Hudson.* New York: Farrar & Reinhart, 1939.

Carse, Robert. *Hilton Head Island in the Civil War.* Hilton Head Island, SC: Heritage Library Foundation, 2002.

Catton, Bruce. *The Civil War.* Boston: Houghton Mifflin, 1987.

———. *The Coming Fury.* Garden City, NY: Doubleday, 1961.

———. *Glory Road.* Garden City, NY: Doubleday, 1952.

———. *Grant Moves South.* Boston: Little, Brown, 1960.

———. *Grant Takes Command.* Boston: Little, Brown, 1968.

———. *Mr. Lincoln's Army.* Garden City, NY: Doubleday, 1951.

———. *A Stillness at Appomattox.* Garden City, NY: Doubleday, 1953.

Cauble, Frank P. *The Surrender Proceedings, April 9, 1865, Appomattox Court House.* Lynchburg, VA: H. E. Howard, 1987.

Centennial History of the United States Military Academy at West Point, New York 1802–1902. Washington: Government Printing Office, 1904. Available at http://digital-library.usma.edu/ libmedia/archives/centennial.

Chamberlain, Joshua L. *The Passing of the Armies.* New York: Bantam, 1993. Originally published 1915 by G. P. Putnam and Sons.

Christian, W. Asbury. *Lynchburg and Its People.* Lynchburg, VA: J. P. Bell, 1967.

Cist, Henry M. *Campaigns of the Civil War: The Army of the Cumberland.* New York: Blue & Gray Press, 1960. Originally appeared in Henry M. Cist, *Campaigns of the Civil War: Volume 7; The Army in Cumberland,* New York: Scribner and Sons, 1882.

Coffey, David. *Sheridan's Lieutenants.* New York: Rowman & Littlefield, 2000.

Coles, David J. *Men and Arms: Sketches of the Commander of Units of the Olustee Campaign, Vol. II.* Gainesville, FL: Renaissance Printing, 1995.

Conley, Robert J. *A Cherokee Encyclopedia.* Albuquerque: University of New Mexico Press, 2007.

Cormier, Steven A. *The Siege of Suffolk.* Lynchburg, VA: H. E. Howard, 1989.

Coski, John M. *The Army of the Potomac at Berkeley Plantation: The Harrison's Landing Occupation of 1862.* Richmond, VA: John M. Coski, 1989.

Cozzens, Peter, ed. *Battles & Leaders of the Civil War.* Vols. 5 and 6. Urbana: University of Illinois Press, 2002.

Crackel, Theodore J. *West Point: A Bicentennial History.* Lawrence: University Press of Kansas, 2002.

Crary, Catherine S. *Dear Belle: Letters from a Cadet and Officer to His Sweetheart.* Middletown, CT: Wesleyan University Press, 1965.

Crouch, Richard E. *Brandy Station: A Battle like No Other.* Westminster, MD: Willow Bend Books, 2002.

Crowley, Robert, and Thomas Guinzburg, eds. *West Point: Two Centuries of Honor and Tradition.* New York: Warner Books, 2002.

Crute, Joseph H., Jr. *Confederate Staff Officers: 1861–1865.* Powhatan, VA: Derwent Books, 1982.

Cullum, George W. *Biographical Register of the Officers and Graduates of the U.S. Military Academy, Volume II.* 3rd ed. Cambridge, MA: Riverside Press / Houghton Mifflin, 1891.

———. *Biographical Register of the Officers and Graduates of the U.S. Military Academy, Supplement Volume IV (1890–1900).* Cambridge, MA: Riverside Press, 1901.

———. *Biographical Register of the Officers and Graduates of the U.S. Military Academy, Supplement, Volume VI-A (1910–1920).* Saginaw, MI: Seeman & Peters, 1920.

Cutler, Henry G. *History of South Carolina, Volume 2.* Edited by Yates Snowden. New York: Lewis Publishing, 1930.

Daniel, Larry J. *Cannoneers in Gray: Field Artillery of the Army of Tennessee.* Tuscaloosa: University of Alabama Press, 2005.

————. *Days of Glory: The Army of the Cumberland, 1861–1865.* Baton Rouge: Louisiana State University Press, 2004.

Davis, Burke. *To Appomattox.* New York: Rinehart, 1952.

Davis, William C. *Battle at Bull Run.* Mechanicsburg, PA: Stackpole, 1977.

Davis, William C., and Bell L. Wiley, eds. *Civil War Album: Complete Photographic History of the Civil War.* New York: Tess Press, 2000. Originally published 1981 to 1984 in six volumes.

Detzer, David. *Allegiance: Fort Sumter, Charleston, and the Beginning of the Civil War.* San Diego: Harcourt, 2001.

Dodge, Theodore A. *The Campaign of Chancellorsville.* New York: Da Capo, 1999. Originally published by James Osgood, 1881.

Doubleday, Abner. *Reminiscences of Forts Sumter and Moutrie in 1860–'61.* Charleston, SC: Nautical and Aviation Publishing, 1998. Originally published 1876 by Harper Brothers.

Dowdy, Clifford. *The Land They Fought For.* Garden City, NY: Doubleday, 1955.

Downey, Fairfax. *The Guns at Gettysburg.* New York: David McKay, 1955, 1956.

————. *The Sound of the Guns.* New York: David McKay, 1958.

Driver, Robert J. *The 52nd Virginia Infantry.* Civil War Series. Lynchburg, VA: H. E. Howard, 1986.

Dyer, Frederick H. *A Compendium of the War of the Rebellion.* Des Moines, IA: Dyer Publishing Co., 1908. Digital copy is part of *The Civil War* CD-ROM, Oliver Computing, Indianapolis, IN, 2006.

Eanes, Greg. *Destroy the Junction: The Wilson-Kautz Raid and the Battle for the Staunton River Bridge, June 21, 1864 to July 1, 1865.* Lynchburg, VA: H. E. Howard, 1999.

Eicher, David J. *The Longest Night.* New York: Simon & Schuster, 2001.

Esley, Paula, ed. *Stone Ground: A History of Union Mills* (Fairfax, VA: Fairfax County Historical Commission, 2003).

Evans, Clement A., ed. *Confederate Military History,* extended edition, 19 vols. Wilmington, NC: Broadfoot Publishing, 1987.

Farley, Joseph Pearson. *West Point in the Early Sixties.* Troy, NY: Pafraets Book Co., 1902.

Fiebeger, G. J. *The Campaign and Battle of Gettysburg.* Hagerstown, MD: Barnwood Books, 1980. Originally published 1915.

Five Points in the Record of North Carolina. Raleigh: North Carolina Literary and Historical Association, 1904.

Foote, Shelby. *The Civil War.* 3 vols. New York: Vintage Books, 1986. Originally published 1958.

Fox, William F. *Regimental Losses in the American Civil War.* Albany, NY: Randow Printing Company, 1889.

Freehling, William W. *The Road to Disunion: Volume II.* New York: Oxford University Press, 2007.

Freeman, Douglas Southall. *Lee's Lieutenants: A Study in Command.* Abridged by Stephen Sears. New York: Simon & Schuster, 1998.

———. *Robert E. Lee.* New York: Scribner & Sons, 1934.

French, William H., William F. Barry, and Henry J. Hunt. *Instruction for Field Artillery.* New York: Van Nostrand, 1864.

Frey, Donald J. *Longstreet's Assault: Pickett's Charge.* Shippensburg, PA: White Mane Books, 2000.

Frye, Dennis E. *12th Virginia Cavalry.* Lynchburg, VA: H. E. Howard, 1988.

Furgurson, Ernest B. *Ashes of Glory.* New York: Knopf, 1996.

———. *Chancellorsville 1863: The Soul of the Brave.* New York: Knopf, 1992.

——— *Freedom Rising.* New York: Knopf, 2004.

———. *Not War but Murder: Cold Harbor, 1864.* New York: Knopf, 2000.

Gallagher, Gary W., ed. *Fighting for the Confederacy: The Personal Reflections of General Edward P. Alexander.* Chapel Hill: University of North Carolina Press, 1989.

Goolrick, William K. *Rebels Resurgent: Fredericksburg to Chancellorsville.* Alexandria, VA: Time-Life Books, 1985.

Gould, John M. *Joseph K. F. Mansfield, Brigadier General of the U.S. Army.* Portland, OR: Stephen Berry, 1895. Found at www.gutenberg.org/files/32258/.

Grant, Ulysses S. *Personal Memoirs of U.S. Grant.* New York: Dover Publications, 1995. Originally published 1885 by Charles L. Webster, New York.

Griffin, Richard N., ed. *Three Years a Soldier.* Knoxville: University of Tennessee Press, 2006.

Gutek, Gerald L. *Historical and Philosophical Foundations of Education.* 2nd ed. Chicago: Merrill, Prentice Hall, 1991.

Hardee, William J. *Rifle and Light Infantry Tactics.* Philadelphia: J. B. Lippincott, 1860.

Harrison, Maureen, and Steve Gilbert, eds. *Abraham Lincoln Word for Word.* San Diego: Excellent Books, 1994.

Harrison, Noel G. *Chancellorsville Battlefield Sites.* Lynchburg, VA: H. E. Howard, 1990.

Haskell, Frank A. *The Battle of Gettysburg.* Cambridge, MA: Riverside Press, 1957.

Haskin, William L. *History of the First Regiment of Artillery.* Portland, ME: B. Thurston, 1879.

Henderson, William D. *41st Virginia Infantry.* Lynchburg, VA: H. E. Howard, 1986.

Hendrickson, Henry. *Sumter: The First Day of the Civil War.* Chelsea, MI: Scarborough House, 1990.

Hennessy, John J. *Second Manassas Map Study.* Lynchburg, VA: H. E. Howard, 1991.

———. *Return to Bull Run.* Norman: University of Oklahoma Press, 1999.

Hess, Earl J. *Pickett's Charge at Gettysburg.* Chapel Hill: University of North Carolina Press, 2001.

Holland, Lynwood M. *Pierce M. B. Young: The Warwick of the South.* Athens: University of Georgia Press, 2009.

Hood, John Bell. *Advance and Retreat.* Secaucus, NJ: Blue & Grey Press, 1985. Originally published 1880 by Burke M. Petridge.

Horn, John. *The Destruction of the Weldon Railroad, Deep Bottom, Globe Tavern, and Reams Station.* Lynchburg, VA: H. E. Howard, 1991.

Houch, Peter W. *Lynchburg: Prototype of a Confederate Hospital Center.* Lynchburg, VA: Warwick House, 1986.

Hsieh, Wayne W. *West Pointers and the Civil War.* Chapel Hill: University of North Carolina Press, 2009.

Hughes, Nathaniel Cheau, Jr. *Bentonville.* Chapel Hill: University of North Carolina Press, 1996.

Hunt, Roger D., and Jack R. Brown. *Brevet Brigadier Generals in Blue.* Gaithersburg, MD: Olde Soldier Books, 1990.

Hyde, Thomas, W. *Follow the Greek Cross: Memories of the Sixth Army Corps.* Columbia: University of South Carolina Press, 2005. Originally published 1898 by Houghton Mifflin.

Ingrisano, Michael N., Jr. *An Artilleryman's War: Gus Dey and the 2nd United States Artillery.* Shippensburg, PA: White Mane Books, 1998.

Johnson, Curt, and Richard C. Anderson Jr. *Artillery Hell: The Employment of Artillery at Antietam.* College Station: Texas A&M University Press, 1995.

Kennedy, Francis, ed. *The Civil War Battlefield Guide.* 2nd ed. New York: Houghton Mifflin, 1998.

Kirshner, Ralph. *The Class of 1861.* Carbondale: Southern Illinois Press, 1999.

Kleese, Ricard B. *49th Virginia Infantry.* Lynchburg, VA: H. E. Howard, 2002.

Ladd, David L., and Audrey J. Ladd, eds. *The Bachelder Papers: Gettysburg in Their Own Words.* Vols. 1–3. Dayton, OH: Morningside House, 1994.

———. *John Bachelder's History of the Battle of Gettysburg.* Dayton, OH: Morningside House, 1997.

Large, George A., and Joe A. Swisher. *Battle of Antietam: The Official History by the Antietam Battlefield Board.* Shippensburg, PA: Burd Street Press, 1998.

Leech, Margaret. *Reveille in Washington (1860–1865).* New York: Harper & Brothers, 1941.

Lewis, Thomas A. *The Guns of Cedar Creek.* New York: Dell, 1988.

Long, A. L., and Marcus Wright. *Memoirs of Robert E. Lee.* Secaucus, NJ: Blue & Grey Press, 1983. Originally published 1886.

Long, Everette Beach. *The Civil War Day by Day: An Almanac 1861–1865.* New York: Da Capo, 1985. Originally published 1971 by Doubleday.

Longacre, Edward G. *Army of Amateurs: General Benjamin F. Butler and the Army of the James, 1893–1865.* Mechanicsburg, PA: Stackpole, 1997.

———. *General John Buford.* Cambridge, MA: Da Capo, 1995.

———. *Lee's Cavalrymen.* Mechanicsburg, PA: Stackpole, 2002.

———. *The Man behind the Guns: A Military Biography of General Henry J. Hunt, Chief of Artillery, Army of the Potomac.* Cambridge, MA: Da Capo, 2003.

Longstreet, James. *From Manassas to Appomattox: Memoirs of the Civil War in America.* New York: DaCapo Press, 1992. Originally published 1896 in Philadelphia.

Lowry, Thomas P., ed. *Swamp Doctor: Diary of a Union Surgeon in the Virginia and North Carolina Marshes.* Mechanicsburg, PA: Stackpole, 2001.

Luvaas, Jay, and Harold W. Nelson. *The U.S. Army War College Guide to the Battlefield of Antietam.* New York: Harper & Row, 1987.

———. *The U.S. Army War College Guide to the Battles of Chancellorsville and Fredericksburg.* Lawrence: University Press of Kansas, 1994.

Martin, David G. *The Chancellorsville Campaign: March–May 1863.* Conshohocken, PA: Combined Books, 1991.

Marvel, William. *Five Flags over Fort Sumter.* National Parks Service Civil War Series. Fort Washington, PA: Eastern National, 1998.

———. *Lee's Last Retreat.* Chapel Hill: University of North Carolina Press, 2002.

Matloff, Maurice, ed. Office of the Chief of Military History, US Army. *American Military History.* Washington, DC: Government Printing Office, 1969.

McClellan, George B. *Report on the Organization and Campaigns of the Army of the Potomac.* New York: Sheldon, 1864.

McDonald, William N. *A History of the Laurel Brigade.* Edited by B. C. Washington. Baltimore: Johns Hopkins University Press, 2002. Originally published 1907 by Sun Job Printing Office.

McKinney, Joseph W. *Brandy Station: Driving Tour and Battlefield Guide.* Brandy Station, VA: Brandy Station Foundation, 2005.

McMurray, Richard M. *Virginia Military Institute Alumni in the Civil War.* Lynchburg, VA: H. E. Howard, 1999.

McPherson, James M. *Crossroads of Freedom: Antietam.* New York: Oxford University Press, 2002.

———. *Ordeal by Fire: The Civil War and Reconstruction.* 3rd ed. New York: McGraw-Hill, 2001.

McPherson, James M., and Patricia R. McPherson. *Lamson of the Gettysburg.* New York: Oxford University Press, 1997.

Miller, Francis T., ed. *Photographic History of the Civil War.* Vol. 3. Secaucus, NJ: Blue & Grey Press, 1987. Originally published 1911 in ten volumes.

Moore, Frank, ed. "History of the Campaign of the Cavalry Corps in Alabama and Georgia." In *Rebellion Record.* Vol. 11. New York: D. Van Nostrand, 1868.

Moore, Robert H. *The Richmond Fayette, Hampden, Thomas, and Blount's Lynchburg Artillery.* Lynchburg, VA: H. E. Howard, 1991.

Morison, Samuel E. *The Oxford History of the American People.* New York: Oxford University Press, 1965.

Morrison, James L., Jr. *The Best School: West Point, 1833–1866.* Kent, OH: Kent State University Press, 1986, 1998.

Murray, R. L. *The Redemption of the "Harper's Ferry Cowards."* Wolcott, NY: Benedum Books, 1994.

Naisawald, L. VanLoan. *Grape and Canister.* 2d ed. Mechanicsburg, PA: Stackpole, 1999.

Nelson, Lankford. *Richmond Burning.* New York: Penguin, 2003.

Nesbitt, Mark. *Saber and Scapegoat.* Mechanicsburg, PA: Stackpole, 1994.

Netherton, Nan, and Whitney Von Lake Wyckoff. *Fairfax Station: All Aboard.* Fairfax, VA: Friends of Fairfax Station, 1995.

On Campaign with the Army of the Potomac: The Civil War Diary of Theodore Ayrault Dodge. New York: Cooper Square Press, 2003.

O'Neil, Robert F. *The Cavalry Battles of Aldie, Middleburg, and Upperville.* Lynchburg, VA: H. E. Howard, 1993.

O'Reilly, Francis A. *The Fredericksburg Campaign: Winter War on the Rappahannock.* Baton Rouge: Louisiana State University Press, 2003.

Palfrey, Francis W. *The Antietam and Fredericksburg.* Campaigns of the Civil War. New York: Da Capo, 1996. Originally published 1882 by Scribner.

Pappas, George S. *To the Point: The United States Military Academy 1802–1902.* Westport, CT: Praeger, 1993.

Patch, Joseph D. *The Battle of Balls Bluff.* Leesburg, VA: Potomac Press, 1958.

Pfanz, Harry W. *Gettysburg: The First Day.* Chapel Hill: University of North Carolina Press, 2001.

———. *Gettysburg: Culp's Hill and Cemetery Hill.* Chapel Hill: University of North Carolina Press, 1993.

———. *Gettysburg: The Second Day.* Chapel Hill: University of North Carolina Press, 1987.

Phisterer, Fred K. *Statistical Record of the Army of the United States.* New York: Scribner & Sons, 1882.

The Photographic History of the Civil War. 5 vols. Secaucus, NJ: Blue & Grey Press, 1987. Originally published 1911.

Pierce, Michael D. *The Most Promising Young Officer.* Norman: University of Oklahoma Press, 1963.

Powell, William H. *The Fifth Army Corps (Army of the Potomac): A Record of Operations during the Civil War in the United States of America, 1861–1865.* Dayton, OH: Morningside Bookshop, 1984.

Priest, John Michael. *Antietam: The Soldiers' Battle.* New York: Oxford University Press, 1989.

———. *Before Antietam.* New York: Oxford University Press, 1992.

———. *Into the Fight: Pickett's Charge at Gettysburg.* Shippensburg, PA: White Mane Books, 1998.

Pyne, Henry A. *Ride to War: A History of the First New Jersey Cavalry.* Brunswick, NJ: Rutgers University Press, 1961. Originally published 1871 by J. A. Beecher as *The History of the First New Jersey Cavalry.*

Raiford, Neil Hunter. *The 4th North Carolina Cavalry in the Civil War.* Jefferson, NC: McFarland, 2003.

Reed, Hugh T. *Cadet Life at West Point.* 3rd ed. Richmond, IN: Irvin Reed and Son, 1911.

Reese, Timothy J. *Sykes Regular Infantry Division: 1861–1864.* Jefferson, NC: McFarland, 1990.

Register of Graduates and Former Cadets of the United States Military Academy. West Point, NY: Association of Graduates, West Point, 2006, 2010.

Rhea, Gordon C. *The Battle of the Wilderness.* Baton Rouge: Louisiana State University Press, 1994.

Robbins, James S. *Last in Their Class.* New York: Encounter Books, 2006.

Roberts, Robert B. *Encyclopedia of Historic Forts.* New York: Macmillan, 1988.

Robertson, William. *The Battle of Old Men and Young Boys.* Lynchburg, VA: H. E. Howard, 1989.

Robinson, Charles M., III. *Bad Hand: A Biography of General Ranald S. Mackenzie.* Austin, TX: State House Press, 1993.

Roemer, Jacob. *Reminiscences of the War of the Rebellion 1861–1865.* Flushing, NY: Press of the *Flushing Journal,* 1897.

Schaff, Morris. *The Battle of the Wilderness.* Boston: Houghton Mifflin, 1910.
————. *Jefferson Davis: His Life and Personality.* Boston, MA: John Luce, 1922.
————. *The Spirit of Old West Point.* New York: Houghton Mifflin, 1907. Also serialized in the *Atlantic Monthly* the same year.
————. *The Sunset of the Confederacy.* Boston: John W. Luce, 1912.
Schiller, Herbert M. *The Bermuda Hundred Campaign.* Dayton, OH: Morningside House, 1988.
Schmidt, Lewis G. *The Civil War in Florida: A Military History, Vol. 2—The Battle of Olustee.* Allentown, PA: Lewis G. Schmidt, 1989.
Schneider, Richard H. *Taps: Notes from a Nation's Heart.* New York: HarperCollins, 2002.
Schultz, David. *Double Canister at Ten Yards.* Redondo Beach, CA: Rank and File Publications, 1995.
Sears, Stephen. *Chancellorsville.* New York: Houghton Mifflin, 1996.
————. *Gettysburg.* New York: Houghton Mifflin, 2004.
————. *Landscape Turned Red.* New York: Houghton Mifflin, 2003.
Seigel, Charles. *The Army of the Potomac in Stafford County 1862–1863 Driving Tour.* Stafford, VA: Rappahannock Valley Civil War Roundtable, n.d.
Sergent, Mary Elizabeth. *Growing up in Alabama.* Middletown, NY: Prior King Press, 1988.
————. *They Lie Forgotten.* Middletown, NY: Prior King Press, 1986.
————. *An Unremaining Glory.* Middletown, NY: Prior King Press, 1997.
Sheridan, Philip H. *Personal Memoirs of P. H. Sheridan.* New York: Da Capo, 1992. Originally published 1888 by C. L. Webster in New York.
Sherman, William T. *Memoirs of General William T. Sherman.* Bloomington: Indiana University Press, 1957. Originally published 1875 by Henry S. King, London.
Sherwood, George L. *The Mathews Light Artillery; Penick's Pittsylvania Artillery; Young's Halifax Artillery, & Johnson's Jackson Flying Artillery.* Lynchburg, VA: H. E. Howard, 1999.
Shue, Richard S. *Morning at Willoughby Run.* Gettysburg, PA: Thomas Publications, 1998.
Sifakis, Stewart. *Compendium of the Confederate Army: Virginia.* New York: Facts on File, 1992.
Smith, Charles H. *The History of Fuller's Ohio Brigade (1861–1865).* Cleveland, OH: Press of A. J. Watt, 1909. Digitized by Google and available at GoogleBooks.com.
Smith, Derek. *The Gallant and the Dead: Union and Confederate Generals Killed in the Civil War.* Mechanicsburg, PA: Stackpole, 2005.
Snowden, Yates. *History of South Carolina, Volume II.* Chicago: Lewis Publishing Company, 1930.

Sommers, Richard. *Richmond Redeemed*. Garden City, NY: Doubleday, 1981.

Speer, Lonnie J. *Portals of Hell: Military Prisons of the Civil War*. Mechanicsburg, PA: Stackpole Books, 1997.

Spencer, Warren F. *Raphael Semmes: The Philosophical Mariner*. Tuscaloosa: University of Alabama Press, 1997.

Stackpole, Edward J. *The Fredericksburg Campaign*. 2nd edition. Mechanicsburg, PA: Stackpole Books, 1991.

———. *They Met at Gettysburg*. 3rd ed. Harrisburg, PA: Stackpole Books, 1982.

Stern, Philip Van Doren. *Soldier Life in the Union and Confederate Armies*. New York: Gramercy Books, 2001. Includes *Hardtack and Coffee* by John Billings and *Soldier Life in the Army of Northern Virginia* by Carlton McCarthy.

Stewart, George R. *Pickett's Charge: A Microhistory of the Final Attack at Gettysburg, July 3, 1863*. Dayton, OH: Morningside Books, 1983.

Strong, George C., and Bernard Lossing. *Cadet Life at West Point*. Boston, MA: T. O. H. P. Burnham, 1862.

Sutherland, Daniel E. *Fredericksburg and Chancellorsville*. Lincoln: University of Nebraska Press, 1998.

Swinton, William. *The Army of the Potomac*. New York: W. S. Konecky Associates, 1995. Originally published 1866.

Taylor, Paul. *Discovering the Civil War in Florida*. Sarasota, FL: Pineapple Press, 2001.

Tobie, Edward P. *History of the First Maine Cavalry*. Boston: Emery and Hughes Press, 1887.

Tremain, Henry E. *Last Hours of Sheridan's Cavalry*. New York: Bonnell, Silvers, and Bowers, 1904.

———. *Sailor's Creek to Appomattox Courthouse*. New York: Charles H. Ludwig, 1885.

Trotter, William R. *The Civil War in the Mountains of North Carolina*. Winston Salem, NC: John F. Blair, 1988.

Trout, Robert J. *They Followed the Plume*. Mechanicsburg, PA: Stackpole, 1993.

Trudeau, Noah A. *Gettysburg: Testing of Courage*. New York: HarperCollins, 2002.

———. *The Last Citadel: Petersburg, Virginia, June 1864–April 1865*. Baton Rouge: Louisiana State University Press, 1993.

Tucker, Glenn. *Hancock the Superb*. Dayton, OH: Morningside Press, 1980.

Urwin, Gregory J. W. *Custer Victorious*. Lincoln: University of Nebraska Press, 1983.

Vail, Theodore F. *History of the Second Connecticut Volunteer Heavy Artillery*. Charleston, SC: BiblioLife, 2009. Originally published 1868 by Winsted Printing Company.

Vandiver, Frank E. *Jubal's Raid*. Lincoln: University of Nebraska Press, 1960, 1988.

Walker, Francis A. *History of the Second Army Corps in the Army of the Potomac*. Gaithersburg, MD: Olde Soldier Books, 1987. Originally published 1887 by Charles Scribner.

Wallace, Lee A. *A Guide to Virginia Military Organizations*. Lynchburg, VA: H. E. Howard, 1986.

Warner, Ezra J. *Generals in Blue*. Baton Rouge: Louisiana State University Press, 1964.

Waugh, John C. *The Class of 1846 from West Point to Appomattox: Stonewall Jackson, George McClellan and Their Brothers*. New York: Warner Books, 1994.

Weigley, Russell F. *A History of the United States Army*. Bloomington: Indiana University Press, 1967, 1984.

Weinert, Richard P., Jr. *The Confederate Regular Army*. Shippensburg, PA: White Mane, 1991.

Wert, Jeffery D. *From Winchester to Cedar Creek*. New York: Simon & Schuster, 1987.

———. *Gettysburg: Day Three*. New York: Touchstone Books, 2001.

———. *The Sword of Lincoln*. New York: Simon & Schuster, 2005.

Whitehorne, Joseph W. A. *Battle of Cedar Creek*. 3rd ed. Middletown, VA: Cedar Creek Battlefield Foundation, 2006.

Wiley, I. B. *The Life of Billy Yank*. Baton Rouge: Louisiana State University Press, 1983.

Williams, T. Harry. *Lincoln and His Generals*. New York: Grosset & Dunlap, 1952.

Wise, Jennings C. *The Long Arm of Lee*. New York: Oxford University Press, 1959. Originally published 1915 by W. P. Bell.

Wittenberg, Eric J. *Glory Enough for All: Sherman's Second Raid and Trevilian Station*. Washington, DC: Brassey's, 2001.

———. *Little Phil: A Reassessment of the Civil War Leadership of Gen. Philip H. Sheridan*. Dulles, VA: Potomac Books, 2002.

Woodbury, Augustus. *Ambrose E. Burnside and the Ninth Army Corps*. Providence, RI: Sidney S. Rider & Brother, 1867.

Woodworth, Steven E. *The Art of Command in the Civil War*. Lincoln: University of Nebraska Press, 1998.

———. *Nothing but Victory: The Army of the Tennessee, 1861–1865*. New York: Vintage Books, 2006.

Articles

Aimone, Alan, and Barbara Aimone. "The Civil War Years at West Point." *Blue & Gray Magazine* (December 1991).

Ambrose, Stephen. "Letters of Henry A. Du Pont." *Civil War History* 10, no. 3 (September 1964).

Anderson, Edward W. "Letters of a West Pointer, 1860–1861." *American Historical Review* 33 (October 1925–July 1928).

Archer, John M. "Remembering the 14th Connecticut Volunteers." *Gettysburg*, no. 9 (July 1993).

Bartlett, William C. "Incident of Fredericksburg." *The United Service: Monthly Review of Military and Naval Affairs* 2 (1889): 467–71.

———. "Knoxville's Memorable Night." *Journal of Military Service Institution of the United States* (January–June 1911): 259–63.

Bateman, Robert L. "Sawyer's Gettysburg Charge." *America's Civil War* (July 2004).

Boyd, Mark. "The Federal Campaign of 1864 in East Florida." *Florida Historical Quarterly* 29, no. 1 (July 1950).

Brennan, Patrick. "Hell on Horseshoe Ridge." *North & South*, March 2004.

Calef, John. "Gettysburg Notes: The Opening Gun." *Journal of Military Service Institution of the United States* 40 (January–June 1907): 40–58.

———. "The Regular Artillery in the Gettysburg Campaign." *Journal of Military Service Institution of the United States* 45 (July–November 1909): 32–38.

Campbell, Eric. "We Have Here a Great Fight." *Civil War Times* (August 2009).

Carman, Ezra A. "The Antietam Manuscript of Ezra Ayres Carman." Article available at http://kperlotto3.home.comcast.net/~kperlotto3/carman/EzraCarman.pdf.

Conklin, Augustus H. "History of Twenty-fourth Regiment Connecticut Volunteer Infantry." Available at http://archiver.rootsweb.ancestry.com/th/read/CTNEWHAV/2001-07/0994054785.

Coulter, Merton. "The Life and Death of James Barrow CSA." *Journal of Southern History* 23, no. 1 (February 1957).

Dupuy, Ernest. "West Point 100 Years Ago." *Assembly* 20, no. 1.

Ferry, Richard J. "The Battle of Olustee." *Blue & Gray Magazine* (February–March 1986).

Fuger, Frederick. "Cushing's Battery at Gettysburg." *Journal of the Military Institution of the United States* 41 (November/December 1907).

Gott, K. D. "Gateway to the Heartland." *North and South* 7, no. 2 (March 2004).

Hunt, Ezra M. "West Point and Cadet Life." *Putnam's Monthly* 4 (August 1854).

King, Charles. "Cadet Life at West Point." *Harper's New Monthly Magazine* 75, no. 446 (July 1887).

Kobrick, Jacob. "No Army Inspired: The Failure of Nationalism at Antebellum West Point." *Concept* 27 (2004).

Lake, Virginia T. "A Crisis of Conscience: West Point Letters of Henry A. Du Pont." *Civil War History* 25, no. 1 (1979).

Longacre, Edward. "The Port Hudson Campaign." *Civil War Times* 10, no. 2 (February 1972).

McCrea, Tully. "Light Artillery: Its Uses and Misuses." *Journal of the Military Institution of the United States* 22 (1898).

McEnany, Brian R. "John Brown's Raid and West Point." *Assembly* 48, no. 1 (October–December 2009).

———. "War Comes to West Point." *North & South* (December 2010).

McMurry, Richard. "The President's Tenth and the Battle of Olustee." *Civil War Times* (January 1978).

Morgan, Michael. "Surprise at Ocean Pond." *America's Civil War* (March 2000).

Morrison, James L. "The Struggle between Sectionalism and Nationalism at Ante-bellum West Point, 1830–1861." *Civil War History* 19, no. 2.

Nicholson, Robert J. "West Point's First Captains." *Assembly* 28, no. 4 (1970).

Niderost, Eric. "We Gained Nothing but Glory." *Gettysburg Magazine*, Special Edition (Summer 2005), 62–69.

O'Reilly, Frank A. "'The Battle of Chancellorsville Was Lost Right Here': McLaws versus Sykes on the Orange Turnpike May 1, 1863." *Fredericksburg History and Biography*, vol. 1. Fredericksburg, VA: Central Virginia Battlefields Trust, 2002.

Petruzzi, J. David. "Cemetery Hill's Forgotten Savior." *Civil War Times* 49, no. 5 (October 2010).

Ray, Fred L. "Mimic War No More." *Civil War Times* 49, no. 1 (February 2010).

Robertson, William G. "The Battle of Chickamauga." *Blue & Gray Magazine* 24, no. 3 (Fall 2007) and no. 6 (Spring 2008).

Rodenbough, T. F. "History of the 3rd U.S. Cavalry." *History of the Army of the United States*. New York: Merrill, 1896.

Schaff, Morris. "The Explosion at City Point." *Military Order of the Loyal Legion of the United States: Massachusetts Commandery* 53.

Semmes, Oliver J. "First Confederate Battery an Orphan." *Confederate Veteran* 21 (1913).

Shepard, Steven J. "Reaching for the Channel." *Alexandria Chronicle*. Alexandria Historical Society (Spring 2006).

Smith, Dwight. "Cadet Life in the 1860's." *Assembly* 34, no. 1 (June 1975).

Ward, Mary Dearing. "Maj. Gen. James Dearing: The Last Hero." Unknown magazine, vol. 14, no. 1 (March/April 1982), 44–49. Found in M. E. Sergent's records of Class of 1862 provided to the author.

Williams, T. Harry. "The Attack on West Point during the Civil War." *Mississippi Historical Review* 25, no. 4 (March 1939).

Wukovits, John. "There's the Devil to Pay." *Gettysburg Magazine*. Special edition (Summer 2005), 18–25.

United States Military Academy (USMA)

Buchwald, Donald M. "Chronological Listing of Significant Changes to Troop Units at West Point from 1775 to 1978." USMA Library, 1978.

"Circumstances of the Parents of Cadets 1842 to 1870." Special Collections and Archives Division, USMA Library.

"Descriptive Lists of New Cadets 1838–1909." 4 vols. Special Collections and Archives Division, USMA Library.

"Index to Obituaries, Association of Graduates, Volume 1, 1870–1940." Special Collections and Archives Division, USMA Library.

Official Register of the Officers and Cadets of the U.S. Military Academy. West Point, NY: USMA (for years 1858–1866). Special Collections and Archives Division, USMA Library.

"Post Orders, Volume 5, December 1856 to February 1861." Special Collections and Archives Division, USMA Library.

"Post Orders, Volume 6, February 1861 to July 1866." Special Collections and Archives Division, USMA Library.

"Proceedings of the Medical Board, June 1856 to August 1862." Special Collections and Archives Division, USMA Library.

"Register of Delinquencies, Volume 11, 1858 to 1859." Special Collections and Archives Division, USMA Library.

The Register of Graduates and Former Cadets of the U.S. Military Academy. West Point, NY: Association of Graduates (for years 2002–2010).

"Register of Punishments, Volume 3, October 1857 to February 1865." Special Collections and Archives Division, USMA Library.

"Remarks Prepared for the Superintendent about the Class of 1862 for Ring Hop, August 1961." Special Collections and Archives Division, USMA Library.

"Report of the Academic Board." United States Military Academy Staff Records, vol. 7 (1859–1865). Special Collections and Archives Division (SCAD), USMA Library.

"Report of the Board of Visitors," included in "Report of the Secretary of War for 1863." Copy held by the Special Collections and Archives Division, USMA Library.

Report of the Committee of the Academic Board of the United States Military Academy in Relation to the Restoration of Cadets Who Have Been Discharged from the Institution. New York: D. Van Nostrand, 1862.

"Report of the Working Committee on the Historical Aspects of the Curriculum for the Period 1802–1945," July 31, 1958. Special Collections and Archives Division, USMA Library.

A Synopsis History, Lineage and Honors of the 1st Infantry, Its Battalions under the Combat Arms Regimental System, and of the Garrison of West Point, New York. West Point, NY: USMA, 1975. Document published in celebration of the US Army's two hundred years of service at West Point.

"U.S. Military Academy Staff Records, 1817–1875," 9 vols., Special Collections and Archives Division, USMA Library.

US Government Documents

"The Abraham Lincoln Papers." Series 1, General Correspondence, 1833–1916. Library of Congress, Washington, DC. Available on Internet.

"Compiled Service Records of Confederate Soldiers." War Department Collection of Confederate Records (Record Group 109). National Archives, Washington, DC.

"Compiled Service Records of Soldiers Who Served in Organizations Raised Directly by the Confederate Government" (M258). War Department Collection of Confederate Records (Record group 109), Washington, DC: National Archives.

Cope, E. B., and H. W. Mattern. *Atlas of the Battlefield of Antietam.* Washington, DC: AGO, 1904.

Davis, George B., et al. *The Official Military Atlas of the Civil War.* Washington, DC: Government Printing Office, 1891–1895, as edited and published by Barnes and Noble Books, 2003.

"Engineer Department Letters Received Related to the U.S. Military Academy." November 1860 to May 1861. Record group 94, microfilm publication 2047 (M2047), rolls 40 and 41. National Archives, Washington, DC.

"Engineer Department Records Related to the US Military Academy." Record group 94 (RG94), microfilm publication 91 (M91), 29 rolls. National Archives, Washington, DC.

"Enlistment Records of the U.S Army (1798–1914)." Microfilm publication M233, 81 rolls. National Archives, Washington, DC.

Heitman, Francis B. *Historical Register and Dictionary of the United States*

Army, from Its Organization, September 29, 1789, to March 2, 1903. Washington, DC: Government Printing Office, 1903.

Official Army Register for 1862 (January and August 1862). Washington, DC: Adjutant General's Office.

"Personal Reports of Retired Officers, 1864–1913." Record group 94, M1064 (Letters Received by the Commission Branch of the Adjutant General's Office, 1863–1870), 527 rolls, Washington, DC: National Archives.

"Records of the 1st–7th Artillery Regiments." Preliminary Inventory of the Records of United States Army Mobile Units (1821–1942), record group 391.2.1, National Archives, Washington, DC.

Register of Officers and Agents Civil, Military and Naval in the Service of the United States. Washington, DC: Government Printing Office, 1862.

"Returns from Regular Army Artillery Regiments, June 1821–January 1901." Microfilm M727, 38 rolls, and Records of the Adjutant General's Office, 1780s–1917, record group 94, National Archives, Washington, DC.

"Returns from Regular Army Engineer Battalions, Sept. 1846–June 1916." Microfilm M690, 10 rolls, and Records of the Adjutant General's Office, 1780s–1917, record group 391.4, National Archives, Washington, DC.

Swift, E. *Medical History of the War of the Rebellion.* Washington, DC: Government Printing Office, 1870. Part first, appendix.

Tilberg, Frederick. *Antietam.* Washington, DC: National Park Service, Government Printing Office, 1960.

US Congress. "American Battlefield Protection Program Civil War Site Advisory Commission Battle Summary (CWSAC) Report on the Nation's Civil War Battlefields." Technical Volume 2: Battle Summaries, Prepared for the Committee on Energy and Natural Resources, United States Senate; Committee on Natural Resources, United States House of Representatives; and the Secretary of the Interior, 1997.

———. "Annual Report of the Secretary of War." Message of the President to Both Houses of Congress, Second Session, 35th Congress, vol. II, part 2, House Executive Document, US Congress, Washington, DC.

———. "Annual Report of the Secretary of War." Thirty-seventh Congress, First Session, Senate Executive Documents, vol. 1, no. 1., US Congress, Washington, DC.

———. *Report of the Joint Committee on the Conduct of the War: Army of the Potomac, Part 2, Second Session, 38th Congress.* Millwood, NY: Kraus Reprint Co., 1977. Extracted from *US Congress Joint Committee on the Conduct of the War: Report of the Joint Committee.* Washington, DC: Government Printing Office, 1865.

———. *Report to the Secretary of War on the Organization of the Army of the Potomac.* Report of General George B. McClellan. Thirty-fifth Congress, First Session, Executive Document No. 15. Washington, DC: Government Printing Office, 1864.

US Congress, Senate. *Report of the Committee to Examine the Organization, System of Discipline, and Course of Instruction of the United States Military Academy.* Report prepared by Sen. Jefferson Davis. Thirty-sixth Congress, Second Session, Senate Misc. Doc. No. 3, December 13, 1860.

"U.S. Military Academy Cadet Application Papers (1805–1866)." Record group 94 (RG94), microfilm pub M668 (M688), 242 rolls. National Archives, Washington, DC.

US War Department. *The War of the Rebellion: A Compilation of the Official Records of the Union and Confederate Armies.* 128 vols. Washington: Government Printing Office, 1880–1901.

Manuscripts/Letters/Photographs

Arnold, Isaac, Jr. Letters held by the Special Collections and Archives Division, USMA Library.

Dearing, James. Family papers and letters held by the Virginia Historical Society, 428 North Boulevard, Richmond, VA, 23221.

Lord, James. Letters held by the Special Collections and Archives Division, USMA Library.

McCrea, Tully. Letters written by McCrea to his cousin Belle McCrea from 1857 to 1867. Special Collections and Archives Division, USMA Library. Selected extracts from 1857 to 1863 are in the possession of the author. These summaries were originally transcribed by Mary Elizabeth Sergent and given to the author in 2005.

———. "Reminiscences of Gettysburg." Unpublished manuscript available at Gettysburg National Military Park and Military History Institute, Brake Collection.

McEnany, Brian R. "A History of the McEnany Family." Unpublished manuscript.

Military Order of the Loyal Legion of the United States: Commandery Series. 38 vols. 1882. US Army Heritage and Education Center, Carlisle, PA.

Military Order of the Loyal Legion of the United States: Commandery of the State of Massachusetts. 136 vols. 1882. US Army Heritage and Education Center, Carlisle, PA.

Rowland, Thomas. "Letters of a Virginia Cadet at West Point, 1859–1861." *South Atlantic Quarterly,* 14–15. Letters were published as a series of five quarterly installments from July 1915 through July 1916.

Warner, Charles N. Unpublished diaries and letters for 1859 to 1865.

Susquehanna Historical Society, 2 Monument Square, Montrose, PA, 18801.

Williams, William. Thirteenth New York Light Artillery, Eleventh Corps. Letter to mother dated May 14, 1863, available at http://www.ny13battery.com/battles/ww630514-chanc.htm.

Other Materials

Aimone, Alan. "U.S. Military Academy Civil War Statistics." West Point: USMA Library, June 2005.

Bachelder, John B. *The John B. Bachelder Gettysburg Map Set.* 28 maps. Dayton, OH: Morningside House, 1997. Maps originally prepared by Bachelder to support location of state monuments at Gettysburg but never published. Sauer, Bearss, and Heiser created an index to the maps for Morningside House.

———. *Maps of the Battlefield of Gettysburg: July 1st, 2nd, 3rd, 1863.* 3 maps. New York: Endicott, 1876. Also available at http://www.loc.gov/item/99447491.

Brager, Bruce L. "The City Point Explosion." Article found at http://www.militaryhistoryonline.com/civiwar/articles/citypoint.aspx (accessed May 21, 2008). Military History Online is a website of community-submitted articles relating to military history.

Burns, Kenneth. *The Civil War.* A documentary prepared for television in eight parts, September 2002. PBS Video.

Civil War Prints and Photographs. Digital Collection, Library of Congress, Washington, DC.

Coates, E. J., Michael J. McAffee, and Don Troiani. *Don Troiani's Civil War Series: Cavalry and Artillery.* 3rd ed. Mechanicsburg, PA: Stackpole, 2006.

Coles, David J. "Far from the Fields of Glory: Military Operations in Florida during the Civil War." PhD diss., Florida State University, 1996. Available at http://palmm.fcla.edu/ as part of the Florida Heritage Collection.

Harper's New Monthly Magazine. Cornell University Library Digital Collection, Ithaca, NY.

Haynes, Donald J. "Wilson's Cavalry Raid." Presentation to the Cincinnati Civil War Roundtable, 1998.

McEnany, Brian R., and James Lewis. *Sunstroke and Ankle Deep Mud: A Self-Guided Tour Guide.* Vienna, VA: 2012.

Meade, George, Jr. Photographic Album. US Army Heritage and Education Center, Carlisle, PA.

O'Reilly, Frank A. *Battle of Chancellorsville Map Set.* 12 maps. United States: John Dove, 1998.

————. *Battle of Fredericksburg Map Set.* 5 maps. Fort Washington, PA: Eastern National, 2001.

Parker, William L. "Brigadier General James Dearing, CSA." Thesis, masters of arts in history, Virginia Polytechnic Institute, 1969. Dearing Family Files, Virginia Historical Society, Richmond, VA.

Pickens, James C. "Reminiscences." Second North Carolina Mounted Infantry website, http://www.2ncmi.org/rem.html.

Rhodes, John H. "*The Gettysburg Gun.*" Gettysburg Discussion Group, http://www.gdg.org/Research/MOLLUS/mollus14.htm.

Wittenburg, Eric. "Brandy Station Seminar." Gettysburg Discussion Group, http://www.gdg.org/Research/people/ Buford/brandy.

————. "The Truth about the Withdrawal of Brig. Gen. John Buford's Cavalry, July 2, 1863." Gettysburg Discussion Group, http://www.gdg .org/Research.

National Park Service Civil War Series

"City Point." Description of area of Grant's headquarters found at http:// www.nps.gov/pete/historyculture/city-point.htm.

Gallagher, Gary. *Chancellorsville.* Fort Washington, PA: Eastern National, 1995.

Greene, A. Wilson. *The Second Battle of Manassas.* Fort Washington, PA: Eastern National, 2006.

Marvel, William. *Five Flags over Fort Sumter.* Fort Washington, PA: Eastern National, 1998.

Pfanz, Harry. *The Battle of Gettysburg.* Fort Washington, PA: Eastern National, 1994.

Rhea, Gordon. *The Battles of Wilderness and Spotsylvania.* Fort Washington, PA: Eastern National, 1995.

Illustration Credits

The illustrations are drawn from the following sources:

AHEC	US Army Heritage and Education Center.
WPAOG	West Point Association of Graduates.
AR (year)	Annual Reports of the Association of Graduates (Year).
BLCW	*Battles and Leaders of Civil War* (4 vols.), 1888 edition.
(Year) CA	Cadet class album photographs provided by the Special Collections and Archives Division, USMA Library, West Point, New York.
Calkins	Chris Calkin's collection. Photo originally from Josephine Pollard, *Our Hero General U.S. Grant, Where When and How He Fought (In Words of One Syllable)* (New York: McLoughlin Bros., 1885).
CULDC	Cornell University Library, Making of America Digital Collection of *Harpers New Monthly Magazine*, 1887.
Lafferty	James Lafferty, great grandson of Charles Warner.
LOC	Library of Congress Civil War Prints, Photographs, and Maps Collections.
MHI	Military History Institute MOLLUS Collection, AHEC.
NA	National Archives, Washington, DC.
OCHS	Ontario County Historical Society and Museum.
SCAD	Special Collections and Archives, US Military Academy Library.

All cadet photographs were found in the 1862 class album held by the Special Collections and Archives Division (SCAD), USMA Library, at West Point, NY. Historic West Point scenes and buildings were found and scanned from the 1857, 1867, 1868, 1869, 1870, and 1878 class albums in SCAD. Only three photographs (of McCrea, Warner, and Schaff in the biographical sketches appendix) were not in the public domain, and permission to use them has been received. All other photographs came from public domain sources, and, where known, the artist or photographer has been identified.

Index

59 *fig. 3.2;* grading scale, 93; graduations, 87–88; Grant West Point visit and, 330; hazing ("deviling"), 29–30; holiday activities/leave, 41–42, 72, 76, 96; housing, 32–34, 32 *fig. 2.5;* leadership of, 63, 97; Lincoln assassination and, 299; meals, 40–41; military training, 30, 118, 142; mock presidential election (1860), 67–68; North/ South polarization in, 49–53, 63–64, 67–68, 348–49; oath of allegiance administered to, 82–83, 102–3; postwar, 336 *fig. 20.1;* regulation changes, 169; riding classes, 65–66, 75, 108; size of, 332; Southern members of, 69; Southern resignations from, 69, 77, 81–85; summer camps, 23–24, 24 *fig. 2.4,* 46–47, 93, 103–4

Couch, Darius N., 160, 166, 176, 178

courts martial, 53–54, 107, 109

Covington (KY), 370

Cox, James Piper, 347 *t. 20.4*

Cozzens, William B., 40, 123

Crook, George: Appomattox Campaign (1865), 301, 304, 305–6, 307, 308; Lord as aide to, 328, 332, 371; Shenandoah Campaign (1864), 280, 284

Crossing the Rappahannock (painting; Waud), 158 *fig. 7.1*

Cullum, George W., 331, 335, 353

Culpeper (VA), 159, 160, 313

Cumberland Gap (TN), 358

Cushing, Alonzo H., 95, 207, 211, 213

Custer, George Armstrong: Appomattox Campaign (1865), 302, 305, 307–8; as Cavalry

Division captain, 146; Cold Harbor (1864), 254; in Grand Review (1865), 328; North/ South friendships of, 348; Shenandoah Campaign (1864), 280, 286, 287, 309; volunteer units joined by, 339; as West Point cadet, 19, 33, 76, 215; West Point graduation of, 95

Dallas (GA), Battle of (1864), 271, 356, 380

Dalton (GA), 389

Dalton, Battle of (GA), 270

dances, 27, 47, 98–99, 103–4, 107, 120

Davies, Henry F., 308

Davis, Jefferson: capture of (1865), 323; as CSA president, 75–76; Fort Sumter attack ordered by, 79; postwar search for, 313; as senator, 61, 63

D Company, 31, 47, 62–63, 72, 76

Dearing, James Griffin: appointment, 8, 10; Appomattox Campaign (1865), 294, 295–96, 297–98, 297 map, 303 map; at Bull Run (1861), 100; Civil War assignment/commands of, 344, 345 *t. 20.2;* as Class of 1862 resignee, 344; death of, 289, 309, 344; education of, 8, 10; family background of, 7–8, 31; furlough travels of, 60; Gettysburg (1863), 93, 193 map, 194, 204–6, 209, 214, 289; holiday activities/ leave, 41–42; as Laurel Brigade commander, 293–94; Mackenzie and, 309, 348; marriage of, 289, 290–91, 292; musical talent of, 63, 104; Overland Campaign (1864),

McCrea, Harriet Camp (wife), 378
McCrea, John (father), 5
McCrea, Mary Jane Galbraith (mother), 5, 90
McCrea, Percy (brother), 5–6, 61
McCrea, Tully, 311; appearance of, 13; birth of, 5; on Bolles's death, 172; early employment of, 6–7; education of, 6; family background of, 5–6, 325, 377; on Ft. Sumter attack, 81; Grant West Point visit and, 330–31; leadership positions held, 346, 348; postwar career of, 349; postwar promotion of, 332, 340, *378;* relocation to Ohio, 6; relocation to West Point, 11–12, 14–17; temperament of, 97–98, 119; as West Point math instructor, 3, 13–14, 57–58, 93–94, 127, 141–42, 169, 191, 215–16, 223–24, 239, 247, 277, 289, 325, 378–79
—AS WEST POINT CADET, 4 *fig. 1.1, 377;* academics, 34–38, 48–49, 64–65, 104–7, 119; appointment, 7, 9, 10, 61, 98, 377; cadet ranks held by, 46, 62, 88, 94, 95, 97, 104, 377; cadet warrant, 44; career aspirations, 67, 93–94, 101; class ranking of, 54, 377; dances attended by, 103–4, 107; discipline/punishment, 28–29, 39, 53, 55, 62, 69–70, 97–98, 377; drills, 38–39, 45; entrance examination, 22–23; examinations, 43–44, 54, 120; family pressure to resign, 89–90; financial difficulties of, 119; furlough travels of, 60–62; graduation, 100–101, 112–14, 119–20, 121–24, 128; guard

details, 29–30, 108–9; holiday activities/leave, 41–42, 76, 110–11; horses assigned to, 106, 112; initial processing, 17–21; lady friends of, 98–99, 107; meals, 26, 27, 101; military training, 30, 142; nickname of, 49; postgraduation travels, 128–31, 136; riding classes, 65–66; on Southern resignations, 84–85; summer camps, 25–28, 46–47, 93, 94–99, 377; transportation/arrival, 11–12, 14–17; tutoring of, 21; West Point North/South polarization and, 85–86; winter activities, 42–43
—CIVIL WAR SERVICE: Antietam (1862), 153–56; army manpower program criticized by, 338; assignment overview, 144 *t. 6.1,* 249 *t. 13.1,* 342 *t. 20.1,* 378; battle wounds of, 3, 127, 234, 277, 378; brevetting of, 156, 213, 237; Chancellorsville (1863), 169, 172, 178, 188; Department of the South, 224–25, 251; Florida Expedition, 226–29; Fredericksburg (1862), 157, 163; Gettysburg (1863), 193 map, 194, 204, 205, 207, 209–11, 212–13; Harrison's Landing encampment, 130–37; hospital/sick leave, 138–40, 145, 235–37, 249 *t. 13.1,* 378; Maryland Campaign (1862), 145–48, 149–50; Olustee (1864), 224, 233–34; promotions of, 225, 337
McCrea, Wallace (uncle), 6, 237
McCrea, Walter (brother), 5
McCrea, William (uncle), 6, 7, 10
McDowell, Irvin, 99
McEnaney, Thomas, 75, 108

Rorty, James J., 207, 208
Rosecrans, William S.: Burroughs
on staff of, 357, 358; Tennessee
Campaign led by, 270, 358;
Wharton on staff of, 390
Ross, Ebenezer ("Rube"), 60, 84,
345 *t. 20.2*
Rosser, Tom: Appomattox
Campaign (1865), 293, 294,
296, 297–98; desire to resign,
70–71; resignation of, as cadet,
84; as West Point cadet, 76, 78
Roswell (GA), 272
Rowland, Tom, 50, 71, 81
Ruff's Station, Battle of (1864),
380
Russell, David A., 256
Russell, E. Kirby, 31, 54, 95, 347
t. 20.3
Russell, John, 7, 10, 98, 109

Sabine Crossroads, Battle of
(1864), 242–43
Sailor's Creek, Battle of (1865),
365
Salem Church, Battle of (1863),
183–88, 185 map
Sanderson (FL), 228, 231, 234
Sanderson, James A.: appointment,
23, 382–83; biographical sketch,
382–83; as cadet lieutenant,
104; Chancellorsville (1863),
169, 170, 171, 173, 174,
179–80, 181, 241; Civil War
assignments, 138, 144 *t. 6.1*,
249 *t. 13.1*, 343 *t. 20.1*, 383;
as Class of 1862 member,
30–31, 33, 47; class ranking
of, 383; death of, in battle,
239–40, 246, 249 *t. 13.1*, 251,
383; Department of the Gulf,
240–41; discipline/punishment,
54, 383; leadership positions

held, 346; New York draft
riots (1863), 241; Red River
Campaign (1864), 243, 244
map, 245–46
Sandy Hook (NJ), artillery trials at,
361
San Francisco (CA), 387, 390
Savannah (GA), 265
Schaff, Morris: as author, 19–20,
51, 309, 348, 385–86; family
background of, 385; leadership
positions held, 346
—AS WEST POINT CADET, *385;* as
acting English professor, 105,
111; on Bull Run, Union defeat
at (1861), 99; cadet ranks held
by, 101, 104; class ranking of,
385; on dinner formations,
19–20; discipline/punishment,
111; entrance examination,
21–23; Fourth of July oration
of, 96; furlough travels of, 60,
61–62; graduation, 121; hazing
of, 29; holiday activities/leave,
42; as McCrea's friend, 3;
nickname of, 49; political views
of, 63–64; roommates of, 47,
62–63, 77, 358; summer camps,
28, 96; transportation/arrival,
16; as tutor, 54; on West Point
North/South polarization, 51
—CIVIL WAR SERVICE: assignment
overview, 144 *t. 6.1*, 249 *t. 13.1*,
331, 342 *t. 20.1*, 386; brevetting
of, 264; City Point Ordnance,
248, 251, 262–64, 263 *fig. 13.2;*
as Hooker aide, 171; as Meade
aide, 194, 250; Watertown
Arsenal, 264; the Wilderness
(1864), 248, 251, 262, 264
Schell, F. S., 216 *fig. 10.1*
Schofield, John M., 267, 270, 272,
319, 340, 355–56

CPSIA information can be obtained
at www.ICGtesting.com
Printed in the USA
BVOW09s0931140817
491989BV00001B/5/P